Thank you for shopping VCB

# Textbook Return Policy:

1. You must have your receipt
2. You must not write in or use the book
3. Return dates are:

with just your receipt by

## Jan. 27th

with receipt & drop slip by

## Feb. 10th

D0391607

## Save Your Sales Receipt!

# General Merchandise Returns

### SOFT GOODS, GIFTS, SCHOOL SUPPLIES

A. All items MUST have receipt to be returned.

B. Returns MUST be made within two weeks from date of purchase.

C. All items MUST be in saleable condition, unwashed and not worn, complete with tags.

D. Packaged items unopened.

E. No refunds on sale items; exchanges for correct sizes only.

F. No returns on markers, spray paint or pens.

G. All refunds subject to departmental approval.

VILLAGE COMMONS BOOKSTORE

Across from the field house

901 Lucinda, 758-0613

# Toward a Political Economy of Development

California Series on Social Choice and Political Economy

*Edited by Brian Barry, Robert H. Bates, and Samuel L. Popkin*

1. *Markets and States in Tropical Africa: The Political Basis of Agricultural Policies* Robert H. Bates
2. *Political Economics* James E. Alt and K. Alec Chrystal
3. *Abortion and the Politics of Motherhood* Kristin Luker
4. *Hard Choices: How Women Decide about Work, Career, and Motherhood* Kathleen Gerson
5. *Regulatory Policy and the Social Sciences* Roger Noll, editor
6. *Reactive Risk and Rational Action: Managing Moral Hazard in Insurance Contracts* Carol A. Heimer
7. *Post-Revolutionary Nicaragua: State, Class, and the Dilemmas of Agrarian Policy* Forrest D. Colburn
8. *Essays on the Political Economy of Rural Africa* Robert H. Bates
9. *Peasants and King in Burgundy: Agrarian Foundations of French Absolutism* Hilton L. Root
10. *The Causal Theory of Justice* Karol Sołtan
11. *Principles of Group Solidarity* Michael Hechter
12. *Political Survival: Politicians and Public Policy in Latin America* Barry Ames
13. *Of Rule and Revenue* Margaret Levi
14. *Toward a Political Economy of Development: A Rational Choice Perspective* Robert H. Bates, editor

# Toward a Political Economy of Development

## A Rational Choice Perspective

*Edited by*
*Robert H. Bates*

UNIVERSITY OF CALIFORNIA PRESS

*Berkeley   Los Angeles   London*

University of California Press
Berkeley and Los Angeles, California

University of California Press, Ltd.
London, England

© 1988 by
The Regents of the University of California

Library of Congress Cataloging-in-Publication Data

Toward a political economy of development.

　　(California series on social choice and political
economy ; 14)
　　　Bibliography: p.
　　　Includes index.
　　　1. Developing countries—Economic policy.
2. Developing countries—Economic conditions.
3. Developing countries—Politics and government.
4. Social choice.　I. Bates, Robert H.　II. Series.
HC59.7.T7376　1988　　338.9′009172′4　　87-10870
ISBN 0-520-06051-2 (alk. paper)
ISBN 0-520-06052-0 (pbk.)

Printed in the United States of America

1　2　3　4　5　6　7　8　9

*To Jane*

# Contents

*Acknowledgments*    x
*Introduction*    1

## Part I                                                           5

The Political Economy of International
Capital Markets    *Robert H. Bates*    7

1. The International Organization of Third
World Debt    *Charles Lipson*    12

2. On Persuading a Leopard to Change His
Spots: Optimal Strategies for Donors and
Recipients of Conditional Development Aid
*Paul Mosley*    47

3. The Political Economy of Stabilization:
Commitment, Capacity, and Public Response
*Joan Nelson*    80

## Part II                                                          131

The State and Development: Taiwan,
Argentina, and Central America
*Robert H. Bates*    133

4. Taiwan's Economic History: A Case of *Etatisme*
and a Challenge to Dependency Theory
*Alice H. Amsden*    142

5. State and Alliances in Argentina, 1956–1976
*Guillermo O'Donnell*    176

**6.** Fissures in the Volcano? Central
American Economic Prospects
*Clark W. Reynolds*    206

**Part III**                                                        237

Toward a Political Economy of Development
*Robert H. Bates*    239

**7.** Public Choice and Peasant Organization
*Samuel L. Popkin*    245

**8.** The Development of Property Rights in
Land: A Comparative Study
*David Feeny*    272

**9.** Structure, Growth, and Power: Three
Rationalist Accounts    *Ronald Rogowski*    300

**10.** Governments and Agricultural Markets in
Africa    *Robert H. Bates*    331

*Selected Readings    359*
*Contributors    381*
*Index    383*

# Acknowledgments

*Toward a Political Economy of Development* consists of a series of papers that deal with the economics and politics of development.

The idea for the volume was conceived jointly by myself and Samuel L. Popkin, and it has received the help of numerous members of the academic profession. In the spring of 1982, we sent a letter to over two hundred fellow academics asking them to nominate the "ten best" articles on development that they had read in "the past few years." We secured copies of the articles thus nominated, read and discussed them, and, over a succession of semesters, taught them to students.

Many pieces that have had a significant impact on the profession have had to be omitted from this collection. Limitations of space restricted the number of pieces that could be republished, and obvious complementarities between pieces also structured the selection process.

I wish to acknowledge the support of the National Science Foundation (Grant no. SE–582–16870), the Social Science Research Council, the Division of Humanities and Social Sciences of the California Institute of Technology, and the Center for Advanced Study in the Behavioral Sciences. I owe special thanks to the Haynes Foundation for helping to defray the costs of completing this work. While at the center, I was supported by Duke University, the Guggenheim Foundation, the Exxon Foundation, and the National Science Foundation (Grant no. BNS–801–1495). The project placed extraordinary demands on the librarians of the California Institute of Technology, who responded with their usual cheerful competence. It also posed special challenges to a succession of secretaries: Jill Irby, Chris Price, Catherine Heising, Leslie Lindzey, and Gerald Florence. I thank them all.

Special thanks go to all who took the time to respond to the letter that initiated this project: Barry Ames, David Becker, Bela Belassa, Clive Bell, Roger Benjamin, Henry Bienen, Leonard Binder, Gary Brewer, Valerie Bunce, Bruce Cain, David Cameron, James Caporaso, Daniel Chirot, John Cohen, Wayne Cornelius, Peter Cowhey, Ann Craig, Bruce Cumings, Alfred Diamant, Carlos Diaz-Alejandro, Jorge Dominguez, Raymond Duvall, Peter Evans, Richard Fagan, David Feeny, John Ferejohn, Thomas Ferguson, Morris Fiorina, John Freeman, Walter Goldfrank, Michael Hechter, Ronald Herring, Douglas Hibbs, Albert Hirschman, Raymond Hopkins, Samuel Huntington, Chalmers Johnson, Bruce Johnston, Kenneth Jowett, Terry Karl, Robert Keohane, Stephen Krasner, Nathaniel Leff, René Lemarchand, Margaret Levi, Ronald Libby, Seymour Martin Lipset, Charles Lipson, Cynthia McClintock, Jeffrey Paige, Ithiel de Sola Pool, Adam Przeworski, Lucian Pye, Clark Reynolds, Ronald Rogowski, Carl Rosberg, Robert Rotberg, Vernon Ruttan, Michael Schatzberg, Susan Shirk, Richard Sklar, Theda Skocpol, Duncan Snidal, Barbara Stallings, Richard Stryker, Sidney Tarrow, Gordon Tullock, Norman Uphoff, Myron Weiner, Miles Wolpin, Crawford Young, and Aristide Zolberg. It should be noted that all the additional articles suggested by these "coeditors" are listed in the bibliography of selected readings.

I wish to thank Peter Cowhey, Robert Keohane, and Myron Weiner for their incisive editorial criticisms, and Jane-Ellen Long and Paulette Higgins for their superb assistance in preparing this manuscript for publication. And I wish to offer special thanks to the students who have responded to different versions of this volume over the last several years and thereby helped to shape it into its final form.

Jane Danielson, to whom this book is dedicated, knows as well as I the things I thank her for.

# Introduction

In no other field of the social sciences are politics and economics so closely intertwined as in the study of development. Despite the prominence given in each discipline to forces that traditionally fall within the domain of the other, economists studying developing societies rarely train in political science, while political scientists too often remain unschooled in economics.

Economists fundamentally skeptical of government intervention in markets treat politics as a source of economic "distortions." While they acknowledge that peace and stability may be purchased through the expenditure of scarce resources, they strongly convey the impression that the developing areas would be better off with "less politics."[1] The ethical stance of such economists is clear; far less clear is their theory of politics. Why do politicians behave the way they do? What drives them to make such costly choices? Why do they not adopt policies that would achieve desired objectives at less cost? The failure to address such questions underscores the failure of such economists to develop a satisfactory theory of politics.

The deficiencies in the political analysis advanced by economists who advocate less government is matched by the lack of sophistication on the part of those who endorse an activist role for governments. Particularly in societies where markets are held to be underdeveloped, governments must take an active role in economic life, they argue; the public sector must do the things private agents fail to accomplish. Economists who advocate this position are clearer in prescribing what governments should do than they

---

1. See, for example, Deepak Lal, *The Poverty of "Development Economics"* (London: Institute of Economic Affairs, 1983).

are in explaining why they expect governments to behave in the ways they advocate. They fail to ask such obvious questions as: Why would governments undertake the tasks they posit for them? And when public officials make economic decisions, why should their choices be in any sense superior to those made by economic agents? Condemning political intervention on one side, endorsing it on the other, economists debate the role of government while lacking a sophisticated understanding of politics.

Political scientists, for their part, exhibit major deficiencies in their understanding of economics. Too often they remain blind to economic facts. Illustrative is that for a decade or more, political scientists championed models of underdevelopment that related foreign investment to economic decline and international trade to economic stagnation—this during a time that saw the rise of the newly industrialized economies, which welcomed foreign investment and relied on foreign trade. Not only do political scientists often fail to get their economic facts right, they also frequently fail to comprehend how economies and markets work. Some confound "nationalization" with "socialism," for example. Others blithely argue that government price controls "lower prices," thereby revealing their lack of even an elementary understanding of markets.

Clearly, then, materials are needed to educate economists who study the developing areas in politics, and political scientists in economics. This volume responds to that need. The book is composed of a collection of essays, most of which have been published elsewhere. The timeliness of the topics addressed by the articles furnished one criterion for selection: thus the emphasis given to the analysis of Third World debt, to the politics of economic adjustment, to the political determinants of economic performance in African agriculture, and to the economic origins of political violence in Central America. Even more important than the currency of the topics, however, are the analytic approaches taken. Preference was given to pieces that attacked problems of interest to development specialists in ways from which both political scientists and economists could learn. The volume seeks, in short, to present papers that teach ways of doing political economy.

The volume purposely fails to cover established forms of political economy, be they of the "Warrenite," *dependencia*, or mode-of-production persuasion.[2] In recent years these approaches have

2. Bill Warren, "Imperialism and Capitalist Industrialization," *New Left Review* 81 (September–October 1973): 3–44. Good review essays are Gabriel Palma, "De-

tended to dominate development studies. They are familiar to a broad audience and many of their leading articles have already been assembled in published collections.[3] Instead, this volume seeks to promote an approach to political economy that, while well established in some portions of the social sciences, is poorly established in development studies. The special focus here is on the "collective choice" approach: one that recognizes that markets are imperfect; that institutions other than markets allocate resources; and that "economic reasoning" can be employed to explain the way political processes and political institutions affect how individuals' desires for valued but scarce resources aggregate into outcomes for entire societies.[4]

---

pendency," *World Development* 6 (1978): 881–924, and Aidan Foster-Carter, "The Mode of Production Controversy," *New Left Review* 107 (1978): 47–77.

3. See the superb volume edited by Charles K. Wilber: *The Political Economy of Development and Underdevelopment* (New York: Random House, 1973).

4. See the discussion in Martin Staniland, *What Is Political Economy?* (New Haven: Yale University Press, 1985), and the conclusion to Robert H. Bates, *Essays on the Political Economy of Rural Africa* (Cambridge, England: Cambridge University Press, 1983).

# Part I

# The Political Economy of International Capital Markets

## *Robert H. Bates*

At least since the time of Lenin and Hobson, scholars have emphasized the importance of international capital for the development of Third World nations.[1] Certainly during the 1960s and 1970s, attention focused on the role of foreign investment, which acted as the prime mover in theories of imperialism. During this period, scholars analyzed the impact on development made by foreign firms, in particular, multinational corporations.[2] More recently, attention has focused less on direct investment and more on capital markets, and rather than examining the impact of foreign firms, scholars have instead analyzed the impact of foreign debt. The articles in this section examine the origins of international capital markets, their organization, and their impact on the politics of developing countries.

1. J. A. Hobson, *Imperialism: A Study* (London: Allen and Unwin, 1938); V. I. Lenin, *Imperialism: The Highest Stage of Capitalism* (London: Lawrence and Wisehart, 1948).

2. See, for example, Peter Evans, "Recent Research on Multinational Corporations," *Annual Review of Sociology* 7 (1981): 199–223.

The section begins with a work by Charles Lipson. Lipson's article was published in 1981, and some of the language will therefore appear incongruous and some of the analysis anachronistic. But it is an important article. For Lipson's study provides a history of the origins of contemporary capital markets. It stresses the role of government regulations and the financial incentives to commence off-shore operations. It analyzes the shift of capital from the developed world to the "petrodollar market," under the impact of the OPEC-inspired jump in petroleum prices. The article is notable as well for its presentation of the institutional structure of the international capital market: the interrelations among private banks, the role of syndication, and the monitoring of relations between debtor and creditor nations by international agencies.

Analytically, Lipson's piece is important because it offers an alternative to the tendency to transfer the command-and-control approach of political analysis to economic settings. Much of the radical literature on capital markets focuses on banks or bankers. It approaches the problem of Third World debt as if the agents who supply capital control the operation of capital markets.[3] Lipson, by contrast, focuses not on agents but, rather, on markets. The relevant factors, he assumes, are not the individual actors—the banks, the bankers, or the firms—but the structure of the market environments within which such agents make choices. There are actors, and Lipson educates us about them. There are outcomes, one of which is Third World debt. But, Lipson demonstrates, the relationship between the preferences of actors and the nature of the outcomes is mediated by markets. The relevant level of analysis is that of the market.

Lipson is no conventional market economist, however, for his concern is not so much with the operation of markets as with their formation. Lying behind all credit markets is the problem of risk; and this problem is particularly great in international markets, where there is no government able to secure property rights and thereby generate collateral for loans. It would be individually rational for a debtor to take a loan and then not repay it; and given the absence of an international government to sanction such behavior, it would be feasible for a foreign debtor to do so. In such circumstances, why would people offer loans? How can credit mar-

3. See, for example, Cheryl Payer, *The Debt Trap: The IMF and the Third World* (New York: Monthly Review Press, 1974).

kets be formed? By addressing such questions, Lipson pushes beyond conventional market economics and examines the ways rational agents compensate for potential market failures.[4]

The oil price shock precipitated a recession in the developed nations, leading to declines in imports from Third World countries. And because of the rise in oil prices, developing nations were compelled to use increasing amounts of the foreign exchange to import petroleum products. Development programs were therefore threatened with an inability to import capital goods, spare parts, and equipment. To maintain their development programs, Third World countries borrowed heavily in capital markets and many rapidly reached the limit of their ability to repay their debts. As Lipson makes clear, a major role of the International Monetary Fund (IMF) has been to manage the resultant debt crisis.

The World Bank has also become involved in the problem of Third World debt. Through a program of structural adjustment lending, the Bank offers credits which enable development programs to proceed; but it does so only if the debtor country agrees to restructure its domestic policies in ways that enable it to generate greater export earnings. Rather than seeking to "deflate" the domestic economy so as to reduce the demand for imports and foreign balances, as the IMF does, the World Bank lends funds for programs designed to promote increased exports and thereby greater foreign earnings.[5] As a result of the debt crisis, then, both the IMF and the World Bank undertake major roles in the formulation of development policies and in the politics of Third World nations.

The essay by Paul Mosley explores the process by which international lenders seek to exercise leverage over the domestic policies of developing nations.[6] Mosley's article is notable for both the

4. Lipson thus opens a line of inquiry later pursued by Robert Axelrod and Robert Keohane, two scholars who seek to advance the application of rational choice analysis to international relations. See Robert Axelrod, *The Evolution of Cooperation* (New York: Basic Books, 1981), and Robert Keohane, *After Hegemony* (Princeton: Princeton University Press, 1984).

5. An excellent collection of essays is contained in Tony Killick, ed., *Adjustment and Finance in the Developing World: The Role of the International Monetary Fund* (Washington, D.C.: International Monetary Fund in association with Overseas Development Institute, 1982). See also M. B. Connolly and Alexander Swoboda, *International Trade and Money: The Geneva Essays* (Toronto: University of Toronto Press, 1973).

6. For additional materials, see the collection of papers in *International Organization* 39 (Summer 1985).

quantity and the quality of the materials it presents. Examining the history of structural adjustment lending by the World Bank, he defines what is meant by *conditionality*—the policy requirements placed on borrowers as a precondition for loans—and presents a detailed portrayal of the conditions set for twenty-five loans to thirteen developing countries. By so doing, Mosley conveys a clear image of just what policy issues form the center of controversy between creditors and debtors in international capital markets.

Equally interesting is Mosley's analysis of the bargaining between the Bank and the debtor governments. He defines a variable, T, which stands for the "tightness" of the policy requirements set as preconditions for Bank lending. The creditors, indexed as $i$, are presumed to favor tighter conditions than are the borrowers, indexed as $j$ ($T_i > T_j$). Both the borrower and the lender encounter risks. The level of each party's risk (which is labeled $r_i$, $r_j$), Mosley argues, is determined by the difference between the amount it will suffer as a result of the imposition of its opponent's conditions for the loan and the amount if it fails to secure a mutually acceptable loan package. Given a player's risk, its opponent then chooses a bargaining strategy (labeled $O_i$ for the lender; $O_j$ for the borrower) in order to secure its preferred level of "tightness" in the conditions for the loan.

Some of the determinants of the risks are measurable, and Mosley uses that fact to evaluate his analysis. The borrower's vulnerability (that is, the degree to which it encounters risks) is greater the higher its balance-of-payments deficit and the greater its debt-service payments as a proportion of total exports. The lender's vulnerability is determined by the degree to which the borrower is dependent on it for foreign assistance. Using data from published sources, Mosley tests his model, finding that the variables (save one) that predict the level of "tightness" discriminate between the "tightest" and "least tight" loan agreements. Mosley also examines the degree of slippage in the actual implementation of loan conditions, that is, the degree to which the debtors abide by the conditions agreed upon.

Mosely focuses on the international dimension of the politics of international capital markets. He largely omits from consideration the domestic political costs of economic adjustment. The third paper in this section, written by Joan Nelson, concentrates on just this issue.

Nelson's concern is with the political sustainability of economic policies, and she focuses on those factors that affect governments' willingness to initiate stabilization programs and their capacity to implement such programs. She draws on the political experiences of five countries—Ghana, Zambia, Kenya, Sri Lanka, and Jamaica—as they underwent the economic adjustments prescribed by the IMF.

Nelson portrays the subjective factors affecting a government's assessment of the risks of economic policies. Among the points she makes with particular force is that those who bear the costs of economic reform lack any means for assessing what their welfare would have been in the absence of the changes in policy. In the face of such uncertainty, disagreements inevitably arise; in addition, advocacy and persuasion play a major political role. And given that in the short run those who benefit from the reforms are not the ones who pay the costs, policy reform completely loses its technical nature. Clouded by uncertainty and controversy, it becomes a matter of politics.

Nelson discusses the factors that shape the subsequent course of political controversy. She stresses that the policies that lead to "excess demand" for foreign exchange tend to lead to rationing as well, and thus create opportunities for patronage politics. And where rationing by public bureaucracies replaces markets, she notes, public-sector interests stand among those most likely to oppose the imposition of market methods for allocating scarce resources. In the face of opposition by politicians with clients and organized interests, technocrats initiating "economic reforms" face strong political resistance. Nelson thus deftly introduces the political considerations affecting governments' ability to change economic policy.

It should be noted that those concerned with the politics of structural adjustment will find other articles of value in this volume. Of particular interest is the work of Guillermo O'Donnell. While not addressing the subject directly, Alice Amsden explores the way the government of Taiwan imposes "market-conforming" policies, and I discuss the political forces that promote "market-distorting" policies in Africa. These three articles therefore give further insight into the role of politics in influencing the behavior of markets and, thus, into the domestic determinants of structural adjustment in Third World nations.

# 1

# The International Organization of Third World Debt

*Charles Lipson*

Throughout the 1970s, Third World states borrowed heavily from international banks. Faced with sharply increased costs for energy and manufactured imports, many states began to compete for commercial loans. The most creditworthy, from Brazil to Korea and Taiwan, have used these funds to offset their growing current-account deficits while maintaining relatively strong economic growth. But with the world economy sagging and interest payments rising, many less developed countries (LDCs) must cope with enormous debt burdens.

The size of these debts and the financial trouble they pose can be illustrated briefly. In 1970 the twelve largest nonoil LDC

Reprinted with permission from *International Organization*, volume 35, Charles Lipson, "The International Organization of Third World Debt." © 1981, The M.I.T. Press.

An earlier version of this paper was presented at the 1980 American Political Science Association convention in Washington, D. C. I wish to thank Robert Z. Aliber, Jonathan Aronson, Benjamin J. Cohen, Jeff Frieden, Peter Katzenstein, Robert Keohane, Kenneth Oye, Susan Strange, John Zysman, and an anonymous reviewer for their comments. This research was supported by a Rockefeller Foundation Fellowship in International Relations.

borrowers[1] paid $1.1 billion in interest on their external debt, which amounted to slightly more than 6 percent of their export earnings. In 1980, by contrast, their interest payments totaled $18.4 billion and absorbed over 14 percent of export earnings.[2] As early as 1982 or 1983, these still-mounting figures led some economists to warn of serious debt problems. Already some weaker economies, from Zaire to Jamaica, have failed to meet repayment schedules; the largest recent case was that of Turkey, whose $3 billion debt had to be rescheduled in 1980. Overhanging all these cases are potential problems in much larger borrowers such as Brazil, which owes over $60 billion and has interest payments equivalent to one-third of its exports.[3]

This mountain of debt was built mainly in the offshore capital markets. The astounding growth of these markets is one of the most striking developments in the modern world economy—barely noticeable in 1960, two decades later they had a gross size of nearly $1.5 *trillion*. Their rapid growth began in the mid-1960s as depositors, borrowers, and major banks all learned to exploit their unique advantages. Their main advantage is lower cost, due mostly to less regulation. Domestic banks in the United States, for instance, are required to hold some assets idle as reserves, but their offshore branches and subsidiaries operate under no such restrictions. They can earn returns on all their assets. As a result, they can profitably offer higher deposit rates and slightly lower loan charges than their domestic counterparts. This near-absence of costly regulations has proven a powerful attraction to most large financial intermediaries and their customers.

By 1973, the year of OPEC's embargo, the offshore markets had already become a prominent component of world capital markets. Yet the embargo and subsequent oil price hike were to have a substantial impact on their growth: they stimulated the demand for payments financing and led to a much larger role for Third World borrowers.

Oil-importing states in the Third World faced immediate and severe balance-of-payments problems as soon as oil prices quad-

1. Brazil, Argentina, South Korea, the Philippines, Chile, Thailand, Taiwan, Colombia, Turkey, the Ivory Coast, Bolivia, and India. Until the recent oil discoveries there, Mexico was grouped with these countries; with over $34 billion in outstanding commercial loans, it is second only to Brazil as an LDC borrower.
2. Morgan Guaranty Trust, *World Financial Markets* (January 1981): table 6.
3. Ibid., table 5.

rupled. To elect to reduce imports swiftly by austerity measures was a politically unattractive strategy that implied sharply lowered growth. Many LDCs, especially those with ambitious development programs, chose to adjust more slowly: they maintained that industrial growth financed the ensuring deficits in the lower-cost credit markets.[4] This basic policy choice, combined with a shortage of official financing for deficits, granted the offshore markets a critical role in balance-of-payments financing.[5]

The huge payments imbalances of the mid-1970s and early 1980s meant, in effect, that oil producers had surplus revenues to invest abroad while oil consumers needed substantial financing. Between these surplus and deficit states stood the major commercial banks, operating in the virtually unregulated Euromarket.[6] By accepting massive short-term deposits (many from oil producers) and making medium-term loans (many to oil consumers), these banks "recycled petrodollar surpluses."

It was a booming business, and a quite profitable one. By the late 1970s the largest banks were deriving as much as half of their operating earnings from international activities. When oil prices doubled again in 1979, the Eurobanks expanded their lending still further, although this time they acted more cautiously, in recognition of the growing risks. Even so, it was commercial banks, not aid donors or official multilateral lenders, that performed the basic recycling function.

4. This strategy of indebted growth is discussed in detail in Jeff Frieden, "Third World Indebted Industrialization: International Finance and State Capitalism in Mexico, Brazil, Algeria, and South Korea," *International Organization* 35, no. 3 (Summer 1981): 407–31.

5. Much of this bank lending was not made to finance balance-of-payments deficits specifically, even though it released other funds for that purpose. Typically, the credits were meant to finance corporate investments or the budgetary deficits of parastatal enterprises. Thus, while Eurolending played a crucial role in financing aggregate deficits, it is not always easy to distinguish resource flows from payments financing. For a comprehensive analysis of these issues see Benjamin J. Cohen and Fabio Basagni, *Banks and the Balance of Payments: Private Lending in the International Adjustment Process* (Montclair, N. J.: Allenheld Osmun, 1981).

6. The term *Euromarket* is commonly, if somewhat inaccurately, used to refer to all offshore credit markets. In this article, I shall use the two terms interchangeably. The distinctive feature of these markets is that they deal in Eurocurrencies, which can be defined as bank deposits denominated in any currency that is not native to the country where the deposit is located. Dollar deposits in the Cayman Islands, for example, are Eurodollars, Deutsche Marks on deposit in Luxembourg are Euro-DMs, and so on for all the major convertible currencies. The market for these offshore currencies is based in London but stretches as far as the Asia-dollar markets in Singapore and Hong Kong and includes a number of financial centers and tax havens in between.

In only a few years, then, the Euromarket had assumed a central role in mediating international capital flows and financing world trade. In the process, private banks had become major creditors of sovereign states, not only in the Third World but also in eastern and southern Europe.[7]

The quality of these international loans has attracted increasing attention from borrowers, lenders, central bankers, and aid officials. Bank economists, in particular, have looked closely at borrowers' projected foreign-exchange earnings, at their debt ratios, and at other macroeconomic data. Globally, they have considered the growth of aggregate payment imbalances and the resulting demands on credit markets and foreign-exchange reserves. Their central aims are to forecast financing needs and debt-service capacity.

As important as these factors are, however, the soundness of international debt depends on more than the financial condition of the borrower—it depends equally on the willingness of sovereign states to repay. The debts, of course, are formal contractual obligations. But it is commonplace to observe that in the international arena the performance of all obligations and the enforcement of all claims must be considered problematic. The reason is fundamentally Hobbesian. There is no overarching sovereignty, no sure enforcement of claims (judicial or otherwise), no "common power," as Hobbes observed, "to keep them in awe." Yet the principle of self-help and the metaphor of anarchy, so often used to describe the underlying condition of international relations, should not be interpreted as an absence of structures that constrain state behavior and give rise to stable expectations. What must be explored in this particular case, then, is the character of the international political structures that have thus far prompted debt service by sovereigns, even when they have found it onerous to continue payments.

What is most compelling about these structures is that sover-

---

7. Bank credits are not the only source of private international lending, but they are by far the most important source of medium- and long-term credits. International bond markets have been much less receptive to underdeveloped states and have remained the preserve of "name" borrowers from the United States and Europe. In recent years, nonoil LDCs have borrowed about $2.6 billion annually in foreign bonds and Eurobonds. They have borrowed ten times that amount in publicized Eurocurrency bank credits (plus a small but growing amount in unpublicized credits). In addition, suppliers' credits, which are frequently furnished by exporters and sometimes subsidized by their governments, are a major source of short-term trade financing.

eigns are constrained less by other sovereigns than by sanctions and incentives organized primarily by multinational banks and official multilateral lenders. These structures include the deterrent threat of effective economic sanctions and the incentive of continued access to credit.

Commercial banks are crucial actors here. Bank lending syndicates are the source of powerful and virtually self-sufficient sanctions against default by solvent borrowers. Because syndicates are well organized, with an agent bank primarily responsible for collection of the loan, and because there are extensive ties between syndicates, willful default threatens to cut off all sources of commercial credit. This implicit sanction stands behind all relations between Eurobanks and their Third World borrowers. Its implementation, it should be noted, depends on the capacity of large numbers of independent banks to take concerted action.

When the problem stems from insolvency rather than unwillingness to pay, resolution may be more complicated. It may, for example, require substantial new credits plus fiscal and monetary restraints by the debtor. In such cases, market-based sanctions and incentives are typically supplemented by the International Monetary Fund. Besides providing technical advice and some financing, the Fund evaluates the debtor's proposed economic program and monitors its implementation. The usual result, worked out jointly by the debtor, the creditors, and the Fund, is a stabilization program and a "work-out" package for the debt, including a delayed repayment schedule and some new credit.

These structures of sanctions and incentives, built around non-state actors, form the basis of a stable expectation that debts are to be serviced promptly if there is any economic possibility of doing so. Debts are to be honored even if economic conditions are hard, even if the debts were incurred by defunct governments now in disrepute.

This definition of obligations implies substantial constraints on state action: debts are to be assumed and serviced by incumbent governments; they are not to be repudiated (and they very seldom are).[8] In practical terms, economic collapse by the debtor may require some readjustment of loan terms, and bargaining over the

---

8. One possible exception, so far untested, might be in the case of fraud or some other clearly illegal act by lenders. As yet, debtors have not advanced such claims as a way of escaping their debt burdens and that in itself is noteworthy.

new terms may be very tough indeed. The norm in such cases is that renegotiations require mutual agreement; they are not to be set unilaterally by the debtor. The broad acceptance of this behavioral standard is demonstrated repeatedly in the careful statements of impoverished debtors and even revolutionary governments. Exceptions, such as North Korea's unilateral suspension of debt service after the oil embargo,[9] are quite rare. Much more common— and indicative of the strength of the debt regime—are incidents such as the refusal of the Sandinistas to repudiate Somoza's debts.[10] Iran under the Ayatollah Khomeini is another compelling example of the strength and domain of these basic norms and related rules, and their backing by effective sanctions and incentives. According to the *New York Times*, "Many European bankers . . . argue that throughout the revolution, Iran has sought to meet its financial obligations, within the limits imposed by the Carter freeze."[11] What is extraordinary is not that some Iranians wanted to disown the debts but that key officials did not. Their efforts to repay were made even though the debts were contracted under the Shah, despite questions about their legality under local law, despite Islamic objections to interest payments, despite serious economic difficulties, and despite the obvious failure of state sanctions to secure Iran's compliance on other issues. The failure of state sanctions also suggests that the rewards and punishments related to debt service may be organized not by capital-exporting states but by the private creditors themselves.

Indeed, the most distinctive element of the debt regime is the peripheral role played by capital-exporting states. To understand this role, and its limits, one must distinguish clearly between the operation of offshore capital markets (which give rise to credit flows) and the supervision of outstanding debt (a stock problem).

Advanced capitalist states, where the major banks are headquartered, have unquestionably played a vital role in the growth of the Euromarket. To begin with, their domestic regulations stimulated the Euromarket as a less costly source of funds. Moreover, as the

9. "Pyongyang Buys More Time," *Far Eastern Economic Review* 7 (September 1979): 56, 59.
10. Steve Downer, "Nicaragua: The Recovery Is Only Just Beginning," *Euromoney* (December 1980), especially p. 129; John Dizard, "Why Bankers Fear the Nicaraguan Solution," *Institutional Investor/International Edition* (November 1980), especially p. 54.
11. Paul Lewis, "Iran's Loan Status Seen Recovering," *New York Times*, 21 January 1981, p. 25.

market developed, monetary authorities in the United States generally avoided actions that might have stunted its growth. If the United States was concerned with its capital account, Britain was concerned with London's role as an international financial center. They welcomed the Euromarket's development in the City. In these ways, state action and inaction shaped the institutional context of credit flows.

But aiding the development of the Euromarket, or even regulating the banks within it, is different from supervising Third World debt. That task has fallen largely to the commercial banks and the International Monetary Fund. Together they have developed informal but effective means of ensuring debt service—even when that involves domestic austerity or complex refinancing. These two nonstate actors have played the central roles in developing rules and procedures related to troubled debt. These arrangements, which currently center on ad hoc creditor conferences, are still relatively new. They are likely to evolve as the volume of debt grows, and they may be strained to the breaking point if prospective defaults are widespread. Still, they have developed over more than a decade and now comprise a coherent and distinctive regime for Third World debt.

## The Structure and Development of the Euromarket

To clarify the basic features of this regime it is essential to understand an antecedent phenomenon, the buildup of sovereign debt to private banks via the Euromarket. The development of the Euromarket is important to our study for several reasons. First, it was the privatization of balance-of-payments financing that reduced the role of official aid donors and elevated the importance of commercial banks in debt negotiations. Second, some arrangements for handling commercial debts are linked directly to Euromarket lending procedures. Finally, to understand pressures for change within the regime—especially pressures for institutional changes at the IMF and World Bank—it is necessary to consider the overall problem of deficits and their financing. If the debt regime cannot be reduced to the credit markets, neither can it be understood without paying close attention to them.

Although the Euromarket is virtually unregulated, its growth has certainly been sensitive to state controls over *domestic* capital markets. In fact, the offshore markets began their rapid growth in the mid-1960s after the United States limited capital exports for balance-of-payments reasons. As American strictures were progressively tightened, multinational corporations were forced to look beyond New York and Chicago for worldwide financing. They found it when familiar money-market banks began producing dollar-denominated deposits in their London branch offices.[12]

As the profit potential was recognized, the number of branch banks in the City began to multiply. "Name" banks from the United States and Europe were soon followed by their regional counterparts. Today, all but six of the world's one hundred largest banks are represented in London.[13] This influx produced a highly competitive capital market, led by some two dozen U. S. and European banks but joined by over four hundred other banks, insurance companies, and other private financial institutions.[14] As the market grew, it also spread—to other financial centers and other currencies. The result was a market for foreign currency liabilities that doubled every three or four years, reaching a net size of $775 billion by December 1980.[15]

As the market grew, its functions expanded from simple commercial lending to balance-of-payments financing. Offshore banks confronted substantial new risks, for throughout the 1970s both interest rates and currency movements were volatile. Borrowers with major industrialization programs began seeking larger loans for longer periods, typically packages of more than $50 million for over seven years. Perhaps more important, many potential borrowers were state agencies or parastatal enterprises. Unlike corporate customers, these state enterprises traditionally claimed sovereign

12. For an examination of U. S. banks' entrance into the Euromarkets, see Janet Kelly, *Bankers and Borders: The Case of American Banks in Britain* (Cambridge, Mass.: Ballinger, 1977).

13. Eighty-nine banks are directly represented and five more participate through shareholding in a consortium bank: Carol Parker, "Foreign Banks in London: New Opportunities for Expansion," *The Banker* (November 1980): 97.

14. Some estimates of the number of Euromarket financial institutions run much higher. Saeed Abtahi, for one, has put the number at around seven hundred. See Abtahi, "Financial Flows to the Developing Countries: The Case of Eurodollar Credits," D.B.A. dissertation, Harvard Business School, 1976, p. 86. As of 1980, 401 foreign banks were registered in London, according to *The Banker* (November 1980): 87. In addition, Singapore, one of the two centers of the Asiadollar market, now has more than 100 licensed operators with total assets and liabilities of about $39 billion. *Wall Street Journal*, 26 March 1980, p. 18.

15. *World Financial Markets* (April 1981): 13. Net size differs from gross size by excluding cross-deposits among banks.

immunity from foreign commercial laws. The novel character of this loan demand and the risks it posed were serious obstacles to greater commercial lending for balance-of-payments purposes.

Eurobanks responded by developing new procedures, which were soon deeply imbedded in the markets' daily operations. To begin with, standard loan agreements require that sovereign immunity be waived. Beyond that, two technical innovations helped open the market to LDCs. The first, copied from equity and bond underwriting, was credit syndication. Larger loans, instead of being made by a single bank, were shared among several major banks and scores of smaller ones. This technique was especially useful in lending to sovereign borrowers, because lenders were less experienced in that area, often knew little about the specific state enterprises involved, and had no accurate way of judging the political and commercial risks. By using syndicated loans, essentially unknowable default risks could be spread over large numbers of banks.

The second important development came in 1969, when short-term interest rates soared above long-term rates. This reversal of the typical yield curve had a sharp impact on loan profits because banks were using short-term liabilities to fund their medium-term assets.[16] Learning from the experience, they introduced floating-rate loans, shifting to the borrower the uncertainty over interest rates. After that, credits were committed to the borrower for several years but their price changed every few months to reflect the cost of short-term funds.

These innovations broadened lender participation and so facilitated sovereign borrowing on a truly massive scale. They still characterize the market. LDC borrowing is overwhelmingly in the form of syndicated Eurodollar credits with fluctuating rates, which include a base interest charge, a lending margin (or spread), and a one-time syndication fee for the lead manager, which arranges the credit. If it is a revolving credit instead of the more usual term loan, a small commitment fee is paid for the unused portion of the loan. The spread, usually between 0.25 percent and 2 percent, is set for the life of the agreement. The base interest charge, on the other hand, is recalculated every three or six months to match the rate London banks pay for Eurocurrency deposits. This base rate

16. M. S. Mendelsohn, *Money on the Move: The Modern International Capital Market* (New York: McGraw-Hill, 1980), p. 80.

THIRD WORLD DEBT     21

is widely known by its acronym LIBOR, for London Inter-Bank Offer Rate. To supervise the repayment of the loan, the lead manager usually takes on the additional role of agent, for which it is paid a small annual fee. With these technical features in place and with interest rates persistently more attractive (to both depositors and borrowers) than those in domestic markets,[17] the supply of Euromarket funds has expanded steadily.

The market's efficiency in attracting these deposits is noteworthy because the sources have varied so markedly, and the shifting sources of Euromarket funding illustrate the complexity of commercial lending to Third World states. It is oversimple to reduce these flows to petrodollar recycling, as important as that is. Actually, Third World borrowers (principally sovereign states, parastatal enterprises, and private corporations with state guarantees) are matched with a variety of ultimate savers via several layers of cross-depositing among Eurobanks. Twice when OPEC ran large surpluses, after the oil price rises of the mid-1970s and again more recently, this banking system funneled credit from petroleum producers to consumers—petrodollar recycling. At other times, when advanced capitalist states were in surplus, they supplied much of the market's funding and, in effect, provided credit for their own industrial exports. For example, they supplied around three-quarters of new Eurodeposits in 1978.[18] For symmetry, we might call this "metrodollar recycling."

Meanwhile, the Euromarket continues to play an entrepôt role, mediating between savers and investors from the same state (or group of states). Eurobank deposits from Tanzania, for instance,

---

17. In 1978, for instance, Eurodollar deposit rates commanded a premium of 0.375 percent to 0.5 percent over U. S. certificates of deposit. That differential moved slightly higher in 1979 and 1980: see Bank for International Settlements (BIS), *BIS 1979 Annual Report,* pp. 127–28, and *BIS 1980 Annual Report,* p. 109. Deposit rates in the two markets co-vary, with Euromarket premiums largely a function of U. S. reserve requirements, Federal Deposit insurance costs, and the non-infinite elasticity of funds with respect to small interest-rate differentials. See Robert Z. Aliber, "Monetary Aspects of Offshore Markets," *Columbia Journal of World Business* 14 (Fall 1979): 8–16, and Ian H. Giddy, "Why Eurodollars Grow," ibid., pp. 54–60.

18. *IMF Survey,* 3 September 1979, p. 274 (table). The Euromarket has thus continued to grow rapidly despite significant redistributions of current-account surpluses. The growth, however, does not mean that Euromarket size is unaffected by the distribution of surpluses. It would be affected if savers in different countries had different marginal propensities to buy Euromarket deposits. I am indebted to Robert Aliber for this point.

are almost identical to Eurobank loans there.[19] The Euromarket's advantage over local capital markets is especially prominent when those markets are thin, monopolized, legally restricted, or otherwise costly. Thus, while the Euromarket does indeed recycle petrodollars, this hardly exhausts its more general functions of mediating between diverse depositors and borrowers and between all surplus and deficit states.

## A Profile of Third World Debt

Among the most important deficit borrowers have been less developed, oil-importing states, especially those with more complex economies and extensive development programs. Since the early 1970s their participation in the Euromarket has grown even faster than the markets themselves. In 1973–1974, for instance, about 20 percent of all Eurocurrency credits went to nonoil LDCs. Within five years that percentage had doubled, an increase even more striking because the market itself had doubled.[20]

This lending has overturned traditional patterns of external finance as private credits have far outpaced grants and loans. During the 1960s, non-OPEC states received over half their net external resources on concessional terms (and much of the rest in the form of foreign direct investment). Between 1974 and 1979, however, development aid and official export credits accounted for less than one-third of their external financing. Fully 60 percent came from commercial bank credits.[21] That translates, predictably enough, into a substantial debt burden. Even if we exclude Mexico's substantial borrowing from the total because of its newly discovered oil, the figures are striking: the twelve largest nonoil borrowers had external debts of $199 billion at the end of 1980. Of that, they owed $120 billion to private banks.[22]

This rise in bank lending to less developed states has been heavily concentrated in fast-growing, semi-industrialized countries. Brazil alone accounts for over 30 percent of all nonoil LDC debt

19. BIS, "International Banking Developments—Second Quarter 1980," 19 November 1980, table 7.

20. *The Banker* (August 1979): 113; *World Financial Markets* (November 1979): 12. These figures refer to publicized Eurocurrency credit. Very few LDCs participate in the international bond market, and their share is typically less than 10 percent of that market.

21. *BIS 1980 Annual Report*, p. 102. The BIS figures include Mexico, so they are designated non-OPEC in the text rather than nonoil or oil-importing.

22. *World Financial Markets* (January 1981): 4, table 5.

and over 38 percent of debt to banks.[23] A handful of states in Latin America and East Asia account for much of the remainder. By contrast, all the nonoil underdeveloped states of Africa together owe less than 9 percent.[24] Except for a few countries with extensive mineral deposits, the least developed states have received virtually no bank financing except for secure, short-term trade credits.[25]

The redirection of aid toward poorer recipients and the stagnation of aid flows as a whole have left countries with higher per capita incomes increasingly dependent on the Euromarket for development and balance-of-payments financing. Taken together, the relative decline of aid, the swift rise of offshore capital markets, and more active market participation by certain LDCs have transformed the basic character of international resource flows and balance-of-payments financing. The IMF puts the matter clearly: "There was a time when official agencies would have been expected to be the principal intermediaries between surplus and deficit countries. When the need arose, however, private international markets had already developed to the point at which they were able to perform this function effectively for a number of countries and have continued to do so."[26]

This private financing has much larger public consequences. At a time when official lending was growing slowly, the Euromarket significantly increased the credit available to the largest LDCs. Heavy borrowing by these states allowed them to maintain growth while adjusting slowly to current-account deficits. By using liability financing, they avoided any immediate reallocation of resources. For the moment, at least, their real absorption of goods and services could remain high relative to production. There is a price, of course; and borrowers have to pay it in both the short and the long term. The immediate price is sharply higher debt service. Not only have debts grown, interest rates have soared; as a result, the interest payments of the twelve major nonoil LDCs have doubled every two years since 1973, from $2.9 billion at the time of the embargo to $18.4 billion in 1980.[27] Interest payments on external debt are also absorbing a much higher percentage of export earnings. For

23. Ibid.

24. *BIS 1980 Annual Report*, p. 119.

25. *Euromoney* (March 1978): 45.

26. Quoted in Gabriel Hauge, Erik Hoffmeyer, and Lord Roll of Ipsden (commentator), *The International Capital Market and the International Monetary System* (Washington, D. C.: IMF, 1978), p. 11.

27. *World Financial Markets* (January 1981): 4, table 5.

the twelve largest nonoil LDCs, interest payments on external debt were less than 6 percent of export earnings in the early 1970s. In 1980, by contrast, 16 percent of export earnings went to interest repayments, and the figure could rise to 20 percent in 1981.[28] On top of these interest charges are substantial obligations to repay (or refinance) loan principal—obligations that are growing as loans from the mid-1970s come due.[29] These developments point to a longer-term price. If debts are ever to be reduced, future absorption must be curtailed relative to production. These countries, in other words, must generate more foreign exchange by higher net exports. The newly industrializing countries (NICs) are likely to pursue this goal by exporting aggressively, a strategy that implies more fractious trade disputes and higher adjustment costs in developed markets. In any case, the need for more foreign exchange earnings gives the NICs a profound stake in the continued openness of the world trading system—a stake they share with their Euromarket creditors. Commercial debts, then, may play a growing role in the trade politics of advanced states, stimulating NIC exports and providing them with some political support from lenders.

The mixture of commercial financing and slow adjustment has had other global repercussions. None is more important than the impact on the distribution of current-account balances. Because creditworthy states could finance their oil deficits, they were more likely to accommodate them and less likely to confront other states. Unlike the situation in the 1930s, there was to be no self-defeating scramble of nations shifting their current-account problems onto others. In fact, Western governments had recognized this danger soon after the embargo and had pledged to forego beggar-my-neighbor policies. Their expressed aim was to accept and finance OPEC surpluses rather than shift the counterpart deficits by external restrictions or excessive retrenchment. They achieved their largest goal: Europe, America, and Japan, despite domestic pressures, did avoid severe restrictions. As a group, however, they

28. *World Financial Markets* (December 1980): 11–12.
29. Amortization payments now add over $15 billion annually to nonoil LDCs' gross financing requirements. Total 1980 outlays for oil imports, gross interest payments, and amortization for the twelve major nonoil LDCs reach approximately $73.7 billion, over 56 percent of exports (calculated from *World Financial Markets* [January 1981]: table 5, and [September 1980]: table 2). The figure for Brazil is a staggering 107 percent of exports: *Wall Street Journal,* 10 February 1981, p. 26.

moved rapidly into current-account balance and provided little new financing for others who bore the deficits. In the end, it was the Eurobanks, not the major central banks, that recycled the petrosurplus. That, too, carried a price, since it accommodated not only the collective deficit but also the OPEC surplus. Thus, the offshore credit markets sustained and reinforced this remarkable transfer of global wealth.

Repeating the recycling process over the next several years may be more difficult. The prospects depend on three uncertain factors: the size and durability of OPEC surpluses, the willingness of advanced states to absorb counterpart deficits, and the capacity of international financial markets. The picture is mixed. Advanced economies are absorbing quite large deficits, having moved from a surplus of around $30 billion in 1978 to a deficit of $46 billion in 1980.[30] Another positive sign for nonoil LDCs is that their combined current-account deficit is smaller in relation to their income than in the mid-1970s: about 4.5 percent of gross domestic product instead of 6 percent.[31] On the other hand, their deficit in absolute terms is large and growing, from $38 billion in 1978 to $80 billion in 1980, and the IMF anticipates $100 billion deficits by 1982.[32] Since these deficits are closely connected to OPEC's surpluses, the future of OPEC's surplus is critically important to nonoil LDCs. After the 1973–1974 oil shock, weak oil prices and OPEC's massive imports rapidly reduced the surplus. In one year alone, OPEC's $68 billion surplus was nearly halved, and it continued to decline rapidly until the second round of oil price increases. There is currently a spirited debate over whether OPEC's most recent surplus will follow the same course of rapid decline.[33]

Underscoring all these issues is one sobering theme: the financing needs of the early 1980s come after seven years of substantial commercial lending to Third World states. The new debt burden differs from the last precisely because it succeeds it and incorporates much of it.

30. Address by J. de Larosière, managing director of the IMF, in *IMF Survey*, 18 May 1981, p. 150.

31. Address by J. de Larosière, *IMF Survey*, 10 November 1980, p. 346.

32. Address by J. de Larosière, *IMF Survey*, 18 May 1981, p. 150. This article was first published in 1981. Keeping the date of publication in mind will help the reader to comprehend statements which may appear incongruous because of the passage of time.

33. See, for example, the address by J. de Larosière, *IMF Survey*, 10 November 1980, p. 346; also *World Financial Markets* (December 1980): 11.

These recycling difficulties are likely to grow more acute over the next several years. They pose at least two major issues for the international organization of Third World debt. The first is the prospect of more debt crises. Until now, these have been managed effectively by informal consortia of creditors. Their immediate aim is to salvage the creditors' assets by deterring default, restructuring debt if necessary, and ensuring timely repayment. Their larger goal is to limit the impact of debt crises on bank assets worldwide. The informal institutions now used will be tested as financing problems grow. Second, there will be tremendous pressure from both creditors and debtors for public institutions to supplement private financing. Thus, the limited capacities of private financial markets are likely to spur innovation at the IMF and World Bank, as well as more government-to-government lending.[34]

### The Role of International Banks in Debt Crises

One of the most intriguing features of individual debt problems is the way the structure of international finance and the procedures of creditors combine to minimize the impact of crises on other debt. Acting in concert, lenders have compelled debt service when borrowers could pay and quietly reorganized obligations when they could not. In so doing, they have deterred defaults on financially sound loans while insulating their worldwide assets from the effects of crises. In other words, a political structure undergirds international debt. Economic sanctions back its commercial security.

To understand this political structure we must first unravel a paradox. How can highly competitive commercial banks, operating in virtually unregulated capital markets, act cooperatively to prevent defaults? The central problem is collective action. To analyze it one must examine certain institutions and conventions of international banking, especially those that apply when default draws near.

While some major banks dominate their local markets, none controls the Euromarket. In 1980, over sixty banks could claim they were lead managers for loans worth more than $1 billion.[35] In

---

34. *Business Week* (19 January 1981): 90.
35. *Institutional Investor/International Edition* (March 1981): 146. These figures allot the full amount of the loan to the lead manager. The top bank, Citicorp Inter-

a market this deep, no single bank or small group can determine interest spreads, loan maturities, or syndication fees. They are set competitively, in the context of overall market liquidity and specific borrower characteristics. But if Eurobanks are competitive deal-makers, how do they manage to cooperate in crises? The answer lies in the formation of syndicates. Syndicate lending, and commercial lending more generally, involves considerable interdependence among banks. They have effective leadership in syndicate agents, ample incentives to cooperate to avert default, and relatively few incentives to cheat on collective agreements.

To begin with, default on any syndicated loan involves a dozen or more syndicate members directly. Cross-default clauses affect still more banks. Written into all syndication agreements, these clauses give every syndicate discretionary power to call its loans in default, even if all payments are current, when another syndicate has called default. The immediate aim is to give each syndicate equal status in protecting its assets. The larger consequence is to deter capricious default by threatening to bankrupt the debtor. Since that entails losses for the creditors, too, cross-default clauses are at best a blunt and dangerous instrument. Their mere presence draws lenders more deeply into each other's disputes, but they are involved only sparingly.

A more common approach is to reorganize troubled debt at creditor conferences. The syndicate structure, with agents responsible for each loan's administration, helps the numerous banks organize for debt restructuring. In negotiations with Peru in 1978, for instance, six large lenders from the United States, Europe, Canada, and Japan represented the 84 banks involved.[36] A subsequent agreement covered 283 banks.[37]

Such tight interdependence does not imply that Eurobanks always agree on how to treat troubled debt.[38] There are some systematic differences among lenders, but formal and informal means have been devised to bridge these differences in order to act collectively. Ultimately, these arrangements are built on the structure of

---

national Group, led seventy-one loans worth over $13 billion. By comparison, the twentieth-largest syndicate manager, Société Générale de Banque, led twenty-two loans worth over $6 billion.

36. *Euromoney* (March 1978): 25.

37. *Wall Street Journal*, 2 January 1979, p. 16.

38. Policy differences arose within lending syndicates in Indonesia, Turkey, Peru, Zaire, and elsewhere. They are discussed by Jonathon Aronson in "The Politics of Private Bank Lending and Debt Renegotiation," in Aronson, ed., *Debt and the Less Developed Countries* (Boulder: Westview Press, 1979).

commercial lending itself: formal contractual arrangements, a dense network of interbank deposits, and reciprocal financial ties among the largest banks.

Differences regarding the treatment of debt can emerge within syndicates or between them. Syndicates with larger loans or worse arrears tend to favor more comprehensive refinancing. Within syndicates, large creditors often counsel patience as long as interest payments are nearly current. If arrearages become serious they prefer emergency refinancing to default. Banks with less at stake are less willing to provide time or money. For them, rescue operations may require undue managerial attention, or, in the case of smaller banks, an excessive share of capital. They may hope larger creditors will simply take over their portion of the loan. In any case, they are more inclined to declare default, recover what they can, and let the resulting damage stand as a warning to debtors.

Lenders resolve these divergent positions in two ways. First, all syndicate agreements have provisions that apply when the agent bank has difficulty collecting the loan. A few permit the agent bank to undertake its own initiatives, at least in limited fashion. Most require the agent to act on instructions from syndicate members, who vote in proportion to their share of the credit.[39] These provisions offer some contractual protection to minor creditors, although the protection can be very weak at times. The best-known example was in several Iranian loans where the largest New York banks simply overrode the minor creditors (European, Japanese, and regional American banks). This experience, and the litigation arising from it, should further clarify the role of syndicate agents and the rights of both participating banks and borrowers.[40]

Besides these contractual provisions, informal ententes often prevail among overlapping syndicates. The danger is that once arrears are large, one or two syndicates might call a default rather than restructure the loan or accept slow payments. Since other creditors lack preferred status, they would have strong incentives to invoke cross-default clauses and claim what assets they could. Thus, a case of poorly performing loans could be transformed swiftly into a serious debt crisis, with some loss of bank assets certain. That prospect gives all banks pause, and it gives debtors some bargaining power. Furthermore, large creditors, bound together

39. Mendelsohn, *Money on the Move*, p. 90.
40. See "Euro-Law Left in Limbo," *The Banker* (March 1981): 84–85.

by joint lending and cross-depositing, may be reluctant to enforce isolated and contentious positions. The transcendent risk is that the code of cooperation and collective action will dissolve in other cases of troubled debt. This mutual but sometimes strained forebearance has characterized interbank relations in a number of cases, including debt renegotiations with Nicaragua and Zaire.

To summarize, international banks have interlocked but not identical interests in crises, and they have syndicate agents to coordinate their actions. Equally important, if they do organize themselves, the prospect of their collective sanctions is almost certain to deter default among solvent borrowers. Such default—or debt renunciation, which is much more serious and much rarer— would deprive a debtor of virtually all international credit, except (perhaps) public aid from countries with overriding political concerns. Henry Wallich of the Federal Reserve Board emphasizes the grave consequences: "Unless [a country] were willing to undertake the political subservience of total dependence on another bloc," he says, "it would have to pay cash for every power station, every industrial project. That it could do so is beyond belief. Consequently, these countries have to continue to service their debts in whatever way they can."[41] Such severe sanctions, organized privately for the most part, have effectively deterred default by the solvent.

### Managing Debt Crises: The IMF and Creditor Clubs

As important as unified private sanctions are, they do not exhaust the problem of collective action in debt crises. A borrower, fearing retribution, may not renounce its debt but still may not be able to pay. Nations can fall behind in servicing debts because of border wars, plummeting commodity prices, or simple economic mismanagement. As arrearages accumulate, the agenda is set for default or refinancing.

Refinancing is a complicated and difficult operation, involving not only the provision of external resources but the restructuring of domestic economic life. It is a politically delicate task that neither commercial banks nor government creditors can perform autonomously. The pivotal actor is the International Monetary Fund,

41. U. S. Congress, Senate, Committee on Banking, Housing, and Urban Affairs, *Hearings on International Debt*, 95th Congress, 1st session, 1977, p. 88.

which in the 1950s began playing a vital role in renegotiating debt and postponing default. Most significantly, the IMF provides the dominant institutional framework for the ongoing management of troubled debt, including the transfusion of new credit and the supervision of austerity policies. In the telling words of one prominent banker, the Fund plays the "vital 'syndicate leadership' role."[42]

The IMF's role in debt renegotiations has two phases. First, it assesses the relevant economic data and reaches agreement for a standby loan, subject to certain conditions. Second, it continuously monitors and evaluates the debtor's economic policies to ensure its adherence to the conditions.

Typically, an IMF loan agreement requires specific changes in economic policies and sets performance criteria. To guarantee that changes are made, the Fund provides credit in several stages as the borrower adapts to agreed stabilization guidelines. The guidelines are essentially stock recipes for improving current and capital accounts.[43] The centerpieces are fiscal and monetary restraints, designed to lower demand for foreign goods without direct controls or other price distortions. Some public subsidies may be eliminated, and typically limits are placed on domestic credit expansion.[44] Devaluation has long been standard, although, because resistance has been so fierce, the IMF is now reconsidering its priority. All these basic changes in national policy are masked by the dulling term *conditionality*.

These stern conditions and the IMF's proven ability to oversee them form the basis for debt renegotiation. Both official and private lenders accept the IMF agreement as a signal that the debtor

42. Statement by Frederick Heldring, president, Philadelphia National Bank, in U. S. Congress, House, Committee on Banking, Finance, and Urban Affairs, *Hearings on U. S. Participation in the Supplementary Financing Facility of the International Monetary Fund*, 95th Congress, 1st session, 1977, p. 142.

43. There is a growing literature—and some sharply divergent opinions—on the effects of these stabilization programs. For an IMF staff view, see Thomas M. Reichmann and Richard T. Stillson, "Experience with Programs of Balance of Payments Adjustment: Stand-By Arrangements in the Higher Tranches, 1963–72," *International Monetary Fund Staff Papers*, 25 June 1978, pp. 293–309. A number of useful contributions can be found in William R. Cline and Sidney Weintraub, eds., *Economic Stabilization in Developing Countries* (Washington, D. C.: Brookings Institution, 1981). The effectiveness of IMF programs is challenged empirically by Thomas A. Connors in an unpublished International Finance Discussion paper for the Federal Reserve Board.

44. *Euromoney* (March 1978): 10; International Monetary Fund, Office of the Secretary, "Multilateral Debt Renegotiations—Experience of Fund Members," unpublished internal memorandum, 6 August 1971, p. 25.

intends to crack down on its deficit. Lenders typically renegotiate their own claims on that condition. According to Anthony Solomon, who supervised international financial issues at the U. S. Treasury before his appointment to head the Federal Reserve Board of New York, "Typically, when the Fund reaches an agreement with a country the banks—instead of rushing to ask for their own money . . . are willing to increase their lending because it has entered a period of stabilization under the tight controls of an IMF standby agreement."[45]

By providing resources for debtors on its own conservative terms, the Fund effectively provides public goods for creditors. The Fund acts directly on debtors: it helps organize official debt renegotiations, enforces conditionality, and audits stabilization programs. Indirectly, the Fund acts on creditors. By supervising the adjustment process, the IMF stiffens the resolve of creditors to provide more capital or at least more time. With the IMF monitoring a national program of economic discipline, private capital markets generally become more accessible and existing loans more secure. The Fund, in other words, permits the banks to act in their collective self-interest.

The IMF's involvement in debt negotiations does suggest an indirect role for advanced capitalist states. After all, they dominate the Fund's weighted voting and, as a rule, endorse its advice and surveillance. Still, the IMF should not be considered simply a cipher for state power. To begin with, it is a genuinely multilateral institution. If it generally represents the interests of major capital exporters in debt issues, those interests are at least highly aggregated. They are joint interests rather than those of a single state, and, in most cases, general policy directions rather than specific instructions. The Fund follows routine procedures and its professional staff is given considerable autonomy in individual negotiations. Ultimately, the Fund's role in these negotiations depends less on its financial resources and its general backing from advanced states than on the perceptions of other lenders. Their agreement

45. *Hearings on U. S. Participation in the Supplementary Financing Facility*, p. 72. Richard Cooper, then undersecretary of state, added that the IMF is especially skilled at facilitating domestic stabilization. It is, he says, the catalyst for the politically difficult adjustment process: U. S. Congress, Senate, Committee on Foreign Relations, *Hearings on American Foreign Economic Policy: An Overview*, 95th Congress, 1st session, 1977, especially p. 48. It is clear from these and other hearings that both bankers and policymakers understand the IMF's capacity to compel adjustment and to secure public and private debts through its conditional lending.

that the IMF's advice is prudent, combined with the Fund's unique capacity to monitor stabilization programs, forms the basis for the Fund's role in debt renegotiations.

The debt negotiations themselves now follow an established routine. The debtor approaches the IMF or a major creditor seeking to reorganize its debt. The aim is to postpone impending repayments and secure new financing. As the IMF negotiates its standby agreement, private and official creditors conduct their own separate meetings. Using these informal club arrangements, they make complete inventories of external debts and gather other economic information. Their agreements, which presuppose an IMF standby agreement, typically provide new financing and reschedule old debt. In the case of official debt, the multilateral agreement is not legally binding, but its recommendations form the basis of subsequent bilateral agreements.[46] These ad hoc conferences are convened at the creditors' discretion and conform to the creditors' position that debt relief is an extreme event, forced by traumatic circumstances. Likewise, despite hard bargaining over the size of new credits and the ease of repayment terms, the agreements conform to the creditors' position that such extreme events are best handled by short-term, generally nonconcessionary, debt reorganization.[47]

Whether the agreements involve public or private creditors, their most important convention deals with burden-sharing: creditors must be treated equally. Most-favored-nation clauses have

---

46. Christopher Prout, "Finance for Development Countries: An Essay," in Andrew Shonfield, ed., *International Economic Relations of the Western World 1959–1971*, vol. 2 (London: Oxford University Press for the Royal Institute of International Affairs, 1976).

47. While private creditors may provide new credits and occasionally permit principal repayments to be stretched out over a longer period, they almost always demand that interest payments be kept current. The conventionality of these arrangements is best shown by the controversy over a recent deviant case, that of Nicaragua. As John Dizard writes: "From the dawn of banking—even through the latest period when occasional reschedulings of government debt have been permitted—one rule has remained sacred: . . . never, never give up on interest payments, lest you put the store in jeopardy. . . . Even Zaire, whose repayment problems are legendary, has kept its interest payments more or less current." But in Nicaragua's case, the 115 lenders capitalized and deferred more than three-quarters of its past-due interest. Both the banks and Nicaragua's finance officials went to some lengths to insist that the country is a unique case, requiring unique treatment. Even so, there has been considerable discussion about whether Nicaragua's rescheduling has set a precedent for other troubled debtors: "The Nicaraguan Precedent," *Institutional Investor/International Edition* (December 1980): 110–11.

eliminated side deals with minor creditors and have been extended to nonparticipants such as the Soviet Union.

These procedures developed incrementally in the 1950s and 1960s as official creditors (the so-called Paris Club) worked out joint approaches to debt rescheduling. Private creditor clubs (the London and the New York clubs) are a more recent development and their arrangements are therefore more tentative. While the groups meet separately, their deliberations are inevitably intertwined. Most notably, private lenders often strike bargains that closely resemble the official accords.

Despite these similarities, there are systematic differences between commercial and official debt negotiations. They typically involve complementary forms of debt consolidation: rescheduling and refinancing. Rescheduling, which normally applies to official debts, simply postpones the timetable for repayment. Refinancing replaces maturing debt with new obligations. Commercial banks prefer it because it avoids the implication that loan agreements have not been honored. At least formally, it upholds the sanctity of contracts.

The reorganization of private debt is also less flexible, since it is based on earlier syndication contracts and aims solely at averting private loan losses. Preserving the current discounted value of bank assets is the overriding goal. As a result, these agreements generally offer harder terms than official creditors do. The official creditors have wider aims, more leeway, and more diverse policy instruments. Although they have traditionally favored hard terms and short reschedulings, they have recently been willing to soften their position in the light of widespread payment problems in poor countries.[48]

Whatever their differences, commercial and official debts are sometimes linked in negotiations. The rescheduling of official debt is sometimes made contingent on the renegotiation of private debt.[49] Bilateral agreements may also explicitly protect private debt, even if the lender's home government had not previously

48. For official creditor positions, see the testimony of John Lange, U. S. Treasury, in U. S. Congress, Senate, Committee on Banking, Housing, and Urban Affairs, *Hearing on U. S. Loans to Zaire*, 96th Congress, 1st session, 1979, p. 20; Brian Crowe (of the U. S. State Department), "International Public Lending and American Policy," in Aronson, ed., *Debt and the Less Developed Countries*, especially pp. 33–34; and Albert C. Cizauskas (of the World Bank), "International Debt Renegotiation: Lessons from the Past," *World Development* 7 (February 1979): 202–3.

49. See statement by Richard Cooper in *Hearings on International Debt*, p. 66.

guaranteed it.[50] Perhaps the most difficult issue is whether official creditors will insist on similar concessions from private lenders. The problem will grow as private debt accumulates and can create even sharper divisions if the banks and aid donors are from different countries. The political risk for aid donors is the charge, already raised in congressional hearings, that public funds might be used to bail out bank loans. The thorniest case arose in Zaire when the Paris Club granted a three-year debt moratorium and rescheduled $1 billion in loans. The one hundred private creditors demanded tougher conditions, including continuing service on outstanding loans. "The Paris Club members," according to *Institutional Investor,* "were obviously distressed at this stubbornness by the private sector. . . . But the private arrangements stuck."[51] Until now, such conflicts have been rare. Most governments have not been eager to push for comparability, perhaps out of solicitude for private capital flow, perhaps because it is very difficult to monitor.

These crosscutting links between public and private debts are another way advanced states impinge on the international organization of Third World debt. Unlike domestic banking rules, which mainly affect Euromarket size, the Paris Club arrangements bear directly on individual private debts. But they appear considerably less important than the banks' autonomous procedures and those of the IMF. Still, as private debt continues to grow and as more parallel agreements are reached, ties between public and private lenders may be elaborated.

Formal ties and formal institutions are always possible, but they are unlikely at present. The ad hoc clubs have proved remarkably effective, at least as far as creditors are concerned. They have successfully resisted efforts to change their procedures, including the Group of 77's proposal at UNCTAD V to establish a permanent International Debt Commission.[52]

The record shows why creditors prefer the status quo. Club arrangements isolate debtors while facilitating collective action by

---

50. International Bank for Reconstruction and Development (IBRD), "Multilateral Debt Renegotiations: 1956–1968," unpublished paper, 11 April 1969, p. 29.

51. Vivian Lewis, "Inside the Paris Club," *Institutional Investor/International Edition* (June 1980): 36.

52. Jonathan Aronson, *Money and Power: Banks and the World Monetary System* (Beverly Hills: Sage Publications, 1977), pp. 167–76; *IMF Survey,* 18 June 1979, p. 187.

creditors. Since they are convened only in payments crises, debt relief cannot even be discussed except under extreme conditions. Indeed, that is one of the regime's well-established rules. Yet when emergencies do occur, the clubs can efficiently reschedule and refinance the debt.

This has not often been necessary. Of the countless billions lent by governments and commercial banks between 1956 and 1978, only about $10 billion had to be rescheduled. Fifteen debtors were involved and a total of forty-two reschedulings were undertaken.[53] The pace then picked up slightly, from about two per year to five in 1979. Given the circumstances of the debtors, the terms seem to show the strength of the creditors' position. Until OECD donors eased some aid terms retroactively, interest payments had been forgiven only twice and no principal had ever been cancelled.[54] Nor do the repeated reschedulings for some nations, India and Argentina for example, indicate that the first procedure failed. Rather, they suggest that the creditors were determined to keep the debtor on a short leash. By rescheduling only the debts falling due in one or two years, they kept a tight hold over payments financing and a close watch on the debtor's economic policies.[55]

This kind of effective cooperation has made default prohibitively costly for any nation that can avoid it. A World Bank study of debt renegotiations underlines the point: "[R]ules of the game have emerged in the field of international finance. One such rule is that default by a debtor country is now excluded as a means of adjusting financial obligations to debt servicing capacity."[56]

## New Demands on the IMF

Although creditor clubs have successfully replaced unilateral default with multilateral debt consolidation, it should be stressed that the arrangements for private creditors are still new. So far, they have been involved in fewer than two dozen reschedulings. And sometimes the learning process can be difficult, as it was in Peru. Facing a payments crisis in 1976, the Morales government sought loans from U. S. banks as a substitute for IMF condi-

53. Crowe, "International Public Lending," table 4.
54. IMF, "Multilateral Debt Renegotiations—Experience," p. 13.
55. Robert N. Bee, "Lessons from Debt Reschedulings in the Past," *Euromoney* (April 1977): 34–35.
56. IBRD, "Multilateral Debt Renegotiations: 1956–68," p. 39.

tional credit. The banks agreed, accepting Peru's position that an IMF program would be politically destabilizing. The risk, for both the government and the banks, was a radical nationalist response. With the IMF on the sidelines, Citibank led a refinancing group and formed a steering committee to oversee economic retrenchment. But organizing for surveillance proved difficult, and the banks found themselves involved deeply and visibly in Peruvian politics. They drew the lesson that commercial banks could not impose conditionality; only the IMF could do so.[57] Since then, lenders have refused to depart from that practice.[58]

To ensure that the IMF plays an effective role in the future, banks have proposed reforms for the Fund and additions to its lending resources. These proposals to strengthen the Fund have generally received support from the State Department and Treasury, and from other creditor states.[59] Suggested changes range from Fund-sponsored insurance for private loans[60] to IMF borrowing in commercial capital markets for re-lending purposes. Uniting these diverse proposals is the idea that the IMF and the World Bank should bear more of the private lenders' risks and play a larger financing role.

Both the World Bank and the IMF are, in fact, seeking increases in their lendable resources. In addition, the World Bank has moved beyond its traditional "project" lending to support structural adjustment to higher energy prices. "In its new role," says *Business Week*, "the [World] bank will supplement the IMF in its efforts to recycle petrodollars and will help to provide a safety net under the commercial banks, which will continue to supply the

---

57. G. A. Costanzo, vice-chairman of Citicorp, remarked that "the reaction to this loan was a signal to me that I want *no* part of deals with that kind of discipline in the future." Quoted by Belliveau in "What the Peru Experiment Means," *Institutional Investor/International Edition* (October 1976): 34.

58. Subsequent negotiations with Peru involved the IMF, and lenders have refused to discuss refinancing in Jamaica without direct IMF involvement in a stabilization program.

59. *Hearings on International Debt; Hearings on U. S. Participation in the Supplementary Financing Facility;* U. S. Congress, Senate, Committee on Banking, Housing, and Urban Affairs, *Hearing on IMF Supplementary Financing Facility,* 95th Congress, 1st session, 1977.

60. Xenophon Zolotas, "The Case for an International Loan Insurance Fund," *The Banker* (November 1980): 33–36. Zolotas, a governor of the Bank of Greece, argues that recycling of oil surplus funds should take place primarily through commercial banks and that an international loan insurance fund would strengthen the international banking system.

bulk of balance-of-payments financing."[61] The World Bank and BIS have also led efforts to provide more extensive and disaggregated information about debts. Finally, the World Bank has begun some cooperative financing with private lenders. Such a program potentially multiplies the Bank's resources while lowering commercial risks (by linking private assets to the inviolate claims of the World Bank). So far, the program has been limited in two ways. Its size remains small,[62] and the World Bank refuses to insert an automatic cross-default clause to protect private lenders. Even so, cofinancing provides a near-guarantee for commercial loans.[63]

Such arrangements linking public and private lenders are likely to grow, but they are limited by all lenders' demands for autonomy. Refinancing is an especially sensitive issue in that regard. Private lenders insist, for example, that in some critical cases a standby agreement with the IMF may still not be sufficient reason to extend new bank credits.[64] Yet it seems clear from the course of debate and from the steps taken so far that more cooperation between Eurobanks and multilateral institutions is likely.[65] Discussion has centered on the style and extent of cooperation, as well as the specific forms it should take, but not on its desirability: it can only diminish the risks of private foreign lending to the Third World.

Despite the importance of World Bank lending, reform propos-

61. *Business Week,* 30 June 1980, p. 40.
62. Cofinancing with private lenders was begun after the oil embargo and was loosely modeled on a World Bank program for European reconstruction. The Bank also cofinances with official aid agencies and export credit institutions. The *BIS 1980 Annual Report* states that "the Executive Directors, during the past year, reviewed the Bank's co-financing experience and gave direction to possible ways to expand co-financing opportunities in the future" (p. 68). The program is growing but is still quite small compared to the volume of commercial lending. From fiscal year 1975 to FY 1978, the Bank cofinanced twenty-nine operations involving $900 million in private funds; in FY 1979 it cofinanced sixteen more with $550 million in private funds (*BIS 1980 Annual Report,* p. 69). The bank's new attitude is summed up in the title of a recent article by Roger S. Leeds of the International Finance Corporation, "Why We Need More Co-Financing," *The Banker* (August 1980): 25. See also Christopher Johnson, "Searching for Foundations in Belgrade," *The Banker* (November 1979): 46.
63. Jessica Einhorn, "Cooperation between Public and Private Lenders to the Third World," *World Economy,* 2 May 1979, pp. 236–39.
64. [Rimmer de Vries], "The International Debt Situation," *World Financial Markets* (June 1977): 12.
65. The World Bank, for instance, concludes in its *World Development Report, 1979* (Washington, D. C.: IBRD, 1980), that "there may be advantages to closer coordination between official creditors and commercial banks in debt renegotiation exercises" (p. 33).

als tend to focus on the IMF, since it is a source not just of financing but of ongoing political supervision of debtors. Two issues dominate the various proposals: the level and form of IMF resources, and the political dilemmas of conditionality.

The Fund currently has substantial resources and it is relatively liquid. The Sixth General Review of Quotas increased resources by $12 billion. The Seventh General Review went much further, raising quotas by about $25 billion, a 50 percent increase.[66] The Fund's newly inaugurated Witteveen facility has added another $10.5 billion. But another round of heavy borrowing is building, and that might require still larger increases in IMF resources.

Such increases face serious obstacles, the principal one being the connection between national voting weights and member contributions to general IMF resources. Acutely aware of this link, advanced states have pushed for various "special funds," since such funds can accept OPEC money without shifting the larger voting distribution. Ultimately, this arrangement depends on OPEC's acceptance—and there are some small signs of difficulty. In July 1980, Saudi Arabia raised the political price for its cooperation by demanding observer status for the Palestine Liberation Organization at both the IMF and the World Bank. After the United States blocked this move, the Saudis settled for a more conventional solution. They agreed to lend the Fund SDR 4 billion (about $4.9 billion) at market rates for each of the next two years and again in the third year if their payments position permitted. The Fund's Board of Governors later announced that the Saudis had been allowed nearly to double their quota. With this increase, Saudi Arabia's share in total quotas rises to 3.5 percent (compared to over 19 percent for the United States), a quota that effectively permanently guarantees the Saudis a member on the IMF Executive Board.[67]

Despite this solution, the episode suggests the vulnerability of IMF funding procedures. The recognition of that vulnerability as well as the need for substantially increased resources has led directly to the search for alternative funding procedures. The leading candidate is the World Bank's procedure: borrowing (for relending purposes) in international financial markets. By borrowing in the Eurocurrency markets, the Fund could simultaneously aug-

---

66 *IMF Survey,* 15 December 1980, p. 377; *IMF Survey,* 9 February 1981, p. 33.
67. *IMF Survey,* 4 May 1981, pp. 129, 146; *IMF Survey,* 6 April 1981, pp. 97–101; conversations with Fund officials.

ment its resources, avoid making heavy demands on OPEC members, and lower its need for funding from a reluctant U. S. Congress. Moreover, the IMF already has the legal authority to undertake such borrowing. Its executive board urged consideration of this alternative in 1979. But an active program of borrowing threatened to disrupt the tight links that now exist between each Fund member's quota payments, its voting rights, and its access to credit.[68]

Of course, if the IMF's conditional lending is to have practical significance, it needs more than augmented resources. Borrowers must actually seek Fund aid. Conditionality is, after all, essentially contractual. It is the price of access to the IMF's higher credit tranches. Sovereign borrowers are increasingly reluctant to pay that price unless conditions are dire, and sometimes not even then. As a result, there are pressures to relax the IMF's tough lending standards.

Any shift in IMF standards poses a dilemma for creditors. If the IMF institutes more flexible conditions for its credit, more borrowers will turn to it. That is already the case with the IMF's special funds, which have fewer strings than regular borrowing. On the other hand, debtors often delay borrowing from regular credit tranches until the situation is critical. By weakening conditionality, the IMF is likely to play a larger role in payments financing and to become involved earlier with debtors' problems. For creditors, the price of such flexibility is that they can no longer consider the IMF's standards a proxy for their own. Private creditors, especially, have been perplexed by this dilemma and ambivalent about the choices it poses.

Meanwhile, the Fund has moved ahead to adopt new guidelines on conditionality. The change is gradual but not insignificant. Under Managing Director Jacques de Larosière, the IMF seems willing to extend larger credits over longer periods and under somewhat less stringent conditions. The Fund's conditions are now limited to "macroeconomic variables," for example. This new position is evolving on a case-by-case basis and its impact on debt negotiations is still uncertain. It could weaken the now-close rela-

68. Harvey D. Shapiro, "The IMF's Identity Crisis," *Institutional Investor/International Edition* (September 1980): 105; Hobart Rowen, "The Washington Agenda," ibid., p. 136; John Dizard, "The Flap over the IMF's Market Debut," *Institutional Investor/International Edition* (January 1981): 51–54; *IMF Press Release* 81/34, 8 May 1981.

tionship between IMF standby agreements and private refinancing. On the other hand, a larger IMF role in debt management and an earlier involvement in problem cases could reduce the risks of commercial lending. Whatever the outcome, this new policy is not a dramatic change, and it will not drastically alter the Fund's impact on Third World debt. Rather, it will modify in an incremental way its already crucial role in dampening private risks.

## Conclusion

This analysis of Third World debt suggests a novel and evolving relationship between private lenders and public institutions—a relationship that is at the heart of the debt regime. To understand that relationship, as well as the role played by capital-exporting states, one must distinguish clearly between the stock of debt and the flow of credit.

Demands for payments financing (indeed, for credit flows in general) arise from larger economic and political relationships: the openness of the international trade regime, supply-and-demand functions for traded goods, and the availability of nondebt financing such as foreign aid or direct foreign investments. Moreover, national economic policies are crucial in determining both the size of deficits and the means of financing them. The mediating role of offshore markets cannot be divorced from these political choices and commercial relationships or from the international political framework within which they take place. Here Gilpin's observation is quite pertinent: "What has to be explained are the economic and political circumstances that enable . . . transnational actors to play their semi-independent role in international affairs."[69]

In a general sense, the privatization of payments financing should be set in this larger context of state interaction. To the extent that the offshore markets are demand-driven, policy choices in oil-importing states are a significant source of market growth. More broadly, the markets' mediation between surplus and deficit states depends on the configuration of current-account balances.

At an institutional level, the Euromarket's development has been shaped by still other state actions. We have already mentioned

69. Robert Gilpin, *U. S. Power and the Multinational Corporation* (New York: Basic Books, 1975), p. 39.

its stimulation by U. S. capital controls, its cost advantages due to domestic banking regulations, and the generally passive stance of national monetary authorities toward its growth.[70] National monetary authorities also play a role, because Eurocurrency transactions require final settlement in national money. Although credit may be furnished in some unit-of-account or stateless money, the means of payment is still domestic money. "The great volume of dollar transactions among Eurobanks," says Ronald McKinnon, "results in a mirror image shuffling of dollar claims (usually demand deposits) among American correspondent banks in New York, Chicago, or San Francisco."[71] Because of this "mirror image shuffling," national authorities can suppress the growth of corresponding Eurocurrencies by restricting certain types of domestic financial transactions. At various times the Japanese, British, and Germans have done exactly that. The United States, by contrast, refrained from imposing such limits during its period of capital controls—a nonaction that was vital to the market's growth. In yet another way, the recent freezing and unfreezing of Iranian assets show that major states can intervene decisively in the Euromarket when they choose.

In one important area, however, they have moved quite cautiously. Despite the concerns of central bankers, there is no overall control of the Euromarket, and none is likely. Likewise, banking supervision has been left to national authorities, although some efforts at cooperation have been made under the auspices of the Bank for International Settlements. The BIS Standing Committee on Banking Regulations and Supervisory Practices (best known by the names of its successive chairmen, Blunden and Cooke) has encouraged consolidated reporting of global bank activities and quietly urged common standards for evaluating bank assets. To go beyond that has proved difficult. Almost any new set of regulations

70. Monetary authorities were not always passive, however, and those decisions also affected market size. In June 1971, for example, the major central banks agreed not to increase their official reserve holdings in the Euromarket. This agreement was based on the supposedly inflationary effects of such deposits. For a theoretical critique, see Gunter Dufey and Ian H. Giddy, *The International Money Market* (Englewood Cliffs, N. J.: Prentice-Hall, 1978), pp. 169–77.

71. Ronald I. McKinnon,, *Money in International Exchange: The Convertible Currency System* (New York: Oxford University Press, 1979), p. 209. McKinnon's view is widely, but not universally, held. In private communication, Robert Aliber has challenged the necessity of final settlement in national monies.

would entail extensive harmonizing of banking laws.[72] Achieving that is virtually impossible because it depends fundamentally on national control over money supplies. This obstacle has not precluded less extensive agreements to preserve the integrity of domestic banking systems. Most notably, the major central banks have devised a plan (the so-called Basle Concordat), as yet untested, to provide emergency liquidity in case a major Eurobank fails.[73]

In all these ways, the Euromarket is connected to national economies, national capital markets, national governments. Helmut Mayer, an economist at the BIS, underscores this basic relationship:

> The Euro-currency market does not . . . act as a self-contained banking system but as a link between the various national markets. This means that although the Euro-market is not subject to centralized control by a central bank, its development will nevertheless be determined in large measure by the policies followed in the main participating countries and by general economic developments in these countries.[74]

But if state policies have shaped the broad outlines of the Euromarket, they have not shaped the disposition of commercial debts. Even now, when central banks and regulatory authorities are keenly aware of Third World debt problems, their actions have been directed primarily at prudent supervision of bank portfolios and the provision of emergency liquidity. Other than the freeze on

72. Jessica P. Einhorn, "International Bank Lending: Expanding the Dialogue," *Columbia Journal of World Business* 13 (Fall 1978), especially pp. 126–29; Ian Giddy and Deborah Allen, "International Competition in Bank Regulation," *Banca Nazionale del Lavoro Quarterly Review*, no. 130 (September 1979); Cohen and Basagni, *Banks and the Balance of Payments*, chapter 5.

73. The 1975 Basle Concordat was developed in the aftermath of two significant bank failures, those of Bankhaus Herstatt and Franklin National. See H. J. Muller, "The Concordat," *De Nederlandsche Bank, N.V., Quarterly Statistics* (September 1979): 84–91; Allen B. Frankel, "The Lender of Last Resort Facility in the Context of Multinational Banking," *Columbia Journal of World Banking* 10 (Winter 1975), especially pp. 120–22; Joan E. Spero, *The Failure of the Franklin National Bank* (New York: Columbia University Press, 1980), chapter 6. For a chilling description of the potential ineffectiveness of international cooperation see John Dizard, "How the Interbank Market System Could Come Tumbling Down," *Institutional Investor/International Edition* (October 1980): 71–83.

74. Helmut Mayer, "Credit and Liquidity Creation in the International Banking Sector," Bank for International Settlements, Basel Economic Papers no. 1, November 1979, p. 21; Robert Z. Aliber, "The Integration of the Offshore and Domestic Banking System," *Journal of Monetary Economics* 6 (1980): 509–26.

Iranian assets, they have not sought to ensure the repayment of loans. Nor have they refinanced debtors, except in their limited capacity as foreign-aid creditors.[75]

Instead, the supervision of debt has largely been a function of commercial banking arrangements and the IMF's conditional lending. The key procedure has been ad hoc creditor conferences, which began among aid donors in the mid-1950s but is no longer limited to them. As the composition of capital flows changed, private banks developed a substantial stake and their own parallel creditor-club framework. As the problems of surveillance became clearer, creditor states and, later, private banks demanded a role for the IMF in stabilization programs. The Fund's role is vital not because it provides capital but because it provides free collective goods and, indirectly, aids in creditor coordination. By signaling the creditworthiness of troubled debtors, it provides important information to all creditors. By monitoring its own conditional loans, it provides essential political surveillance. Private lenders, though they control the main spigots of international capital, cannot easily provide such collective goods for themselves.

As important as the IMF is in supervising debt crises, the coordination of private lenders is substantially a function of their own reciprocal relationships and the contractual character of their international lending. Most significantly, the vast majority of loans to Third World states are made through multinational banking syndicates, which have their own conventions and legal obligations. Relying on these contractual provisions and established procedures, agent banks then oversee the repayment of debt. If the loan is nonperforming, the agent is well placed to organize the syndicate for collective action.

In debt crises, these lending arrangements provide formal avenues for reconciling creditor preferences within syndicates. Should differences arise between syndicates, collective action is less certain but still common. Its basis is the far-reaching interdepen-

75. Where security issues are highly salient, one might expect greater state involvement in debt issues. Specifically, one would expect financial support for allies suffering debt problems. The only recent example is Turkey, where several NATO states played an especially active role in reorganizing debts. Indeed, the OECD (which has a considerable overlap with NATO's membership) replaced the IMF as the organizer of the creditor conference: *The Banker* (August 1979): 15. The pole of military power is still the pole of states.

dence of the largest Eurobanks, with its implications of mutual support or retribution.[76] Finally, should the informal codes of lender conduct fail, the debt's contractual character at least gives each bank some recourse in case of illegal usurpation by other banks.[77] Together, these features of Eurocurrency lending markedly reduce the incentives for otherwise competitive banks to pursue beggar-my-neighbor policies in debt crises.

This political structure for collective action ensures that no state will default unless it is insolvent or is willing to accept a radical rupture with the capitalist world economy.[78] The debts are politically secure becaue they are backed by a network of mutilateral banks, private lenders, and (more marginally) advanced capitalist states. They are jointly capable of consolidating debts in emergencies and severely punishing those who default without sufficient cause.

The sanctions available to these institutions are powerful not only because they are coherent, but because of a basic structural feature of international finance: nations that expect to conduct multilateral trade require short- and medium-term financing plus other bank services. Thus, to deny access to credit is a powerful sanction. We might term it an "intrinsic sanction," since it is substantively related to the action being sanctioned and involves an issue-bounded relationship among the actors.[79] Because debt sanctions are intrinsic and because they do not generally require creditors to inflict special costs on themselves, coordination problems are simplified. The close interdependence of international banks, their capacity to coordinate, and the IMF's permanent institutional framework virtually assure collective action in cases of impending default. Thus, there is an effective structure for the supervision of

76. The communication that is required for collective action is undoubtedly facilitated by the sociological context of international banking: the physical proximity of key actors in London and New York, their long-standing working relationships, and their similar patterns of education, recruitment, and training.

77. The contractual form of debt is another residual role of state authority.

78. See Cheryl Payer's discussion of "The Breakaways: Chile, Ghana, North Korea," in Payer, *The Debt Trap: The IMF and the Third World* (New York: Monthly Review Press, 1974). Two of those cases are also examined by John Odell in "The Politics of Debt Relief: Official Creditors and Brazil, Ghana, and Chile," in Aronson, ed., *Debt and the Less Developed Countries*.

79. It can be differentiated from extrinsic sanctions, which involve some form of compulsion not closely tied to the specific substance of the dispute, as in tactical issue linkage. An extrinsic reward would be a side-payment.

sovereign debt—a structure built not on state power but on private sanctions and multilateral oversight.

The strength of these arrangements lies in the capacity to isolate individual debt problems and, treating them in isolation, to resolve the discrete cases. That may also be the regime's greatest limitation. So far ad hoc arrangements have been sufficient. But their scope is necessarily too limited to anticipate and cope with a much larger agenda of troubled debt. There are no mechanisms to assure any given level of payments financing in the private markets. Nor do the IMF and the World Bank have sufficient resources to offset any major change in the provision of private credit. As a result, a flurry of debt problems or, worse, a few major defaults could produce a self-defeating spiral of credit contraction. In such a risky environment, banks would be reluctant to lend freely, so still more debt crises would emerge. The intervention of central banks would dampen some of the consequences. Lender-of-last-resort facilities might prevent illiquidity from spreading through the banking system, permitting some rollover credits for troubled debtors. Nothing, however, would ensure the provision of such credits on a substantial scale. None of this is meant as a forecast; rather, it is designed to show the institutional limits of the debt regime. So far, common action has been needed only to avoid very specific outcomes in a limited number of deviant cases. Perhaps as a result, the debt regime is poorly institutionalized.[80] Certainly it is ill equipped to cope with larger dilemmas in which the avoidance of default and the global provision of credit merge.

Whatever its limitations, the debt regime is surely distinctive. The configuration of nonstate actors seems to contravene Oran Young's claim that "in formal terms, the members of international regimes are always sovereign states, though the parties carrying out the actions governed by international regimes are often private entities (for example, fishing companies, banks, or private airlines)."[81] For most issues, Young's statement holds. The state system does provide the basic framework for private economic transactions. It does so even in the case of offshore credit markets, as

80. A relationship between the degree of institutionalization and the form of collective interests is suggested in Arthur Stein, "Global Anarchy, State Interest, and International Regimes," paper delivered at the September 1980 Convention of the American Political Science Association.

81. Oran Young, "International Regimes: Problems of Concept Formation," *World Politics* 32 (April 1980): 333.

we have seen. But in the case of LDC debt, the central actors are the IMF and the major money-market banks, operating through integrated networks of foreign branches and subsidiaries. They are not simply carrying out regime-governed actions, as Young would have it. Having become essential intermediaries in the international transmission of credit, they have also become the source of most regime rules, norms, and procedures.

Not only are these arrangements distinctive, they are relatively autonomous. That autonomy is striking because the debts themselves are so closely tied to other economic transactions. Yet shifts in larger political and economic relationships and even changes in closely related issues do not seem to have diminished the security of Third World debts. The international monetary regime, for instance, has undergone profound and sometimes turbulent change since 1971. Likewise, the rules governing the treatment of foreign direct investment (the most obvious alternative to international lending as a source of long-term finance) have changed dramatically. While direct investment was increasingly subject to idiosyncratic national control, the debt regime has been characterized by coherent global rules and unified sanctions. Even the decline of hegemony has not weakened the political supervision of debt, although the ebbing of U. S. economic leadership has surely contributed to the relative decline of aid and the rise of offshore lending. All this suggests that the debt regime's structure and evolution do not coincide with developments in other issue areas, even those that are closely related, or to broad changes in the international power distribution.

This does not imply that Eurolending and the allied structure of debt supervision could survive a traumatic rupture in international economic relationships. We have already indicated that the regime is premised on the rarity of debt problems, which are effectively insulated from the larger stock of global debts and treated as deviant cases. Within these limits, however, the debt regime has a singular, relatively autonomous issue structure. Although capital movements are partly a function of other economic flows, the international organization of debt is largely independent of these other issues. Its rules and procedures, its actors and their conventions are all distinctive. Without relying on the diplomacy of military resources of advanced capitalist states, independent of hegemony or its gradual decline, they have provided solid political backing for foreign capital.

# 2

# On Persuading a Leopard to Change His Spots:

## Optimal Strategies for Donors and Recipients of Conditional Development Aid

*Paul Mosley*

In recent years international aid and finance agencies dealing with Third World countries have devoted enormous attention to increasing the effectiveness, or productivity, of the capital resources they supply. One of the main policy instruments that they have used for this purpose is the practice variously known as *conditionality, leverage,* or *policy dialogue;* that is, the negotiation, in consultation with the recipient government, of a set of changes in economic policy that the recipient government must

Reprinted with permission from Paul Mosley, "On Persuading a Leopard to Change His Spots: Optimal Strategies for Donors and Recipients of Conditional Development Aid," University of Bath, Papers on Political Economy, Working Paper no. 0485 (1985).

implement in return for a loan or grant. Conditionality is, of course, nothing new in itself. It is a standard feature of loans by banks to individuals or to domestic companies; the condition in such cases normally consists of a legally binding undertaking by the borrower to hand over a security or negotiable capital asset to the lender if he cannot otherwise pay the loan back. When financial institutions lend to overseas governments, the conditions often become more complex, because the borrower is a sovereign body on whose assets the lender has no legal claim. The International Monetary Fund (IMF), for example, normally asks the governments to which it lends to adhere to specified targets for the growth of bank credit and government expenditures and for the exchange rate.[1] The conditionality remains, as in the case of an ordinary commercial loan, an instrument intended to maximize the probability that the loan will be repaid; but its application becomes a more controversial matter, both because the link between that instrument and the ultimate target is less certain and because the application of the instrument may hurt influential interest groups and thus be politically destabilizing.[2]

Whereas the IMF provides short-term finance keyed, in general, to policy measures that reduce demand, the World Bank and certain bilateral development agencies have since the late 1970s made money available for long-term development keyed to policy measures designed to augment supply, such as the raising of food and energy prices and the lowering of protective barriers on external trade. It is the contention of this paper that this development raises new analytical issues. The link between instrument and target remains loose and the application of the instrument arouses political

1. For a discussion of IMF conditionality see Tony Killick and associates, *The Quest for Economic Stabilization: The IMF and the Third World,* 2 vols. (London: Heinemann, 1984), especially chapter 6.

2. Both these points can be illustrated by reference to exchange-rate devaluation, a common IMF condition. An influential literature argues that in less developed economies the elasticity of supply of exports and the elasticity of demand for imports are too low for the Marshall-Lerner condition to be satisfied (see, for example, Lance Taylor, *Structuralist Macroeconomics* (New York: Basic Books, 1983), in which event devaluation may worsen rather than assist the balance of payments. Moreover, devaluation is notoriously unpopular politically. Witness the finding of Richard N. Cooper, "Currency Devaluation in Developing Countries," in Gustav Ranis, ed., *Government and Economic Development* (New Haven: Yale University Press, 1971), that devaluation trebled the risk that the finance minister responsible would lose his job within the year and doubled the risk that the entire government would fall within that time.

opposition, as in the case of the IMF. But, first, the target of conditionality is now no longer simply to maximize the probability of repayment of the loan. Much bilateral development aid and the World Bank's International Development Agency (IDA) credits are given on grant of near-grant terms,[3] and even "hard" development aid lent on market terms is expected to fulfill purposes other than the mere development of a healthy cash-flow—for example, the development of export potential, the growth of GNP, and the reduction of poverty. Second, it often takes a long time for the donor[4] of supply-augmenting finance to see whether the recipient is acting in accordance with the spirit of the policy measures it wants implemented. It takes longer for the World Bank to find out whether a recipient is genuinely rationalizing its structure of protection, given the time required to commission, complete, and implement the necessary studies, than it does for the IMF to find out whether a recipient has kept domestic credit expansion within the negotiated limits. This offers opportunities for "exploitation" of a donor by a recipient that needs short-term help but is reluctant to offend the vested interests that would be hurt by the application of the donor's conditionality. These two characteristics, we shall argue, weaken the bargaining power of the donor of aid that is conditioned on the "supply side" in relation to the commercial banker or even the IMF. A summary of the differences among the three types of conditional financial transfer is provided in Table 1.

## An Outline History of Conditional Development Aid

The main development agencies to have shown interest in conditionality as a means of enhancing the effectiveness of aid are the bilateral Canadian International Development Agency (CIDA), U. K. Overseas Development Administration (ODA), and the United States Agency for International Development (USAID), and among multilateral agencies, preeminently the World Bank.

3. The World Bank's IDA credits are free except for an annual service charge of ¾ percent. Most bilateral aid by OECD countries consists of grants (for example, U. S. aid in 1983 had a grant element of 94 percent, and U. K. aid a grant element of 98 percent): OECD, *Development Assistance: Efforts and Policies of the Members of the Development Assistance Committee in 1983* (Paris: OECD, 1984), table V1–4.

4. We shall for convenience use the term *donor* for the provider of conditional finance, even though much of that finance is in fact provided on nonconditional terms.

**Table 1.** *Financial Transfers: Three Types of Conditionality*

| Loan | Instrument (condition) | Target (purpose of condition) | Link between Instrument and Target | Monitoring of Compliance | Legal Enforceability |
|---|---|---|---|---|---|
| By bank to individual | Collateral must be transferred to bank to extent of loan default | Maximize probability of repayment | Very tight | Instant | Yes |
| By IMF to sovereign country | Various, usually including ceilings on central bank credit and public spending | Maximize probability of repayment; reduce aggregate demand | Fairly tight | After delays (usually 1–3 months) involved in publication of statistics | No |
| By World Bank or bilateral aid donor to sovereign country | Various, usually including increases in agriculture and energy prices, reductions in rate of protection | Increase aggregate supply by improvements in economic efficiency | Rather loose | Often not for several years | No |

Each of these agencies has increased its ratio of program to project-aid disbursement during the 1970s.[5] In part this behavior is a response to sudden deterioration in recipient countries' balance of payments, caused by the oil shocks of 1974 and 1979, and to perceived limits to their "absorptive capacity" for projects. In addition, however, it reflects a growing perception that the failure of projects at the micro level is frequently due to an unfavorable policy environment at the macro level, as when a well-planned and well-executed agricultural project nonetheless fails, because the price paid to producers for the crop is too low to give them an incentive to market it.[6] Such program aid has, therefore, been made conditional on improvements to this "policy environment." Among the four agencies mentioned there is considerable consensus on what kinds of improvements are necessary. Prices to agricultural producers, especially exporters, must be modified (usually, raised) to give them an incentive to produce for the market; the financial performance of public enterprises must be improved by a redirection of resources from the creation of new capacity to the maintenance of existing capital or by outright privatization; and trade policy must become more outward looking by removal of controls or exchange rates and by a reduction of the economy's rate of effective protection against imports.[7] The common thread running through this package is that a reduction is required in the degree of state control over the economy. The theoretical and empirical rationale for the package will not be considered here. We shall take it as given that this is the set of reforms desired by those aid donors that wish to achieve policy change through conditionality, and we shall examine the ways they have tried to persuade Third World governments to adopt these reforms.

We shall concentrate our attention on the most important exercise so far in this kind of persuasion, the World Bank's structural adjustment loans (SALs). These were first introduced in early 1980, and thirty of them have now been made in sixteen countries. Their objective has been defined by a World Bank official as "to

5. See OECD, *Development Assistance*, p. 221.

6. See, for example, World Bank, *Rural Development Projects: A Retrospective View of Bank Experience in Sub-Saharan Africa* (Washington, D. C.: IBRD, 1978); World Bank, *Accelerated Development in Sub-Saharan Africa: An Agenda for Action* (Washington, D. C.: IBRD, 1981).

7. See, for example, World Bank, *Accelerated Development in Sub-Saharan Africa*, pp. 3 and 24; World Bank, *Towards Sustained Development in Sub-Saharan Africa* (Washington, D. C.: IBRD, 1984), chapter 5.

provide quick disbursing finance to support measures designed to strengthen recipient countries' balance of payments within five to ten years without severely constraining demand in a manner that unnecessarily sets back economic and social development."[8] Disbursement of SALs is always conditional [on] "the elaboration of an appropriate set of specific actions that the government will take either to increase or save foreign exchange earnings."[9]

Like the IMF,[10] the Bank is at pains to stress that there is no question of a standard package of policy reforms being imposed on any recipient country, that each country's path toward structural adjustment must be tailored to its specific circumstances. Nonetheless, reforms in agricultural pricing policy, in the system of export incentives, and in the ordering of public investment priorities have been requested in over 80 percent of cases. This form of finance has been confined to the faster-growing and more outward-looking developing countries. The average rate of growth of GDP during the 1970s was 5.5 percent among countries awarded SALs, by contrast with 4.6 percent for low- and middle-income countries as a whole,[11] and Yugoslavia is the only socialist country of the sixteen to have received a SAL. In principle, "any country facing a serious medium-term foreign exchange constraint and proposing a viable adjustment programme is eligible" for a SAL,"[12] but in practice those Third World countries with the most deep-rooted economic difficulties appear to have been excluded from the scheme. Some very poor countries have initiated negotiations with the Bank for SAL finance which have then been broken off because agreement on the required package of policy reforms could not be reached; we return to this point later.

For the moment let us examine the logic behind the policy reform packages. In nearly all cases what is involved in implementing these packages is taking away from some interest group a shield against market forces that the government has granted it in order to win its political support. Subsidies on the price of food and energy provide a shield against market forces for urban consumers;

---

8. Peter Landell-Mills, "Structural Adjustment Lending: Early Experience," *Finance and Development* 18 (1981): 17.

9. Ibid.

10. As reported in Killick, *Quest for Economic Stabilization*, vol. 1, p. 192, table 6.2.

11. Data from World Bank, *World Development Report 1984* (Washington, D. C.: IBRD, 1984), Appendix table 1.

12. Landell-Mills, "Structural Adjustment Lending," p. 17.

tariffs, quotas on imports, and overvalued exchange rates, for industrialists supplying the home market; extravagant projects in rural areas, for those who benefit from the services they provide. The additional real incomes these beneficiaries manage to enjoy because of the existence of the shield constitute *rents* to the supply of factors limited only by government fiat, and as such do not have to be paid to keep production at its existing level. The World Bank argues explicitly to countries that receive SALs that if the burden of these rents is lifted, production and exports will increase—sometimes dramatically, as is shown in Table 2. This prospect of enhanced economic growth, along with the SAL finance itself, is the economic benefit that countries receiving SALs are offered by the Bank in order to embolden them to incur the political cost of taking away rents from those who receive them. They are a bribe to Third World governments to buy out some of the restrictive practices by which they currently hold the state together.

Usually—on the limited evidence so far available—the bribe is successful in eliciting the policy changes requested, but sometimes it is not. Among the countries discussed here, Turkey, Jamaica, Pakistan, and South Korea have met nearly all the conditions, and of these Turkey is now into its fifth structural adjustment loan, and Jamaica into its third. Meanwhile, Kenya, Guyana, and Bolivia, in particular, have been remiss in complying with the conditions set, but whereas the two last-named have had one structural adjustment loan only, Kenya has had two. In an intermediate group (Malawi, the Ivory Coast, Thailand, and the Philippines), most, but not all, of the conditions set have been complied with, and the process of dialogue continues: all are some way into their second SAL. The distribution of the eleven countries so far discussed by numbers of SALs received and compliance level is set out in Table 3. To that table, for comparison, are added two African countries that entered into negotiations for SALs but have not so far (i.e., by 1985) received any program finance from the Bank: Senegal was awarded a SAL in 1981 but cancelled it on deciding that it was unable to comply with the conditions set and Tanzania has (as of 1985) been prevented from receiving SAL finance by its inability to conclude a standby agreement with the IMF.

Let us assume for the time being that the cogency of the economic argument for policy reform placed by the World Bank in front of these thirteen countries is equal for all. If that is the case, then the immediate question that emerges from Table 3 is why that

*Table 2.* Output Changes Predicted by World Bank in Recipient
Countries if Conditions of Structural Adjustment Program Are Met

| | FIRST SAL, GNP GROWTH (1980–85) (%) | | SECOND SAL, GNP GROWTH (1981–86) (%) | |
|---|---|---|---|---|
| | *With Structural Adjustment* | *Without Structural Adjustment* | *With Structural Adjustment* | *Without Structural Adjustment* |
| Kenya | | | | |
| total output | — | — | 4.3 | 3.8 |
| agriculture only | — | — | 3.9 | 2.7 |
| exports only | — | — | 4.7 | 4.0 |
| Jamaica | | | | |
| total output | — | — | 4.0 | — |
| exports only | — | — | 6.8 | 5.5 |
| Ivory Coast | | | | |
| total output | 6.8 | 4.9 | 6.5* | 4.5* |
| agriculture only | 4.2 | 1.9 | 6.0* | 4.2* |
| exports only | 7.6 | 5.5 | 5.1* | 2.5* |
| Malawi | | | | |
| total output | — | — | 3.4† | 2.5† |
| agriculture only | — | — | 3.4† | 2.4† |
| exports only | — | — | 5.5† | 4.0† |
| Philippines | | | | |
| total output | 6.4 | 5.5 | 6.5‡ | 4.0‡ |
| agriculture only | 5.0 | 4.7 | — | — |
| exports only | 10.7 | 9.3 | 8.5‡ | 6.5‡ |
| Thailand | | | | |
| total output | 7.3 | 7.0 | 5.4§ | 4.8§ |
| agriculture only | 4.2 | 3.1 | 4.0§ | 3.1§ |
| exports only | 10.0 | 8.1 | 6.8§ | 4.5§ |

*Sources:* World Bank, *Report and Recommendation of the World Bank President to the Executive Directors on a Proposed Second Structural Adjustment Loan to Kenya,* Report P–3322–KE (Washington, D.C.: IBRD, 1982); World Bank, *Report of the World Bank to the Executive Directors on a Proposed Second Structural Adjustment Credit to Malawi,* Report P–3663–MAI (Washington, D.C.: IBRD, 1983); World Bank, *Report of the World Bank President on a Proposed Second Structural Adjustment Loan to the Ivory Coast,* Report P–3613–IVC (Washington, D.C.: IBRD, 1983); World Bank, *Report of the World Bank President on a Second Structural Adjustment Loan to Thailand,* Report P–3481–TH (Washington, D.C.: IBRD, 1983); World Bank, *Report of the World Bank* (Washington, D.C.: IBRD, 1983); World Bank, *Report of the World Bank President on a Second Structural Loan to Jamaica,* Report P–3559–JM (Washington, D.C.: IBRD, 1983).

* 1985–1990 †1983–1987 ‡1986–1989 §1982–1990

**Table 3.**  *Thirteen Less Developed Countries: Status of World Bank Structural Adjustment Operations, March 1985*

| Recipient Government | Granted 2 or More SALs | Granted 1 SAL Loan | Negotiations Only |
|---|---|---|---|
| Has complied with all or nearly all conditions requested by Bank (index of compliance 90% or more) | Turkey Jamaica South Korea | Pakistan | |
| Has complied with some but not all conditions requested by Bank (index of compliance 60– 90%) | Malawi Thailand Ivory Coast Philippines | | |
| Has complied with few conditions requested by Bank (index of compliance 9– 60%) | Kenya | Guyana Bolivia | Tanzania Senegal |

*Source:* Materials gathered from the records of the World Bank.

argument experienced such differential success in persuading governments and overcoming the political vested interests arrayed against policy reform. A subsidiary question, of course, is why the Bank appears not to have applied the principle of equal treatment of equals, awarding two SALs to Kenya, which has a compliance index of 38 percent, and only one to Pakistan, which has a compliance index of 90 percent.

We can begin our search for an answer by referring back to two specific features of conditional development aid discussed in Table 1. First, the conditions are likely to cause serious economic hurt to certain pressure groups; and, second, failure to comply with them may not come to the attention of the donor for several years, because policy changes of the structural adjustment type have a long gestation period. These two features may tempt a recipient government to promise to comply with the conditions proposed by the donor and then to renege on that promise, if it does not expect to need program finance beyond the point at which its failure to comply has been demonstrated. In other words, it may see aid negotiations as a *game* whose object is to obtain specific sums of money without complying with the associated conditions. The donor, in such a situation, needs strategies to discourage such behavior without embittering relationships to the point where all possibility of influence over the recipient is lost.

## Policy Dialogue as a Non-Zero-Sum Game

### A Simple Two-Person, One-Stage Game

The simplest model of negotiations between a donor and a recipient of aid describes the case where the options for both parties are all or nothing, threats are binding, and compliance with conditions can be instantly monitored. That is, the donor has two possible strategies (to give a development loan,[13] or not to give it); the recipient also has two possible strategies (to comply with the conditions which the donor has proposed for the loan, or not to comply); the donor is committed to disbursing the loan if the recipient complies with this condition and to carry out its threat of not disbursing the loan if it does not; and the donor can reliably assess, before disbursing the loan, whether or not the recipient has complied with the conditions. In this event the "game" between donor and recipient can be portrayed as in Table 4. This model more or less describes the first case of conditionality mentioned above: the one-tranche loan by a bank to an individual, which is conditional on the transfer of collateral (or a legal claim to it) by the individual to the bank. In this model, off-diagonal outcomes, involving exploitation of one of the parties by the other, are excluded by the rules of the game. Outcome (2), where the recipient gets its money and escapes the discipline of complying with the conditions, is excluded by the donor's binding threat to refuse to disburse if the conditions are not met, and outcome (4) by its binding promise to disburse if the conditions *are* met. The only aspect that is indeterminate is the recipient's subjective assessment of whether the ex-

13. We assume in what follows that the donor gives his assistance in loan form. In fact many bilateral transactions between rich and poor countries are in grant form.

**Table 4.**    *Conditional Lending, Simplest Case*

| Donor | Recipient Complies with Donor's Conditons | Recipient Does Not Comply with Donor's Conditions |
|---|---|---|
| Disburses loan | 1 | (2) |
| Does not disburse loan | (4) | 3 |

pected short-term cost of complying with the conditions exceeds the expected long-term economic benefit from receiving the loan. If so, negotiations collapse, and we are in position 3; if not, the deal is done, as in position 1.

The situation where the World Bank or a bilateral donor offers conditional program aid differs from the above in a number of ways. First, both donor and recipient may employ complex strategies, that is, the recipient may comply with some but not all of the conditions set by the donor, and the donor may disburse some but not all of a planned loan—for example, by giving it out in several tranches, each of which is contingent on satisfactory performance in the previous period.

Second, the donor of conditional aid cannot assess whether the recipient has complied with the conditions before disbursing the loan. All that can be negotiated before disbursing the loan is a *promise* by the recipient to comply with the conditions; whether the recipient actually has complied cannot be ascertained. Above we argued that the lag between the promise being given and the first moment when fulfillment of the promise could be reasonably tested was much longer (often as long as three or four years), given the complexity of the changes in policy instruments required for loans such as World Bank SALs, which are intended to boost the supply side of the economy. This long lag opens up the possibility of exploitation of the donor by a recipient that needs finance only for a short period and discounts the long-term consequences of a deterioration in its relationship with the donor: such a recipient can promise to comply with particular performance criteria, receive its money, and then fail to comply.[14] The donor can try and

14. This behavior corresponds to the off-diagonal element (2) in Table 4, which becomes attainable if and only if we relax the assumption that compliance with conditions can be instantly monitored.

defend itself by disbursing its finance in a series of loans, each of which can then be divided into tranches, rather than a lump sum; this happens, as we saw, with World Bank SALs.

Third, the donor may not wish to be bound by its initial threat to cut off program aid if it finds at the end of a loan (or tranche) that its conditions have not been complied with so far. It may prefer to give the recipient the benefit of the doubt, that is, to allow a slower transition toward fulfillment of the conditions of the loan than was originally agreed—particularly if external circumstances such as weather or world crop prices have intervened in an adverse way in the interim, if the donor still trusts the recipient to comply eventually with the conditions set, or if it needs to sustain a relationship with the recipient for some other reason. However, this relationship is asymmetric: the donor may have good reasons for not implementing its threat to cut off aid if conditions are not met, but it has no good reason for not implementing its *promise* to provide aid if conditions are met.

### A Two-Person, Multistage Game with Non-Binding Threats

In the light of the previous discussion, realism requires us to divide the game between the donor and the recipient of conditional aid into three "acts," which are consecutive in time:

1. An initial negotiating process in which donor and recipient try to agree on the conditions to be attached to a development loan. If successful, this process culminates in a set of promises by the recipient to undertake certain policy actions.
2. A period, which may be up to four years long, in which the recipient decides how far to honor its promises made in Act 1.
3. A period in which the donor grants or does not grant further finance to the recipient, depending on the recipient's performance in Act 2.

We shall assume that Act 1 proceeds in the following manner. The donor begins by asking the recipient to offer a set of reforms that will assist economic recovery. The recipient, which is suffering from serious balance-of-payments problems and foreign indebtedness, offers a package of reforms $T_j$ which it considers its best initial offer.[15] We can think of this as a point of tangency between

15. T is mnemonic for *tightness;* here and throughout the paper, we use the subscript $i$ for the donor and $j$ for the recipient.

an "economically feasible" set of policy options and a welfare function that balances the long-term economic benefit from harsh stabilization measures against the short-term political cost of those incomes.[16]

The donor now makes a counteroffer $T_i$, consisting of the package of reforms it would like to see the recipient implement. This normally goes further (that is, involves more and tighter reforms) than the recipient's initial offer. In the exceptional case where it does not ($T_i = T_j$), the game collapses into an immediate agreement.[17]

In the third scene of Act 1, the donor and recipient deploy bargaining strategies. These consist partly of threats (forecasts of how they will behave if negotiations break down) and partly of persuasive statements designed to alter the other party's perception of the cost of settling on its opponent's terms. The donor's main available threat is, of course, to provide no money if the conditions are not complied with, and its main persuasive strategy is to remind the recipient of the economic benefits that will flow if it incurs the political cost of defying vested interests, for example, by citing figures such as those contained in Table 2 above, accompanied by economic analysis.[18] The recipient cannot easily utter threats against a

16. Only in an exceptional case will the recipient's indifference curve be vertical; i.e., the recipient, however principled his opposition to outside interference with his economic policy, will normally be forced by sheer fear of default on external debt to implement some stabilization measures. Even President Nyerere of Tanzania, one of the most unbending Third World political leaders in negotiations with the Bank and the IMF, offered considerable measures of devaluation and public-expenditure reductions in negotiations with the Fund in 1978 when faced with a balance-of-payments crisis. Indeed, it will normally be in the recipient's interest to offer, at this initial bargaining stage, some of the stabilization measures *which he would have implemented anyhow* and to represent these as concessions to the donor, saving other similar concessions for later stages of the negotiating process. If this happens, then the impact of conditionality will be less than it might otherwise appear to the donor. What we are saying is that fungibility operates at the level of conditions as well as at the level of amounts of money. Just as a donor's financial aid may lose leverage if it pays for projects the recipient would have implemented in any case, with domestic resources, so his conditionality may lose leverage if it consists of policy reforms the recipient would have implemented even without external aid.

17. In this event the donor becomes a policy adviser to the recipient, working out detailed modalities by which the recipient can carry through policies he has already committed himself to implement; but in this event it becomes inappropriate to speak of the donor as having exerted leverage on the recipient's policies.

18. As an example of economic analysis arguing a correlation between absence of price distortions and economic growth, and justifying the removal of such price distortions as a precondition for the fixing of aid, see World Bank, *Report of the World Bank President on a Second Structural Adjustment Loan to Thailand,* R.P. 3481-TH (Washington, D.C.: IBRD, 1983), part 2.

multilateral donor such as the World Bank, but when dealing with a bilateral donor with geopolitical interests in his country it can threaten, for example, to withdraw military facilities from that donor,[19] or to discriminate against that country in placing government contracts for imports.[20] Its persuasive statements may rest on an attempt to get the donor to take its own view of the ultimate goals of economic policy (for example, it can stress the need for giving an incentive to producers of food crops, against a donor's argument that it should give priority to producers of cash crops) or, alternatively, on administrative and political feasibility (for example, it can suggest that a donor's proposed timetable for liberalization of imports is not realistic and should be extended).

We now apply a strengthened form of Zeuthen's Principle, which is that if concessions are made, the first concessions must always come from the player that is less willing to face the risk of conflict. We shall define the *risk limit* for each player $i$ as the ratio between the cost to it of reaching an agreement on its opponent's terms and the cost to it of reaching no agreement at all. Define risks $(r_i, r_j)$ as:

$$\text{Risk limit for Player } i = r_i = \frac{U_i(T_i) - U_i(T_j)}{U_i(T_i) - U_i(C)} \tag{1}$$

where

$U_i(T_i)$ = utility level associated by player $i$ with his own offer $T_i$

$U_i(T_j)$ = utility level associated by player $i$ with his opponent's offer $T_j$

$U_i(C)$ = utility level associated by player $i$ with reaching no agreement[21]

Zeuthen's Principle states that

19. This strategy can be used, for example, by Kenya against the United States (which is trying to persuade Kenya to liberalize its economy by means of conditional aid, but also maintains naval facilities at Mombasa on which the United States is heavily dependent); see Paul Mosley, "The Politics of Economic Liberalization: USAID and the World Bank in Kenya, 1980–1984," Bath University Papers in Political Economy, in *African Affairs* 30 (October 1985).

20. This strategy was implemented by Malaysia in 1982: Britain withdrew a subsidy on overseas students' fees, and Malaysia retaliated by announcing that its government would thenceforward follow a policy of "buying British last."

21. As long as $U_i(C) < U_i(T_i) < U_i(T_j)$ where $(j = 1, 2$ and $i \neq j)$, it follows from (1) that $0 < r_i < 1$.

if $r_i > r_j$,   then player $i$, that is, the donor, has    (2a)
to make the first concession

if $r_i < r_j$,   then player $j$, that is, the recipient,
has to make the first concession

if $r_i = r_j$,   then both players have to make concessions

if $r_i > r_j$,   then player $i$, that is, the donor,    (2b)
makes a *bigger* concession the higher
the ratio is of $r_i$ to $r_j$

if $r_i < r_j$,   then player $j$, that is, the recipient,
makes a *bigger* concession the higher
the ratio is of $r_j$ to $r_i$

If this principle is applied at every stage of the bargaining process, then a set of policy reforms will eventually be agreed upon
that maximizes the "Nash product," that is, the product of the donor's and the recipient's gain in utility in relation to the deadlock
payoff $C$;[22] and this agreed-upon set of policy reforms will be closer
to the donor's demand $T_i$ the greater is the cost to the recipient of
going without a loan rather than accepting the policy conditions
set by the donor. The determinants of these costs will be investi-

---

22. According to Zeuthen's Principle, player $i$ ($i = 1,2$) will always make a concession to the other player whenever

$$r_i = \frac{U_i(A_i) - U_i(A_j)}{U_i(A_i) - U_i(C)} \leq \frac{U_j(A_j) - U_j(A_i)}{U_j(A_j) - U_j(C)} = r_j$$

This condition is equivalent to $\pi(A_i) = [U_i(A_i) - U_i(C)] [U_j(A_i) - U_j(C)] \leq [U_i(A_j) - U_i(C)] [U_j(A_j) - U_j(C)] = \pi(A_j)$. That is, player $i$ will always make a concession whenever $\pi(A_i)$, the Nash product associated with his own last offer $A_i$, is smaller than $\pi(A_j)$, the Nash product associated with his opponent's last offer, $A_j$. The bigger the gap, the larger the concession. When player $i$ comes to propose and offer $A^*_i$ associated with a *larger* Nash product $(A^*_i)$ than the Nash product $\pi(A_j)$ associated with his opponent's last offer, $A_j$, then player $j$ will have to take over the task of making concessions; the bigger $(\pi(A^*_i) - (A_j))$, the larger the concession player $j$ now has to make. Thus at every stage of the bargaining process, of the two parties' last offers, the offer corresponding to the *smaller* value of the Nash product $\pi$ will always be retained until the next stage. At this stage one of the two parties will introduce a new offer associated with an even larger $\pi$ value than the one surviving from the previous stage, and so on until one of the two parties introduces an offer corresponding to the largest possible value of $\pi$; this offer will be accepted by both parties, since the other party will not be able to counter this by an offer correspond-ing to a still larger value of $\pi$. Hence under Zeuthen's model the final agreement will be reached at the point at which the Nash product takes its maximum value. This proof combines the argument by John C. Harsanyi in *Rational Behaviour and Bargaining Equilibrium in Games and Social Situations* (Cambridge, England: Cambridge University Press, 1977), p. 153, with assumption (2b) above.

gated in the next section, and the resulting hypothesis will be tested below.

Two implications of the analysis so far, however, may be noted. First, the less easy it is for the donor to monitor the policy package it proposes, the smaller the subjective cost $[U_j(T_i) - U_j(C)]$ to the recipient of settling on its opponent's terms, since all it has to give before the money is handed over is a promise, not the implementation of that promise. As we saw above, the monitoring problem is most acute in the case of what we called Type-3 conditionality (World Bank SALs and the like); hence in the case of such loans we may expect the agreed upon policy package T* to be close to the donor's demand, $T_i$. The second implication is that bilateral donors, as we saw, have substantial commercial and political reasons, which multilateral donors do not have, for not breaking off an aid relationship with the recipient; that is, $U_i(T_j) - U_i(C)$ may be lower for them than it will be for a multilateral donor. Hence if bilateral donors attempt to conclude conditional aid packages independently with a given recipient, those packages will be less tight, that is, closer to $T_j$, than loans negotiated by a multilateral donor with the same country.

The analysis so far depends on the assumption that the weaker party in the bargaining process will make concessions when its risk limit is less than its opponent's, and will not treat his offer as an ultimatum. If it does choose to give an ultimatum, then the bargaining set collapses to a single point, and the only possible outcomes of this part of the game are acceptance of the ultimatum or the breakdown of negotiations, that is, retreat by both parties to their conflict payoff C.[23] Certainly both parties in conditional-aid negotiations are under psychological pressure to treat the bargaining game of Act 1 as though it were an ultimatum game, the recipient out of national pride,[24] and the donor because it knows it is

23. If, and only if, $U_i(C) < U_i(A_j)$ and $U_j(C) < U_j(A_i)$, then this is "cutting off one's nose to spite one's face." Otherwise it is perfectly rational behavior.

24. The classic case of this form of behavior so far is the attitude taken by President Nyerere of Tanzania. Rejecting IMF proposals for liberalization of the economy in the midst of a balance-of-payments crisis, he announced in his New Year's Address of 1980 that

Tanzania is not prepared to devalue its currency just because this is a traditional free market solution to everything and regardless of the merits of our position. It is not prepared to surrender its right to restrict imports by measures designed to ensure that we import quinine rather than cosmetics, or buses rather than cars for the elite.

involved in a series of negotiations with separate aid recipients[25] and fears that its bargaining position in the next set of negotiations will be damaged if the next recipient learns of concessions made in the previous set. However, a reading of the record suggests that, at least in the case of World Bank structural adjustment loans, the parties involved have treated Act 1 negotiations as ultimatum games only in a minority of cases.

We now move into Act 2, in which the recipient decides what proportion to implement of the policy reform program it has promised, at the end of Act 1, to implement in full. It has to decide, in other words, how much *slippage* there will be on commitments made to the donor. This decision, it must be stressed, is in fact a series of decisions, widely distributed both over time and over the diverse executive agencies of government responsible for the implementation of different parts of the economic reform package, but for expository convenience we will treat this cluster of decisions here as one action.

We must first of all distinguish between factors influencing the recipient's willingness to carry out the provisions of the agreed reform program, and those affecting its ability to do so. The recipient's willingness to carry out the conditions depends partly on how much it genuinely wishes to do so (that is, has been persuaded that they are genuinely necessary for the recovery of the economy, instead of having been coerced into accepting them simply because it needs the money) and partly on how much it needs to do so in order to get a second loan from the donor.[26] The recipient's ability to implement the conditions is partly a matter of administrative capacity and partly a matter of the strength of political opposition:

My government is not prepared to give up our national endeavour to provide clean water for all our people. Cuts may have to be made in our national expenditure but *we* will decide whether they fall on public services or private expenditure. Nor are we prepared to deal with inflation and shortages by relying only on monetary policy regardless of its relative effect on the poorest and the less poor. Our price control machinery may not be the most effective in the world but we will not abandon price control; we will only strive to make it more efficient. And above all we shall continue with our endeavours to build a socialist society. (Quoted in C. Payer, *Tanzania and the World Bank* DERAP Working Paper A285 [Bergen, Norway: Christian Michelsen Institute, 1982])

25. For example, the World Bank is currently involved in structural adjustment loan negotiations with the nine countries that have had two or more structural adjustment loans.

26. This in turn depends on the current and expected future behavior of *other* donors giving money to that country; see below.

thus, the conditions attached to World Bank SALs frequently call for the losses of public corporations to be eliminated, but a less developed country's ability to prevent a grain marketing authority being a drain on its public finances depends both on whether it can produce a coherent plan for getting out of the red and on whether the withdrawal of subsidies on the consumer price will lead to riots in the streets. All these four factors influencing degree of implementation relate to the recipient's behavior. However, the degree of implementation in Act 2 is also influenced by extraneous factors; for example, a fall in the world price of the recipient's primary export can reduce general public revenue and hence the recipient's ability to remove a supply bottleneck that it has promised to remove. It is clearly important for a donor to discriminate accurately between internal and external causes of slippage if it is to make a fair assessment of performance in Act 2.

Act 2—the period that must elapse between disbursement of conditional finance and the first moment that the donor can make a genuine assessment of the level of "slippage"—lasts for four years or so.[27] After this the recipient must decide whether to seek another conditional program loan. If it decides to do so, the donor must in turn decide whether it is willing to enter into negotiations. (It would be tempting to interpret such willingness as inversely proportional to the level of slippage, or at least of internally induced slippage, but this could be misleading, particularly in the case of bilateral donors. Even a unilateral donor may feel that, rather than abandon a Prodigal Son, it should educate the delinquent recipient into a better awareness of the rationale for its conditions; but a bilateral donor, in addition to this, may have compelling commercial and geopolitical reasons for continuing to lend even if slippage in Act 2 has been high.) If the donor decides to negotiate, it asks the recipient for a draft stabilization program, as in Act 1; it makes a reply, which will be related to the degree of fulfillment achieved in Act 2; and a negotiation process then gets underway, exactly as in Act 1 except that a great deal of information about the behaviors of both parties in Acts 1 and 2 will have been fed into the expectations, and thus into the negotiating behavior, of both parties during Act 3.

We now face the task of specifying the conditional aid game in

27. We interpret Act 2, in the case of World Bank conditional finance, as lasting for a period of two SALs.

a form that will enable it to be tested against the data and of considering rather more precisely the concept of optimal strategies for each player at different points in the game. This is done in the following section; the test proper is conducted below.

### Optimal Threat-and-Inducement Strategies for Donor and Recipient: Hypotheses to Be Tested

When it initiates the process of bargaining over a conditional development loan, the donor has three potential negotiating instruments: the size of the loan, the terms of the loan (interest rate, grace period, and so on), and the conditions attached to the loan. In what follows we shall assume that the first two of these are not used as actual negotiating instruments, in the sense that a softening of these instruments is traded for a tightening of conditionality or vice versa.[28] Rather, the only issue is the tightness of the conditions attaching to the loan: if and only if this can be agreed upon by the negotiating parties, the other features of the loan follow according to mechanical formulas.

We shall assume that the tightness of the conditions attaching to a particular loan, $T_{ij}$, can be measured along a continuous arithmetic scale. The measure of tightness is based on the number of specific conditions that have been imposed requiring alterations in such policy areas as agricultural pricing, interest rates, and the management of public enterprises. Historically, conditionalities involve policy reform in a maximum of twenty such areas. The measure represents the number of such conditions required by the SAL and has been calculated for each of the SALs negotiated for each country. The data yield a distribution of scores running from a low of six out of twenty (for Bolivia) to fifteen out of twenty (for the first of Turkey's four structural adjustment loans). If an agreement can be negotiated between two parties in Act 1, then the measure of tightness agreed upon in Act 1, $T^*_{(1)}$, will be somewhere between the tightness of the conditions proposed by the donor, $T_i$, and the tightness of the conditions proposed by the recipient, $T_j$. Thus if $T^*$ exists,

$$T_{i(1)} \geq T^*_{(1)} \leq T_{j(1)} \tag{3}$$

---

28. The figures suggest that for World Bank SALs, loan sizes are fairly rigidly keyed to the size of the recipient's balance-of-payments deficit and that loan terms are the same for every country in a given year.

We have already suggested that the outcome of the negotiations between donor and recipient could be represented by a Nash-Zeuthen bargaining process. That is,

$$T^*_{(1)} = f\left(\frac{r_i}{r_j}\right) \tag{4}$$

where $r_i$ is the risk limit of the donor and $r_j$ is the risk limit of the recipient, as was defined in Equation 1.

The risk limits of each party, that is, the utility to them of settling on their opponent's terms rather than not settling at all, are then determined by the threat-and-inducement strategies,[29] $\theta_i$, of each of the negotiating parties. The threats are intended to reduce the other player's subjective estimation of the conflict payoff, $C$; the inducements are intended to raise the other player's subjective estimation of settling on its opponent's terms, $U_i(A_j)$. Thus the problem for the recipient player $j$ is to

$$\text{choose } \theta_j \text{ so as to maximize } U_i(A_j) - C_i \tag{5a}$$

and for the donor player, $i$, it is to

$$\text{choose } \theta_i \text{ so as to maximize } U_j(A_i) - C_i \tag{5b}$$

We turn now to the problem of giving empirical content to the threats and inducements that each player in the conditional aid game can make. The recipient has relatively few strategies it can deploy against a multilateral donor, as discussed earlier,[30] except for the threat of getting the money from another source, but against a bilateral donor it can threaten withdrawal of military support or trade links. The donor meanwhile can threaten by drawing attention to the recipient's balance-of-payments position and/or debt-service ratio and can induce by promising the recipient a large improvement in production or exports if its draft conditions are accepted,[31] an inducement which will seem more attractive the

---

29. We use this term rather than the more familiar term *threat strategies* used by, for example, Harsanyi in *Rational Behaviour,* p. 167, since much of the persuasion applied by donors consists not of threats but of measures designed to reduce the recipient's estimate of the long-run costs of complying with their conditions.

30. This assumption oversimplifies; for individual members of the multilateral aid agency there will be considerable personal costs to initiating conditions and negotiations that subsequently collapse.

31. As the World Bank has done in the case of SALs; see above.

greater the degree of trust between the negotiating staffs of the donor and the recipient country[32] and the lower the degree of anticipated opposition from interest groups whose rents would be reduced under the terms of the donor's proposed conditionality. We have, then,

$$\theta_i = \alpha\left(B_j, \frac{D_j}{X_j}, M_j\right)_0 \tag{6a}$$

and

$$\theta_j = \beta\left(\frac{F_i}{\sum_{k \neq i} F_k}\right)_0 \tag{6b}$$

where

$B_j$                      = balance of payments of recipient country

$D_j$                      = debt-service payments of recipient country

$X_j$                      = exports of recipient country

$M_j$                      = "miscellaneous" factors affecting the recipient country's perceptions of the conditionality package $T_i$, in particular the strength of anticipated political opposition, its degree of trust in the donor's package, and the size of improvement in economic conditions offered to it by the donor

$F_i$                      = concessional-aid flows from donor institution

$\sum_{k \neq i} F_k$      = concessional-aid flows from all other donor institutions $(k \neq i)$

subscript 0 = the year before negotiations commence (year 1)

32. This is partly a matter of personal relationships but comes down ultimately to the recipient's trust in the economic analysis he is being offered by the donor, that is, his degree of belief that conditional predictions such as those made in Table 2 are valid.

We now move forward into Act 2, the implementation phase. During this period, if a conditional loan agreement was agreed upon in Act 1, the recipient implements a proportion $p$ ($0 < p < 1$) of the set T* of conditions that were agreed upon at the conclusion of Act 1.[33] What will determine the size of $p$? An extreme assumption would be that "leopards never change their spots," hence that the recipient will fail to implement all the conditions which were coercively imposed on it at the end of the Act 1, that is, the entire set that fall in T* but not in $T_j$. Such an assumption precludes, however, both the possibility of "learning" by the recipient during the process of policy dialogue,[34] and the possibility of the recipient acting in anticipation of Act 2, when it may want another loan from the donor. The first of these is hard to quantify or to model except as a random disturbance, but the recipient's balance-of-payments position and dependence on the donor for concessional money presumably determine whether or not the recipient will need another program loan from that donor. As a behavioral equation for Act 2 we therefore suggest:

$$P_{j(2)} = \gamma \left(T^*_{(1)} - T_{j(1)}, \; B_{j(2)}, \; \frac{F_i}{\sum\limits_{k \neq i} F_{k(2)}}\right) \tag{7}$$

the first term on the right side of which represents the coercion of which it desired to rid itself at the end of Act 1, and the second and third terms of which are proxies for its need for further finance from that donor at the end of Act 2 and hence of its need to subject itself to further coercion during Act 3.

Finally, at the start of Act 3 the recipient makes a decision as to whether it will need another loan, and if it decides to seek one the donor makes a decision about whether it will enter into negotiations. If the donor does decide to enter into negotiations we may take it as an initial hypothesis that the set of conditions it proposes

33. The amount $(1-p)$ can be interpreted as the degree of slippage on the conditions.

34. "Learning" (that is, a flattening in the indifference curve during the course of Act 2) can occur either because policymakers become more convinced that the economic analysis underlying the donor's proposed conditions is correct or because the vested interests opposing the implementation of those conditions weaken in the course of Act 2. For example, those vested interests may move out from under a protective umbrella when it no longer gives them effective shelter.

will be directly related to the amount of slippage during Act 2. Thus

$$T^*_{i(3)} = \delta p_{j(2)} \text{ if and only if } p_j > p^*_j \qquad (8)$$

This completes the model. We now proceed to test it against data for the World Bank structural adjustment loans.

## Interim Tests of Hypotheses

The story is told of the England cricket player Wilfred Rhodes that he was once bowling to a raw seventeen-year-old recruit in the Yorkshire nets. The youth took a wild swipe and hit his first ball out of the ground.

"Look where your legs are!" shouted Rhodes in disgust.

"Never mind my legs," the youth replied. "Look where the bloody ball's gone."

He was sacked on the spot; but he had made his point. You can judge any operation in two ways: in terms of the technical correctness with which it was carried out, and in terms of its ultimate success. In the next section we shall apply both modes of evaluation to the most important case of Type-3 conditionality, the structural adjustment loans of the World Bank. We have looked at the determinants of conditionality and of compliance with it; we move on to consider whether it has had any visible effect, *so far,* on what it is meant to influence, namely, exports, balance of payments, and gross national product.

In the previous section we argued that the tightness of the conditions a donor sets on a loan depends on the relative costs to donor and recipient of settling on the other party's terms rather than not settling at all (Equation 4) and that these relative costs for each party depend on the effectiveness of the threat-and-inducement strategies that the other party was able to deploy. In the special case of multilateral aid, the donor would be able to threaten more effectively the more desperate was the recipient's debt-service and balance-of-payments situation, and induce more effectively the greater the improvement in economic performance it was able to offer. Meanwhile, the recipient could threaten more effectively to withdraw from the relationship the smaller the percentage of total official financial flows it derived from that one donor. We may write our hypothesis in general terms as

$$T^*_{ij(1)} = h(\overset{+}{B_j}, \frac{\overset{+}{D_j}}{X_j}, M_j, \left(\frac{\overset{-}{F_i}}{\sum_{k \neq i} F_k}\right) \tag{9}$$

where the arithmetic signs written above coefficients denote the kind of impact expected.

Table 5 sets out a measure of the tightness of the conditions negotiated by the Bank on the SALs studied in this project, together with measures of the other variables in Equation 9. The measure is a simple arithmetic sum of the *number* of conditions imposed on each country, and as such does not capture tightness perfectly, although an examination of the data does suggest that the countries that had a large number of separate conditions imposed on them were also those where the individual conditions were politically and administratively demanding.[35]

The table shows that tight conditions were negotiated, in general, with the poorest countries in the sample, those with the worst balance-of-payments problems, and those that were most dependent on SAL finance for official capital flows from abroad.[36] All this is consistent with the theory set out in Equation 9. Whether a country that is offered the inducement of a high increase in its national income will thus be motivated to accept proportionately harsher terms for policy reform cannot be effectively tested against the six cases in the table; the verbal testimony of World Bank staff who had been involved in SAL negotiations was that the "with and without" figures of Table 2 were seldom important elements in conditionality negotiations. Finally, we must stress that the burden

35. As a measure of this, we imagine that most readers would accept the following scale of priorities: elimination of subsidies is "tougher" than reduction of subsidies; elimination of quotas is "tougher" than reduction of tariffs; privatization of agricultural marketing is "tougher" than alterations of agricultural prices. The only countries to have been subjected to the "tough" conditions in the left-hand column are: elimination of subsidies—Pakistan, Malawi; elimination of import quotas—Jamaica, the Philippines, the Ivory Coast, Turkey, Kenya; privatization of agricultural marketing—Kenya, the Ivory Coast. All of these countries are in the tightest group of Table 5 except for the Philippines and the Ivory Coast.

36. We use the value of SALs rather than the total flow of funds from the World Bank group as the numerator in the final column of Table 5 because it is the World Bank's normal practice to continue with project finance in a country even if negotiations on a SAL break down (examples: Guyana in 1982; Kenya in 1984).

of debt service, according to the figures in Table 5, had an *opposite* effect to that predicted by the theory: the gentlest terms appeared on the average to be negotiated with countries that had the worst debt-service problems, and the gentlest of all were negotiated with Bolivia, which between 1978 and 1980 had an average debt-service ratio of 36 percent, well over twice the sample average, and which was indeed forced to default on a part of its overseas debts in 1983. The reason why fear of default failed to influence the tightness of conditions negotiated is not obvious; in the case of Bolivia, the World Bank's own internal assessment certainly suggests that more pressure for policy reform on the Bolivian authorities would have been desirable, both in negotiating the initial conditions and in conducting a review of policies before the release of the second tranche of the loan.[37]

First impressions therefore suggest that the relative bargaining strengths of donor and recipient may have exerted an influence on the content of the Bank's conditional-aid packages. Before exploring this proposition further, however, let us consider a contrary *technocratic* hypothesis, which appears to be held by the Bank itself.[38] This hypothesis is that the content of the policy-reform packages negotiated with each borrower is determined purely by the Bank's assessment of the quality of that borrower's economic policies and not at all by its bargaining strength. One measure of the Bank's assessment of the economic policies of different developing countries is provided by its price distortion index, published in the 1983 *World Development Report,* which summarizes the effects of state intervention across a number of markets and reports a marked negative correlation between the distortion index and the growth rate of GDP across a sample of less developed countries.[39] If the technocratic hypothesis is correct, then the value of the price distortion index ought to correlate positively with the tightness of the policy packages negotiated with individual borrowers. It does not.

As Table 6 shows, tight conditionality was imposed on Malawi,

37. See World Bank, *Program Performance Audit Report: Bolivia Structural Adjustment Loan,* Rep. no. 5155, Operations Evaluation Department (Washington, D.C.: IBRD, 1984), p. 19.

38. See Landell-Mills, "Structural Adjustment Lending"; Ernest Stern, "World Bank Financing of Structural Adjustment," in John Williamson, ed., *IMF Conditionality* (Washington, D.C.: Institute for International Economics, 1983), pp. 87–108.

39. World Bank, *World Development Report 1983* (Washington, D.C.: IBRD, 1983), pp. 60–62.

**Table 5.**  *World Bank Structural Adjustment Loans: Tightness of Loan Conditions and Its Possible Determinants*

| | FIRST SAL | TIGHTNESS TO DATE[a] | POSSIBLE DETERMINANTS OF TIGHTNESS | |
|---|---|---|---|---|
| | | | Per Capita GDP, 1980[b] | Recipient's Balance of Payments (average 1978–80 as % of GNP)[c] |
| 1. Guyana | 1981 | 13 | 660 | − 15.8 |
| 2. Jamaica | 1982 | 11 | 1,140 | − 5.5 |
| 3. Bolivia | 1980 | 6 | 580 | − 5.9 |
| 4. South Korea | 1981 | 11 | 1,400 | − 6.2 |
| 5. Thailand | 1982 | 11 | 660 | − 6.3 |
| 6. Philippines | 1980 | 6 | 700 | − 5.2 |
| 7. Turkey | 1980 | 13 | 1,130 | − 3.8 |
| 8. Pakistan | 1982 | 12 | 310 | − 4.3 |
| 9. Kenya | 1980 | 12 | 350 | − 11.4 |
| 10. Malawi | 1981 | 12 | 190 | − 20.1 |
| 11. Ivory Coast | 1981 | 10 | 1,050 | − 14.5 |
| $x_1$ = average of five tightest (1, 7, 8, 9, 10) | | | 528 | 11.1 |
| $x_2$ = average of six loosest (2, 3, 4, 5, 6, 11) | | | 920 | 7.2 |
| $t$ − statistic = $\dfrac{\bar{x}_1 - \bar{x}_2}{\sigma_{\bar{x}_1 - \bar{x}_2}}$ | | | 3.15** | 1.96* |

*Difference between sample means significant at 10% level ($t_{0.05}$ with 10 d.f. = 1.81)

**Difference between sample means signficant at 5% level ($t_{0.25}$ with 10 d.f. = 2.22)

[a]Tightness of SALs is a simple arithmetic sum of the number of areas in which conditions were imposed in successive loans.

[b]Figures from World Bank, *World Bank Development Report 1982* (Washington, D.C.: IBRD, 1982).

POSSIBLE DETERMINANTS OF TIGHTNESS

| Recipient's Debt-Service Ratio (average 1978–1980, as %)[d] | Increase in GDP Growth Rate Forecast (%)[e] | SAL $ as Percentage of Borrower's Gross Public External Capital Flow in Year-of-Issue Average of All SALs[f] |
|---|---|---|
| 20.5 | n.a. | 22.9 |
| 12.9 | 23.6 | 16.6 |
| 36.3 | n.a. | 11.3 |
| 12.0 | n.a. | 4.5 |
| 15.5 | 4.2 | 11.1 |
| 21.1 | 16.3 | 17.0 |
| 13.1 | n.a. | 14.6 |
| 19.7 | n.a. | 20.8 |
| 8.2 | 13.1 | 20.3 |
| 3.2 | 36.0 | 38.4 |
| 18.0 | 38.7 | 12.8 |
| 13.0 | (24.5) | 23.4 |
| 19.3 | (26.2) | 12.2 |
| 2.17* | 0.46 | 3.75** |

[d]Ratio of debt, outstanding and disbursed, to exports of goods and services, as given in World Bank, *World Debt Tables* (Washington, D.C.: IBRD, 1984 and 1985).

[e]Increase in growth rate forecast by World Bank staff.

[f]OECD Development Assistance Committee, *Geographical Distribution of Financial Flows to Developing Countries, 1977–1980* (Paris: OECD, 1981), and subsequent issues.

[c]On *current account* as given in International Monetary Fund, *International Financial Statistics Yearbook 1984* (Washington, D.C.: IMF, 1984).

**Table 6.**  *Measures of Price Distortion and Tightness of Policy Packages Negotiated in SALs.*

| | Distortion Index | Tightness of Terms Negotiated for SALs (range = 1–20) |
|---|---|---|
| Malawi | 1.14 | 12 |
| South Korea | 1.57 | 11 |
| Thailand | 1.43 | 11 |
| Philippines | 1.57 | 6 |
| Kenya | 1.71 | 12 |
| $\bar{x}_1$ = Average, "low distortion" group | 1.48 | 10.4 |
| Ivory Coast | 2.14 | 10 |
| Turkey | 2.14 | 13 |
| Pakistan | 2.29 | 12 |
| Jamaica | 2.29 | 11 |
| Bolivia | 2.29 | 6 |
| $\bar{x}_2$ = Average, "high distortion" group | 2.23 | 10.6 |
| $t$ − statistic $= \dfrac{\bar{x}_1 - \bar{x}_2}{\sigma_{\bar{x}_1 - \bar{x}_2}}$ | 1.87* | 0.10 |

*Sources:* Distortion index from World Bank, *World Development Report 1983* (Washington, D.C.: IBRD, 1983), pp. 60–61; "tightness" from Table 5 above.

*Difference between sample means significant at 10 percent level ($t_{0.05}$ with 10 d.f. = 1.81)

which is at the very top of the Bank's "distortion" league table, and loose conditionality on Bolivia, which is close to the bottom. If we take together the ten countries for which data exist, there is no statistically significant difference between the tightness of the terms imposed on the low-distortion group, which, on the Bank's assessment, had relatively enlightened policies, and the terms imposed on the high-distortion group, whose policies were judged far less favorable to growth. There is, therefore, little support from the data presented here for the view that the tightness of the policy packages recommended by the Bank to borrower countries was dependent on the quality of the recipient's economic policies rather than its bargaining position in relation to the lender.

We now consider the performance of borrowers in what we have called Act 2, that is, the phase in which they decide how much of the conditionality package to implement. The decision is not always fully voluntary; borrower governments often do not have absolute power to implement things they have undertaken to do. For example, a borrower that has undertaken "to reduce the public sector financial deficit from 9% to 6% over three years"[40] may not be able to do this if its forecasts of the tax base turn out to be wrong as a result of the weather or some other uncontrollable variable. However, we have argued that the controllable part of their actions can be explained by the hypothesis of Equation 7, that is, the borrower is less likely to implement agreed-upon policy conditions imposed by a given donor, the less its dependence is on that donor at the end of the loan period (as measured by its balance-of-payments deficit and the share of the donor in the total concessional-aid flow), and the greater the perceived coercion, that is, the gap between the reform package it would have liked to implement in the first loan period and the package it agreed to implement. The first two of these variables are easily quantified; perceived coercion is not. Our approach to devising a suitable proxy variable is as follows. First, other things being equal, it seems reasonable to assume that perceived coercion will be greater the greater the tightness of the policy-reform package. Second, however, the main factor that may render other things unequal is whether the reform package was reluctantly agreed to by an old government in contradiction of its previous policies, or whether it was enthusiastically offered by a new government as part of its manifesto commitment. In the first case the implementation of the reform involves a reversal of declared policies, and this will humiliate the government; in the second no break with past practice need be involved, and the new government can present such sacrifices as the reforms do impose on people as part of a consistent strategy rather than as a last desperate expedient. The degree of tightness of the original loan and whether or not the government was a new one at the time that loan was negotiated appear, therefore, to be the most obvious a priori determinants or perceived coercion.

A preliminary test of these hypotheses is carried out in Table 7. The results are patchy. As predicted, slippage is greater among countries whose balance-of-payments problems are relatively minor and whose need of special assistance has become smallest: the

40. This was a condition accepted by the Kenya government when negotiating its first SAL.

**Table 7.**  *World Bank Structural Adjustment Loans: Slippage and Its Possible Determinants*

|  | First SAL Disbursed | Slippage, to End 1984 (%)[a] | Tightness of First SAL (range 1–20)[b] |
|---|---|---|---|
| 1. Guyana | 1981 | 42 | 13 |
| 2. Jamaica | 1982 | 5 | 11 |
| 3. Bolivia | 1980 | 80 | 6 |
| 4. South Korea | 1981 | 5 | 11 |
| 5. Thailand | 1982 | 18 | 11 |
| 6. Philippines | 1980 | 19 | 6 |
| 7. Turkey | 1980 | 4 | 13 |
| 8. Pakistan | 1982 | 10 | 12 |
| 9. Kenya | 1980 | 61 | 12 |
| 10. Malawi | 1981 | 37 | 12 |
| 11. Ivory Coast | 1981 | 18 | 10 |
| $x_1$ = Average of five *highest* (1, 3, 6, 9, 10) | | 47.8 | 9.8 |
| $x_2$ = Average of six *lowest* (2, 4, 5, 7, 8, 11) | | 9.2 | 11.1 |
| $t$ − statistic = $\dfrac{\bar{x}_1 - \bar{x}_2}{\sigma_{\bar{x}_1 - \bar{x}_2}}$ | | 7.87* | 0.98 |

*Difference between sample means significant at 5 percent level ($t_{0.025}$ with 10 d.f. = 2.22)

[a]Slippage on agreed-upon SAL conditions is measured as a percentage of the agreed-upon policy changes that are actually implemented. See Table 4 of the original text.

[b]Transcribed from Table 5 above.

average balance-of-payments deficit among countries whose slippage was high is under 4 percent of GNP in 1983 and falling, whereas the average deficit among countries whose slippage was low is over 6 percent and rising. However, tightness on its own has no significant correlation with slippage, and those countries whose slippage is high, contrary to our hypothesis, are more heavily de-

| Recipient's Balance of Payments (% GNP in 1983; ↑ ↓ = trend since 1980)[c] | SAL as % of Borrower's Gross Public External Capital Flow in Year of Issue (average of all SALs)[d] | New Government in Year before SAL Package Agreed? |
|---|---|---|
| −2.6; ↑ | 22.9 | |
| −11.8; ↓ | 16.6 | Yes |
| −3.0; ↓ | 11.3 | |
| −2.1; ↑ | 4.5 | |
| −7.3; ↓ | 11.1 | |
| −8.1; ↓ | 17.0 | |
| −3.7; ↑ | 14.6 | Yes |
| +0.04; ↑ | 20.8 | |
| −3.1; ↑ | 20.3 | |
| −2.3; ↑ | 38.4 | |
| −12.3; ↑ | 12.8 | |
| −3.8; ↓ | 21.9 | |
| −6.2; ↑ | 13.4 | |
| 1.21 | 2.95* | |

[c]Balance of payments 1980 and 1983 measured on current account from International Monetary Fund, *International Financial Statistics Yearbook 1984* (Washington, D.C.: IMF, 1984), supplemented where necessary by IMF, *International Financial Statistics* (Washington, D.C.: IMF, April 1985).

[d]From OECD, Development Assistance Committee, *Geographical Distribution of Financial Flows, 1977–80* (Paris: OECD, 1981), and subsequent issues.

pendent on SALs for external finance than the low-slippage group. Perhaps the most significant datum in Table 7, however, is the fact that the countries whose policy-reform packages have been most faithfully implemented, Turkey and Jamaica, both underwent changes of government in the year before the SAL agreement was concluded. In the former case the new government was mili-

**Table 8.** *World Bank Structural Adjustment Loans: Tightness in relation to Slippage in Previous Period*

| | SLIPPAGE, FIRST SAL (%) | SECOND SAL | | SUBSEQUENT SALS |
|---|---|---|---|---|
| | | Granted? | Tightness (range = 1–20) | Slippage to End 1984 (%) | |
| Bolivia | 80 | No | | | |
| Guyana | 42 | No | | | |
| Kenya | 40 | Yes | 14 | 78 | |
| Malawi | 30 | Yes | 11 | 44 | * |
| Thailand | 30 | Yes | 13 | 12 | * |
| Ivory Coast | 20 | Yes | 11 | 16 | * |
| Jamaica | 16 | Yes | 11 | 16 | 2 |
| Pakistan | 10 | No | | | |
| Philippines | 10 | Yes | 7 | 30 | * |
| South Korea | 0 | Yes | 10 | 5 | |
| Turkey | 0 | Yes | 15 | 4 | 3 |

*Source:* Slippage from Table 7.

*Third SAL under discussion.

tary and in the latter, civil; the important point is that neither government was significantly obligated to the groups who could be expected to lose from a liberalization of domestic and foreign trade, or could be accused of inconsistency or betrayal of those groups if it went ahead with an economic stabilization program. When the SAL agreements were signed in those countries, indeed, they did little more than codify the program that their government had said it intended to implement in any case.[41] There and only there among SAL countries, the leopard had formally committed himself to change his *dirigiste* spots before the question of conditional aid even arose. By that same token, however, the range of

41. This is conceded by the World Bank's evaluation of the Turkish structural adjustment program: World Bank, *Program Performance Audit Report: Turkey First Structural Adjustment Loan* (Washington, D.C.: IBRD, 1982), pp. 3–4, 28–31. For the case of Jamaica see *Sunday Times* (New York), 4 July 1980.

policy reforms in both countries since 1980 cannot be listed among the achievements of conditional development aid.

Finally we consider Act 3, the phase in which the lender decides to grant or not to grant a further loan to the borrower. Our model (Equation 8) states that a further loan will be granted only if slippage falls short of some critical level, and in this event the tightness of the new loan will be directly related to the level of such slippage in the previous period. Table 8 shows that only a part of this hypothesis is confirmed by experience. Pakistan, which had only 10 percent slippage on the first SAL, was refused a second loan of this type,[42] and Turkey, whose fulfillment of the conditions of the first SAL was exemplary, nonetheless had tight conditionality, by our measure, attached to its second and indeed its third. In general, there is no perceptible relationship between slippage on the first loan and tightness of the conditions attached to the second, although this may reflect the limitations of our tightness measure rather than the way the World Bank saw the matter.

42. It was, however, offered a clutch of conditional sector loans in compensation.

# 3

# The Political Economy of Stabilization: Commitment, Capacity, and Public Response

## *Joan Nelson*

Since 1979, the second oil price increase, the worldwide recession, rising interest rates, and related trends in the international economy have brought a surge in the number of developing nations facing acute financial difficulties. Such difficulties usually result from efforts by the public and the government to spend more than available resources permit. In the early 1980s many developing countries found that their exports earned less, their imports cost more, interest rates on accumulated foreign debt rose sharply, production dropped, and government revenues

Reprinted with permission from Joan Nelson, "The Political Economy of Stabilization," *World Development,* vol. 12. © 1984, Pergamon Press, Ltd.

The research on which this discussion is based was mainly funded by the Agency for International Development. The World Bank provided supplementary funding, and the Overseas Development Council provided invaluable logistic support and dwindled, while government ministries tried to continue their operations and ordinary people tried to maintain their earlier (often very modest) standards of living. Typical symptoms of the crisis were the drying up of foreign exchange reserves (sometimes to the point where only a few days of imports could be financed), acute scarcity of imported goods for production and consumption, accumulation of overdue payments to creditors abroad, budget deficit on the order of 15, 20, or even 30 percent of GNP, and accelerated inflation. The standard prescription for such symptoms is a stabilization program, designed to bring consumption in general and demand for imported goods and services in particular into better balance with available resources, while encouraging investment, production, and greater foreign-exchange earnings. To that end, governments may need to impose a series of difficult austerity measures, such as cuts in government expenditures and/or increases in taxation, wage freezes in the public and the private sector, devaluation, credit restrictions (particularly on public-sector borrowing from the banking system), and increased real interest rates. Such measures are politically difficult for leaders to adopt, and to implement once adopted. This chapter focuses on the political factors affecting the success or failure of economic stabilization programs.

The discussion starts from the assumption that despite the painful nature of stabilization programs, the alternative to planned and guided adjustment is chaotic ad hoc adjustment, entailing even higher costs in terms of debt, controls, scarcities, inflation, unemployment, and atrophied output and growth. This holds, unfortunately, regardless of whether the root causes of the crisis are within or beyond the country's control. In some countries, a good case can be made that the main causes of the crisis are beyond the country's control. Examples include extended drought, a catastrophic drop in the price of the country's major export product(s), sharply rising costs of imports, unanticipated increases in the servicing charges on variable-interest-rate debts, or instability and war

intellectual stimulation. Special thanks are due to Princeton Lyman and Costas Michalopoulos for early encouragement, and to Alan Gelb, Gerald Helleiner, John Lewis, Jacob Meerman, and Norman Uphoff for particularly thorough comments and suggestions. Many others generously provided information and interpretation for the country case studies, or specific suggestions on the general analysis. The study would not have been possible without such broad support, but I alone am responsible for the views and interpretations it sets forth.

in surrounding countries, which may cut transport links or otherwise harm noncombatant neighbors. In most developing countries, internal policies and practices have also contributed to the crises of the early 1980s, often through the cumulative, unanticipated, and sometimes unrecognized effects of measures adopted years or decades earlier (such as high protection for import-substituting industries). But regardless of whether the main responsibility lies within or outside the nation itself, a financial crisis means that consumption cannot continue at current levels. The choice is not whether to tighten belts, but whether to attempt to guide and control adjustment so as to limit the damage to welfare, equity, and growth and to accelerate recovery, or to let the contraction take place willy-nilly.[1]

Since stabilization is essential, clearly it is desirable to make the measures as effective as possible. But the batting average of planned stabilization programs has not been good, especially in the poorer countries. A high percentage of such programs are abandoned in midstream. Others are technically completed, in that performance targets are met and all loan installments drawn, but serious difficulties often recur within a matter of months.

There are many explanations for such a record, including such completely uncontrollable events as adverse weather or shifts in the terms of trade; occasional failure of expected supplementary external finance or support (for instance, private capital inflows or rescheduling, or aid from bilateral sources); and, possibly, shortcomings inherent in the approach to stabilization itself. The most common of all the reasons for failure are internal political pressures and politicians' fears of such pressures, which lead governments to postpone corrective action until the economic crisis is acute and/or to dilute or abandon programs before the necessary economic adjustments are accomplished.

Theorists and practitioners involved in stabilization efforts are well aware of the importance of politics to the success or failure of those efforts. References to political constraints crop up repeatedly in studies of specific countries' experiences and, to some extent, in

---

1. In many countries, austerity measures directed to stabilizing the economy are not sufficient to trigger renewed growth, with changed patterns of production and consumption so as to avoid a recurrence of the same problems. Changes in the international economic and financial system and structural adjustment measures in the countries concerned are also essential. But such measures will not obviate the need for stabilization in the short run, nor, often, in the medium run.

broader theoretical analyses. But it is fair to say that there has been little systematic or comparative analysis of the politics of stabilization efforts.[2]

It is often argued that as international organizations and bilateral aid agencies ought not to become involved in recipient nations' political affairs, they have no business explicitly considering political dimensions of the programs they assist. But the argument is both illogical and impractical. There are sound moral and practical reasons why neither international organizations nor other nations should deliberately intervene in internal politics (though in fact, of course, governments regularly do try to intervene in other nations' affairs). But anticipating political reactions and adjusting one's own action accordingly is not tantamount to intervention. In the case of stabilization programs, an attempt to anticipate political and administrative obstacles and to design the program so as to cope with those obstacles is no more than practical. Failure to do so, in fact, is irresponsible, both vis-à-vis the government concerned and with respect to effective use of the resources of the external agency. In practice, experienced analysts and advisers do try to anticipate political constraints informally, although the main responsibility properly falls on the government concerned.

Sometimes, too, political issues are conveniently dismissed as a

2. David Finch, "Adjustment Policies and Conditionality," in John Williamson, ed., *IMF Conditionality* (Washington, D.C.: for International Economics, 1983), offers an excellent general discussion by a senior Fund official that repeatedly and explicitly refers to political pressures and considerations. An early effort at a systematic, though narrow-gauged, assessment of the political risks associated with devaluation (not with stabilization more generally) used the criterion of whether or not the government or the finance minister falls within the year following a devaluation: Richard N. Cooper, "An Assessment of Currency Devaluation in Developing Countries," in Gustav Ranis, ed., *Government and Economic Development* (New Haven: Yale University Press, 1971), pp. 500–503. More recently, Donald Keesing includes in his study of trade policy for developing countries a substantial discussion of political factors supporting or inhibiting trade liberalization: *Trade Policy for Developing Countries*, World Bank Staff Working Paper no. 353 (Washington, D.C.: World Bank, 1979), pp. 143ff. John Sheahan offers a more extensive analysis of political obstacles to market-oriented policies in general—for example, devaluation, decontrol of the economy, trade liberalization—in Latin America, focused on the hypothesis that effective pursuit of such policies often requires authoritarian methods: "Market Oriented Economic Policies and Political Repression in Latin America," *Economic Development and Cultural Change* 28, no. 2 (January 1980): 267–92. David Denoon, in *Devaluation under Pressure: India, Indonesia, and Ghana* (New York: New York University Press, forthcoming), has prepared a study of the politics of devaluation in India, Indonesia, and Ghana in the late 1960s. Alejandro Foxley and Laurence Whitehead organized a series of studies on the politics of stabilization in Latin America, published as a special issue of *World Development:* 8, no. 11 (November 1980).

matter of sufficient political "will" on the part of the government concerned. Either the government has sufficient will or it does not. If it does, political analysis is unnecessary; if it does not, there is not much to be done about it. But this is a simplistic attitude. Commitment to stabilization on the part of the top political leaders of a country is indeed crucial. But that commitment itself is a variable on which outside agencies can have some influence. Commitment is also a matter of degree, and different degrees of commitment may call for differently designed programs. Still more important, even strong commitment may not be sufficient to overcome political obstacles unless programs are also designed in a manner that addresses those obstacles.

The importance of considering political sustainability is buttressed by the high costs of failed programs. Failures are costly in terms of resources expended and in terms of sacrifices suffered for little or no lasting gain. Failures may also create a legacy of cynicism and bitterness that seriously complicates future efforts. Disappointing experience with stabilization efforts has prompted an intense debate regarding program design, and considerable experimentation both within developing countries and on the part of multilateral and bilateral agencies seeking to assist (and often to guide) them. In general, policy and (perhaps in lesser degree) practice have moved toward programs that are longer in duration, rely less on monetary instruments, and give more explicit attention to structural adjustment on the supply side. Stabilization and adjustment can usefully be viewed as a continuum, with stabilization programs focused on demand management and potential short-run gains in foreign-exchange earnings or savings, while structural adjustment programs emphasize supply-side changes that usually take several years to bear fruit. The boundary between the two is not well defined, and actual programs usually include elements of both (indeed, the same reforms may promote both). But some programs clearly approximate "pure" stabilization, while others have a much stronger adjustment element.

Increased emphasis on structural adjustment makes it all the more urgent to take steps to assure political sustainability. Over a period of several years, opposition can coalesce. The costs and risks of relying on coercive suppression of opposition are correspondingly heightened. But the longer time horizon also provides more opportunity for phasing, for gradual application of measures, for manipulation of the sequence in which measures are introduced, and for mid-course adjustments to respond to both technical and political signals. Thus the mixed record of past efforts, the pressing nature of current problems, and the evolving nature of stabilization and adjustment programs all point toward the need for more systematic political analysis.

One important reason for the comparative neglect of political analysis within the on-going reassessment of stabilization policies is the absence of a useful framework for such analysis, and the absence of information for specific countries needed to make reliable assessments. There are no neat and realistic "models" available to predict and analyze the interactions of politics and alternative stabilization packages for a specific country. Even if such theoretical models existed, most of the country-specific data needed for such a model would not be available. Indeed, some of the crucial information is closely held, especially information on goals and perceptions of key factions and individuals in the highly personalistic politics of many countries. Nevertheless, both general knowledge and theory about political behavior and the wealth of case material now available permit analysis that moves beyond the back-of-the-envelope (or seat-of-the-pants?) approach to political considerations.

## Factors Determining Political Sustainability

Three sets of factors directly affect the political sustainability of a stabilization effort—that is, the odds that it will not be abandoned or seriously diluted in mid-course because of leaders' political concerns or popular political pressure. These factors are:

> The strength of political leaders' commitment to the program
>
> The government's capabilities
>
> The political response the program evokes from influential groups

These factors are not independent of each other; indeed, they interact dynamically. Each is also of course influenced by the anticipated and actual economic impact of the program. And each reflects a number of more basic attitudes, institutions, and relationships, some of which are discussed in this chapter.

The conceptual approach and many of the more specific observations in this discussion are based on a comparative study of five countries, completed in mid-1983. The cases included:

> Ghana, from the overthrow of Nkrumah in 1966 through the military and the civilian regimes that followed, to the coup of January 1972

> Zambia, from the adoption of a two-year Standby Agreement with the IMF in April 1978 to January 1983

> Kenya, from Kenyatta's death in 1978 and Moi's succession to the presidency through 1982

> Sri Lanka, from the mid-1977 landslide election of a United National Party (UNP) committed to a more market-oriented economy through the reelection of the president in the autumn of 1982

> Jamaica, from the initial adoption of a stabilization package by the Manley government in early 1977, through several unsuccessful efforts, to the electoral victory of the Seaga government in 1980 and its initial reforms

With the exception of Jamaica, these are all quite poor nations. In 1980, GNP per capita was $270 in Sri Lanka and ranged up to $560 in Zambia (where distribution, however, leaves the bulk of the population extremely poor); Jamaican per capita GNP was $1,040. Kenya, with just under 16 million people in 1980, is the largest of the five; Jamaica, with 2.2 million, the smallest. All case studies covered at least five years; they were not confined to a single "stabilization episode" (usually defined as the duration of a standby agreement with the International Monetary Fund). One of the most interesting aspects of the cases is the ways experience during earlier periods affected later decisions and political responses.[3]

Why focus on small, poor, highly trade-dependent countries? There is a hot debate among development specialists as to whether conventional stabilization approaches work adequately in such countries. The logic of a stabilization program is not merely to cut trade and budget deficits by reducing consumption and production, but to shift the incentives and thereby the structure of pro-

3. The AID study includes the country case descriptions and the full list of sources consulted. See Joan Nelson, "The Political Economy of Stabilization in Small, Low-Income, Trade-Dependent Nations," Research Report for the United States Agency for International Development, Washington, D.C., 1983 (typescript).

duction and consumption in an economy so as to increase ability to earn foreign exchange and reduce requirements for using it. Such adjustments are particularly important in small countries, which typically rely heavily on trade, because their own internal resources and markets are limited. Generally, however, small, poor countries are dependent on one or a few export goods. They cannot switch rapidly into entirely different items, nor can they readily start producing a wide range of domestic substitutes for basic imported items. They do not usually produce products that are tradable but not already traded; therefore, cutting domestic demand and increasing incentives to export cannot prompt a rapid shift from domestic to foreign markets. Even expansion of such traditional exports as tree crops may have long lead times due to technical factors. Moreover, since their people are already, for the most part, very poor, and government expenditures are limited, an austerity program may mean real hunger for households, lack of the simplest medicines for clinics, deterioration of roads and other infrastructure for lack of maintenance, and more generally the breakdown of institutions and facilities essential for a modicum of welfare and for resumed growth.

This chapter does not try to judge the validity of these criticisms about the economic impact of stabilization measures in poor countries, and especially in small poor countries. But the chapter does take into special consideration some of the political factors that may be particularly important in such countries and may therefore affect the prospects for stabilization. In many ways the politics of stabilization is similar in any country, advanced, semi-industrialized, or poor, small or large, heavily or only moderately trade-dependent. But just as the more detailed economic issues of stabilization differ in these different settings, so do political and administrative constraints and opportunities. This chapter thus pursues two themes simultaneously. It suggests a conceptual framework for analyzing the political sustainability of economic stabilization programs in any setting. It also gives special attention to one category of cases: small, poor, highly trade-dependent economies.

Two points should be noted about the scope of this discussion. First, the study is concerned with factors affecting the political sustainability of stabilization efforts and with ways to improve political sustainability. Political sustainability overlaps but is by no means the same as distributional equity. Improved design of stabilization with respect to equity requires reducing the losses suffered by the poorest groups. Improved design of stabilization programs with respect to political sustainability may require reducing the losses (or increasing the gains) to the most politically relevant groups. The two goals may, and often do, conflict.

The second caveat: the study focuses on the effects of politics on stabilization, rather than the impact of stabilization on politics. A number of analysts have argued that stabilization measures, because they impose hardships on many groups within society and they challenge the position of vested interests, are most readily carried out by authoritarian regimes. More disturbing, they suggest that advocating stabilization measures or, more generally, urging market-oriented policies of decontrol and liberalization in nations characterized by extensive "populist" state intervention implicitly encourages and endorses authoritarian political tendencies. These issues are extremely important, but they are not systematically considered here.

## Leaders' Commitment to Stabilization

The country cases on which this discussion is based certainly confirm the importance of committed leadership for effective stabilization. Will alone is not sufficient, but it is clearly necessary. Reluctance to adopt firm stabilization measures is generally prompted either by fear of political repercussions or by lack of confidence that such measures will in fact improve the situation— or both. Commitment is usually born of duress—the painful recognition that the economic and political costs of failure to act are probably greater than the costs of action. The strength of leaders' commitment is determined by the perceived margin of advantage, that is, the degree to which the expected results of stabilization are preferred to available alternatives. Commitment that grows out of desperation will fade if any aspect of the situation becomes less binding—for example, if prices improve for a major export good.

Occasionally the stabilization package may include features that are positively preferred by political leaders, particularly if the package includes structural adjustment components consistent with leaders' own goals or ideological leanings. For example, in Sri Lanka a new government was elected by a sweeping majority in 1977. That government, headed by J. R. Jayawardene, was committed to dismantling much of the elaborate structure of government controls and regulations accumulated over three decades, and particularly in the seven years of the previous administration, and it also sought a much more dynamic, outward-looking growth strategy. Positive commitment of this kind is more durable, but much less common.

## Obstacles to Commitment: Leaders' Political Fears

Politicians are damned if they do and damned if 'they don't, when it comes to the political consequences of their stabilization decisions. A firm stabilization program will predictably provoke protest. But so will continued economic deterioration. Leaders' decisions may be influenced by a less obvious consideration. The public will evaluate government policies on the basis of events that follow adoption of a program (a before/after comparison) rather than trying to gauge what would have happened had the program not been adopted (a with/without comparison). Once the government adopts stabilization measures, the public is likely to attribute to the government the responsibility for economic hardship that would have occurred (perhaps even more acutely) in the absence of those policies. Therefore, politicians are likely to view adoption of stabilization measures as accelerating or accentuating public reactions to economic hardship and focusing those reactions on the government itself instead of on exogenous forces such as rapacious foreign creditors. Moreover, to the extent that stabilization measures shift the incidence of economic hardship to the detriment of groups capable of concerted protest (for instance, civil servants), adopting a program may intensify the political risks inherent in the tight economic situation. Finally, in those cases in which stabilization entails a Standby or Extended Fund Facility Agreement with the IMF, adopting a stabilization program may sometimes ignite political opposition, because elements of the public or opposition parties can seize on IMF involvement and government "capitulation." In other cases, however, IMF involvement may be politically convenient to the government, as a scapegoat and/or as reassurance to some elements of the public.

Political leaders must balance their fear of intensified protest, more sharply focused on the government itself, against the possible political benefits of increased foreign exchange available through a standby agreement (and possibly from other public and private sources whose support is contingent on the IMF seal of approval).[4] Obviously the volume, timing, and conditions attached to foreign financial support affect its political value. Assistance that can be used only to reduce overdue foreign debt, for example, is considerably less attractive than assistance that can be used to increase imports.

Leaders' assessment of their own political security or lack thereof affects the weight they attach to anticipated risks. Leaders may feel secure because they believe (rightly or wrongly) that they are popular and legitimate, or because they can rely on well-organized political support bases and face little organized opposition, or because they count on loyal and effective police and military. New regimes, elected or not, often can count on a brief "honeymoon" during which much of the public will suspend judgment and adopt a wait-and-see stance toward policy changes. The newly elected UNP government in Sri Lanka capitalized on that advantage in the 1977–1979 period to introduce a vigorous reform program. Jamaica in late 1980 appeared to be in a similar situation. After years of economic decline, a new government had been elected with a strong majority, promising extensive reforms. In fact, however, the Seaga government in Jamaica made much less vigorous use of its "grace period" than did the Jayawardene regime in Sri Lanka. Long-established governments whose popularity and legitimacy have gradually eroded may rely heavily on a fairly narrow political support base of high-level bureaucrats and party officials and their circles of clients. Measures that threaten these relationships can be highly risky. This was the situation in Zambia in the late 1970s and early 1980s.

Sometimes, of course, leaders badly misjudge their security: among the cases examined as background for this study, Ghana in late 1971 offers an example. A civilian government headed by Prime Minister Busia had been elected in the autumn of 1969, following several years of military rule and fairly severe stabilization policies under the National Liberation Council. The new government had hoped to preside over resumed growth and was reluc-

4. Some stabilization programs are undertaken without IMF guidance and assistance, but most developing countries facing financial crises need the assistance and therefore must accept some guidance. Moreover, private banks, bilateral aid donors, and sometimes the World Bank may be willing to provide fresh loans to a financially precarious nation only after it has entered into a standby agreement with the IMF, in principle committing itself to take corrective measures.

tant and slow to address a deteriorating economic situation. It also alienated important segments of the public by actions unrelated to economic policy. When Busia finally became convinced in late 1971 that he must take painful corrective action, he decided on a drastic devaluation which nearly doubled the price of imported goods. At the time, he and the cabinet probably did not realize the extent of public alienation. The devaluation touched off protest demonstrations and was the catalyst for a military coup.

Leaders' aspirations for the future also bear on their aversion to risk and therefore on their willingness to make a firm commitment to stabilization. A military leader (or council) that plans to return the government to civilian rule fairly soon (as in Ghana under the National Liberation Council in the mid-1960s) can afford measures that governments with longer time horizons would avoid. Similarly, a last-term elected leader may be able to take political risks, especially if the division of powers between the executive and the legislative branch of government does not make that leader a "lame duck."

### Obstacles to Commitment:
### Leaders' Economic Doubts

Economists often assume that fear of political risk is the most important deterrent to strong commitment from political leaders. Evidence from the five cases examined in this study challenges this assumption. In all these cases, doubts about the economic benefits of stabilization measures played a major role in the delay in adoption or the vacillating or half-hearted implementation of measures. This evidence is all the more striking because (with the exception of the Manley era in Jamaica) none of these were countries with strong ideological obstacles to stabilization measures. Indeed, in Ghana at the end of the 1960s, in Kenya, in Sri Lanka since 1977, and in Jamaica since late 1980, fairly free market activity has been favored in principle. Skepticism about the economic benefits of stabilization in these cases can fairly be taken to represent much more widespread and intense skepticism in many other countries. Therefore it is worth examining the roots of leaders' economic skepticism.

In some cases, ministers and political leaders simply have very limited economic background and understanding. This can be true in any country (including highly industrialized ones), but it is more likely in countries with a short history of independence and comparatively few highly educated people.

Moreover, some aspects of conventional stabilization and adjustment programs are counterintuitive. This is perhaps particularly true of devaluation. All but a handful of the most economically sophisticated officials and members of the public find it hard to understand why a shortage of foreign exchange (expressed as a balance-of-payments deficit and import restrictions) will be relieved by lowering the value of their currency vis-à-vis those of others. Prices in general are widely viewed as normative, a value to be politically determined, not a variable with a unique market-clearing magnitude which it is important to approximate. (The same attitude, incidentally, prevailed in earlier centuries in Western Europe, and is widely encountered today in Eastern Europe: prices of grain, for instance, were often set in terms of what urban consumers were thought to be able to afford.) The exchange rate in particular is not viewed as an economist views prices; it is implicitly assumed that the supply of and demand for foreign exchange are inelastic to price, that is, the exchange rate. Hence the widespread public conviction, shared by many politicians and officials, that devaluation is a formula forced on developing nations by the IMF, for obscure theoretical reasons that have little application to their own circumstances or, worse, to protect the interests of rich international financiers.

Countries are often urged not only to devalue, as part of a stabilization effort, but also to reduce or dismantle controls over various internal prices, such as producer and consumer prices for staple foods, or interest rates on credit. Such controls often distort incentives and result in scarcities, black or "parallel" markets, extensive smuggling, and other problems that aggravate the financial difficulties. But the potential benefits of freeing internal prices are also not obvious. As Killick observes with reference to public opinion in Ghana, "Who except an unholy alliance of trading houses and a few academic economists could be in favour of removing price controls?"[5] Interest-rate reform is also widely misperceived. Sheahan's comments, based on observations in Latin America, also apply elsewhere:

> The fact that the main group which gains from selective credit allocation at below-market interest rates is the business sector [and es-

5. Tony Killick, *Development Economics in Action: A Study of Economic Policies in Ghana* (New York: St. Martin's Press, 1978), p. 438.

pecially the larger firms], for which investment is effectively subsidized, is not emphasized either by equalitarian reformers or by the business sector itself. It is more directly evident that small borrowers without special influence are badly hurt by excessively high interest rates than it is that controls in regulated financial markets are in part responsible for the exaggerated rates elsewhere.[6]

Even where the economic rationale of stabilization is well understood, political leaders often lack confidence in that rationale. Skepticism flows in part from the linkage of stabilization with economic liberalization. Many IMF-supported programs and all World Bank structural adjustment loans stress reduced direct government intervention in the economy and greater reliance on market incentives for public corporations and services. These prescriptions run counter to deep-rooted statist, anti-market biases. Throughout the developing world, as was true historically in Western Europe, most officials and intellectuals and much of the public tend to doubt that the profit motive can be socially constructive, view middlemen as unproductive and exploitative, and place considerable confidence in the efficacy of state economic controls to pursue national goals.

These attitudes bear on leaders' receptivity to stabilization and structural-adjustment prescriptions in two ways. First, to the extent that stabilization is viewed as a stalking-horse for privatization of the economy, and to the extent that it is perceived as conflicting with social goals and needs, stabilization will be resisted. Second, statist biases inhibit acceptance of stabilization and adjustment prescriptions, through what might be labeled the illusion of control. These prescriptions imply reduced direct government control of economic forces—at precisely the moment when those forces are most overwhelming and frightening. Even though government regulations and controls are often not effective or are even harmful, sharply reducing them is a difficult step. Killick observes that Ghana's minister of finance, J. H. Mensah, opposed the 1971 devaluation partly because "it would remove the discretion of economic management from the government."[7]

Disappointing experience with past stabilization efforts frequently reinforces politicians' tendency toward statist, anti-market biases. For example, the National Liberation Council that ruled Ghana in the mid-1960s undertook a series of austerity measures

6. John Sheahan, "Market Oriented Economic Policies," pp. 275–76.
7. Killick, *Development Economics in Action*, p. 320.

to stabilize the economy, brought to the edge of collapse during Nkrumah's last years in power. The effort included a devaluation in 1967, which was widely regarded as merely having raised prices without stimulating exports or producing other benefits. Though technicians would dispute this interpretation, the legacy of the 1967 devaluation in the public mind contributed to the successor government's reluctance to devalue again in 1970 or 1971 and probably sharpened public anger when devaluation finally came. Similarly, Jamaica experienced a sizable devaluation in 1978, followed by small devaluations for several months, which were generally interpreted as having failed and which, until late 1983, inhibited the successor Seaga government from adjusting the exchange rate. India's 1966 experience with devaluation has colored public attitudes to the present time.

As was noted earlier, interpretations of past experiences are often based on a "before/after" comparison.[8] But some past efforts were indeed inadequate in design or execution, even in terms of the appropriate "with/without" evaluation. Remedial measures have sometimes failed to take sufficient account of structural or institutional rigidities in supply response or have been unduly optimistic (or, perhaps, reasonable but proved wrong by events) in their assumptions about international prices, weather, or other exogenous factors. Such experiences undermine confidence in the whole approach.

An additional factor contributing to lack of commitment is the overriding importance attributed to *forces beyond the individual country's control.* In Zambia, for example, both the public at large and political leaders were convinced that the fall in copper prices throughout the 1970s and the war in Zimbabwe (which severely disrupted the landlocked nation's transport arteries and also entailed other burdens) were the main causes of the acute economic pressures in the late 1970s. When the war ended and copper prices briefly recovered, neither politicians nor the public were at all prepared for continuing difficulties. In Ghana during the Busia administration, most people were convinced that the root cause of the nation's problems was the large and wasteful debts incurred by Nkrumah in his last years in power. These obligations (which the

8. J. Clark Leith's analysis of the 1967 devaluation and liberalization efforts in Ghana explicitly notes that the later assessments of those efforts were based on before/after comparisons: *Foreign Trade Regimes and Economic Development: Ghana* (New York: National Bureau of Economic Research, 1974), p. 112.

NLC and the Busia government both decided to honor, despite some public pressure to abrogate) made devaluation and stabilization measures still more distasteful than they would have been in any case. Where politicians and publics are convinced that the main causes of their difficulties lie beyond their control, it seems fruitless to adopt painful policies to try to correct the situation. If political leaders adopt corrective policies that go beyond short-run, essential reactions (such as rationing foreign exchange as reserves fall), they will have assumed a larger degree of responsibility for what happens to the country—and therefore they will be correspondingly held liable if the effort fails.[9]

Sharply divergent lines of advice on how to interpret and cope with economic crises have constituted still another obstacle to commitment. Experiences in Zambia, Ghana, and Jamaica illustrate the point. In Ghana, as late as the autumn of 1971, Minister of Finance Mensah was still arguing that cocoa prices would rise soon and that drastic measures were not needed. In Zambia early in 1980, Kaunda was confronted with totally different assessments from the conservative team that had guided the stabilization program of 1978–1980, on the one hand, and the new head of the National Planning Office and those around him, on the other. And in Jamaica in 1978–1979, high-level economic officials of the Manley government were divided between moderates and radicals, with sharply divergent interpretations of trends and prospects, hence of appropriate policy.

Conversely, in most cases of effective adjustment programs, one or a few highly committed technocrat-politicians with strong (though sometimes temporary or contingent) backing from top political leaders have played a crucial role. Among clear-cut instances are Indonesia in the late 1960s with Widjojo Nitisastro leading a group of highly competent advisers, and Turkey from 1980 to 1982, where Turgut Ozal played the central role.

### Factors Encouraging Commitment

This list of reasons why so many decisionmakers in poorer countries have little faith in stabilization measures (not to mention

9. Keesing notes also that "teetering from crisis to crisis" may have political advantages, demonstrating apparent skill in maneuver—and also muting criticism, since attacking management in the midst of externally imposed crisis is unpatriotic: *Trade Policy for Developing Countries*, p. 149.

their concerns about political risks) includes little that is new or startling. But the list is formidable. However, there are also countervailing forces that may improve the prospects for the necessary commitment from leaders over the difficult years of the mid-1980s.

In many countries, experience with past unsuccessful or only partially successful measures has paved the way for more effective efforts. John Odling-Smee notes in a review of adjustment experience in seven countries assisted by the IMF, "The first attempts at stabilization and adjustment were not always successful (as Korea in 1979, Peru in 1976–77, and Portugal in 1977), mainly because the extent of the problem was underestimated. After some success in adjusting was achieved, further problems came close to reversing it in these cases."[10] Christine Bindert notes that successful stabilization programs in Portugal, Peru, and Turkey were preceded in each country by two or three abortive attempts.[11] Osman Okyar's account of Turkish experience spells out the successive policy attempts under three different administrations: under Ecevit in 1978 and again in 1979; under Demirel in early 1980; and under the new military regime in late 1980.[12]

In this study, the new policies introduced in Sri Lanka in 1977 and in Jamaica in 1980 were directly related to past policy failures. Several Sri Lankan officials prefaced discussions of specific reforms (trade liberalization, food subsidy reductions) by recounting a history of failed reform efforts. A similar process was evident in Zambia by the beginning of 1983. But, as was noted just above, past failures can also be interpreted as ruling out, or making highly undesirable, measures, such as devaluation, that may in fact be essential components of a fresh reform effort.

Sri Lanka has been independent since early 1948. Ghana gained its independence in 1957; the other three countries in this study became independent in the early 1960s (Zambia not until 1964). It is hard to weigh the importance to the learning process of Sri Lanka's longer post-independence history. But it is worth noting that in Jamaica, and in many sub-Saharan African countries, the first decade after independence saw brisk growth. Both exogenous

10. John Odling-Smee, "Adjustment with Financial Assistance from the Fund," *Finance and Development* 19, no. 4 (December 1982): 30.
11. Christine A. Bogdanowicz-Bindert, "Portugal, Turkey, and Peru: Three Successful Stabilization Programs under the Auspices of the I.M.F.," *World Development* 11 (January 1983): 65.
12. Osman Okyar in Williamson, ed., *IMF Conditionality*.

shocks and the cumulative ill effects of domestic policies have been concentrated in the decade since 1974—not a very long time to gain experience with the implications of complex and difficult policies. It is also hard to weigh the longer-term contribution to the learning process of analyses that seem to have little initial practical impact. The Kenyan government has produced a number of penetrating assessments of its own policies and institutions, including the Sessional Papers of 1975 and 1980 and the more recent Ndegwa Report. These studies have produced much praise but, thus far, little action. Similarly, the International Labor Organization's Jobs and Skills Program for Africa undertook two probing studies of basic needs and employment in Zambia, in 1975 and 1980. Such studies may produce their main results indirectly and after some years' lag, by influencing the outlook of younger Kenyan and Zambian officials, academics, and politicians. In short, the sifting and interpreting of experience takes time.

Perspectives within a nation may be influenced not only by its own experience but also by changes in international currents of opinion and the experience of other countries. In discussing the factors that made possible Sri Lanka's reorientation since 1977, two Sri Lankan observers commented that the leftist opposition parties were not only disorganized and disheartened by the UNP's sweeping victory but also disoriented and put on the defensive by changes in the wider global scene. Specifically, they cited the disarray among the European Communist movements; the major shifts in theory and practice in the People's Republic of China and in some of the Eastern European nations; and the shift in perspective that changed Singapore from a "bad" to a "good" model. For groups with other points of reference, the changing policy emphasis within Western professional development circles is probably having an impact. Those shifts in emphasis of course reflect the world economic crisis, but they also flow from a growing recognition of the cumulative costs of two decades of statist intervention. Even if there had not been so severe an international recession, it seems likely that the World Bank, for instance, would be placing more emphasis on realistic pricing policies and improved efficiency of public corporations than it did in the 1970s. In short, changes in international intellectual currents do affect attitudes in developing countries, even if slowly and somewhat indirectly.

In addition to these diffuse outside influences, international organizations and bilateral agencies have of course long sought to play more direct roles in evolving economic policy, through their programs of training and technical assistance and through policy dialogue. The urgency of policy reform in the mid-1980s suggests the need to increase emphasis on such efforts, to reassess their focus, and to look for additional ways to narrow the gap between outside agencies' judgments about necessary changes and governments' own convictions. One approach might be increased use of joint analysis, with host-country analysts working in collaboration with World Bank, IMF, or other outside specialists to assemble and assess information on key areas of persistent disagreement—for instance, exchange-rate management or grain-marketing systems. Such studies carry their own risks but can contribute to a new consensus within countries. They have the further merit of responding to the widespread perception that the IMF and the World Bank, and perhaps other donor agencies, tend to apply standard remedies without close consideration of country-specific conditions and constraints.

Another, quite different approach to improved consensus and commitment focuses on the process of designing and implementing stabilization programs. Negotiations to arrange a stabilization program with IMF (or other external) assistance are usually conducted under intense time pressure and virtually always involve only a small circle of top-level economic ministers and officials, plus the highest political authorities. Agreements are expressed in technical language. Those outside this small circle (and sometimes those within it) may not understand aspects of the program; they are likely to be surprised, angry, and resistant. Some decisions must be kept secret before public announcement to minimize speculation (although in reality devaluation often has been anticipated for some months and many of the defensive actions secrecy is designed to avoid have already occurred). But fuller briefing of a wider circle is likely to be helpful, if possible in advance of announcing a program or at any rate immediately after announcement. Particularly in countries where there are only a few well-trained economic officials and they are working under immense pressure, the negotiating team itself should include among its responsibilities the preparation of simple, clear, written explanations of the program which the government can use at its discretion to promote fuller understanding. In some cases outsiders, at the invitation of the government, might even play a direct role in dis-

cussing and explaining the program. The (perhaps unique?) experience of the IMF team in Jamaica in 1978, which met at the
government's request with leaders of unions and other interest
groups, offers a precedent, though such a high-profile role may
not often be desirable. The main point is that in order to improve
the prospects for commitment and political sustainability, the efforts of the negotiating team in many cases should not end with
the formulation of a program that is appropriate (in the judgment
of the team and, it is hoped, of key economic officials in the government), but should extend to paving the way for fuller understanding on the part of the political leadership, a broader governmental elite, and even the public.

Overall program design, including the attempted speed of adjustment and the level, content, and conditions of assistance, are
additional factors that obviously shape leaders' commitment, by affecting both their confidence in the program's economic rationale
and their assessment of its political risks. These issues are discussed at the end of this chapter. Here it can simply be noted that
strong commitment from political leadership is more likely for a
program that includes not only stabilization but longer-run structural-adjustment elements that leaders are convinced will be constructive for their nations. The cases of Sri Lanka and Jamaica are
the obvious examples in this study. The logic is clear: stabilization
is mainly a negative set of prescriptions designed to correct certain
key imbalances in an economy. While leaders may sometimes be
convinced that the medicine is necessary, it is hard to be enthusiastic about taking it. A more fundamental readjustment program,
although also painful, elicits more creative and constructive ener-
gies and corresponding psychological involvement. It also can be
presented to the public in a more positive and persuasive manner
than can a straight austerity program.

Most of the instances of ambitious readjustment programs have
been undertaken when a new regime takes office and is in a position to repudiate or depart sharply from the policies and orientation of its predecessor. It is obviously easier for Jayawardene or
Seaga to announce a bold new program than for Zambia's Kaunda
to declare, in effect, that many of his government's earlier decisions
had unanticipated and adverse results. Certain moments in the political history of a nation are advantageous for a fresh departure.
Such moments can be seized or let pass.

## Government Capabilities

Commitment is crucial, but it is no guarantee of ability to implement a program. Even committed leaders face an array of constraints, including, in many instances, divisions and challenges within their own elite circles, inadequate central financial control mechanisms, and other problems of bureaucratic management and efficiency, as well as resistance from specific interest groups or the public at large.

### Elite Unity

The degree of unity and discipline within elite political circles is one crucial component of governmental capacity. The term *government* implies a coherent entity capable of taking decisions and acting on them, but of course there are usually divisions and rivalries within a government. These may be contained and subdued by firm leadership and a shared sense of purpose, or they may be open and highly disruptive.

Among the cases providing background for this chapter, Sri Lanka offers the clearest example of a cabinet in part preselected for consensus on many issues and reinforced by deference to the president. The other four cases all lacked such high-level unity and discipline. In Kenya and in Zambia, cabinet and party executive or central committee members represent geographic and ethnic interests primarily and may be quick to protest adverse effects of macroeconomic policies on their constituents. They may also seize on controversial policies to maneuver for advantage in inner-circle politics. In Ghana in the late 1960s, while the cabinet operated somewhat more as a collegial body, economic policy was almost wholly determined by Minister of Finance Mensah for the first year and a half of the Busia administration. Thereafter there was a growing split between Mensah and other senior economic officials in and out of the Cabinet, but Prime Minister Busia did not step in decisively until so late that draconian measures were almost inevitable. Jamaica under Prime Minister Manley was a still more striking case of bitter divisions and outright power struggles between two ideological factions within the Cabinet and the party's National Executive Council. The result was repeatedly to abort decisions about to be made or to reverse those already taken.

### Managing the Bureaucracy

A second key component of governmental capacity is the adequacy of management of the bureaucratic and parastatal machinery itself. Paradoxically, although the public sector should in theory be more responsive to political guidance and broad public policy (this is one of the main rationales for expanding the public sector), public corporations and even central government agencies may be more difficult to control or influence than parts of the private sector. Price and incentive mechanisms that may change private behavior (that is, devaluation, interest rate adjustment, changes in taxes and tariffs) have much less leverage on the public sector. And direct control is often evaded or eroded.

Budget discipline has proved perhaps the most difficult aspect of stabilization programs for governments to observe. This was surely true of the cases on which this study is based, but it applies much more generally. A survey of 70 IMF standby arrangements during the period 1963–1972 and a second review covering 105 standbys between 1969 and 1978 concurred that "most unsuccessful financial programs failed because of fiscal problems." By 1977 and 1978, expenditures were contained as planned in fewer than a fifth of the programs.[13] Public pressure to maintain or expand benefits makes it hard to contain government expenditures. The quasi-autonomy of public corporations and even of ministries (in fact if not in law) is also a major factor, perhaps still more important in some cases.

Why, then, is there apparently so little interest at top levels in substantially strengthening financial and budgeting control mechanisms? In part the explanation may be that such matters are both arcane and dull, but after the experiences of the past few years the need should be apparent. In some cases, titular leaders may lack real power to control powerful ministers. Or leaders may have adequate power but not be particularly eager to establish powerful, institutionalized procedures and staffs for advance coordination and on-going vetting of expenditures. They prefer to keep most of that authority in their own hands. Among the cases in this study,

---

13. Thomas Reichmann and Richard Stillson, "How Successful Are Programs Supported by Stand-by Arrangements?" *Finance and Development* 14, no. 1 (March 1977): 293–309; W. A. Beveridge and Margaret R. Kelly, "Fiscal Content of Financial Programs Supported by Stand-by Arrangements in the Upper Credit Tranches, 1969–78," *IMF Staff Papers* 27, no. 2 (June 1980): 213–16.

this pattern has been evident in Kenya and Zambia. It is a direct result of the reliance on patronage politics discussed below. Where top political leaders depend on their control over allocation of resources to maintain the loyalty of faction-ridden or personally ambitious lieutenants, they cannot lightly relinquish such control to an anonymous group of technical bureaucrats. Thus even where the benefits in terms of greater fiscal discipline are evident, political leaders may not be willing or able to move toward such a system.

## Political Support Bases

The third and broadest set of factors determining governmental capacity to implement a stabilization program is the scope and nature of its political support base. The concept of a support base is not identical with popularity, which usually fluctuates, and predictably falls if stabilization is pursued—and also if it is not pursued. Rather, the term refers to groups bound to the regime by more durable ties of ethnic identity, ideological compatibility, ingrained party loyalties, and/or patron-client networks (to name the major kinds of links). Among the cases on which this discussion is based, both the scope and the nature of the support bases varied substantially. In several of the cases, the bases were seriously eroded over time. In all of them, patron-client links played a substantial (in some cases dominant) role, with implications for stabilization policy.

It seems clear that the absence of broad and varied bases of support constrained both Kenya's President Moi and Zambia's President Kaunda with respect to economic policy in the periods reviewed. Moi lacks a large ethnic base (and was early viewed as a stalking-horse for Kikuyu domination). During his first year in office after independence leader Kenyatta's death in 1978, Moi generated an initial popularity that surprised observers, using a triple strategy of ethnic conciliation and national unity appeals, populist gestures, and "new broom" anti-corruption proclamations. This first flush, however, faded (due in good part to a grain scandal in 1978–1979), and for several years Moi's popular support shrank, leaving him increasingly dependent on the elite political and administrative circles surrounding him. However, he continued to build a patron-client network, operating mainly through the dominant party, the Kenya African National Union (KANU). His victory in the September 1983 elections is in large part attributed to these tactics, but turnout was low.

In Zambia, Kaunda was immensely popular for years, reflecting his anti-colonial role, his ability to appeal to various tribes while not being solely identified with any, and his skill in manipulating ethnic representation in the party and government. But by the mid-1970s, much of that popularity had eroded. The grassroots organization within the United National Independence Party, active in the pre- and early post-independence era, withered. Efforts to mobilize ideological enthusiasm through the espousal of Kaunda's philosophy of humanism never made much headway. Much of the political history of the late 1970s and early 1980s increasingly suggests dependence on a narrow circle of retainers from the highest levels of the party, the army, and the civil service. The stabilization program of 1978–1980 was tolerated (despite many outbursts, mainly by unions) as a sacrifice required by Zambia's support of Zimbabwe's struggle for independence. But when that situation was resolved in 1980, Kaunda could count on little backing if he persisted in austerity policies.

In Ghana, Busia and his administration had a fairly broad constituency among the electorate in 1969, though there was a readily identifiable regional/ethnic core within the Ashanti cocoa-growing area. Many looked hopefully to the new government to inaugurate a better era after the fiasco of the final Nkrumah years and the economic austerity and political moratorium of the military National Liberation Council's three years in office. But during its twenty-seven–month rule the Busia regime alienated almost all major political groups in the population except, perhaps, its core support base. In good part this occurred through measures unconnected to economic policy: for example, appointments, promotions, and dismissals in the civil service and military that were widely viewed as ethnically biased and were made more offensive by an apparent challenge to the autonomy of the courts; the flouting of a constitutional requirement to declare assets on entering office; heavy-handed treatment of students protesting this behavior; and poor handling of relations with the large and independent unions. The loss of legitimacy and support also reflected economic policies: tight urban wage restraint (applying to minimum-wage as well as better-paid workers and defended as necessary to narrow the urban-rural gap, but probably excessive in view of the serious erosion of real wages over the past decade); the attempted introduction of a National Development Levy in 1971; and substantial cuts in the military budget and in military and civilian officials' perquisites in each of the two budgets. Thus the devaluation of December 1971 was the crowning blow to many groups in the population already alienated from the Busia regime.

In both Jamaica and Sri Lanka, long-established and hotly competitive political parties and a proliferation of highly organized and vocal interest groups permit broad-gauged political support but also facilitate opposition activity. Both Jayawardene's UNP in Sri Lanka after 1977 and Seaga's Jamaica Labour Party (JLP) after late 1980 enjoyed considerable popular support, in part a reaction to economic stagnation or (in the case of Jamaica) decline under previous administrations. Both governments also benefited from disarray within the opposition parties, though that disarray was much more thorough and lasted longer in the Sri Lankan case, giving Jayawardene correspondingly greater freedom. Both regimes also had the advantage of extensive foreign aid. The Jayawardene administration further benefited from good weather and high export prices in its first years. As a result, both governments were able to offer some prompt economic gains to many groups within the population (again, to a greater extent in Sri Lanka). Thus the question of the durability of broad support was less pressing than it would have been if more severe austerity measures had been necessary.[14]

One conclusion to be drawn from the brief survey of political support bases in these cases and from the evidence from other countries is the importance of patron-client ties in the informal political structures of many developing countries. In a broad sense, the popularity of any government depends on its ability to maintain conditions under which most of the population can prosper. But patron-client parties rely much more explicitly and directly on a continuing stream of favors and benefits flowing directly from the patron to his designated client, rather than reaching parts of the population as a result of the impersonal operation of institutions and policies. All countries, wealthy and poor, democratic and authoritarian, have patron-client networks as aspects of their political systems, but in many countries patronage is a fairly minor ele-

14. Sri Lanka's tragic communal riots of the summer of 1983 and their aftermath have clouded both political and economic prospects, but this analysis focuses on the political factors that permitted economic reorientation after 1977 and partial stabilization in 1981, not on the causes or consequences of the 1983 riots.

ment in the overall political sense, while in others it is central to the governing elites' support. In countries in which the government relies heavily on patron-client ties, stabilization (particularly stringent budget discipline) therefore cuts not merely at a government's general popularity but at the resources needed for it to maintain its support base. To the extent that parties atrophy (as, for example, in Zambia), the leadership finds itself increasingly dependent on fairly narrow circles of retainers, who may also openly or implicitly make their continued support contingent on a flow of benefits.

The point sounds academic, but it is not. In Kenya, support for rival candidates for party and national office at both local district and higher levels is generated by distribution of concrete benefits—for communities (for example, school buildings, small public works) and individuals (jobs, land, contracts). Command over such resources translates directly into political support. The point has recently been underscored in analyses of the elections held in September 1983.[15] The short-lived parties in Ghana in the late 1960s relied heavily on links between political candidates and hometown or local "improvement associations," youth associations, and the like: "There was a pervading feeling in the country that a close, functional relationship existed between the origin of a parliamentary candidate and local economic development."[16] The decline of Zambia's main party, the United National Independence Party (UNIP), at local levels in the late 1960s and early 1970s was partly a result of the refusal to expand patronage opportunities, including paid jobs for local party workers.[17] Even in Jamaica, where other factors enter into support for both of the two major parties, massive job turnover at low as well as high levels is expected with each change in party government.[18]

The extent to which political leaders depend on patron-client

15. *Washington Post*, 29 September 1983, pp. 1, 26.
16. Yaw Twumasi, "The 1969 Election," in Dennis Austin and Robin Luckham, eds., *Politicians and Soldiers in Ghana 1966–1972* (London: Frank Cass, 1983), p. 151.
17. Ian Scott, "Party and Administration under the One-Party State," in William Tordoff, ed., *Administration in Zambia* (Manchester: Manchester University Press, 1980), pp. 143–48.
18. See Arthur Lewin, "The Fall of Michael Manley: A Case Study of the Failure of Reform Socialism," *Monthly Review* 34 (February 1982): 51, and Carl Stone, *Class, Race, and Political Behavior in Urban Jamaica* (Mona, Jamaica: Institute of Social and Economic Research, University of the West Indies, 1973), p. 80, for data on the high proportions of small businessmen, white-collar workers, the working class, and, especially, lower-class people who seek personal aid and favors from politicians.

networks thus bears directly on their ability to implement stabilization measures. The same considerations affect their willingness and capacity to adopt adjustment measures that move away from direct controls and toward greater reliance on market mechanisms, including more realistic pricing within the public and parastatal sectors. If a politician's main means of building and maintaining political support is the direction of the jobs, contracts, licenses, foreign exchange, subsidized goods and services, and other benefits to his political friends and away from his political enemies, he cannot lightly relinquish such control to price mechanisms that do not distinguish supporter from opponent.[19] If alternative channels and methods of generating and holding political support are poorly developed, as is the case in many of the poorer and less politically experienced nations, then even farsighted and personally honest leaders must rely substantially on patronage to maintain their positions. Thus, not only vested economic interests and, in some cases, ideological leanings but also the very structure of political support mechanisms become obstacles to economic reforms involving decontrol.

Like the discussion of leaders' commitment, this brief survey of governmental capacities suggests both some modest implications for policy and the limits of outside intervention. Outsiders can do little to influence elite unity or the scope and nature of a government's support base. However, outside assistance clearly can improve government management of the bureaucracy. Training and technical assistance in budgeting and related functions are, of course, long-established areas of donor activity. Much more recently, some World Bank structural adjustment loans have incorporated improvements in central financial and budget control mechanisms and other specific administrative reforms as *conditions* of aid.[20] Some means must be found to make such improvements a high-level priority and to gain backing and attention from top political leaders. Otherwise, in the highly personalized bureau-

19. For a detailed discussion of this theme, see Robert H. Bates, *Markets and States in Tropical Africa: The Political Basis of Agricultural Policies* (Berkeley and Los Angeles: University of California Press, 1981); also Warren Ilchman and Norman Uphoff, *The Political Economy of Change* (Berkeley and Los Angeles: University of California Press, 1969).

20. Killick, "IMF Stabilization Program," ODI Working Paper No. 6 (London: Overseas Development Institute, 1981), discusses the desirability of substituting specific procedural, legal, or institutional reforms for macroeconomic targets, with reference to IMF practice.

cratic politics of many small countries, there will be little progress. One danger of such conditioning is the temptation to include too wide a range of reforms, encouraging or even pressing the government to overstretch its administrative and political resources.

## Assessing and Managing Political Risk

### Determinants of Public Reactions to Stabilization

The discussion thus far has focused on one side of the political equation determining political sustainability: governmental commitment and capacity. The political responses of interest groups and the general public constitute the other side. Their reactions are determined by the actual impact of the policies, their interpretations of those policies, and their varying political capabilities.

A fundamental determinant of public reaction is, obviously, who gains, who loses, and when. To be useful for political analysis or prediction, winners and losers must be identified in terms of socially meaningful groups, not quartiles or other statistical aggregates. It is often a complex task to assess the impact of stabilization on particular groups, since different aspects of the package bear differently on the same group. Effects may cumulate for some groups—for example, civil servants may face simultaneously increased prices for imported consumer goods (due to devaluation), declining real wages (due to wage freezes), cuts in perquisites (due to budget reductions) and frustrating shortages of funds and inputs for the programs for which they are responsible. The impacts of stabilization on other groups may partly offset one another. Thus producers of agricultural export crops may gain from strengthened foreign demand for their products but may also have to pay more for imported fertilizer and pesticide—both effects resulting from devaluation. A further complication is the fact that for some groups, gains and/or losses may not be solely or primarily material but may involve power and authority, security, autonomy, or relative status. Despite these caveats, even a rough assessment of major winning and losing groups is an essential starting point for understanding political reactions to stabilization programs.

However, there is no neat one-to-one correspondence between economic impact and political response. People's perceptions and interpretations of policies also shape their reactions. Subjective interpretations that are crucial for political reactions include:

>   The attribution of responsibility for losses (or gains) to such forces as government, foreign creditors, or fate (for example, bad weather)
>
>   The expected duration of losses: short- , medium- , or long-run
>
>   The degree of confidence that policies will help solve economic problems
>
>   The perceived equity of impact, among classes and, in many countries, among ethnic groups and/or regions

Because these interpretations are so important, the government's presentation and explanation of stabilization measures can significantly affect sustainability—a point to which we will return.

Actual effects and interpretations of effects determine how people feel about stabilization. What they do about how they feel depends on their political capabilities. Not all categories of people affected similarly by stabilization measures constitute groups in the sense that they are capable of politically effective joint or coordinated action; some are divided among themselves by regional, ethnic, religious, factional, or party allegiances, or they may lack organization and leadership. Even groups conscious of their shared interests and to some degree organized may lack political resources (information and contacts, control over economic or other assets, numbers and/or discipline, sympathy or support from a wider public) adequate to exercise significant influence.

The term *interest group* often connotes private-sector groups. But in many developing nations, especially the poorest, few private-sector groups are organized or influential enough to exert much pressure. However, civil servants, officials of public corporations, and the military all constitute potentially crucial interest groups, both because of their organization, awareness, and control over important assets and because of the absence of powerful private groups.

Political responses to stabilization are partly the reactions of specific interest groups and of organized opposition parties in countries where these operate. Another important element is more elusive: the public mood with respect to economic policies. There are times when a broad swath of public opinion is convinced that basic changes are unavoidable. That conviction often grows out of years of economic stagnation or decline, perhaps punctuated by repeated but limited and ineffective stabilization efforts. Among the clearer examples are Peru in the late 1970s and Turkey in the years just before and after 1980. Sri Lanka in 1977 and Jamaica in 1980 demonstrated at the polls the public sense that a change of direction was imperative. A public mood prepared for economic reform improves the prospects for temporary toleration of austerity, a grace period during which the government has a contingent grant of confidence. Such a mood is also likely to inhibit protests by specific groups that might otherwise create serious problems.

Reactions to stabilization are also muted or heightened by the security or precariousness of the government and by the nature and strength of opposition. Regardless of the source of security or lack thereof, protest directed to a secure government is presented differently than to a precarious one. In Sri Lanka, the Bandaranaike government in office from 1970 to 1977 was beset by internal divisions, an early rebellion, and economic stagnation; it was increasingly indecisive and insecure. Unions expressed their opposition with repeated, widespread, and often violent strikes which contributed to undermining the government by the mid-1970s. In contrast, Jayawardene's successor administration was coherent, overwhelmingly dominated parliament, built up additional support through its initial economic successes, and was accordingly self-assured and decisive. As inflation and other economic problems began to worsen by 1980, unions (especially those affiliated with opposition parties) became increasingly disgruntled, but the sole attempted general strike of mid-1980 was firmly squelched and there was virtually no further labor unrest.

In addition to these very general factors shaping the public response to stabilization, one specific issue should be highlighted: the burden of external debt. Where payments due on foreign debt are widely viewed as a major source, or the primary source, of the need for austerity, and particularly where the burden is attributed to a profligate earlier regime (as in Ghana in the late 1960s and early 1970s) or to soaring interest rates (as in Brazil currently), it is easy to view the debt payments as literally starving the poor in order to fatten the accounts of distant and extraordinarily wealthy creditors. Political leaders may themselves share the perception of a massive violation of basic equity. Even if they take a different view, they cannot readily alter the public perception. Thus the debt issue has played, and is playing, a special role in shaping the public mood and the political prospects for stabilization—a fact perhaps not adequately appreciated by creditors and their governments in their attitudes toward rescheduling.

### Special Features of the Politics of Stabilization in Poorer Countries

Leaders' commitment, governmental capabilities, and public responses determine the political sustainability of stabilization and adjustment measures in any country, be it France, Brazil, or Zambia. But certain characteristics of the poorer (and especially the small poor) nations' economic structure and institutions have implications for the politics of stabilization.

First, in quite poor countries, a high proportion of urban wage and salary workers are employed by the government or parastatals and will be directly harmed by fiscal stringency. In small poor countries, even basic staples for urban consumers often are imported, making those consumers particularly vulnerable to losses through devaluation. And urban industrial workers are more likely than their counterparts in semi-industrialized countries to be employed in forms dependent on imported intermediate goods. Thus urban populations are particularly vulnerable to the immediate impact of stabilization measures. Conversely, in at least some of the poorer countries the more remote segments of the rural population are comparatively loosely linked to national and international institutions and markets. They pay low or no taxes, receive few government services or benefits, sell little of what they produce, and buy few imported items. While they do not entirely escape the impact of stabilization, many rural dwellers may be less deeply affected than their counterparts in rural areas of more advanced countries.

Another, related characteristic of most poorer countries operates through the relative importance of various interest groups. Devaluation and other measures to encourage exports and discourage imports most directly benefit producers of exportables, and also, in principle, producers of import-substituting products. Many poorer countries rely on agricultural products as their major exports. Producers of key export crops may or may not be well organized politically; growers of import-substituting foods often are not vocal in politics. Often, also, the government monopolizes or dominates the purchase and export of key crops, thereby controlling a major or main revenue source. It may or may not be willing to pass on to producers most of the gains from devaluation. Firms producing import-substituting manufactures also, in theory, benefit from devaluation, but in the poorer countries these firms usually both are heavily protected already by high quantitative or tariff barriers and are themselves highly dependent on imported inputs. Thus the major groups that theoretically benefit from devaluation are often either weak politically or do not in fact benefit much; indeed, in the short run some may lose. In contrast, in NICs like Mexico, more diversified export- and import-competing sectors are likely to benefit and are also more likely to be politically influential.

Still a third feature of the poorer countries bears on the politics of stabilization. Such countries generally lack well-developed financial intermediary institutions, and a large proportion of their credit is provided directly through government programs and agencies. But many stabilization programs entail restriction of credit, often to both the public and the private sector. The absence of arms-length or anonymous mechanisms for alerting and containing credit flows and the reliance on direct loans mean that those implementing the credit squeeze must directly confront the victims of the squeeze. As a result, both the administrative and the political aspects of implementation are likely to be more difficult.[21]

Finally, it is broadly true that the less developed an economy, the less its ability to adjust rapidly to altered international economic conditions. Exports are usually concentrated in one or a few products, and there are no or few products that are tradable but not in fact traded, hence available to increase exports quickly if relative prices (including the exchange rate) are changed. Increased production and diversification of exports and larger and more efficient import-substitution may require five or more years of investment, reorganization, and training. Both the public and the private sector are thin in trained and experienced managers and entrepreneurs to guide and direct such transformations. Therefore the timetable for stabilization and adjustment must be longer

21. I am indebted to Alan Gelb for this point.

in the poorer countries, if "stabilization" is to mean more than the narrowest (and most brutal) shrinking of imports and public and private consumption to fit sharply diminished earning capabilities and to accommodate heavy debt burdens.

In sum, in the poorer countries as compared to NICs and advanced nations, stabilization may affect a smaller part of the population more intensely. There are fewer groups—often, none—that believe they might gain from stabilization and can therefore serve as counterweights to losers. Because credit flows largely through direct public channels, manufacturing, construction, and commercial firms are more likely to seek relief from the squeeze by special exceptions and less likely to direct their efforts to changes in general policy. The outcome may be no less a threat to sustained and effective stabilization policies. Finally, the longer timetable essential for meaningful adjustment puts an immense strain on public patience and leaders' commitment. The political problems of stabilization and adjustment are not necessarily more difficult than those in, say, Brazil and Argentina. But they are different in certain systematic ways, which should in turn affect program design and implementation.

The perceived gains and losses and therefore the political responses to stabilization measures may be different in one special subset of cases: countries in an extreme state of economic disintegration (often accompanied by social and political unraveling that has been going on for years, as in Uganda). In such extreme cases the consumption level of most of the population is already very depressed, and most large and medium-sized manufacturing and business establishments (including public corporations) have already virtually halted operations, though small-scale parallel market activity may be considerable. Legal exports have largely ceased. Imports are being sold at black-market exchange rates and/or have been smuggled into the country, so that even drastic nominal price changes resulting from devaluation will not greatly affect the actual prices paid by most people and enterprises. Where there are official subsidies for consumer goods, either the goods themselves are virtually unavailable or the limited supplies are resold, by those few individuals or firms receiving them, at prices many times above the subsidized level; thus again the removal of the subsidies harms only a small group. If the opposition of the small circle that benefits inordinately from the existing arrangements can be overcome, then rapid strides may be made. "It may well be that it is when the most disorderly conditions prevail that the recovery [or, more conservatively, improvement?] can be most rapid."[22]

## Techniques for Managing Political Risk

Despite the usual array of hostile interests, some governments have been quite effective in generating public tolerance of difficult measures. Basically, governments have four broad techniques at their disposal to reduce resistance to and win support for stabilization measures, both in advance of implementation and once the measures are in effect. These techniques are partial compensation, persuasion, diversion or obfuscation, and containment. The potential of the techniques varies according to a country's circumstances, and therefore the mix of techniques that is likely best to promote political sustainability will differ in different countries.

*Partial Compensation*  Partial compensation is the technique for reducing opposition to stabilization that occurs most naturally to economists accustomed to thinking in terms of costs and benefits. The technique is widely used, mainly in the form of wage adjustments and in concessions and exceptions of various kinds for specific businesses and firms. While the background cases for this study are too few to permit generalization, two contrasting experiences suggest the limits of compensation and offer clues on how to maximize its political benefits.

In Ghana under the Busia administration, the devaluation of December 1971 was announced simultaneously with several sweeteners, including abolition of the import surcharges imposed over the past few years, elimination of the recently imposed and much resented National Development Levy, a 33 percent increase in the minimum wage, and a 25 percent increase in the producer price of cocoa. The minimum-wage hike was more than twice as large as the predicted impact of the devaluation on the urban cost of living.[23] Since unions in particular had been pressing for an increase in the minimum wage and had been particularly bitter over the National Development Levy, these concessions might have been ex-

---

22. Finch, "Adjustment Policies and Conditionality," p. 19.
23. Leith states that the actual provision for an increased minimum wage applied only to the public sector and called for a progressive increase ranging from 33⅓ percent for the lowest-paid workers to zero for those earning over N.C. 1,000 a year. But the public generally thought that there had been an increase in the minimum wage for all workers: *Foreign Trade Regimes*, p. 152.

pected to win labor acquiescence. However, the devaluation took the public by surprise and was poorly explained and defended. It also came at a moment of widespread political alienation. Any softening of political reactions resulting from the sweeteners was short-lived, evaporating in the face of the doubling of prices for imported goods.

It is interesting to contrast this experience with that in Jamaica in the second half of 1978. In July the Manley government announced a sizable devaluation (plus unification of the exchange rate; the weighted overall devaluation was 15 percent) and associated stabilization measures. This package was not accompanied by significant sweeteners, and its net effect was to reduce real wages by about 25 percent. But its announcement was promptly followed by a vigorous and extensive program of explanation in which the prime minister and members of his cabinet took the lead. The stabilization program was beset by broader economic and political pressures and collapsed inside of a year. But it is noteworthy that for seven or eight months, labor unions confined their reactions to public grumbling, restraining their members from more active protest. By the spring of 1979, the earlier economic decline had been virtually halted. Arguably, had the government been able to point to positive economic gains the unions and other segments of the public might have accepted continued austerity. A vigorous and clear campaign to explain stabilization measures might, then, be more helpful in avoiding initial outbursts than are sweeteners. Conversely, partial compensation may be most useful later in the process, used selectively to dampen cumulating opposition and extend the period of reluctant acquiescence until economic benefits begin to become evident.

Sometimes it may be possible to offer partial compensation of a noneconomic nature for the public or some part of it. In Peru, beginning in late 1976, President Morales Bermudez gradually established a link between successful economic stabilization and the restoration of civilian political rule. A three-year schedule was established for the political transition, coinciding with the expected period of economic recovery. The initial stabilization efforts foundered. When new and stringent measures were announced in May 1978, various groups threatened a general strike. The government responded by announcing the postponement of scheduled constituent assembly elections—a veiled threat that confrontation over economic policy would end the political transition. Favorable export prices and other factors permitted some easing of austerity by 1979. During this period, at least, the sense of political progress reinforced the feeling that the economic program, for all its unpopularity, was producing some results and offered hope for broader benefits later.[24] In 1983 and 1984, stabilization efforts in Brazil and particularly in Argentina have been somewhat similarly linked to redemocratization, with varying effectiveness. Increased physical security is another benefit that governments can offer concomitantly with economic stabilization. In Jamaica after 1980 and in Turkey at the same time, new governments cracked down on widespread political violence, to the relief of large parts of the population.

*Persuasion* While compensation or sweeteners are often mentioned as a means to soften opposition to stabilization, many economists and technicians are more skeptical about the utility of persuasion. Yet the cases used as background to this study, as well as clues from elsewhere, suggest that frank and vigorous campaigns of explanation and persuasion can be quite effective in winning temporary public acquiescence and gaining union acceptance of wage restraint. The scope for effective persuasion obviously varies with trust or mistrust of the government and perceptions of its honesty and efficiency. A new government's "honeymoon" period is precisely a period during which much of the public is willing to suspend adverse judgments. A broad consensus that basic changes are needed, as in 1977 in Sri Lanka and in 1980 in Jamaica, increases receptivity to persuasion.

Among the clear-cut examples of cases where unions were persuaded to accept major cuts in real wages are Jamaica in 1978, Portugal in the same year,[25] and Venezuela in the 1960s; union cooperation was also successfully elicited in Italy in 1977.[26] All four cases are ones in which government had strong ties with but did not control major segments of organized labor.

As the last observation suggests, governments with open chan-

24. Ernest J. Preeg, "The Evolution of a Revolution: Peru and Its Relations with the United States, 1968–1980" (Washington, D.C.: National Policy Association, 1981).
25. Lopes Jose de Silva, "IMF Conditionality in the Stand-by Arrangements with Portugal of 1978," in Williamson, ed., *IMF Conditionality*.
26. Luigi Spaventa, "Two Letters of Intent: External Crisis and Stabilization Policies in Italy, 1973–1977," in Williamson, ed., *IMF Conditionality*.

nels of communication to the groups most likely to be vocal in opposition to stabilization are in a better position to utilize persuasion. The conventional wisdom that argues the advantages of
authoritarian government in imposing difficult reforms fails to
take into account this asset of more open political systems.

But persuasion clearly also has its limits even for governments
with good communication channels. In many cases, unions remained unpersuaded. And the business community may be still
less responsive to persuasion than are unions or the public at large.
This is partly because different responses are sought from labor
and the public than from business. The former groups are basically asked to tighten their belts and continue their work, while
investors and entrepreneurs are asked to consider new options,
take new risks, write off (at least in part) old investments, and generally change their ways of doing business. Large and medium-
scale businessmen may also have good connections in the government, especially in smaller countries where political and economic
elites often constitute small and overlapping circles. It is tempting
for businessmen to use these connections to try to win exceptions,
delays, and modifications in the application of reforms to their
own interests, rather than accepting the changes and considering
how best to adjust their own activities. In short, somewhat paradoxically, the very fact that business circles are often close to political circles may make persuasion less effective in altering their behavior than it is with respect to groups more distanced from the
government.

It is interesting to note that in the accounts of internal discussion
and maneuvers associated with stabilization in this study, the military are almost never mentioned as participants. In Ghana in late
1971, government advisers tried to estimate the impact of the
planned devaluation on various groups, but no one thought to include the military.[27] More generally, there seem to have been remarkably few efforts to keep military leaders briefed on the evolving economic situation in order that policy adjustment might come
less as a surprise and be better understood. The omission may be
a serious mistake.

27. Michael Roemer, "Ghana 1950–1980: Missed Opportunities," paper prepared for the Conference on World Economic Growth Problems, sponsored by the
Institute for Contemporary Studies, Mexico City, April 1983, p. 26 (typescript).

*Diversion or Obfuscation*    As with any unpopular measure, politicians often try to mute opposition to stabilization by pointing to scapegoats or diverting attention to other issues. The IMF is, of course, a frequent scapegoat, sometimes (as in Colombia in the mid-1960s) vigorously lambasted by the same government that is highly cooperative behind the scenes. Recent Moroccan reductions in food subsidies prompted riots, which the government promptly blamed on "Communists, Iranian and Zionist agitators."[28] The increasingly beleaguered Busia government in Ghana in the autumn of 1971 began to accuse its trade-unionist opposition of foreign and Nkrumahist links. And in Zambia during the severe austerity of 1978–1980, the government pointed (with a great deal of justification) to the transport cutoff and direct attacks resulting from the civil war in Southern Rhodesia/Zimbabwe.

Governments may also try to camouflage their actual measures. Egypt and Sudan have both reduced the standard size of subsidized bread loaves in preference to raising the price. In Sri Lanka, at the time of the UNP electoral victory in 1977, the rice ration (partly free, partly at a low, subsidized price) was available to almost the entire population. The ration was a serious economic drain and had been an explosive political issue for twenty-five years. Early in 1978 the government confined the ration to the poorer half of the population. The step was accompanied by extensive explanation; it was accepted with remarkably little protest, partly because of the government's still-fresh mandate and the decimated opposition, partly because general economic conditions were improving, and partly because the action was regarded as equitable. Twenty-one months later, the subsidized ration was converted to a food-stamp system, again carefully explained and administered. The initial value of the stamps was set slightly higher than the current value of the rice ration. But the stamps were denominated in nominal values and therefore were subject to erosion by inflation. Whether this effect was premeditated or not, the effect has been to reduce the subsidy greatly, as it were by stealth. Seaga's handling of Jamaican exchange rates provides another example of camouflage or obfuscation. Reluctant to devalue, he instead gave de facto recognition to and later legalized the existing parallel market in

---

28. *Washington Post*, 23 January 1984, p. A–12. In this case, however, the government rescinded the price increase.

foreign exchange, thus establishing a dual exchange rate without fully admitting the fact.

*Containment*   Even with skillful use of compensation, persuasion, and diversion or obfuscation, stabilization will almost certainly prompt strong opposition. The opposition may or may not break into violence. How the government handles initial protest will strongly affect its future course. Clear boundaries of acceptable protest, backed by prompt and firm action against those overstepping the boundaries, is probably an essential component of effective implementation, even though such containment is in a sense a measure of the failure of alternative techniques of risk management.

Containment is most effective in a broader context of a clear and firm program commitment that has won or is winning acceptance from a good part of the population. In Sri Lanka, as was mentioned earlier, unions had a long history of political activity punctuated by sporadic violence and had played a major role in the crumbling of the Bandaranaike regime in the mid-1970s. The UNP government elected in 1977 promptly initiated a series of statements and White Papers that made it clear that union pressure, especially from public-sector unions, would not be tolerated. When leftist unions did attempt to organize a general strike in July 1980, the government's response was swift and unexpectedly firm. Strikers were promptly fired and (contrary to previous patterns) not rehired except with long delays. There were no further significant labor protests, despite the austerity of 1981. Contrasting experience with containing opposition in Ghana in 1971 suggests the importance of the broader political context and public perceptions of the government's management. A major rail and port workers' strike in July 1971 was handled similarly to the Sri Lanka strike, with detention of leaders and large-scale firings (though not so large-scale as in Sri Lanka). The action merely fed growing tensions between government and labor, leading within a few months to the banning of the powerful and largely autonomous labor federation and to labor's support for the coup of early 1972. The contrasting results reflected much more serious economic grievances than in Sri Lanka, much more widespread public alienation from the government, and the absence of an economic program perceived as credible.

### The Dynamics of Public Response

The skillful use of all these techniques can have a substantial effect on public reactions to stabilization, perhaps especially on responses to initial announcement of painful measures. But more sustained sacrifice by the public at large and a positive response from private-sector entrepreneurs depend on perceptions that the program is working. This raises two key questions: What do people view as indicators of success? And how long are people willing to tolerate severe deprivation? If clear answers were available, they would be highly relevant to the design of stabilization programs.

Economic indicators that are significant to one group are not necessarily significant to others. Central Bank and Ministry of Finance officials focus on cuts in public-sector and trade deficits, reduced arrears in payments on foreign obligations, and/or increased international reserves. Large and medium-sized businesses and the private financial community probably watch the same indicators, and in some countries sophisticated trade union leaders may accept such evidence of progress. Small firms are likely to focus on more immediately tangible concerns, such as availability of credit and foreign exchange for imported inputs. Workers and consumers are also likely to gauge progress by improvements that affect their daily lives. The most important of these fall into four categories:

> Improved availability, first and foremost of preferred staples (that is, rice or wheat or maize rather than yams or millet or barley), and, one step beyond preferred staples, of items that are neither staples nor luxuries but affect the quality of daily life, such as textiles, soap, or batteries

> Slowed inflation

> Reduced unemployment, including not only jobs in the formal sector but quickened activity, hence more earning opportunities, in the informal sector

> More adequate or less often interrupted basic national and municipal services: fewer brown-outs or power stoppages, more regular bus service, simple medicines and supplies in stock in clinics

In Sri Lanka, much of the popular support and sense of optimism in the first years after the 1977 elections reflected the first and third items; in Jamaica, the first and second greatly eased political tensions. But in both cases, the prompt improvements largely resulted from very generous levels of external support. In the absence of such support, and depending also on the severity of the crisis when the measures were adopted, there may be little progress of this "tangible" kind for a year or more.

It would be useful to have some sense of priorities and trade-offs among the various criteria of tangible improvements. Availability of staples is almost surely the highest priority. Beyond this, one can hypothesize that where unemployment is widespread and rising, not only those out of work but those with jobs are frightened. If unemployment can be capped or slightly reduced there may be a significant shift in mood, as employed workers no longer fear layoffs. If this is true, a strategy for inspiring public confidence would place very high initial priority on turning the corner on unemployment. But once unemployment is no longer rising, further reductions may be less important than slowed inflation or expanded availability of widely used consumer goods (above the basic staples level), since both these measures affect the living standards of the entire population. The case studies do not offer enough evidence to confirm or deny such a specific hypothesis, but it might be useful to consider such trade-offs explicitly, in the context of specific country circumstances.

## The Speed of Adjustment, Optimal Assistance Levels, and Political Sustainability

In designing stabilization programs, questions such as the optimal speed of adjustment and appropriate level of assistance bear on all three aspects of political sustainability: leaders' commitment, governmental implementing capacity, and public political reactions. Political considerations must be taken jointly with economic considerations: where the two perspectives conflict, their relative importance must be weighed. This final section considers several well-recognized issues concerning program design and political sustainability. There are no easy solutions to these issues. But it is possible to sharpen some of the political assumptions, to consider the conditions under which the various political assumptions may or may not hold, and to suggest lines of analysis and tentative policy adjustments that may be helpful in some cases.

### Levels and Terms of Assistance and Political Sustainability

One set of issues, often posed as a dilemma for donors, concerns the level of stabilization assistance. If external assistance is generous enough to ease the imminent threat of serious financial crisis, by that very fact it will also remove the main incentive for reluctant politicians to agree and follow through on needed but painful reforms, at least in the short run. But if external assistance is not generous enough, the same leaders will conclude that the game is not worth the candle: the meager and short-lived foreign exchange relief being offered is not sufficient to counterbalance the political risks incurred by undertaking a formal stabilization program, including entering into conditional agreements with the IMF, the World Bank, or other sources of external finance.

A second dilemma about the level and terms of assistance focuses on implementation capabilities rather than commitment: minimum levels and a short leash (frequent performance tests) may buttress the authority of central financial and economic officials vis-à-vis the spending agencies, but the same tactics ensure that the handful of key officials with authority and competence in such matters spend all their time coping with short-term targets and negotiating with external agencies, rather than strengthening their government's institutional and procedural capabilities and designing responsible medium-term policies.

The two dilemmas are least troublesome at the two ends of the commitment spectrum. When political leaders are clearly uncommitted, when they refuse to focus on the issues of stabilization or to face their real options, there is little alternative in the short run to maintaining pressure through restricted aid and frequent performance tests. At the other extreme, when leaders are convinced that stabilization measures are needed and useful, reduced assistance and tight conditions will not increase their resolve. Rather, to the degree that aid can ease political opposition and free key economic officials from chronic crisis pressures, increased aid can facilitate implementation. In such a setting, the key issues concern the design of measures and the uses of financial aid, in order to avoid uses that reduce political obstacles but also undercut the purposes of the reform. Among the cases providing background for this chapter, both the UNP government in Sri Lanka in 1977 and the JLP government in Jamaica in late 1980 were judged highly committed, and donors provided substantial assistance to support reforms and bridge the transition to improved economic performance. In both cases the assistance did indeed relieve economic pressure, permitting a jump in imports and, in the case of Sri Lanka, sharp rises in investment and employment. In Sri Lanka, aid combined with other favorable economic conditions from 1977 through 1979 permitted the government to roll back food subsidies and implement other reforms without strong adverse reactions. In Jamaica, however, despite the aid and the apparent commitment of Prime Minister Seaga, thus far progress on adjustment has been more limited. Seaga initially seemed to be promising the Jamaicans that adjustment could take place without much sacrifice; he explicitly ruled out devaluation and reductions in the civil service. It could plausibly be argued that the generosity and speed of international support for his new administration permitted, or even caused, his government to underestimate the difficulty of the needed measures.

As the case of Jamaica suggests, even apparently committed leaders may need continuing pressure to prompt difficult decisions and actions. The problem is to determine a level of aid (or, more precisely, a combination of level, content, and conditions) that maintains pressure but also allows the government room for maneuver vis-à-vis internal political opposition. Conceptually, there is an optimal level of aid for maintaining commitment. At that level, leaders perceive the economic and political gains from pursuing an appropriate stabilization program as just outweighing the costs and risks. Above that level, there is a temptation to postpone or evade the most painful aspects of the program: the costs of failing to act have been lowered too much. Below that optimal level, political risks look too high or economic gains too low to warrant a serious stabilization attempt. Since the full effects of stabilization and liberalization attempts are usually hard to predict, assistance also serves an insurance function, and therefore the optimal level will depend in part on the leaders' degree of aversion to risk.

Because there are political, administrative, and economic costs associated with highly restrictive levels and conditions of aid, alternative means to encourage leaders' commitment and public acquiescence are desirable. In some circumstances it may be possible to separate out the insurance function of aid. Contingency clauses that specify conditions under which additional support becomes automatic (or at least would be given prompt and favorable attention) might serve this purpose. Such an approach might make sense when leaders are reasonably convinced of the need to stabilize and liberalize but are deeply concerned about particular kinds of economic effects which are difficult to predict. Closely related to this is the need for donors to remain flexible regarding supplementary funding in response to change *exogenous* conditions. Especially where rigidities slow adjustment, bad weather or a further adverse trade shift may sabotage the program before it has had time to take effect. Public opinion, understandably, does not draw fine distinctions as to the sources of its misery. The upshot may be to discredit sound government policies and complicate future attempts by the same or successor governments to stabilize the economy.

Under such circumstances, a strong rationale exists, in terms of political sustainability, for adjusting external finance promptly and adequately to take account of new difficulties beyond the government's control. The Compensatory Financing Facility of the IMF serves this purpose to some degree,[29] and the IMF is also sometimes willing to waive performance requirements if the case is a compelling one. But often the Fund's response to new problems is to insist on greater austerity. Particularly in highly vulnerable economies, where relatively small changes in external conditions can have major repercussions, it would be politically as well as economically helpful if standby agreements explicitly stated the assumptions about major economic variables on which the agreed-upon levels of assistance were based. Appropriate adjustments should then be considered if factors beyond the country's control caused significant departures from the assumed values.[30] The understanding might extend to downward revisions in assistance if events provided an unexpected windfall. Such a device could simultaneously provide insurance against bad luck and increase the

29. The Compensatory Financing Facility was established within the IMF mainly to assist exporters of primary products. It provides loans to help to cover shortfalls in export earnings that are both temporary and due mainly to factors beyond the country's control, such as sharp fluctuations in prices for exports, or bad weather that leads to a very small crop.

30. This follows John Williamson's suggestion for contingency conditions. See Williamson, ed., *IMF Conditionality*, p. 638.

credibility of the effort in the public view, while emphasizing the need for sustained adjustment efforts and countering false hopes that external events might obviate the need for adjustment.

In addition to lowering risks by more adequately addressing the need for insurance, external agencies may be able to ease specific kinds of political risks with specific kinds of support or by the phasing and timing of assistance; bilateral donors, for instance, have used food aid to ease the impact of austerity on the poorest groups (as in Peru in the late 1970s). It may also make sense in some cases to tailor the size of different tranches in multitranche commitments to meet the anticipated waning of public patience.

The fact that external agencies often feel they must use restrictive levels and conditions of assistance to maintain commitment, even when such restrictiveness entails clear costs, underscores the need for more attention to means for bolstering understanding and commitment, discussed earlier in this paper. To state the same point differently, in addition to seeking means to reduce the risks of stabilization as perceived by leaders, it is also important to increase the perceived benefits and the confidence with which leaders (and the public) await those benefits, especially if the gains will emerge only gradually.

### The Speed of Adjustment and Political Sustainability

A second debate regarding the design of stabilization, with implications for political sustainability, focuses on the optimal speed of adjustment. The debate is often encapsulated in the phrase "shock treatment versus gradualism." This debate includes several distinct though interrelated strands: the relationship between speed of adjustment and burden of adjustment (aggregate economic loss, its incidence, its timing); the relationship between attempted speed and credibility of reforms among groups whose behavior must be altered (especially the business community); and the political implications of the alternative approaches to stabilization.

The political assumptions of advocates of the two approaches can be summarized concisely. Proponents of the "shock" approach believe that public tolerance for sacrifice is brief and politicians' capacity for pursuing stringent policies is correspondingly limited. If the adjustment process is too gradual, political opposition will cumulate. Groups that initially do not have a united position or are not organized to protest will get organized and may form alliances with other aggrieved groups. Cumulating political pressure may finally produce a massive outburst or, before that point is reached, politicians will dilute or abandon key aspects of the program. Those advocating gradualism make the opposite assessment. They believe the greatest risks lie with sudden cuts in consumption, employment, and sometimes output. Such shock treatment is likely to prompt massive protests and/or a coup. A more gradual approach may avoid putting enough pressure on any important group to goad it into action, or at least will permit phasing aspects of the program to avoid pressuring too many important groups at one time. If one or a few groups do offer vigorous resistance, the government can then attempt to persuade, partially compensate, or restrain the group in whatever ways seem most effective.

These contrasting sets of assumptions cannot be proved right or wrong a priori. But we can ask what conditions each is likely to apply. The political logic of the shock approach depends on the ability of the economy to respond rapidly to drastically altered signals and resource availability (that is, reduced consumption). A rapid economic turnaround permits some loosening of austerity, while generating hope. Once the initial "hump" is gotten over, the program can be expected to generate considerable support. Thus when economic conditions include sizable excess capacity, especially in export sectors, and/or significant production of tradable goods that are consumed domestically but could be shifted into export trade, or when substantial potential remittances from emigrants abroad are being withheld due to lack of confidence (as in Portugal in 1978–1979), a rapid timetable for stabilization may produce rapid progress. But when economic structure and institutional rigidities preclude a rapid economic response, the political logic of the shock approach obviously does not hold.

Different political structures and circumstances also bear on which of the alternative political assessments sketched above is more likely to be valid. Urban wage-earners and consumers are likely to be hit hard by a shock approach. The short-term political capabilities of these groups (their ability to mount and sustain protest) vary widely, not only from one country to another but also at different times in the same country. The probability of violent outbreaks will be influenced by the general trust or distrust of the government; the degree to which public opinion is prepared (perhaps by earlier unsuccessful programs) for fairly drastic measures; the strength and orientation of organized opposition groups; and the tradition or absence of tradition of large-scale demonstrations in the cities. If there is some significant chance of early large-scale or violent reactions, the ability of the government to contain such protests is a crucial consideration for the prospects for a shock strategy. Even if the economy could in theory respond positively to the strategy, it may not make sense for a weak government to attempt it.

Poorer and less flexible economies, especially in sub-Saharan Africa, confront a cruel dilemma with respect to the attempted speed of adjustment. In many cases their economies are not capable of rapid adjustment. A shock approach can indeed balance the budget and the trade account, but only by reducing consumption, government services, production, and employment far below any level that could facilitate real adjustment, that is, expanded capacity for production and an altered composition of both production and consumption that is more in line with resources and comparative advantage. Indeed, a draconian approach in such economies can impair capacity for real adjustment. But some of these same countries lack the resources—internal and external— to pursue the more gradual yet purposeful course which offers the most promise. Available resources are so badly out of line with needs that there is no avoiding drastic cuts in imports and domestic spending, whatever the costs to progress toward sustainable adjustment and resumed development. Without more adequate financial assistance, debates about the optimal speed of adjustment have a bitter theoretical flavor for such governments.

Having recognized this fact, it is still useful to consider the political dimensions of more gradualist approaches, since some countries do have room for choice, and the pressure on others may ease somewhat with economic recovery in the industrialized nations.

The gradual approach to stabilization is often portrayed as a political "soft option," or, at any rate, softer than the shock approach. Gradualism in principle dilutes political risks, partly by permitting more flexibility in timing and phasing of measures to minimize political backlash and partly by allowing time for real economic adjustments to begin to take hold, thereby reducing real costs. For instance, if higher prices for imported foods (as a result of devaluation and/or reduced direct subsidies) are introduced in stages, the impact can be somewhat cushioned by increased supply and (it is hoped) only moderate increases in the prices of domestic substitutes. But a gradual approach has clear risks. It depends crucially on international financing adequate to cover the continuing trade deficit over several years. It allows more opportunity for producers (public corporations as well as private firms) to seek to evade rather than adjust to new disincentives. Gradualism permits opponents of adjustment measures to become organized and articulate and to join forces with each other. And it calls on politicians to maintain their commitment in the face of cumulating pressures. Far from being a soft option, successful management of a sustained stabilization and adjustment effort over several years requires political leadership and skill of a high order. It is probably more difficult than the challenge of maintaining transitional order and acceptance during a shock program in countries where a rapid economic turnaround is feasible.

Since a gradualist approach (which might include rapid action on one or a few specific measures) is the only course that makes economic sense in many countries, it is important to seek means to cope with the political risks of that course.

As was noted earlier, the combination of adjustment measures with more immediate stabilization steps may win stronger commitment from political leaders, and such a program can be presented to the public in a more positive and persuasive manner. However, many specific adjustment measures hurt some groups (often in a prompt and highly visible manner) while benefiting others (often only after a delay, and sometimes in an indirect or dispersed manner). For example, reduced protection against imports may put high-cost domestic producers out of business rapidly, while the direct gains to consumers and to firms that need the products as inputs to their own production (hence to workers in such firms and to purchasers of their products) are much more dispersed, partly indirect, and partly delayed. Therefore the selection, timing, and phasing of initial adjustment steps must take into account the political strains added to those already imposed by austerity. Combined stabilization/adjustment efforts also put a greater burden on bureaucratic capabilities to plan and implement reforms, even when some of these reforms are intended to reduce government intervention in the economy. The combined approach, in short, can generate stronger commitment and public acceptance but is more likely than a narrower stabilization package to strain the limits of managerial capacity.

The core political problem with a stabilization and adjustment program that must be sustained over several years is usually that middle and upper-middle strata—including civil servants, military officers, organized labor, teachers, professionals, and university students—must bear substantial losses. These are the groups whose living standards have moved most seriously out of line with what the country can afford. Unless some fortunate combination of aid, weather, and international prices permits an expansionary adjustment (as in Sri Lanka in 1978 and 1979), their standards must drop. But they are also the most politically potent groups. While persuasion clearly has its limits, these groups should nonetheless be the targets of the most vigorous attempts at explanation and patriotic appeals. Such appeals are likely to carry more weight if politicians adjust their own lifestyles. Such symbolic gestures are sometimes belittled, but at the very least they remove a target of opposition and cynicism.

While real or apparent equity is no guarantee of acceptance of austerity, in many countries obvious inequity has fueled public bitterness. In poorer countries, where all but the highest-income urban households spend the bulk of their incomes on food, management of food prices is probably crucial. Reductions in subsidies should almost certainly be phased, and the impact of large devaluations on food staples should be cushioned. Selective targeting, as in the case of Sri Lanka, is desirable in principle but usually difficult to administer.

Any initial grace period of public acquiescence is limited, and it is important to be able to point to evidence of progress as patience begins to wear thin. It may be feasible to design programs to tolerate some loosening after several months, in terms both of the vigor of initial government measures and of the timing and quantity of assistance. Thus an initial wage freeze might be lifted after some months for particular categories; drastic cuts in government spending might be selectively and very partially reinstated; a larger fraction of a second tranche of aid might be designated for politically strategic consumer-goods imports. Some preplanned lifting of austerity may not always be optimal from the standpoint of technical economic considerations. But it is certainly preferable to what often happens: the government feels constrained to relax the stringency of measures even at the price of abrogating commitments to the IMF or other donors, the program is abandoned, and a new start is launched after some months or even years of confusion and continued economic deterioration.

Beyond these general observations, a series of more specific issues concern the design and phasing of the many policies that comprise a stabilization and adjustment package. The handling of each of these component policies raises political as well as economic issues. Unfortunately, almost no systematic comparative analysis is available on the political implications of various options. For example, overvalued exchange rates are almost always part of a financial crisis. What are the probable political repercussions of a large one-time devaluation versus several smaller steps? Of various flexible exchange-rate mechanisms, following devaluation, to guard against further erosion of international competitiveness? Conventional wisdom argues that dual exchange rates are usually economically inadequate and administratively awkward, yet political leaders often prefer dual rates to devaluation. Under what conditions does a split rate have real political advantages? There has been remarkably little effort to address such questions.

Similarly, we know very little about the conditions under which a government can successfully reduce costly, unsustainable food subsidies—another common theme in stabilization and adjustment programs recently, and a topic that universally gives politicians nightmares. Such efforts have produced massive riots (for example, in Cairo in 1979 and in Tunisia, Morocco, and the Dominican Republic in 1984) and coups (as in Liberia in 1980), yet elsewhere (as in Sri Lanka in 1978 and 1979; Senegal in 1982 and 1983) major cuts provoked no violent protest. It is common sense to argue that government-mandated price increases should not be timed when domestic food supplies are low (thus Senegal resisted external pressure to cut its subsidies on imported rice in 1981, when drought had shrunk domestic substitutes; Sri Lankan subsidies and rations were successfully slashed during a period when domestic rice supplies and the economy generally were expanding rapidly). In the field of trade liberalization, an initial emphasis on export expansion may (to the degree that it is successful) ease the political repercussions of a broader trade-liberalization effort. But we lack even semi-systematic comparative empirical knowledge to support such plausible suggestions. Despite the recognized importance of politics to the success of stabilization and adjustment efforts, the more specific policy issues and options remain to be explored from a political economy perspective.

Stabilization is inherently risky politically, and no combination of strategy, tactics, and support measures by governments and outside agencies can do more than somewhat reduce the risks. Clearly, too, approaches must be tailored to the conditions of each case: there are no standard formulas. But the disappointing record of most stabilization efforts is a powerful argument for more attention to political sustainability. More explicit and systematic consideration of the political dimensions of proposed programs might permit some improvements. As more systematic comparative analysis of past experiences becomes available, it should be possible to identify the conditions under which particular policy options or combinations are likely to survive politically. Even a modest increase in our grasp of such issues would be a contribution in a largely uncharted field.

# Part II

# The State and Development:

## Taiwan, Argentina, and Central America

### *Robert H. Bates*

Part two of this volume contains three case studies: Alice Amsden's study of Taiwan, Guillermo O'Donnell's of Argentina, and Clark Reynolds's of Central America. No effort has been made to select a geographically representative sample, although when the subsequent chapters by Feeny and Bates are added, a broad coverage is in fact achieved. Rather, the chapters were selected because they examine significant interactions between economics and politics, illustrate the political impact of market processes, and advance powerful lines of reasoning.

Alice Amsden examines one of the success stories of modern development: Taiwan.[1] She explores the way the transformation of Taiwan's agriculture pioneered subsequent growth in its manufacturing and industrial sector. She also discusses Taiwan's pursuit of

1. A compact and broad coverage of the Asian economies is contained in Bruce Cumings, "The Origin and Development of the Northeastern Asian Political Economy," *International Organizations* 38 (Winter 1984): 1–40.

a trade-oriented growth strategy that exploited opportunities for exports and the expanding volume of world trade in the post-war era.

Much of Amsden's analysis serves as a cautionary tale. Taiwan, she argues, is an open economy, welcoming foreign investment and engaging in international trade. One of the major orthodoxies in the political economy of development, the dependency school, would therefore predict that Taiwan would be underdeveloped, with low rates of investment, low rates of productivity growth, and high levels of inequality. Contrary to such expectations, Taiwan has achieved high levels of capital accumulation and investment, and it has achieved high rates of growth. Increases in output have resulted not from increased work effort—what Marx called absolute exploitation—but, rather, from gains in efficiency resulting from the application of new techniques. And while growing more rapidly than most developing countries, Taiwan exhibits less inequality. Programs of land reform have led instead to a relatively egalitarian distribution of income and assets.

Should we, then, abandon political economy, to look for purely economic explanations of Taiwan's performance? Some certainly would advocate such an approach.[2] Pointing to Taiwan's "openness," they would argue that the unbridled operation of the market would account for Taiwan's growth. But Amsden attacks such apolitical explanations. The state, she argues, at every point pioneered Taiwan's economic growth. It manipulated relations between agriculture and the larger economy so as to extract resources from the rural sector. And it promoted the organization of industrial groups so as to extract resources from foreign trade. Market-conforming Taiwan's policies may be; but they were *dirigiste*, not laissez-faire.

In emphasizing the activist role of the Taiwan government, Amsden refers to it as "bureaucratic capitalist," engaged in a process of "revolution from above."[3] O'Donnell analyzes a strikingly different case, that of the role of the state in Argentina. The contrast is best revealed in the basic questions motivating O'Donnell's research: Why has not the government of Argentina promoted accumulation and investment? Why have the economic technocrats proved unable to manipulate the private sector so as to achieve

2. See, for example, Bela Balassa, "The Newly Industrializing Countries after the Oil Crisis," *Weltwirtschaftliches Archiv* 117 (1981): 141–94.

3. The phrase is from Ellen Kay Trimberger, "A Theory of Elite Revolution," *Studies in Comparative International Development* 10 (1972): 191–203.

development and growth? Implicit in O'Donnell's answer to these questions is the existence of two possible growth paths: one in which growth is promoted by a government bureaucracy that has succeeded in fragmenting or co-opting private interests (as through land reform in the case of Taiwan); and one in which growth is led by a coherent bourgeoisie. Argentina fits neither model. The bourgeoisie remains divided, split into agrarian and industrial factions; policies that favor accumulation by one tend to be vetoed by the other. And by "colonizing" the state bureaucracy, major private interests fragment it, thereby crippling the power of the economic technocrats who would champion the course of state-led growth.

While employing the language of class analysis and the now fashionable literature on "the state,"[4] O'Donnell's analysis is grounded on well-thought-out microanalytic reasoning. An economic component emphasizes the role of markets and prices in allocating resources and determining incomes. And a political component emphasizes the public power of private interests and their capacity to form coalitions.

O'Donnell identifies four major private interests: the agrarian (pampean) bourgeoisie; the industrial bourgeoisie; and the popular faction, which itself contains two components—a well-organized labor movement, and owners of small businesses. O'Donnell locates these interests within four major markets: for exports, for food, for labor, and for foreign currency. And he introduces a government that intervenes in these markets, setting prices and thereby determining the real value of incomes.[5] Within the political economic arena populated by these actors, there then takes place a competitive struggle as these interests seek to combine, seize power, and set market prices to their advantage.

The key price in O'Donnell's analysis is the price of foreign exchange, that is, the rate at which Argentinean currency can be exchanged for foreign currencies. The popular faction, according to O'Donnell, favors an overvalued exchange rate. Overvaluation

4. See the recent collection of papers edited by Peter Evans, Dietrich Rueschemeyer, and Theda Skocpol, *Bringing the State Back In* (Cambridge, England: Cambridge University Press, 1985).

5. The real value of an income is the magnitude of the satisfaction that can be attained by spending it; it is therefore a function of the level of prices. If money incomes remain unchanged but prices double, then the real value of incomes will fall by one-half of what they would have been had consumers been purchasing their utility-maximizing consumption bundles in the first place.

takes place when public authorities set the exchange price for the local currency above the level at which supply would equal demand in private markets. Overvaluation is preferred by urban interests in Argentina because Argentina exports grain and cattle; and by raising the foreign-currency price for grain and beef, overvaluation deters foreign purchasers from competing with local consumers for these products. Were the government to devalue the local currency (that is, to lower the exchange rate of Argentina's currency), then a single unit of foreign currency could purchase a larger number of australes and foreigners would be favored when competing with domestic consumers for these goods. The result would be a price rise for food in local markets, which would lower the real value of urban incomes. Adding to the preference of urban consumers for an overvalued exchange rate is that when the Argentinean currency is artificially kept strong, people can purchase imported goods more cheaply, that is, for fewer australes. In terms of the purchase both of domestically produced goods and of foreign products, the Argentinean consumer thus benefits from a strong currency.

The interests of the rural bourgeoisie—the pampean producers of wheat and beef—directly conflict with those of the urban consumer. Whereas the urban consumer wants low food prices, the rural producer wants high ones; therefore while the urban consumer favors the overvaluation of the currency, the rural producer opposes it.

What of the urban bourgeoisie? Both owners of small businesses and those running large industries would like to pay lower wages. And when food prices rise, demands for wage increases are sure to follow. For this reason, both may side with labor in demanding low-cost food, and, consequently, an overvaluation of the currency. But—and this is critical to O'Donnell's reasoning—once the currency has become overvalued, then the interests of small and large businesses tend to diverge.

The industrialists have a greater need for foreign exchange than do owners of small businesses, for they tend to be more reliant on imported parts and equipment. But the overvaluation of the currency prices Argentine exports out of international markets; following an upward valuation of Argentina's currency, the large industries suffer as the supply of foreign exchange dwindles. Moreover, large industries are less affected by wage increases than are small businesses. Labor forms a smaller percentage of their costs, and they may be in a better position to pass on increases in costs in the form of higher product prices. By comparison with small businesses, then, large industries bear greater costs and reap fewer benefits from overvaluation. The economic interests of small and big businesses therefore diverge; and their preferences with respect to government policy diverge as well. Following a decision to increase the strength of the Argentine currency, then, industrialists may come to separate themselves from other members of the urban coalition, align with the rural bourgeoisie, and demand that the government devalue the national currency so as to generate a renewed flow of exports and replenish the reserves of foreign exchange.

But, O'Donnell argues, devaluation is itself unstable. The result of the subsequent devaluation is inflation, as foreign buyers compete with local consumers for meat and grain. Workers strike, demanding higher wages to compensate for the erosion in the value of their incomes. Pressures mount for a change in government policy and, driven by urban unrest, the industrialists may swing back into the urban coalition. Thus, by O'Donnell's account, are governments made and unmade in Argentina. And thus too policies shift, as the major actors—particularly the urban bourgeoisie—alter their coalitional alliances.

O'Donnell thus derives policy preferences from market locations and shows how private interests coalesce in efforts to influence public policy. O'Donnell uses his explanatory framework to reconstruct the history of Argentinean politics: its shifting class alliances, its stop-and-start patterns of growth, and its failure to achieve political stability and enduring policy commitments. Clark Reynolds, in "Fissures in the Volcano," also applies microanalytic reasoning. He too examines the impact of economic forces on private political interests. But rather than looking backward in time in an effort to explain what has happened, he looks forward in time in an effort to predict what may happen. Writing in the mid-1970s, Reynolds examined economic conditions in Central America and warned: Watch out!

In reading the Reynolds chapter, it is important to take into account that it was first published in 1978. Like the Lipson piece which begins the volume, it may therefore appear anachronistic. But, again like the Lipson chapter, Reynolds's possesses a characteristic that virtually dictates its inclusion: it exhibits a mode of reasoning from which both economists and political scientists can learn and it applies that reasoning to a significant topic.

Like O'Donnell, Reynolds links market forces to political preferences. Creating this link, according to Reynolds, is government policy, which can affect the impact of the market on the distribution of income. In Reynolds's analysis, people care about their share of the size distribution of income. Poor people want to become richer and rich people want to remain that way, and a distribution of income in which the top few (say, 10 percent) control a disproportionate share of the income (say, 40 percent) is less stable politically than a more equitable distribution (in which the richest 10 percent earn, say, 10 percent of the income).

Incomes are generated as payments to factors of production. Reynolds examines how economic activity in Central America generates a functional distribution of income, a distribution in the form of wages, profits, rents, and taxes. As people prefer more income to less, the struggle for economic improvement takes the form of competition among the holders of different factors for a greater share of the total income. In particular, Reynolds focuses on the share of labor in total income and warns that forces that lower labor's share may be setting the stage for political conflict in Central America.

A conventional economist might at this point query: Why is this a political problem? Such struggles always take place; but they take the form of economic competition in the market settings.

Reynolds notes three reasons why a market explanation fails to capture the full story of the struggle over the distribution of income. One is that before the market determines the level of payments to the owners of various factors, there first has to take place a political act: the determination of property rights. For many persons in Central America, whether they earn their incomes from wages or rents depends on how those who control government power have allotted rights to land. Second, Reynolds notes that many markets are not competitive. In some, there are monopolists, single economic agents who dominate the market and set prices for the goods they sell; in others, there are monopsonists, single agents who set prices for the goods they buy; and in still others, there are ologopolists, a few agents who restrict competition among themselves and thereby alter market prices. Ologopoly, he stresses, is particularly characteristic of export agriculture, where the owners of land and the suppliers of capital conspire to lower the level of wages. Prices set by agents arise not from market competition but, rather, from market power. The distribution of income thus becomes a political act.

Finally, Reynolds stresses the role of "rents," payments that flow to the holders of productive assets which lie above what they would earn in a perfectly competitive market. In a market equilibrium, each factor would earn in a particular economic activity what it could earn in its next-best use. The payments it could command in its next-best use represent its "opportunity cost," the cost it incurs from remaining in its present activity. In a two-sector economy composed of agriculture and industry, for example, a worker in industry would earn what he or she could earn in agriculture: less than that opportunity cost, and the worker would return to agriculture; more, and other workers would flock from agriculture to industry and the competition would then lower the wage rate. But in some cases, factors employed in an industry can earn a premium over and above their opportunity costs. It could be, for example, that the industry commands an economic advantage that would be so costly to reproduce that competitors could not enter and bring earnings down to the competitive rate of return. Those who supply factors of production could then command a price above what they could earn in their next-best use. Reynolds focuses on one such industry: export agriculture. Climatic, location, and other factors that are costly to reproduce confer on those producing coffee, bananas, and other crops in Central America special economic advantages—which generate significant economic rents.

In such a setting, the problem then becomes: how are these rents to be shared? Given that they cannot be competed away in the marketplace, a political struggle arises over the establishment of property rights over—or entitlements to—these superior returns.

As Reynolds notes, in the 1960s the level of rents in export agriculture increased in Central America. Export prices rose and various innovations, such as the introduction of fertilizers and the creation of cheaper transport routes, lowered costs, thereby increasing the flow of payments to export agriculture. One argument might have been that the rise in export prices was an act of God, and the economic benefits were not earned; they therefore should not be appropriated by people in the export industry. On the basis of this argument, the government would be justified in taxing away the rents and spending them on services that would benefit all citizens. Alternatively, workers could form a union and demand that the rents be shared with them in the form of higher wages. Or landlords could extract them by raising land rents. When rents are created, then, competition for them increases, and with the rise in competition a political struggle takes place.

Reynolds examines the political currents unleashed by economic growth in Central America in the 1960s. In addition to the rise in export prices, the formation of the Central American Common Market gave impetus to the growth of the regional economy. The common market led to trade diversion: goods that had formerly been bought abroad were now purchased locally, though at higher prices. But it also led to trade creation: goods that were not formerly traded were now produced and sold, as new industries were set up and as tariffs on intermediate goods (goods used in production) were lowered, enabling firms to operate at lower cost. In the short run, Reynolds notes, the effects of trade creation outweighed those from trade diversion, and the result was growth in the total value of goods produced and consumed in Central America.

In moving from the economic story to the political, Reynolds focuses not only on the struggle over rents from exports but also on the impact of growth on the distribution of income and, in particular, on the share of labor. Increases in productivity were, he argues, a major source of growth. The gains in total output were not matched by gains in employment. This was particularly true in agriculture, where rapid increases in output were not matched by increases in the number of jobs. Nor were the workers "exported" from agriculture fully absorbed in other sectors. Reynolds therefore documents a shift in the relative position of labor, a shift which, he argues, set the stage for political struggle in Central America.

In retrospect, Reynolds's piece appears prophetic. At least as important for this volume, it illustrates ways of combining economic and political reasoning—ones taken up most notably in recent efforts to combine microeconomic reasoning with class analysis.[6] "Fissures in the Volcano" therefore combines materials of

6. See, for example, Robert Brenner, "Agrarian Class Structure and Economic Development in Pre-Industrial Europe," *Past and Present* 70 (1976): 30–75. See also such works as Jon Elster, *Making Sense of Marx* (Cambridge, England: Cambridge

great substantive interest with materials that teach us how to study political economy. As does the work of Amsden and O'Donnell, it imparts tools by which to study two of the grand themes of political economy: the ways economic location determines political interest and politics influences the behavior of economies.

University Press, 1985); Adam Przeworski, *Capitalism and Social Democracy* (Cambridge, England: Cambridge University Press, 1985); and, above all, John Roemer, *A General Theory of Exploitation and Class* (Cambridge, Mass.: Harvard University Press, 1982).

# 4

# Taiwan's Economic History:

## A Case of *Etatisme* and a Challenge to Dependency Theory

*Alice H. Amsden*

Taiwan distinguishes itself as one of the few nonsocialist economies since Japan to rise from the grossest poverty and to enter the world of the developed. As if this were not enough, and if the figures are correct, income distribution has also been far less inequitable in Taiwan than in other poor market economies. The two phenomena together have earned Taiwan the title of "economic miracle."

In seeking an explanation for these phenomena, which *are* rather miraculous in the context of continued underdevelopment in the rest of the Third World, we have come face to face with two schools of thought: neoclassical and dependency theory. The for-

Reprinted from Alice H. Amsden, "Taiwan's Economic History: A Case of *Etatisme* and a Challenge to Dependency Theory," *Modern China* 5, no. 3 (July 1979): 341–80. © 1979 by Sage Publications, Inc. Reprinted by permission of Sage Publications, Inc.

mer, to generalize somewhat, sees the explanation for the Taiwan "miracle" in the application of free-market principles. The latter ignores Taiwan altogether, probably because it sees it as a "special case" undeserving of attention.

Concerning the popular conception of Taiwan as an economy wherein market forces guide capital accumulation, it is quite true today that government interference does not assume the form it has taken in many other Third World countries, that is, heavy protection and price "distortion" to facilitate industrialization based on the home market. Nevertheless, it is our contention that both in the past and at present, the state in Taiwan has acted as a key agent in the process of capital accumulation—not because it has kept aloof from it, but because it has very much dominated it. In general, the role of the state in Third World economies exceeds that elsewhere. Of late, however, the degree of *étatisme* has been seen to be growing or greater than once believed. Surprisingly, Taiwan appears to fall closer to the end of the spectrum of state activity that is unusual rather than commonplace.

It is particularly with respect to dependency theory that Taiwan emerges as an interesting case history. The major thesis of dependency theory is that the rise of foreign trade and the arrival of foreign capital from the core lie at the heart of underdevelopment on the periphery. Taiwan, however, presents dependency theory with a paradox. It is both more integrated in world capitalism than other poor market economies, and more developed. However miserable the level of real wages in Taiwan (as elsewhere), full employment has emerged, and capital accumulation proceeds on the basis of both relative and absolute surplus-value extraction, with an emphasis on the former. That is, capital accumulation proceeds on the basis of technological innovation and greater efficiency rather than on the basis of longer hours of work and more intensive effort *alone*. This is what we mean by "developed."

We argue that dependency theory is unable to come to grips with the Taiwan paradox because it employs a methodology that elevates imperialism to the primary analytical category. Only when endogenous productive and social relations are taken as primary can both successful and unsuccessful instances of development be understood. Throughout the Third World, trade and investment from the core created pressures to develop the productive forces. But class and productive relations within Taiwan made such pressures general. Specifically, *étatisme* and land reform mediated the effects of imperialism to advantage. Many features made Taiwan an unrealistic model of capitalist development for other Third World countries to copy. They do not, however, render Taiwan constitutionally unsuited for the assessment of the usefulness of dependency theory.

*Etatisme,* law and order, and much else have their roots in the Japanese occupation of Taiwan. The section that follows therefore examines the Japanese interlude in some detail.

## The Colonial Period: 1895–1945

It is a misconception that the Taiwan miracle commenced with the export of labor-intensive manufactures and a reduction of government management of trade and monetary matters in the decade of the 1960s. As Table 1 indicates, Taiwan already enjoyed a relatively fast-rising real gross domestic product in the 1950s, when agriculture was the dominant sector and the economic regime in industry, as in many other underdeveloped countries, was one of protection of infant industries. Growth was also rapid during the years of Japanese domination (1895–1945). Excluding the war years of 1941–1945, the per capita income of the agricultural sector almost doubled in half a century. This is a rather impressive figure, given that population rose by approximately 43 percent.[1]

The economy that the Japanese fashioned in Taiwan was achieved by means of deliberate planning and government ownership of major resources (in partnership with private Japanese capitalists). The dominance of the Japanese colonial administration in Taiwan's economy mirrored the dominant role of the Meiji government in Japan proper, which distinguished it in important respects from the colonial offices of England and France.[2] The "indirect rule" of the British and French colonial offices involved the protection of private property, with the assistance of local satraps. The rule of the Japanese imperialists was much more direct and involved production by the state itself and oppression by a ubiqui-

1. A. Y. C. Koo, *The Role of Land Reform in Economic Development* (New York: Praeger, 1968), p. 8.
2. H. Y. Chang and R. H. Myers, "Japanese Colonial Development Policy in Taiwan, 1895–1906—A Case of Bureaucratic Entrepreneurship," *Journal of Asian Studies* 22, no. 4 (August 1963): 433–49, and S. P. S. Ho, "The Development of Japanese Colonial Government in Taiwan, 1895–1945," in Gustav Ranis, ed., *Government and Economic Development* (New Haven: Yale University Press, 1971).

*Table 1.*   *Leading Economic Indicators of Taiwan*

| | AVERAGE ANNUAL GROWTH RATES (%) | | |
| --- | --- | --- | --- |
| | *1952–1960* | *1960–1968* | *1968–1973* |
| Real GDP | 7.3 | 8.5 | 10.6 |
| Real per capita income | 3.1 | 4.0 | 7.1 |
| Agriculture | 3.6 | 4.2 | 1.2 |
| Forestry/fisheries/livestock | 4.6* | 5.3 | 3.5 |
| Manufacturing | 13.3 | 15.8 | 23.0 |

*Source:* Government of Taiwan, Economic Planning Council, 1975.

   *1953–1960.

tous Japanese police force. The Jiang Jie-shi (Chiang Kai-shek) forces benefited enormously from their inheritance of Japanese state monopolies, and the whole interventionist approach taken by the Japanese to the development of an occupied territory was not lost on the Guomindang.

From the start, Taiwan was regarded as an agricultural appendage to be developed as a complement to Japan. A two-crop economy (sugar and rice) was encouraged, much in the classical imperial pattern. But one aspect that sets Taiwan's colonial experience apart from the rest is that primary production was not confined to a foreign enclave with limited spillover on subsistence agriculture. Many farmers with access to arable land produced rice for market to meet the ever-escalating needs of Japanese consumers. Although sugarcane is frequently cultivated on large plantations in some Third World countries, in Taiwan it was grown by small owner-operators and tenants as well as on large land tracts owned by Japanese sugar manufacturers. Thus, agriculture in Taiwan was quickly and generally commercialized.[3]

Government surveys had revealed that much of rural Taiwan at the turn of the century operated under an archaic three-tier tenancy system. It consisted of the great landlords and the tenant

3. R. H. Myers, "The Commercialization of Agriculture in Modern China," in W. E. Willmott, ed., *Economic Organization in Chinese Society* (Stanford: Stanford University Press, 1972).

landlords, who paid the former a fixed rent and who collected rent in kind from their cultivators (or subtenants). Under this system, property rights were unclear and hence blamed for difficulties in collecting taxes and making land transactions. To end this system, the Japanese administration first undertook an extensive cadastral survey. Two by-products of this inventory were the uncovering of farms that were not on the tax roll and a record of agricultural holdings that would prove of immense usefulness for the land re-form effected by the government of Jiang Jie-shi half a century later. Next, the Japanese administration undertook its own land reform, which left the existing social structure of landlordism in-tact while allowing new farming practices to be assimilated.[4] The land reform had much in common with changes introduced in ru-ral Japan itself after the Meiji Restoration. Landlords were given incentives to produce more, thus minimizing their opposition to taxation, while their tenants were squeezed to the maximum. Under the reform, the tenant landlords became the legal owners of the land, directly responsible for taxes. The clarification of property rights was judged by the Japanese administration to be the key prerequisite for investment in land development under noncommunal farming. A flat tax on land, rather than a propor-tional tax on output, was also viewed as an incentive to greater production. Meanwhile, ground rents amounting to 50 percent and occasionally as much as 70 percent of a tenant's main crop yield were common.

A scientific approach to agriculture was the main ingredient of rural policy. To make it still more profitable for landlords to ex-pand production for the Japanese market, the colonialists pio-neered important technological advances. New seed strains suit-able to the Taiwanese ecology were experimented with and perfected by various research agencies supported by the state. A host of technological advances were achieved (long before the Green Revolution became a twinkle in the eye of the Rockefeller Foundation) and set in motion that application of science to farm-ing which characterizes the rural economy of Taiwan today.[5]

Significantly, the oppressive land-tenure arrangements (which

4. Ho, "Development"; E. B. Wickberg, "Late Nineteenth Century Land Tenure in Northern Taiwan," in Leonard H. D. Gordon, ed., *Taiwan: Studies in Chinese Local History* (New York: Columbia University Press, 1970).

5. S. P. S. Ho, "Agricultural Transformation under Colonialism: The Case of Taiwan," *Journal of Economic History* 28, no. 3 (September 1968): 313–40; R. H. Myers and A. Ching, "Agricultural Development in Taiwan under Japanese Colonial

persisted even after the "great landlords" had been exorcised) seemingly did not obstruct the march of technological progress. Tenant farmers applied improved technology, fertilizers, and other inputs to increase crop yields.[6] Presumably, either tenants' net incomes would have been lower or their leases would not have been renewed had they not done so. By way of encouragement, an elaborate network of agricultural associations, under the aegis of the government and rich landlords, provided peasants with extension education, the cooperative purchase of fertilizers, warehousing, and other services. Where persuasion failed, the police were employed to force modern techniques onto rural communities that resisted change.[7] The experience small tenants gained in experimenting with new seed strains and their familiarization with scientific farming would also prove of immense usefulness to the later land-reform efforts of the Chinese Nationalists. The extensive network of agricultural associations introduced by the Japanese was created to facilitate police surveillance and control over the local population. Today, these associations persist and are an important element in the government's management of agriculture.

In the 1930s, Japan reshaped its policy of transforming Taiwan into a source of food supply for the home market. The shift in policy can be understood only in the context of Japan's increasingly militarism and expansionism in the Pacific. Belatedly and frantically, Japan sought to refashion Taiwan as an industrial adjunct to its own war preparations and ambitions in Southeast Asia and South China:

> Japan had always considered Taiwan the natural base for extending its influence in these two areas. Economically, it was hoped that, at a minimum, more of Taiwan's exports could be directed toward them. With its growing productive capacity, the government realized that Taiwan had to broaden its market, and it had visions of transforming

Rule," *Journal of Asian Studies* 23, no. 4 (August 1964): 555–70; R. P. Christensen, "Taiwan's Agricultural Development," U.S. Department of Agriculture, Economic Research Studies, Foreign Agricultural Economic Report no. 39 (Washington, D.C.: U.S. Government Printing Office, 1968); S. C. Hsieh and T. H. Lee, "Agricultural Development and Its Contribution to Economic Growth in Taiwan," Economic Digest Series no. 17 (Taibei: Government Printer, 1966); and Teng-Hui Lee, *Inter-Sectoral Capital Flows in the Development of Taiwan: 1895–1960* (Ithaca: Cornell University Press, 1971).

6. About 65 to 70 percent of the total crop of Taiwan in the 1930s was produced by peasants on rented land: A. J. Grajdanzev, *Formosa Today* (New York: Institute for Pacific Relations, 1942), p. 76.

7. Myers and Ching, "Agricultural Development."

Taiwan into an industrial center, with South China and Southeast
Asia as its markets as well as its sources of raw materials.[8]

The new economic policy of the Japanese administration resulted in a diversification of agriculture as new crops for industrial
use were introduced. These raw materials were processed in Taiwan, adding to the industrial base there, as did the processing of
raw materials imported into Taiwan from Southeast Asia. While
industry had not been specifically prohibited in Taiwan before the
1930s, the fact that the gains from Taiwan's growth largely gravi-
tated to Japan meant that only those industries with a locational
advantage (for example, cement, sugar refining) could survive in
the absence of a sizable domestic market and the influx of duty-
free Japanese imports. After 1930, however, locational advantages
grew more decisive. The construction of a hydroelectric power in-
stallation in 1934 gave rise to the beginnings of metallurgical and
chemical sectors, both of which rely heavily on low-cost power. As
Japan's military buildup escalated and, finally, as World War II
erupted, the traffic in Japanese goods to Taiwan dwindled and
then ceased. As a consequence there was evidence of the beginnings of local manufacture of some goods that had previously been
imported from Japan. It needs to be added that, as in Japan itself,
it was semi-official enterprise that realized the various industrial
projects on the government's drawing board.[9]

The industrial transformation of Taiwan did not progress much
under Japanese rule. One reason was that the policy to build Taiwan into an industrial bridgehead to South Asia was in effect for
only a short time before World War II brought it to a halt. Moreover, as Ho notes, the early policies of the government frustrated
its later designs.[10] For obvious political reasons, the Japanese colonial authority had underinvested in education. Although alloca-
tions for education were eventually increased, providing Taiwan
with one of the most literate populations among the underdeveloped countries, such expenditures came too late to furnish the
trained manpower required by industrialization. Similarly, Taiwan's infrastructure was initially designed to support agriculture.
While the last-minute efforts to construct transport and harbor fa-

8. Ho, "Development," p. 325.
9. United States Navy, *Handbook*, Economic Supplement (Washington, D.C.: U.S.
Government Printing Office, 1944), chapters 6–9.
10. Ho, "Development," p. 325.

cilities suited to military and industrial needs proved highly beneficial in postwar years, many projects remained on the drawing board when war erupted.

Thus, economic growth in Taiwan under Japanese rule went about as far as it could go, given the internal contradictions of imperialism. Growth included a rise in per capita incomes: indeed, the welfare of the Taiwanese peasant in the first half of the twentieth century may have exceeded that of the Japanese peasant, according to such welfare indices as type of wearing apparel, housing, local bank deposits, and the like.[11] The most enduring legacy of the Japanese occupation, however, was not the betterment of living standards but the building of a foundation for subsequent development. Whereas much of the gain in per capita income was lost as a consequence of war and an influx of Mainlanders following the Communist victory in China (and was not regained until the 1950s and 1960s), the economic structure implanted by the Japanese survived. This structure encompassed agriculture, industry, and social overhead, including law and order—something at which both the Japanese and, later, the Chinese Nationalists excelled.

### The Japanese Interlude and Formosan Nationalism

An interesting feature of the Japanese interlude was its romanticization, after the war and at least through the 1960s, by those of the middle class in Taiwan with a taste for Formosan (that is, Taiwanese) nationalism. Some 80 percent of the island's population of 16 million people is composed of descendants of people who have migrated from China since the early seventeenth century. The remainder is composed of Mainlanders who arrived after 1949.

The Japanese interlude, and Japanese culture in general, were romanticized by Formosan Nationalists, if only to demystify the degree of economic development achieved under Mainlander rule: "'The Nationalists cannot claim credit for those things,' insisted an economics student [in 1962], 'and we could do better under our own system without the incubus of a refugee main-

11. T. Ouchi, "Agricultural Depression and Japanese Villages," *Developing Economies* 5, no. 4 (December 1964): 597–627.

lander government.'" [12] The continued very heavy military expenditures by the Guomindang in the hope of retaking the Mainland were seen by Formosan Nationalists as needless drains on the development effort. The inflation and economic stagnation in postwar Taiwan and, indeed, the fairly lengthy interval before per capita income, and production in certain sectors, recovered their prewar levels were attributed by Formosan Nationalists not so much to wartime dislocations and Allied bombing (which is the Guomindang contention) as to the mass influx of Mainland refugees, and—in the words of George Kerr, a former U.S. State Department official stationed in Taiwan—to "the stripping of factories of equipment and capital goods [for a final battle for the mainland], the drain on the treasury to pay off the hordes of carpetbaggers, the dismissal or bypassing of competent, trained Formosans, and nepotism." [13] Peng Ming-min, a professor of law and a leader of the Formosan independence movement who escaped from Taiwan after his arrest in 1964, writes in his autobiography about the Japanese interlude as follows:

> Under the Japanese, [the Formosans] enjoyed the benefits of a rule of law. The police were strict, often harsh, and the Japanese colonial administration treated Formosans as second-class citizens. However, under Japanese reorganization and direction our island economy had made spectacular gains, and our living standard rose steadily until among Asian countries we were second only to Japan in agricultural and industrial technology, in communications, in public health, and in provisions for the general public welfare. Our grandparents had witnessed this transformation from a backward, ill-governed, disorganized island nominally dependent on the Chinese. They did not like the Japanese, but they appreciated the economic and social benefits of fifty years of peace which they enjoyed while the Chinese on the mainland proper endured fifty years of revolution, warlordism, and civil war. [14]

Disgust with Chinese Nationalist corruption and rapacity after 1945 appears to have cut across classes in Taiwan. According to Kerr:

---

12. D. Mendel, *The Politics of Formosan Nationalism* (Berkeley and Los Angeles: University of California Press, 1970), p. 66.

13. G. H. Kerr, *Formosa Betrayed* (Boston: Houghton Mifflin, 1965), p. 201.

14. Peng Ming-min, *A Taste of Freedom: Memoirs of a Formosan Independence Leader* (New York: Holt, Rinehart and Winston, 1972), pp. 59–60.

> As I went around the Island, I noticed the tension rising, and reports of strikes due to the Formosans being replaced by Mainland Chinese became fairly common. On October 10th in the Takao factory of the Taiwan Steel Manufacturing Company all the workers, comprising 960 men, went on strike as a result of trouble with the police. The workers objected to Chinese being put over them and capable Formosans being replaced. . . . In the Taiwan Alkali Company's plant at Takao on October 28th, 1946, 2,000 men struck for reasons similar to those in the steel manufacturing company, and demanded equal treatment with the Chinese. . . . Similar action took place in the cement factory at Takao.[15]

Unrest spread with the increase of unemployment and of wages being withheld.

Finally, in March 1947, a mass rebellion against the mainland government erupted. The demands of the Formosan Nationalist leaders are indicative of the character they lent to the popular uprising. Demands were avowedly "reformist" (an end to bribes and corruption, management of government monopolies by Taiwanese, and the like), rather than revolutionary or even "rebellious" (the severing of ties with China). One immediate cause of the 1947 uprising had been the effective barring from purchase by Formosans, either by cash or credit, of confiscated Japanese property.[16] But reformist or not, the Guomindang forces quickly put down the uprising at the cost of an estimated 10,000 to 20,000 lives: "Some [Formosans] were beaten and killed on the spot, but large numbers of doctors, lawyers, editors, and businessmen were simply taken away."[17] The Guomindang had taken advantage of a lull in the uprising "to identify the Formosan activists both individually and as types (college students, teachers, and doctors, among others)."[18] Peng Ming-min writes about the events before the massacre as follows:

> Alert citizens in the Hsin-chu area prevented troop movements by tearing up the rails at certain places and stalling the troop trains. Governor Chen's attempt at deception heightened the anger and mistrust of the Taipei people. Riots occurred in some of the principal towns where the governor's men attempted to maintain control. A handful of communists, men and women released from local Jap-

15. Kerr, *Formosa Betrayed*, p. 235.
16. Ibid.
17. Mendel, *Politics*, p. 34.
18. Ibid.

anese prisons in late 1945 on General MacArthur's orders, attempted to take advantage of the confusion. They failed to attract a following. Formosans had become accustomed to fear communism ever since Japan adopted its determined anticommunist policies at the close of World War I.[19]

According to one American academic sympathetic to the Formosan cause (and, like many other academics with similar sympathies, anti-Communist as well), "Naturally, the Japanese regime did its best to suppress, subvert, or disrupt extremist Formosan political movements. It encouraged the moderates."[20] Undoubtedly, "extremist" elements attracted a larger following and were more active in the 1947 uprising than most accounts of the events indicate. Nevertheless, it is clear that, if nothing else, the Japanese colonial authority helped determine that the most vocal liberation movement in Taiwan to date has had a character that is distinctly bourgeois.

### Land to the Tiller

Agriculture was by far the most important sector in Taiwan in the late 1940s, accounting for twice as much of domestic product as industry and for over 90 percent of exports. Not unnaturally, then, the attention of the Nationalists was first turned to reforming the countryside. This is not to suggest that rural Taiwan was at the boiling point when land was redistributed. The 1947 uprising had been largely urban-based. But the threat of an impoverished peasantry had been driven home to the Nationalists on the mainland and they reacted accordingly.

Agriculture was reformed in three stages. First, in early 1949, farm rent was limited to a maximum of 37.5 percent of the total main crop yield. Second, in June 1951, public land formerly owned by Japanese nationals was distributed on easy terms, with preference given to the tenant claimants. Third, in 1953, landlords were obliged to divest themselves of their holdings above a minimal size and sell out to their tenants under the Land-to-the-Tiller Act.[21] This end to landlordism and the creation of a class of smallholders

19. Peng, *Taste of Freedom*, pp. 66–67.
20. Mendel, *Politics*, p. 24.
21. The government purchased all private tenanted holdings in excess of three hectares for paddy land and six hectares for dry land and resold it to tenants. The terms of sale were very liberal and similar to those for public lands: the purchase

was the grand inspiration of Dr. Sun Yat-sen. The Guomindang's land-to-the-tiller program had amounted to sheer rhetoric in China during the 1930s and 1940s because would-be expropriated landlords were stalwarts of the Nationalists. In Taiwan, by contrast, the mainland government was under no obligation to the rural Taiwanese elite. Landlords were given land bonds in kind and stocks in public enterprise in exchange for the compulsory divestiture of their holdings. Some landlords profited from their stock ownership and became successful industrialists. Others went into bankruptcy.[22] The landlord class, however, sank into social oblivion, as the great landlord class had done half a century earlier.

Thus, almost overnight the countryside in Taiwan ceased to be oppressed by a small class of large landlords and became characterized by a large number of owner-operators with extremely small holdings. By 1973, almost 80 percent of the agricultural population were owner-cultivators and another tenth were part-owners.[23] Only 6 percent of farm income accrued to landlords and moneylenders.[24] This undoubtedly underscores the fact that income distribution (by household) in Taiwan is far less inequitable than in most other Third World countries and is more like the pattern in advanced capitalist countries—which is not to say, however, that income distribution is equitable.[25] The average area of cultivated land per farm family has also steadily decreased, from its already handkerchief size in 1953. In 1970, 90 percent of all farms in Taiwan covered less than two hectares.[26]

The fact that parcellation was engineered by an exogenous military force (backed by U.S. aid and hardware) is clearly of immense significance in drawing comparisons between Taiwan's economic history and that of other underdeveloped countries. The issue is treated separately later on. What follows now is a discussion of agricultural performance in the post-reform period.

---

and resale price of land was fixed at 2.5 multiplied by the annual crop yield, and tenant purchasers paid the government in 20 semi-annual installments over a period of ten years: Christensen, *Taiwan's Agricultural Development*, p. 47.

22. Koo, *Land Reform*.

23. Department of Agriculture and Forestry, Provincial Government, *Taiwan Agricultural Yearbook, 1974*.

24. Lee, *Inter-Sectoral Capital Flows*, p. 75.

25. Wan-Yong Kuo, "Income Distribution by Size in Taiwan Area—Changes and Causes," *Industry of Free China* 45 (January–March 1976).

26. And only 0.06 had above ten hectares: *Report of the 1970 Agricultural Census of Taiwan and Fukien Districts*, vol. 2, book 1 (1971).

### Agriculture, 1953–1968

The years 1953–1968 witnessed annual growth rates in agricultural output that were impressive by any standard. Equally impressive was the spillover effect on industry, for however tight the squeeze on agriculture under Japanese rule, it was even tighter under the Jiang Jie-shi administration. Whereas net real capital outflow from agriculture had increased at a rate of 3.8 percent annually between 1911 and 1940, it rose on the average by 10 percent annually between 1951 and 1960.[27] Fast growth and a transfer of agricultural resources to the towns, however, were neither the outcome of free-market forces nor the automatic result of purely technical phenomena—the Green Revolution. Rather, they reflected the structure of ownership in the countryside and state management of almost every conceivable economic activity.

In the decade and a half following the end of World War II, multiple cropping and the use of fertilizer accounted for most of the growth in agricultural output. By contrast, both structural shifts away from traditional crops and the introduction of fixed capital (tractors and livestock) and current inputs other than fertilizer (such as herbicides and insecticides) were mainly responsible for output gains in the 1960s (agricultural output showed signs of stagnation after 1968).[28] Nevertheless, in both periods higher yields per hectare or the expansion of higher-value crops, rather than increased labor input or the expansion of cultivated areas, accounted for the lion's share of growth. This is quite significant. A defining characteristic of production is rising output as a consequence of greater efficiency rather than greater effort: the difference between relative and absolute surplus value, on which Marx elaborated. Taiwan's agriculture has developed in the former, critical sense.

This is not to ignore the fact that over time, Taiwanese farmers have worked longer and perhaps harder. The annual average number of working days per farm worker increased from 117 working days in the period 1911–1915, to 143 working days in 1926–1930; decreased to 115 working days in 1946–1950; and

27. Lee, *Inter-Sectoral Capital Flows,* p. 28.
28. Teng-Hui Lee and T. H. Shen, "Agriculture as a Base for Socio-Economic Development," in T. H. Shen, ed., *Agriculture's Place in the Strategy of Development: The Taiwan Experience* (Taibei: Joint Commission on Rural Reconstruction, 1974).

**Table 2.** Annual Compound Rate of Growth in Agricultural Productivity, 1949–1970 (Five-Year Average, as %)

|  | Worker | Working Days | Arable Land (ha.) |
|---|---|---|---|
| 1946–1951 | 6.8 | 3.6 | 9.2 |
| 1951–1960 | 4.4 | 3.0 | 4.6 |
| 1960–1970 | 3.9 | 3.3 | 3.9 |

Source: Compiled from Teng-Hui Lee and T. H. Shen, "Agriculture as a Base For Socio-Economic Development," in T. H. Shen, ed., Agriculture's Place in the Strategy of Development: The Taiwan Experience (Taibei: Joint Commission on Rural Reconstruction, 1974).

then increased again to 155 working days after the land reform.[29] Nevertheless, labor productivity has risen since the war both per farm laborer and per working day (see Table 2).[30]

It is well known that in developing countries there have been large gains in income among the few (that is, the bigger farmers) when the new technology associated with the Green Revolution has been introduced. But the problem is that the so-called Green Revolution has not been introduced in most developing countries very widely. Small-scale peasants, tenants, and sharecroppers have been restricted to old techniques because for the most part they have not gained access to the complementary inputs which the implementation of the Green Revolution demands. The allocation of resources in agriculture and the efficiency with which they are used are, in theory, unaffected by agrarian structure. It is a matter of indifference in neoclassical theory whether landowners have a sharecropping or leasehold contract with a tenant, farm the land themselves, or hire labor, so long as factor and product markets are competitive. But such markets are typically far from competi-

29. Lee, Inter-Sectoral Capital Flows, p. 58.
30. That Taiwanese agriculture under Japanese as well as Mainlander rule was both capital-intensive and labor-intensive with respect to land is by no means contradictory. Certain capital inputs are complementary with labor rather than substitutive. In particular, working or current capital inputs (which include fertilizer, feeds, and seeds) are labor-absorbing, in contradistinction to some fixed capital inputs (particularly farm machinery, implements, and livestock), which are labor-displacing. Working capital inputs, moreover, may be applied in variable quantities on small farms.

tive and "under rationed conditions, it is the larger farmers who obtain the fertilizer and receive the irrigation water."[31]

By contrast, the Green Revolution in Taiwan has transformed the life of almost every peasant. Furthermore, such an extensive application of science appears to hinge on government control over capital accumulation. The state distributes resources equally among all peasants—as the market mechanism might not do. Hence, there have been large gains among the many. A small class of big landowners has not yet resurfaced (nor, consequently, has a potentially cohesive source of opposition to the state). It is, then, a defining characteristic of Taiwan's agriculture that a multiplicity of peasant proprietors of smallholdings exist in conformity with the bourgeois model of individualistic family farming, while directing this drama is a highly centralized government bureaucracy.

This point was recognized by two anthropologists in a study of rice farming in three Taiwanese villages:

> In this small island with its geographically very mobile population, the arm of the state reaches down to virtually every farmer—outside the mountainous regions. This is a basic social and administrative characteristic of agriculture in Taiwan that has been long in the making.
>
> As a result of [land tenure reforms], the rural landlord social class in the villages disappeared. The power of the state could reach then direct to every villager. The tenants of the past pay land tax now to the state and water fees to the government directly.[32]

In 1965, government agencies or related credit institutions supplied 65 percent of all agricultural loans. Before land reform, private moneylenders, particularly landlords, accounted for 82 percent of credit.[33] With respect to such activities as agricultural education and marketing, the government exerts its control through the elaborate network of agricultural associations laid down by the Japanese.

A cruder form of state power with a purpose altogether unrelated to economic planning was also remarked upon by Wang and Apthorpe:

31. K. Griffin, *The Political Economy of Agrarian Change* (Cambridge, Mass.: Harvard University Press, 1974), p. 30.

32. Sung Hsing Wang and R. Apthorpe, *Rice Farming in Taiwan: Three Village Studies,* Academia Sinica Monograph Series B, no. 5 (1974), pp. 10–11.

33. Christensen, *Taiwan's Agricultural Development,* p. 57.

At least for as long as relations between island and continental China continue in their present form presumably a justification will be found for continuing a form of reliance on the kind of police methods which have now become part and parcel of everyday life. The Minister of the Interior in the Nationalist government used very often in 1971 for instance, to the astonishment of persons familiar with a very different tradition, to speak of the policeman as the most important resource person of all for community development in the island. Villagers, too, speak of the intimacy of police participation in parts of their daily life.[34]

It was especially through its control of fertilizers, which Taiwanese farmers relied on and used intensively, that the government gained leverage over economic matters. Until recently, the distribution (and production) of fertilizers was monopolized by the government. Whether from the perspective of economic management or from the perspective of prolonging egalitarianism in the countryside, the importance of this monopoly cannot be overstated. As W. P. Falcon observed, "It permitted all farmers to obtain *the* key modern input. It provided a source of credit that was an alternative to rural moneylenders. And it reduced price risks to farmers. (Widespread emphasis on risk-reduction is evident in Taiwan's agricultural policies and seems to be one of its important lessons.)"[35] A monopoly on fertilizers made every peasant—without discrimination—beholden to the state. Such a monopoly also allowed the state to determine the crucial equation in economic development: the transfer of surplus from agriculture to industry.

### The Squeeze on Agriculture

The barter of fertilizer for rice was until recently the major mechanism for transferring surplus out of the countryside. Over half the rice collected by the government in the 1950s and 1960s was acquired by this barter arrangement. The barter ratio was highly unfavorable to farmers. The price Taiwanese farmers paid for 100 kilograms of ammonium sulphate in 1964–1965 was higher by almost 40 percent than the price Japanese, Dutch, Belgian, American, or Indian farmers paid.[36]

34. Wang and Apthorpe, *Rice Farming*, p. 10.
35. W. P. Falcon, "Key Issues in Taiwan's Agricultural Development," *Industry of Free China* 41, no. 4 (April 1974): 4.
36. Christensen, *Taiwan's Agricultural Development*, p. 72.

Other mechanisms were also used to transfer real net surplus out of agriculture: land taxes, compulsory rice purchases by the government, loan repayments, and repayment for land resold to tenants under land-to-the-tiller. (See Table 3 for a comparison of the tax burden of farm and nonfarm families.) All such collections were made in kind. All amounted to hidden rice taxes, because the government's purchase prices were considerably lower than implicit market prices. Together, such collections brought more than half of the marketed surplus of rice into government hands after the war.[37] About half of the rice collected by the government was rationed to the military and civil servants, including teachers and their dependents; 20 percent was sold on the free market for revenue and price stabilization purposes; the remaining 30 percent was exported.[38] The government's gains through rice collection were enormous: the hidden rice tax exceeded total income-tax revenue every year before 1963.[39]

It is interesting that in spite of the high degree of commercialization of Taiwanese agriculture, the government placed minimal reliance on market forces to extract a surplus from the countryside. Rice collections were made in kind and rice was *bartered* for fertilizer. Indicative of the government's avoidance of the market mechanism were its attempts (albeit unsuccessful) to barter rice not only for fertilizer but also for cotton cloth, bicycles, soybean cakes, and the like.[40]

In general, the terms of trade have been unfavorable to farmers.[41] Whether for rice or for other crops, the government has manipulated prices through monopsonistic buying arrangements. About 70 percent of the total sugarcane acreage is grown by private smallholders. They contrast with the government-owned Taiwan Sugar Corporation, whose monopoly on sugar refining allows it to set the price for cane. (In 1961–1965, rice and sugarcane together accounted for over 60 percent of the total crop area, excluding acreage devoted to sweet potatoes, a subsistence crop.) The government-owned Tobacco and Wine Monopoly Bureau contracts with individual farmers for the purchase of tobacco leaves.

37. Lee, *Inter-Sectoral Capital Flows*, p. 89.
38. Christensen, *Taiwan's Agricultural Development*, p. 54.
39. Kuo, "Income Distribution."
40. Ibid.
41. Christensen, *Taiwan's Agricultural Development*, pp. 13, 65; Shen, ed., *Agriculture's Place;* Lee, *Inter-Sectoral Capital Flows*, p. 90.

**Table 3.**    *Comparison of Tax Burden of Farm and Nonfarm Families, 1971*

| INCOME BRACKET (NT $) | AVERAGE TAX BURDEN PER FAMILY IN NT $ | |
|---|---|---|
| | *Farm* | *Nonfarm* |
| Under $10,000 | 83.8 | 36.9 |
| 10,000–19,999 | 178.7 | 74.7 |
| 20,000–29,999 | 216.7 | 119.0 |
| 30,000–39,999 | 277.6 | 199.5 |
| 40,000–49,999 | 482.1 | 386.0 |
| 50,000–59,999 | 625.0 | 603.7 |
| 60,000–69,999 | 861.5 | 1,124.6 |

*Source:* Taiwan Provincial Bureau of Accounting and Statistics, 1971.

There are no price support programs for field crops (cotton, wheat, soybeans, corn, and other feed grains) but government import controls affect local prices.[42]

It is proverbial in Taiwan that the goat has been fed as it has been milked. Health, sanitation, and education; caloric intake; overall consumption; and other indices of welfare in the countryside have increased through the years in tandem with surplus extraction. Publication by the government of annual statistics on the percentage of farmers owning such household appliances as electric fans and even color televisions should alert social scientists to the need to discard outmoded conceptions of an impoverished Taiwanese peasantry. Nevertheless, it is well to emphasize the sources responsible for improvements in living standards in recent years. It is highly significant that even in Taiwan, where small-scale agriculture has had such an impressive record, most of the gains in farm household income have come from *non*farm sources. The contribution of off-farm work to farm household income rose from 29 percent in 1962 to 66 percent in 1972.[43] The gap in per capita income between farm and nonfarm families has widened since the

42. W. F. Hsu, "Prices and Pricing of Farm Products," in Shen, ed., *Agriculture's Place.*

43. Statistical tables on Taiwan's economy in Shen, ed., *Agriculture's Place,* pp. 417–35.

1950s. Farm families have entered the factory to close the gap. By 1970, income per capita of farm people was a third lower than that of nonfarm people, and 72 percent of all farms in Taiwan were classified as part-time (see Tables 4, 5, and 6).

### The State and Surplus Extraction

Generally, the private vice of profitability and the public virtue of maximum production are least antagonistic under conditions of competition. But even under competitive conditions, small farms that make minimal use of hired labor may be expected to produce more per acre than farms that routinely use hired labor. This is because labor costs are valued differently by self-employed peasants and by capitalist farmers. Self-employed peas-

**Table 4.**  *Per Capita Income of Farm and Nonfarm Families*

| Year | Farm Family (1) (NT $) | Nonfarm Family (2) (NT $) | (1)/(2) × 100 (%) |
|------|------------------------|---------------------------|--------------------|
| 1954 | 1,661 | 2,216 | 75 |
| 1959 | 2,500 | 2,985 | 84 |
| 1964 | 3,845 | 6,277 | 61 |
| 1966 | 4,509 | 6,464 | 70 |
| 1968 | 4,757 | 8,214 | 58 |
| 1970 | 5,350 | 8,894 | 60 |

*Source:* Teng-Hui Lee and T. H. Shen, "Agriculture as a Base for Socio-Economic Development," in T. H. Shen, ed., *Agriculture's Place in the Strategy of Development: The Taiwan Experience* (Taibei: Joint Commission on Rural Reconstruction, 1974).

**Table 5.**  *Distribution of Full-Time and Part-Time Farms (%)*

| Year | Full-Time | Part-Time |
|------|-----------|-----------|
| 1955 | 40 | 60 |
| 1960 | 48 | 52 |
| 1965 | 32 | 68 |
| 1970 | 28 | 72 |

*Source: Report* of the 1970 Agricultural Census.

**Table 6.**   Net Domestic Product by Industrial Origin, 1952, 1962, 1972 (%) (at current prices)

|                                        | 1952 | 1962 | 1972 |
|----------------------------------------|------|------|------|
| Agriculture                            | 35.7 | 28.8 | 14.9 |
| Manufacturing                          | 10.8 | 16.8 | 31.1 |
| Wholesale and retail trades            | 18.7 | 14.3 | 11.7 |
| Government service                     | 10.8 | 13.2 | 12.8 |
| Other services                         | 5.5  | 5.5  | 6.4  |
| Transport, storage, communications     | 3.8  | 4.5  | 6.0  |
| Electricity, gas, water                | 0.6  | 1.7  | 2.1  |
| Other                                  | 14.1 | 15.2 | 15.0 |

Source: Directorate-General of Budgets, Accounts and Statistics, Executive Yuan, National Income of the Republic of China (various years).

ants may be expected to work long hours to maximize their output per hectare, which is ideal from the viewpoint of the state, whereas the dictates of profitability under capitalist farming may lead to fewer hired working hours of input. Even before the stage is reached at which the implementation of advanced technology requires larger landholdings than the average peasant owns, however, peasant small-farming is typically vexed by two problems. First, it is generally unproductive because it is unscientific. Second (according to an argument popularized by Stalin in defense of collectivization), peasant production frustrates the extraction of a surplus by the state because at a low level of per capita income farmers are said to consume their incremental output rather than market it, that is, they may be more resistant to exploitation. In land-scarce Taiwan the state managed to overcome both problems. The second problem resolved itself as scientific agriculture raised per capita income and forced the peasantry to part with its crop in order to obtain fertilizer and socially necessary items of consumption.

Hla Myint points to an additional problem historically encountered in peasant production. When peasants become full-time producers for the market, they "cease to be self-financing and have to borrow from the chief sources available to them—the moneylenders who charge them high rates of interest. With their ignorance of the rapidly changing market conditions, they tend to get heavily into debt, and where land is alienable, they lose their land in default of loans and get reduced to the status of tenants."[44] Economic history in Taiwan, by contrast, saw the state effectively preserve an agrarian structure of peasant smallholdings by stabilizing prices and by making credit generally available (simulating a perfect credit market by having no market at all). The Jiang Jie-shi government also dispensed with foreign middlemen, who typically exercised monopoly power in rural areas of other economies, by itself buying cash crops cheap from the peasantry and selling them dear.[45]

Thus, a self-exploitative peasantry working long hours to maximize production per hectare and a superexploitative state ticking along effectively to extract the fruits of the peasantry's labor operated hand-in-hand in Taiwan to great advantage until the late 1960s.

The only question that remains is: to *whose* advantage in particular? Taiwan is not a classless entity, and the state acted in the interests of an elite when it squeezed the countryside. Unfortunately, whereas a voluminous amount of statistical information is available about Taiwan, very little class analysis has been published. Clearly, however, the historical roots of the Guomindang's *étatisme*, and its class affiliations, are traceable not only to Japanese colonialism but also to events on the mainland. We may hypothesize that the system of bureaucratic capitalism of late imperial China, with its total interpenetration of public and private interests, was transplanted into Taiwan along with the Mainlanders. Under bureaucratic capitalism, public office (or office in public corporations) provided a source of private gain, and private enterprise was profitable only in close alliance with the state.[46] Initially, the Jiang Jie-shi regime in Taiwan took a direct role in realizing surplus value for the dominant Mainlander bureaucratic capitalist class. Later, the Nationalist government appropriated the surplus value produced by the peasantry and proletariat for the benefit of the increasingly dominant industrial capitalist class (by now composed of Mainlanders as well as Taiwanese and foreign firms). While historical conditions were unpropitious for economic development under bureaucratic

44. Hla Myint, *The Economics of the Developing Countries* (New York: Praeger, 1964).
45. T. H. Shen, "A New Agricultural Policy," in Shen, ed., *Agriculture's Place.*
46. Etienne Balazs, *Chinese Civilization and Bureaucracy* (New Haven: Yale University Press, 1972).

capitalism in China, they were favorable in Taiwan. The 1953 land reform and subsequent agricultural development breathed new life into the Guomindang apparatus, and the bureaucratic capitalism of the Guomindang regime sustained the life of reform and small-scale farming.

In summary, agriculture in Taiwan gave industrial capital a labor force, a surplus, and foreign exchange. Even during the immediate postwar years of economic chaos and a world-record rate of population growth, Taiwan managed to produce a food supply sufficient to meet minimum domestic consumption requirements as well as a residual for export.[47] Good rice harvests have been a major factor in price (and real wage) stability. The foreign exchange saved as a result of high productivity in agriculture has been equally important. Even after the export of laber-intensive manufactures got underway, Taiwan ran a trade deficit. The trade balance remained negative until 1969. It became negative again in 1974, 1975, and 1977.[48] This is a consequence of the fact that per capita income has been growing rapidly and so, too, have imports. Much exporting also relies on imported inputs. Had Taiwan's agriculture not been so productive, the strain on the balance of payments would have been greater. Agriculture also managed to provide an important source of demand for Taiwan's industrial output, particularly chemicals and tools, and a mass market for consumption goods. The agrarian structure provided a degree of political stability sufficient to draw the most timid of foreign firms to the island. Agriculture has been sufficiently productive to set the floor on industrial wages that has lately taken effect. Factory women who returned home to the farm during the depression of 1974–1975 subsequently refused to return to wage employment at the prevailing rates.[49] A labor shortage symbolizes Taiwan's introduction to the problems of capitalist development rather than underdevelopment, and it is to industrialization that we must now turn.

## Industrialization

Taiwan's record in the industrial arena has often been described. Consequently, we are less concerned with detailing it than

47. Hsieh and Lee, "Agricultural Development," p. 90.
48. Economic Planning Council, *Taiwan Statistical Data Book* (1976), table 10-4.
49. *Free China Review* (Taibei) (March 1976).

with dispelling four myths that have surrounded it. The mythology amounts to the following: first, that the seed of industrialization bore fruit in Taiwan because the environment that succored it was free of state interference; second, that Taiwan, unlike the Latin American countries, resisted the temptations of infant industry protection and a regime of import-substitution industrialization; third, that industrialization in Taiwan remains superficial insofar as production is limited to little more than light manufactures; and, fourth, that ownership of the economy rests for all practical purposes in foreign hands.

An OECD study published in 1970, comparing industrialization in Brazil, Mexico, Argentina, India, Pakistan, the Philippines, and Taiwan, made a start toward correcting some of these misconceptions.[50] The study showed that a regime of import substitution preceded the export of labor-intensive manufactures in Taiwan. Nor was infant-industry protection a trivial episode in Taiwan's economic history. A policy of inward-oriented growth was introduced in 1949 partly by default—Taiwan's traditional agricultural exports no longer found protected or preferential markets in Japan and China—and partly by design—it was politically expedient to aid the class of small-scale capitalists who had acquired a portion of the old Japanese facilities. Small enterprises were in serious trouble by 1949 as a result of the loss of the mainland market and the reappearance of competitive Japanese goods.[51] Import, foreign-exchange, and licensing controls were introduced by the government to salvage small establishments from extinction and to ease the critical balance-of-payments situation. The scope and height of such controls in the 1950s rivaled similar measures designed to protect infant industries in the OECD's sample of Third World countries well known for protectionism.[52]

Protectionism in Taiwan soon outlived its usefulness. While it

---

50. I. Little, T. Scitovsky, and M. Scott, *Industry and Trade in Some Developing Countries* (London: Oxford University Press, 1960).

51. Ching-Yuan Lin, *Industrialization in Taiwan, 1946–1972: Trade and Import Substitution Policies for Developing Countries* (New York: Praeger, 1973), p. 43.

52. Taiwan's government, like India's, also resorted to industrial licensing not only to guide the development of private industries but also to shield some from "excessive" competition. A set of administrative controls for certain consumer durables introduced in the 1960s also took the form of progressive local content requirements, in an effort to push the manufacture of these lines beyond the stage of mere assembly. See Lin, *Industrialization;* Mo-Huan Hsing, *Taiwan and the Philippines: Industry and Trade Relations* (London: Oxford University Press, 1971).

conferred high profits on some, it also conferred inflation, monopoly, excess capacity, a reliance on American donations of hard currency, and corruption on all. It was only after manufacturing had made a fair start, however, that the Taiwanese government curtailed its import controls and charted a new course. The economy was propelled in the direction of export-led growth, and instead of protecting private capital from foreign competition the state began protecting exporters from competition with each other. Monetary and fiscal policies were redesigned and inflation was brought under control. These changes have earned the title *liberalization* and have given Taiwan its reputation for successful development with the "right" formulas.[53]

Even under export-led growth, however, production and distribution have been carried out in the shadow of the state. For the Guomindang government has resorted to the free-trade nemesis of cartels wherever expedient. It has also offered both local and foreign exporters an impressive battery of incentives. While economists have viewed a regime of export-led growth as being more in keeping with the wisdom of neoclassical theory, the Taiwanese government has not been guided by any theoretical orthodoxy to turn a profit. A civil servant writes:

> Unorganized production and export often lead to excessive production and cut-throat competition in foreign markets, which inevitably cause a sharp decline in price, deterioration in quality, and finally loss of the export market. To combat these shortcomings, the government has encouraged unified and joint marketing of exports in foreign markets through limitation of production by means of export quotas, improvement of quality, and unified quotation of export prices.[54]

53. The OECD's study of industrialization in seven developing countries compared rates of effective protection and found them to be lowest in Mexico and next lowest in Taiwan (the effective rate of protection measures the percentage by which import restrictions enable the price of the value added in production to exceed what it would be in their absence). The study, however, cautions that while "the average levels of protection for all manufacturing industry . . . in Taiwan were moderate . . . these moderate levels were due to zero or negative protection for exporting, while protection given to production for sale on the home market was much higher than in Mexico." Moreover, rates of effective protection in Taiwan were for the year 1966, after import controls had been liberalized: Little, Scitovsky, and Scott, *Industry and Trade*.

54. H. D. Fong, "Taiwan's Industry, with Special Reference to Policies and Control," *Journal of Hanyang University* 2 (1968).

Subsidy of exports by means of domestic sales, moreover, has not been confined to peripheral products. Cartels, in various guises, have covered many of Taiwan's exports: textiles, canned mushrooms and asparagus, rubber, steel, paper products, and the like. The government has been particularly energetic in trying to get the marketing of all exports into Taiwanese hands because bureaucrats and businessmen alike are sensitive to the inroads into overseas marketing made by large Japanese trading companies.

Taiwan's foreign trade is also characterized by a fair degree of concentration. Many firms participate in the export trade. In 1966, 3,935 firms exported a total of U.S. $569 million worth of industrial and agricultural goods. But over 94 percent of this value was accounted for by fewer than 30 percent of such firms. Among the 629 private industrial enterprises (with annual exports of over $50,000 each) exporting a total of $300 million worth of industrial products in 1966, 46 percent was contributed by only 37 firms.[55]

Rates of growth of GDP, manufacturing output, and both private consumption expenditure and total gross investment accelerated dramatically *after* liberalization was introduced and the exporting of manufactures commenced on a massive scale. These relationships have been seen as a vindication of free-trade theory, but three points need to be stressed in this connection. First, as was just indicated, liberalization should in no way be interpreted as a restoration in Taiwan of a pure market-economy; government management of capital accumulation has continued. Second, growth rates were quite high before massive exporting, and the cumulative effects of long-term developments in agriculture and import substitution under heavy protection must not be minimized. To credit fast growth exclusively to a policy of liberalization is ahistorical. The extent to which full employment is attributable to exporting should also not be exaggerated. Tyler estimated that in 1969 only 16.7 percent of the labor force in Taiwan was employed directly or indirectly in manufacturing for export.[56] Third, Taiwan's export boom and dramatic growth rates coincided with an extraordinarily favorable international situation. Worldwide trade flows were growing at an unprecedented rate and credit

55. Fong, "Taiwan's Industry."
56. W. G. Tyler, "Employment Generation and the Promotion of Manufactured Exports in Less Developed Countries: Some Suggestive Evidence," in Herbert Giersch, ed., *The International Division of Labour: Problems and Perspectives* (Tübingen: J. C. B. Mohr, 1974).

availability in the Eurodollar market was exceptionally easy in the late 1960s and early 1970s. The Vietnam war was also very good business for Taiwan. Growth rates might well have been lower (as they subsequently were) had the international situation not been so propitious. Indeed, it may be unrealistic to hold Taiwan up as a model for other Third World countries to aspire to, if only because the exceptional international boom that provided Taiwan with a critical advantage cannot be counted on to reoccur.

### State Enterprise

To appreciate the extent of bureaucratic capitalism in Taiwan, we must focus our attention on ownership of the means of production as well as on policies that affect capital accumulation.

In 1952, as much as 56 percent of total industrial production (value added at 1966 prices) and 56 percent of manufacturing output were accounted for by public corporations.[57] Partly under the persuasion of USAID, majority or 100 percent equity in four public corporations (one highly profitable, two others distinctly less so) was transferred to landlords in 1954 as partial compensation for confiscations carried out under the 1953 land reform. Recently there has been mounting pressure for denationalization from local capital, who want to share in the action of lucrative state enterprises. But enthusiasm for denationalization wanes as profitability decreases, especially in the case of unprofitable state enterprises with externalities that subsidize the private sector. Government policy toward public enterprise mirrors these divergent demands. Thus, on the one hand, in some new industries (such as plate glass) the government, as in Japan, has built new factories which, once they are in the black, are transferred to private owners.[58] On the other hand, in industries deemed essential for industrialization but in which private capital has been reluctant to invest, the government has stepped in. Plans to nationalize the China Shipbuilding Company and a huge integrated steel complex were recently announced. Both undertakings had had private capital participation before takeover, but fear that "profitability would be slow"

57. Economic Planning Council, *Taiwan Statistical Data Book*. table 5–6. For an early account of state enterprise, see U.S. Department of Commerce, Bureau of Foreign Commerce, *Investment in Taiwan (Formosa)* (1959). The distribution of loans and discounts of all banks, by borrower, also suggests the importance of public enterprise, particularly in the early period: ibid., table 7–7b.

58. Hsing, *Taiwan*, p. 201.

prompted divestiture by the private partners (both foreign and local).[59]

The government has been slow to divest itself of its holdings for
additional reasons. In the postwar years, as was noted above, public
enterprise served to consolidate the power of the Mainlander bureaucracy. In recent years, public enterprise has allowed the
Guomindang to buttress its own power vis-à-vis foreign capital.
One of the fundamental consequences of public enterprise has
been the control of key sectors in the economy by the state rather
than by the multinationals. This is not to belittle the power of the
multinationals, nor to suggest the absence of an organic solidarity
between the productive activities of the state and foreign investors.
In many sectors, particularly petroleum, they have allied to form a
nucleus of expansion. But the state has held its own in several crucial respects. The government did not abandon its traditionally
conservative attitude toward foreign investment until the export
boom of the late 1960s had gotten underway. Only then did foreign firms begin arriving in Taiwan in significant numbers. By
1971, overseas Chinese and other foreign investments were substantial, together amounting to roughly one-seventh of the total
registered capital (about the same proportion as in Brazil).[60] Foreign investments, however, are concentrated in electronics, chemicals, and textiles destined for export. The Jiang Jie-shi government
cannot be said to have delivered Taiwan into foreign hands, either
by letting merchant capital dominate foreign trade or by letting
monopoly capital dominate manufacturing. Key manufacturing
sectors remain wholly or partly under state control. Automobile
production, which in other Third World countries is the bastion of
foreign domination, in Taiwan is controlled by a partnership of
Japanese capital and a Mainlander firm which has long enjoyed the
support of the Guomindang machine. Still other sectors in Taiwan,
such as food processing, are shielded from foreign influence either
by the relatively small size of the Taiwanese market or by the en-
durance of indigenous tastes for traditional goods. What the Jiang
Jie-shi regime did allow foreign (and local) capital to do was to
exploit Taiwanese labor. What it provided for capital were favor-

59. *Free China Weekly* (Taibei)(16 June 1977).

60. *Industrial and Commercial Census of Taiwan and Fukien.* vol. 3: *Manufacturing
(Taiwan Area)* (1971), table 16; E. L. Bacha, "Issues and Evidence on Recent Brazilian Economic Growth," *World Development* 5, no. 1–2 (January–February 1977):
47–67.

able investment terms and political stability (underwritten by U.S. and Japanese aid).

By the early 1970s, the share of the public sector in manufacturing production had fallen to less than 20 percent. Nevertheless, the government remains dominant in such fields as heavy machinery, steel, aluminum, shipbuilding, petroleum, synthetics, fertilizers, and, last but not least, banking. Almost all banks in Taiwan are wholly or partially owned by the state (until 1969, foreign banks were not allowed to establish operations). The lending activities of all financial institutions have been under strict state supervision.[61] If the government in Taiwan does not quite "control the commanding heights," it goes a long way toward doing so.

As far as capital formation is concerned, the public sector is still very important. The state accounted for as much as 40 percent of gross domestic investment in 1972 (down from a high of 60 percent in 1958).[62]

In an environment made more rational and remunerative by the state, manufacturing in Taiwan, both public and private, has grown in breadth (the percentage of manufacturing in GDP) and in depth (the percentage of "sophisticated" products and processes in the total manufacturing output). Whereas in 1952 agriculture accounted for 35 percent of net domestic product and industry for only a tenth, agriculture now accounts for only 15 percent and industry for almost 40 percent (see Table 7). By 1973, 23 percent of all workers aged 15 and over were engaged in the industrial sector.[63] Since the early 1970s there has been a decline in the *absolute* number of workers in the agricultural labor force. In historical perspective, this is highly significant. In the United States, absolute declines in the farm population did not begin until the 1930s.[64]

Nor has manufacturing been confined to "wigs and wallets," as myth would have it. In 1974, for example, Taiwan ranked twenty-eighth among world producers of machine tools. The world's third largest ship, a 445,000-ton oil tanker, is nearing completion in the Gaoxiong yards.[65] In the course of five indicative plan periods, im-

61. Hsing, *Taiwan*, p. 224.
62. Economic Planning Council, *Taiwan Statistical Data Book* (1974), table 3–8b; *Wall Street Journal*, 24 March 1977.
63. Economic Planning Council, *Taiwan Statistical Data Book* (1974).
64. S. Lebergott, "Labor Force and Employment, 1802–1960," *Output, Employment and Productivity in the United States after 1800*, vol. 30 of Studies in Income and Wealth (New York: National Bureau of Economic Research, 1960).
65. *Free China Weekly* (Taibei) (9 January 1977).

**Table 7.** *Contribution of Production Increase, by Sector, to Total Increase in Manufacturing in Four-Year Plans, 1953–1968*

|  | FOUR-YEAR PLAN | | | |
|  | *1st* *(1953–1956)* | *2d* *(1957–1960)* | *3d* *(1961–1964)* | *4th* *(1965–1968)* |
|---|---|---|---|---|
| Nondurable consumer goods | 66% | 56% | 66% | 24% |
| Intermediate goods | 25 | 30 | 26 | 41 |
| Capital goods and durable consumer goods | 9 | 14 | 8 | 35 |
| Total manufacturing | 100% | 100% | 100% | 100% |

*Source:* Teng-Hui Lee, *Inter-Sectoral Capital Flows in the Development of Taiwan: 1895–1960* (Ithaca, N.Y.: Cornell University Press, 1971).

portant structural changes have occurred within manufacturing. Along with these changes in product mix have come changes in input mix: capital-intensive production techniques, and especially skill-intensive production techniques, have grown in importance. Textiles and food processing were the leading sectors during the first two plan periods (1953–1956 and 1957–1960).[66] During the second plan period, however, the relative contribution of nondurable consumer goods, particularly processed foods, declined, while intermediate goods (cement and paper) expanded. Chemicals (fertilizers, soda ash, plastics, pharmaceuticals) assumed major importance during the third plan period (1961–1964). Capital and durable goods (electrical and nonelectrical machinery such as radios and sewing machines and transport equipment such as bicycles and ships) as well as petroleum products grew enormously during the fourth and fifth plan periods (1965–1968 and 1969–1973) and continue to expand. Although textiles and clothing remain important in total output, food processing has declined sharply.

Thus, there is no denying the ever-increasing sophistication of production within the manufacturing sector at the aggregate level.

66. The analysis of industrialization that follows is based on T. H. Lee, *Industrial and Commercial Census* (1974).

Nevertheless, it should be emphasized that serious structural weaknesses do persist at the level of the firm. The existence of a large number of very small firms which do not appear to be upgrading their technology is the Achilles' heel of industrialization in Taiwan. The problem takes the form of the small firm's failure to merge or grow amid the scarcities created by fast industrialization economy-wide, but failure also altogether to disappear, quickly and obligingly. The growth in breadth and depth of manufacturing in the aggregate must be qualified (as it must be to a lesser degree in many advanced capitalist countries) in the light of the persistence of "industrial dualism."

## The Taiwan Case and Dependency Theory

Dependency theorists have produced a voluminous literature describing the exploitation and consequent underdevelopment of the Third World by the advanced capitalist countries. Divergent nuances and refinements have been articulated by different members of this school (such as Paul Baran, Andre Gunder Frank, Samir Amin, and Immanuel Wallerstein), but one central theme unifies them all: that underdevelopment exists because the situation of the Third World (the periphery) in capitalism on a world scale has left it dependent on the advanced capitalist countries (the core).[67]

The first target of attack of dependency theorists was the conventional explanations for chronic poverty provided by neoclassical economists. Such explanations featured the misguided interventionist policies of Third World Nationalist governments which impeded the market from doing its job, along with primitive social structures which awaited "modernization." Clearly, this ignored important lessons in economic history and the realities of Third World economies, and dependency theorists took the very welcome step of introducing imperialism into the growth equation.

Nevertheless, when foreign trade and investment, two concrete expressions of imperialism, are seen as the primary categories by which exploitation is perpetrated and by which dependency and underdevelopment are perpetuated, much is left unexplained. For

67. For a representative collection of writings of dependency theorists, see Charles K. Wilber, ed., *The Political Economy of Development and Underdevelopment* (New York: Random House, 1973).

if, in fact, participation in foreign trade and the presence of foreign investment are useful categories for understanding the failure of Third World countries to develop, then a case like Taiwan, where development has succeeded, should be explicable by the absence of foreign trade and investment. But clearly this is incorrect. Taiwan's political economy is a tableau of the petty and profound maneuvers of international diplomacy. Taiwan is a popular place for the investment of foreign capital. Of all Third World countries, Taiwan's economy is perhaps the most open to foreign trade.[68] It is also true that development and unequal exchange have occurred simultaneously in Taiwan, if unequal exchange is operationalized as adverse movements in the terms of trade. In only three years between 1953 and 1973 did the net terms of trade turn in Taiwan's favor.[69] The case of Taiwan, therefore, argues against dependency theorists' use of the primary categories of foreign trade and investment as explanations for persistent poverty.

Whereas dependency theorists see all events in the periphery as the outcome of external forces—trade and foreign investment determine what is produced, by what methods, how income is distributed, and the like—the Taiwanese experience suggests just the reverse. First and foremost, class and productive relations within the periphery are decisive in how foreign trade and investment affect development. Such relations mediate the impact of foreign penetration, although they invariably bear its imprint. Thus, the roots of underdevelopment can be seen to lie not so much in surplus extraction through unequal exchange and the repatriation of profits as in local class relationships. These relationships will ultimately decide the effects of the pressures unleashed by imperialism.

## A Special Case

The economic history and geopolitics of Taiwan have been so affected by a confluence of unusual circumstances that they mark this island economy as a special case. It would be idle, therefore, to hold Taiwan up as an example of capitalist development for other poor countries to follow.

What sharply distinguishes Taiwan from other Third World economies are the scientific advances that agriculture made under

68. Lin, *Industrialization*, p. 6.
69. Economic Planning Council, *Taiwan Statistical Data Book.* (1974), table 10–2.

Japanese imperialism and the subsequent success of the 1953 land reform. We have argued that this reform helped mediate the effects of exporting labor-intensive manufactures to advantage. Yet there is much to suggest that land reforms in other Third World countries are unlikely to materialize except under revolutionary conditions. Taiwan's land reform was engineered exogenously, by the Guomindang, in alliance with the Americans. The Taiwanese landed aristocracy could be expropriated because the Americans and Mainlanders were under no obligation to it. This most unusual situation was unlikely to be repeated.

Although a redistribution of land to the peasants in Taiwan undoubtedly strengthened the Guomindang, its authority was also guaranteed by U.S. foreign aid, in military and other forms. There is dispute as to how economically effective U.S. aid to Taiwan in fact was, in part because so much of it went for the most unproductive activity of all—militarism, and because another large fraction went for infrastructure projects based on faulty investment criteria and evaluation methods (agriculture was relatively ignored by U.S. aid.)[70] What is indisputable is the increase in consumption which American relief made possible in the dismal years after World War II. Although the economic situation in Taiwan today is probably good enough to allow the Guomindang to stay in power with only tacit U.S. support and without the Japanese loans which have in fact partly replaced American donations, U.S. aid kept the regime in power in its earliest years.[71] A champion of American policy reminds us: "U.S. economic assistance helped to preserve the cohesion of the Mainlander minority and to consolidate its political power. Had no external assistance come to douse the fires of inflation and improve the material conditions of the Taiwanese during the early 1950s, it is doubtful whether the ROC would have endured in its present form."[72]

### A Crisis of Labor

We have characterized Taiwan as an economy standing at the threshold of development partly because, beginning in the

---

70. K. Griffin, "An Assessment of Development in Taiwan," *World Development* 1, no. 6 (June 1973): 31–42.

71. J. Halliday and G. McCormack, *Japanese Imperialism Today: Coprosperity in Greater East Asia* (London: Penguin, 1973).

72. N. Jacoby, *U.S. Aid to Taiwan* (New York: Praeger, 1966), p. 164.

early 1970s, full employment became a reality. A small amount of unemployment persists and cyclical unemployment remains very much a fact of life. But the general situation in the labor market and the rapid rise in wages in the last few years indicate that the era of an "unlimited" labor supply is at an end.

A high secular level of employment promises to create as many new problems for Taiwan as it solves old ones. Cheap labor can no longer provide the main ingredient for growth. Consequently, small-scale industry and agriculture, which use labor intensively, face serious crises in the coming years.

In the period 1968–1973, the growth rate of agricultural output slowed considerably. (A series of bumper harvest after 1973 make it difficult to assess the most recent period.) In part, the slowdown reflected the fact that earlier growth had drawn heavily on agronomic research developed in the 1920s and 1930s. No breakthrough of such major proportions has occurred since. More important, slower growth reflected the fact that the number of rural workers declined absolutely, beginning in the early 1970s, and the real wages of agricultural labor rose. Labor shortages have threatened the multiple cropping system, and, indeed, the very logic of agrarian organization. An ever decreasing area of winter crops and the over 20,000 hectares of farmland lying idle in the fertile Western Plain evince the seriousness of the crisis.[73]

To cope with the crisis, the government has adopted a series of new agricultural policies. Mechanization is to be encouraged by means of subsidizing credit for the purchase of farm machinery (principally low-horsepower tillers, power sprayers, and grain dryers). But small farms, the leading actor in Taiwan's golden age of agriculture, now present an obstacle to mechanization. Even before the crisis, the government had attempted to facilitate selective mechanization without disturbing the agrarian structure. It urged voluntary consolidation of farms and the growth of machine pools. Neither policy was especially successful in a capitalist milieu. The only real option remaining is mechanization *with* the disturbance of the agrarian structure. In fact, the government's newest agricultural policy, however low in profile, amounts to creating an ever-expanding subsector of large-scale, capital-intensive, commercial farms. The smallholders who manage to survive will be forced either to farm jointly or to farm part-time (as many already do).

73. Hung-Yu Hu, "Agricultural Policy and Labor Absorption in Taiwan," *Industry of Free China* 45, no. 4 (April 1976): 20–30.

The problem in industry parallels that in agriculture. If manufacturing output continues to grow at anywhere near the rate it has grown in the past decade, the labor situation for small firms will deteriorate still further. In general, small-scale industry in underdeveloped countries is the victim of competitive imports or foreign investment. In Taiwan, at its current stage of development, the death process is more indirect. Big business threatens small local capital in Taiwan not by supplying competitive goods but by demanding labor at competitive prices. The future of this class of petty producers is pointed in the direction of paid employment. The transition from self-employment to wage labor is likely to be as socially explosive in manufacturing as in agriculture.

For most Third World countries, the relationship between the equality of income distribution and the growth process has been found to be U-shaped: income distribution worsens in the early phase of development and improves only much later on.[74] Taiwan has attracted attention because its pattern has been different: household income distribution since the early 1960s appears to have improved in association with development. The demise of the small-scale farmer and small-scale manufacturer, however, may signify a reversal of this pattern. As concentration and centralization of capital increase, that is, as capitalism expands, class differences may be expected to intensify and income distribution to worsen. Taiwan may prove to be as interesting a case for study in the future as it has been in the past.

74. H. Chenery, M. Ahuwalia, C. L. G. Bell, J. Duloy, and R. Jolly, *Redistribution with Growth* (London: Oxford University Press, 1974).

# 5

# State and Alliances in Argentina, 1956–1976

## Guillermo O'Donnell

Certain features of Argentina's incorporation into the world capitalist system gave rise to the country's peculiarity in comparison with the rest of Latin America.[1] These differences continue to bear on certain characteristics of Argentine capitalism and class structure and also—centrally for our subject—on the power resources and on the political alliances available to the popular sectors. The following are the most crucial features for our analysis.

First, as in the rest of Latin America, the pact and characteristics of Argentine capitalist expansion were fundamentally determined by the incorporation of some of its regions as exporters of primary products. This allows us to make an initial distinction between those vast regions of Latin America with no direct linkage to the world market (such as the Andean *haciendas*) and those which were

Reprinted by permission of Frank Cass and Co. Ltd. from *Journal of Development Studies,* volume 15, Guillermo O'Donnell, "States and Alliances in Argentina, 1956–1976," pp. 3–33. © 1978, Frank Cass and Co. Ltd. The first version of this paper was prepared for the Conference on the State and Economic Development in Latin America, Cambridge University, 12–16 December 1973. It has been translated by Guillermo Makin and David Lehmann.

1. And to that of Uruguay, to which I shall briefly return.

directly linked to such a market as exporters of primary products.[2] Among these the *estancia* of the Argentine pampas and Uruguay differed substantially from the enclaves and plantations which were the principal form of incorporation elsewhere in the continent. The main differences were: (1) the *estancia* was less labor-intensive than the plantation and the *hacienda;* (2) it was less capital-intensive than the plantation and the enclave; (3) largely because of the latter, the control of land, the principal productive resource, was left, in the Argentine pampas and in Uruguay, in the hands of an early domestic agrarian bourgeoisie, while the enclave and the plantation were usually directly owned by international capital, and the *hacienda* was left in the hands of an oligarchy with hardly any capitalist traits; (4) this pattern, combined with a high differential rent, endowed the pampean and the Uruguayan bourgeoisie with an important capital accumulation base of their own; and (5) this bourgeoisie did not escape dependence on European capital via the transport, finance, and international marketing of its products, but its base of capital accumulation did foment a significantly wealthier and more diversified urban, commercial, and incipient industrial sector than was to be found in those economies that revolved around the *hacienda,* the enclave, and the plantation. These characteristics are well known,[3] but others, to which less attention has been given, stem from them.

The second feature is that the cereal, wool, and, later, also beef-exporting economy covered a relatively larger portion of the national territory than the exporting sectors of other countries. Above all, in Argentina the areas not directly incorporated in the world market carried much less economic and demographic weight than in the rest of Latin America. Furthermore, in Argen-

2. When I speak of direct incorporation or linkage I refer to the role some regions played as part of the world capitalist system. This of course does not imply that regions not linked to the world capitalist system were not importers of products from the center, nor that they were not subject to the effects of world capitalist expansion, often through directly incorporated regions.

3. Above all since Fernando H. Cardoso's and Enzo Faletto's book *Dependencia y desarrollo en América Latina* (Mexico City: Siglo Veintiuno Editores, 1971), where we find the characterization of the types of exporting economy I have mentioned. An important recent contribution is that of Albert Hirschman, who adapts elements of staple theory to his concept of linkages, widened to include not strictly economic relationships, and from there explores the consequences of the type of export product through which incorporation into the international market took place; unfortunately, this author does not deal with pampean and Uruguayan products. See Albert Hirschman, "A Generalized Linkage Approach to Development, with Special Reference to Staples," Princeton: Institute for Advanced Study, 1976 (typescript).

tina and Uruguay the peasantry subject to precapitalist relations of production was a small proportion compared with much of the continent. The insertion of a much larger proportion of the population into the export economy meant that, from the end of the nineteenth century, Argentina exhibited a significantly greater homogeneity than the rest of Latin America,[4] a homogeneity which, in spite of later mishaps, continues to be noticeable.[5]

Third, in addition to the sizable base of local accumulation due to direct control of land, the high productivity of land in international terms until approximately 1930[6] and the low labor requirements of extensive farming contributed decisively to the greater diversification and prosperity of the pampa region and its urban centers—compared to the regions dominated by the enclave, the plantations, and the *hacienda*. Suffice it to say that wages in the pampa region and the Argentine urban centers, until approximately World War II, were higher than in many European countries,[7] while those of the rest of Latin America—if and when wage

4. With the exception of Uruguay, a case of even greater intranational homogeneity, since practically all its territory and its population were incorporated in the world market under conditions similar to those of the Argentine pampean region. Another exception, though partial and more complicated, is that of Chile; here, in the last third of the nineteenth century, the highly homogeneous agrarian economy of the central valley, partly oriented toward the export of foodstuffs, underwent (in contrast with Argentina and Uruguay) a decline, and the mining enclaves of the north emerged. But, in contrast with other cases, those enclaves were inserted in a national market and a national state already constituted around the central agrarian region. See Marcelo Cacarozzi, *The State and the Industrial Bourgeoisie in Chile* (forthcoming). Uruguay's greater intranational homogeneity allowed the earlier and fuller development of a liberal and welfare state. But for this very reason the problems concealed by the initial bonanza exploded earlier than in Argentina. Besides, the smaller absolute size of the Uruguayan internal market was decisive in interrupting its industrialization much earlier and thus, in recent decades, the relative weight of its working class has been significantly less than in Argentina.

5. For data and references on Argentina's intranational homogeneity compared to that of most of Latin America, see Guillermo O'Donnell, *Modernization and Bureaucratic Authoritarianism* (Berkeley and Los Angeles: University of California, 1972), chapter 1. For an analysis of the differences in the distribution of income and its political correlates in Latin America, see Jorge Graciarena, "Estructura del poder y distribución del ingreso en América Latina," *Revista Latinoamericana de Ciencia Política* 2, no. 2 (August 1971).

6. Since then the increasingly capital-intensive modalities of the production of wool, cereals, and beef in the world market implied that agrarian activity in Uruguay and Argentina rapidly fell behind that of other exporters: Carlos Díaz Alejandro, *Essays on the Economic History of the Argentine Republic* (New Haven: Yale University Press, 1970).

7. Lucio Geller, "El crecimiento industrial argentino hasta 1914 y la teoría del bien primario exportador," in Marcos Giménez Zapiola, ed., *El regimen oligárquico:*

relationships were established—were much lower. Thus, not only was international homogeneity higher, but also the region of Argentina that was directly incorporated into the world economy was more diversified and generated a significantly higher income for its popular sector than in the other Latin American countries.

This, in turn, has other consequences. Around the beginning of the twentieth century, the existence of a fully capitalist and relatively wealthy urban (and, largely, also pampean) consumer market induced an industrialization which received further stimulus from the import restrictions resulting from World War I. Argentine industrialization did not begin with the world crisis of 1930; it began earlier, and it proceeded faster than in the rest of Latin America.[8] Also, an early working class therefore also emerged, which developed organizational patterns autonomous both of the state and of the incipient industrial bourgeoisie, although it entered the political arena only later.[9] The strong demand for labor, in the absence of a large peasantry providing cheap labor, could only favor such an outcome. Because of the specific characteristics of Argentina's inclusion in the world capitalist system, its economic growth was powered fundamentally by its civil society and its relationships with the international market. The dynamizing impulse did not depend on the state, as generally occurred—with many difficulties—in the other Latin American economies. This point must be developed in greater detail.

In the period between roughly 1870 and 1930,[10] the Argentine state had certain features in common with the liberal states of the great world centers: although it was a more ostensibly fraudulent

---

materiales para el estudio de la realidad argentina hasta 1930 (Buenos Aires: Amorrortu, 1975).

8. The exception to this generalization is Brazil's São Paulo industrialization, based on the dynamizing stimulus of the coffee economy, which does not correspond to any of the generic types I have employed (see Hirschman, "Generalized Linkage Approach"). But its original use of slave labor, its labor-intensive character compared with the pampa economy, and—most important for our argument—its location in a national context in which the slave system predominated contributed to the low degree of autonomous organization and political weight of the Brazilian working class compared with Argentina's.

9. This is related to the Spanish and Italian immigration, which nourished that class, and the anarchistic ideology that prevailed in it until approximately 1920. The main source on this point continues to be Gino Germani, especially Política y sociedad en una época de transición (Buenos Aires: Paidos, 1962).

10. That is, between the strongly exogenous impulse of the incorporation of the pampa region in the international market and the world crisis that altered the main basis of the system.

political democracy, the level of electoral participation was not lower,[11] and the state machine did not go beyond providing crucial, though limited, general conditions for the functioning of the economy.[12] But this state was the creation of the pampa bourgeoisie and its financial and commercial appendages, by means of a process which also entailed the making of that bourgeoisie, and of the system it dominated, in a marginal yet integral corner of the world capitalist market. To clarify this statement we must resort to some comparisons.

The pampa bourgeoisie and its urban branches directly constituted a national state, not the regional state which was the main political power base of the dominant classes in so many Latin American countries.[13] The Argentine national state also eliminated—earlier, and with greater ease and completeness—the autonomy of the regions not directly linked to the world market, largely because those regions carried much less weight in the country as a whole than was true in most other Latin American countries.[14] This implied that the state was an expression of changing power-relationships between those regions directly incorporated in the world market and others marginal to it to a much smaller extent than in the rest of Latin America.

Thus the pampa bourgeoisie and its urban tentacles held both a central economic position and, through the national state, a central

11. Cf. Atilio Borón, "El estudio de la movilización electoral en América Latina: movilización electoral en Argentina y Chile," *Desarrollo Económico* 2, no. 48 (July–September 1972).

12. Above all, the transport and warehouse network necessary for shipping the pampas' production, international capital's capture of which was generously subsidized by the state. If the small technology requirements of direct exploitation of the pampean region permitted domestic control of the land, the much greater requirements of such a network (and, later, of the meat-packing industry) determined a high and early inflow of international capital.

13. I am not concerned here with the details of the respective historical processes. In particular the imposition of nationalization on Buenos Aires by a coalition of provinces of the interior against the opposition of a sizable part of the pampa interests was no obstacle, once the vigorous exogenous impulses of the European demand for foodstuffs were felt, to the processes discussed in the text.

14. Even in Brazil, characterized by relatively early industrialization and by the great weight of the state bureaucratic apparatus inherited from the imperial period, the subordination of the dominant classes of the northeast and the elimination of the barriers interposed by the regional states to the effective functioning of a national market were only completed after 1930: Centro Brasileiro de Analise e Planejamento, *Estado y sociedad en el Brasil: la planificación regional en la época de SUDENE* (São Paulo: CEBRAP, 1976). It should be borne in mind that I am excluding Chile and Uruguay from these generalizations.

political position as an internally dominant class burdened by other regions. Furthermore, the shifts in the relative importance of export products took place within the pampean zone and among its bourgeoisie,[15] and not, as in most other cases, by means of the incorporation of new products from new regions leading to shifting alliances with existing locally dominant classes and established segments of international capital.

Nevertheless, the pampa bourgeoisie and the national state became the principal channels of internationalization of both society and economy, because of the nature of their inclusion in the world market. The liberal characteristics of the Argentine state and the strong relative weight of its civil society can only be understood as consequences of the position of the state at the point of intersection of the pampa bourgeoisie with international capital—which had deeply penetrated the economy through its control of the financing, transportation, and external marketing of pampa production. The Andean oligarchy or that of Brazil's northeast could directly and diaphanously control "their" regional state apparatus, while international capital, based on enclaves and plantations, controlled a state which was less an emanation from than a graft imposed on a society that lacked a local bourgeoisie endowed with its own accumulation base. Instead, in Argentina, the existence of such a bourgeoisie arising from the very process of incorporation into the international market created a situation in which the regional states had little weight; furthermore, the national state was one of the crucial channels of the rapid and early internationalization, which, due to the weight of the pampa economy, covered much more of the country than in other Latin American states. That is why—not in spite of, but as a very condition of, its centrality—the relationship between the pampa bourgeoisie and the state did not exhibit the transparency and immediacy which the regional oligarchies and international capital induced in a large portion of Latin America's regional and (for a long time, mostly nominal) national states.[16]

15. Of course, economic factors were not the only ones operating in this. The pampean bourgeoisie's greater weight, condensed in the national state, with respect to the oligarchies of other regions allowed it to discourage, by means of diverse economic and political mechanisms, the emergence of other dynamic exporting industries.

16. If instead of making these comparisons with other Latin American countries we had made them with Australia and New Zealand, the dimensions Argentina and

Although the liberal Argentine state did not survive the crisis of the 1930s, the factors summarized above allowed it to recover from the economic impact of that world crisis more quickly and easily than most other Latin American countries. The crisis induced a new wave of industrialization through import substitution (helped by a comparatively broad internal market)[17] and the absorption of a large part of the still available work-force from the nonpampa regions, thus reducing their relative weight even further. However, this is not the place to analyze how this affected the emergence of *peronismo;* instead, we turn to the central theme of the paper.

## Dilemmas

I have already mentioned the emergence in Argentina of a popular sector, which included a politically significant working class, with larger economic and organizational resources than those of the rest of Latin America.[18] This in turn resulted from the combination of large available economic surpluses and the negligible pressure exerted on the urban labor-market by an almost nonexistent peasantry. If this was an advantage for Argentina's capitalist development, it also strengthened its popular sector. When the bonanza disappeared and the economic conditions approached zero-sum, there was no sizable peasantry to bear a substantial part of the costs of agreements negotiated between the classes located within the fully capitalist region.

The second point to be considered arises from another peculiarity of this economy: its main export products, cereals and beef, are wage goods, foodstuffs that constitute the main consumption items of the popular sector. Let us initially note some general consequences of this peculiarity. Other Latin American primary export products have less influence on the consumption of the pop-

---

Uruguay had in common with the other Latin American countries would be more noticeable. For some comparisons in that direction, see Geller, "El crecimiento industrial argentino," and Hector Diéguez, "Argentina y Australia: algunos aspectos de su desarrollo económico comparado," *Desarrollo Económico* 8, no. 32 (January–March 1969).

17. The effective market is a function not so much of the total population as of that part of the population subject to capitalist relationships and with a monetary income sufficient for the purchase of mass-consumption industrial goods; cf. O'Donnell, *Modernization,* chapter 1.

18. As always, with the exception of Uruguay and partly—in a way too complicated to be dealt with here—of Chile.

.

ular sector and, therefore, on the relative prices of their consumption baskets. Furthermore, the way their price-changes influence popular consumption is, in most cases, indirect, generated by mechanisms that are difficult to apprehend; in contrast, a change in the relative prices of foodstuffs is immediately perceptible. In addition, this perception occurs in a popular sector with a significantly higher level of income (and, presumably, of expectations) and organizational autonomy (and therefore greater capacity for resistance) than in the other Latin American cases. We are now in a position to analyze more concrete processes.

The world crisis of the 1930s depressed the prices of pampean goods. Subsequently the *peronista* government (1946–1955) offered a foretaste of the problems that would explode later. First (1946–1950), the state appropriated a substantial part of the proceeds of pampean exports, kept internal foodstuff prices depressed, and thus increased the income of the popular sector and provoked an expanding demand for other goods, especially industrial ones. But this was to generate a balance-of-payments squeeze, due to the "discouragement" effect of low prices on pampa production and to increasing internal consumption of exportable foodstuffs. Subsequently (1952–1955), agricultural prices improved, whereupon—because of the operation of the inverse joint effect—the balance-of-payments situation improved. But this in turn generated political troubles, due to the regressive redistribution of income it entailed and to the reduction of the domestic demand on which the urban bourgeoisie depended.

Following this, around 1960, a wave of direct foreign investment in industry and services provoked a rapid internationalization of the urban productive structure (by means of capital sources and activities different from those involved in export).[19] Contrary to the developmentalist hopes, this new stage resulted in a marked increase in demand for imports, which outran the growth rate of GNP, exports, and pampa production.[20] Faced with this situation,

19. It is impossible to quote here all the pertinent bibliography. The data and main sources can be found in Pablo Gerchunoff and Juan Llach, "Capitalismo industrial, desarrollo asociado y distribución del ingreso entre los gobiernos peronistas," *Desarrollo Económico* 15, no. 57 (April–June 1975); and Juan Sourrouille, "El impacto de las empresas transnacionales sobre el empleo y los ingresos: el caso de Argentina" (Geneva: International Labour Office, 1976).

20. See, above all, Juan Ayza, Gerard Fichet, and Norberto González, *América Latina: integración económica y sustitución de Importaciones* (Mexico City: CEPAL and Fondo de Cultura Económica, 1976).

the only economically evident solution—repeatedly expounded—lay in a large increase in exports, which would have provided the urban productive structure with the imports necessary for "self-sustained development." Assuming the capitalist parameters of the situation, this solution entailed, fundamentally, an increase in pampean production (and productivity) and/or a reduction in real wages, so as to free exportable surpluses of food. But the Cartesian simplicity of these solutions—which were indeed attempted—ran into political complications which we must now analyze.

## Cycles

Several consequences arose from the fact that wage goods were also the main export products. In the first place, it offered an objective basis, which was also subjectively acknowledged,[21] for repeated alliances among many of the weaker segments of the urban bourgeoisie and the popular sector. These alliances were based on the defense of the internal market against the recessive effects (via an increase in domestic food prices) of every significant rise in the price of pampa products. In the second place, mobilizations of the popular sector in defense of its consumption levels reinforced its capacity for organizational and political action through particular but repeated victories. A third consequence was that the above-mentioned alliances again and again spotlit and widened a deep horizontal cleavage within the urban bourgeoisie, between its oligopolistic fractions and those weaker ones which found a welcome ally in the popular sectors. Fourth, these same processes determined the appearance of another fundamental intrabourgeois cleavage, by separating the economic interests and political goals of the urban bourgeoisie (including its oligopolistic fractions) from those of the pampean bourgeoisie. These changing alliances underlie the economic and political cycles on which students of Argentina have fastened their attention.[22]

21. This was one of the constant themes of the CGE and the CGT after 1955.
22. The subject of the stop-go cycle has elicited important contributions from various theoretical perspectives. See, above all, Carlos Díaz Alejandro, *Devaluación en la tasa de cambio en un país semi-industrializado: la experiencia argentina, 1955–1961* (Buenos Aires: Editorial del Instituto, 1966); idem, *Essays;* Marcelo Diamand, *Doctrinas económicas, desarrollo e independencia* (Buenos Aires: Paidos, 1973); Mario Brodersohn, "Política económica de corto plazo, crecimiento e inflación en la Argentina, 1950–1972," in Consejo Professional de Ciencias Económicas, *Problemas económicos argentinos, diagnóstico y política* (Buenos Aires: Macchi, 1974); Juan Sourrouille and

The solution of Argentina's balance-of-payments bottlenecks requires a substantial increase of pampean exports. However, around 1960, when the demand for imports rose rapidly, the exports themselves rose much less. This was due to an increase in the internal consumption of exportables and also to a slow rate of improvement in the pampean region's productivity.[23] Neither the space available nor my knowledge allows for a satisfactory explanation of this failure, but it seems obvious that, assuming the capitalist parameters of the context, a necessary (but not sufficient) condition for rising production of pampean goods lies in satisfactory prices for the pampean bourgeoisie. The meaning of *satisfactory* is complex, but it includes at least two further necessary conditions. One is that prices should make feasible the investments necessary to increase the capital density of the pampean regions and their productivity. The second condition, less obvious but more important, is that those prices should be stable and that they should be perceived as such at the microeconomic level. I do not know of any studies that establish this, but there is no reason to suppose that in the 1956–1976 period the profit rate of the pampa bourgeoisie was lower than that of the urban bourgeoisie. However, historical data clearly shows the enormous instability of the main pampean wholesale prices (cereals, linseed, and beef), measured in relation to wholesale urban prices.

A substantial increase in pampean production (and exports) cannot take place without converting the *estancias* into a much more capital-intensive agribusiness. Discarding explanations based on the economic "irrationality" of the pampa bourgeoisie—which

Richard Mallon, *Economic Policy-Making in a Conflict Society* (Cambridge, Mass.: Harvard University Press, 1974); Aldo Ferrer et al., *Los planes de estabilización en la Argentina* (Buenos Aires: Paidos, 1969); and Javier Villanueva, "Una interpretación de la inflación argentina," *Revista de Ciencias Económicas* (April–September 1972). Adolfo Canitrot, in "La experiencia populista en la redistribución de ingresos," *Desarrollo Económico* 15, no. 59 (October–December 1975), has a different viewpoint, but nevertheless makes an important contribution. For attempts to connect this type of analysis with a more specifically political level, see Oscar Braun, "Desarrollo del capital monopolista en la Argentina," in Braun, ed., *El capitalismo argentino en crisis* (Buenos Aires: Siglo XXI, 1973); and O'Donnell, *Modernization*. From another angle, the literature already mentioned on the political stalemate in Argentina is relevant to this subject. However, not much has been done so far to capture the formation and shifts of political alliances that have stimulated those cycles.

23. On this subject the principal source is Díaz Alejandro's important *Essays*, where the slow growth in the physical quantity of these exports and the spectacular lag of pampean productivity with respect to its principal competitors in the world market are shown. Also see Sourrouille and Mallon, *Economic Policy-Making*.

are an implicit avowal of their author's ignorance—it seems clear that the answer must be found at the level of the parameters that govern microeconomic decisions. These parameters do not spring from some economic necessity but from political struggles and from the swings of the state, which in turn result from the specificities of a class structure whose origins I have summarized in the previous sections. This is what we must analyze.

The conversion of the pampean *estancia* into a capital- and technology-intensive agribusiness entails making rather long-term investment decisions.[24] The instability of pampean relative prices, the historical awareness of this and, above all, the difficulty of forecasting future price instability have prevented those decisions.[25] Thus, the pampa bourgeoisie, once dynamic (even in international terms, during the period before 1930), has become less and less so in recent times. The basic reason is that relative prices made it microeconomically rational to maintain the extensive exploitation of the land.[26]

In the short term the rise in relative internal prices of pampean production entails an almost equivalent net loss for the whole of the urban sector. The income redistribution and the recessive effect on the urban economy that (*ceteris paribus*) this entails increase

24. I hope it is clear that I am speaking at the class level. That is, the change toward an agribusiness would surely displace more than the few individuals who at present constitute the pampa bourgeoisie.

25. The pampa bourgeoisie's demands and declarations, at least of the last twenty years, constitute a repeated complaint that it does not receive profitable or stable prices.

26. Cf. the microeconomic studies quoted in the works I mentioned below. The issue is, however, more complicated, as appears from the controversy that took place in *Desarrollo Económico* between Guillermo Flischman ("Modelo de asignación de recursos en el sector agropecuario," *Desarrollo Económico* 10, no. 39–40 [October–December 1970], and "Nuevamente en torno de la eficiencia en el uso de la tierra y la caracterización de los grandes terratenientes," *Desarrollo Económico* 14, no. 54 [July–September 1974]), Oscar Braun ("Comentario al trabajo de Guillermo Flischman," *Desarrollo Económico* 10, no. 39–40 [October–December 1970], and "La renta absoluta y el uso ineficiente de la tierra en la Argentina," *Desarrollo Económico* 14, no. 54 [July–September 1974]), and Carlos Martínez et al. ("Nuevamente en torno al problema de asignación de recursos en el sector agropecuario pampeano," *Desarrollo Económico* 16, no. 61 [April–June 1976]). The central point of these for our analysis is that the differential rent which the pampean region still enjoys and, especially, the great fluctuations of the whole economy and the high (and erratic) inflation rate made a defense against the effects of inflation—for the urban and agrarian capital surpluses. This combines to reinforce the microeconomic rationality of maintaining the region's extensive exploitation. But, from the perspective of this analysis, the subject that these authors discuss seems to be a consequence (although in time it nourishes them in turn) of the economic and political factors I analyze here.

the export surpluses (via their immediate effect on the internal consumption of exportables) and might induce a medium-term increase of pampa production by satisfying the necessary condition of "satisfactory" prices. This would not be too onerous for the oligopolistic elements of the urban bourgeoisie. They have an objective interest in increasing the balance-of-payments surplus because of their high import coefficient.[27] The recessions and redistributions of income which usually accompany increases in food prices are less harmful for these oligopolistic sectors than for the weaker ones. In effect, the former have greater economic resources and preferential access to internal credit,[28] and this position enables them to shoulder the burden of the recession and, indeed, to promote capital concentration to their advantage at the same time.[29] Besides, the urban bourgeoisie's oligopolistic groups aim much of their production and supply of services at the relatively high-income strata, whose income is less affected, both absolutely and proportionately, by rises in food prices.

Although this generalization would require qualification in a more refined analysis, it clearly provides an objective basis for a long-term alliance between the large urban bourgeoisie and the pampa bourgeoisie that could guide the modernization of Argentine capitalism simultaneously through capital concentration in the urban sector and the development of capital-intensive agribusiness in the countryside. However, at least until 1976, this alliance only lasted for short periods, dissolving rapidly in situations that repeatedly put these two dominant sectors of the Argentine bourgeoisie in different political camps.

Why this deviation from economic logic? Fundamentally, because this alliance has been confronted again and again by another—basically made up of the popular sectors and the weaker elements of the urban bourgeoisie—which, in spite of its economic subordination, has been able to prevent the other from holding together beyond the short term. In the Latin American context this

27. Not only is the coefficient high but it grows with elasticity greater than 1.0 with increases in its production level; cf. Ayza et al., *América Latina.*
28. For data on this point see especially Fundación de Investigaciones Económicas América Latina, *La financiación de las empresas industriales en la Argentina* (Buenos Aires: FIEL, 1971); and Mario Brodersohn, *Financiamiento de empresas privadas y mercados de capital* (Buenos Aires: Programa Latinoamericano para el Desarrollo de Mercados de Capital, 1972).
29. On this point and others closely connected with it, see Guillermo O'Donnell and Delfina Linck, *Dependencia y autonomía* (Buenos Aires: Amorrortu, 1973).

has been one of Argentina's (and, with its own characteristics, Uruguay's) peculiarities, which can only be understood in terms of the historical perspectives summarized in the previous sections. But we still have new elements to introduce into our analysis.

Which processes posed these dilemmas and conflicts? The periods of low internal prices of foodstuffs and stable foreign exchange rates have, not by chance, been those of the highest growth rates and—until the approach of the end of the cycle—the lowest inflation rates.[30] But they have also led to balance-of-payments crises, which brought about the introduction of controls, especially on internal prices and the foreign-exchange movements, although these were not enough to stave off the crises. Once a balance-of-payments crisis was unleashed, it was dealt with by means of devaluations which (with the exception of the 1967–1969 period) implied a correlative increase in the internal prices of exportables. These devaluations formed part of stabilization programs that accentuated the recessive and redistributionary effects of the devaluation by means of a restriction of money supply, reduction of the budgetary deficit, wage freezes, and increases in the real interest rate, tending, on the one hand, to consolidate the transfer of income to the exporting sector and, on the other, to adjust the internal level of economic activity to meet the balance-of-payments restrictions.

The effects were not only recessive and redistributive but also inflationary ("stagflation" is no novelty in Argentina), through the rise in domestic food prices caused by the growth of their export value, and the rising cost of imported goods and credit—at times when, in contrast, wages and salaries were kept frozen or systematically lagging and recession increased unemployment. In the short term (and, as we shall see, in these processes there was never more than a short term), the transfer of income toward the exporting sector did not induce an increase in pampean production,[31] but the stabilization programs were instrumental in easing the balance-of-payments squeeze.

True, such successes were due to factors very different from those proclaimed in official speeches, in the "recommendations" of

30. Cf. the pertinent data in Brodersohn, "Politica económica."
31. Actually, the price elasticity of pampean production is nil or slightly negative in the short term. This is because for cattle "an increase in relative prices reduces supply and increases the stocks. Besides, an increase in the cattle stock implies a greater use of land due to the rigidity in the supply of land. . . . Therefore an in-

the International Monetary Fund and in the exultant statements of the organizations of the pampa bourgeoisie. They were achieved not by an increase of exportable production but by recession, which diminished the demand for imports and increased the exportable surplus, especially of foodstuffs. This generated resistance among the many penalized by these policies, but the resultant easing of the balance of payments made economic reactivation policies possible. The liquidity increase, relaxing of controls on the fiscal deficit, availability of foreign exchange, growth in employment, and salary increases that followed ended the downward phase of the cycle and inaugurated the upward phase. But the latter led into a new balance-of-payments crisis,[32] after which further devaluations, and the consequent stabilization program, opened up another downward phase. . . .[33]

## Pendulums

In each phase of the cycle, the large bourgeoisie has played on the winner's side. I have already pointed out that the recessions provoked by stabilization programs have, at the very least, not damaged that sector: at the same time, as a direct appendage of (or intimately linked to) international capital, it is the large bourgeoisie that best perceives—and most fears—the costs of international insolvency.[34] It has the most direct interest in an improve-

crease in the relative prices of beef also negatively affects the production of cereals since to the lesser supply of beef is to be added the smaller area for cultivation": Brodersohn, "Política económica," p. 20.

32. In contrast with what I noted above concerning exports, the income elasticity of imports is extremely high. It was estimated at around 2.6 for the 1947–1967 period (see Díaz Alejandro, *Devaluación*, p. 356); for the period after 1966, Ayza et al. (*América Latina*, p. 13), with a different methodology, estimate an elasticity of 1.8. One piece of information that indicates how internal consumption causes this pincer movement to close on the balance of payments in the upward phase of the cycle is that the wage earners' marginal propensity to consume exportable goods (foodstuffs, drinks, and tobacco) is 0.36 and that of nonwage earners is 0.16: Díaz Alejandro, *Essays*, chapter 4.

33. This is the briefest of summaries of the principal theme of the works quoted in footnote 22, to which I must refer. A useful presentation of the economic mechanisms operating in the upward and downward phases of the cycles—which, unfortunately, came to my attention only when this work was substantially finished—is Marcelo Diamand, "El péndulo argentino: empate político o fracasos económicos?" 1976 (typescript).

34. As the upward phase approached the balance-of-payments crisis, state controls were imposed on prices and foreign exchange, thus particularly troubling this faction. I cannot deal with these points at greater length here; suffice it to point out

ment of the balance of payments.[35] Furthermore, the free international movement of capital enhances the privileged position, in an ever narrower domestic credit market, of this most internationalized sector, while at the same time reopening the "normal" channels for the transfer of capital accumulation toward the center of the system,[36] and thus toward this internally dominant faction. In the final stretch of the upward phase of the cycle, these factors turned the large bourgeoisie into an ally of the pampa bourgeoisie (and of the whole of the exporting sector) in the clamor for the devaluation and deflationary policies which launch the downward phase. Thus, faced with the onset of the balance-of-payments crisis, the large bourgeoisie swung toward the objective interests of the pampa bourgeoisie, favoring and supporting stabilization programs that transferred a mass of resources toward the latter, mostly at the expense of the urban sector.

But the regressive and recessionary impact of these measures generated a reaction among the weaker factions of the urban bourgeoisie and of the popular sector at the same time that the improvement in the foreign exchange position made feasible the economic reactivation measures for which they were clamoring.[37]

---

that, as far as price controls, which are typical of the final movements of the upward phase, are concerned, they could only really be attempted with the "leading firms." In other respects, when the balance-of-payments crisis occurred, the imposition of foreign-exchange controls and of restrictions on capital transfers abroad became a serious hindrance, particularly to firms more closely connected with the centers of world capitalism. Admittedly, none of these controls achieved their goals, nor did they prevent massive flights of capital, but many of the high-ranking staff of large firms, both national and transnational, whom I interviewed in 1971 and 1972 said that for that reason they "had" to act "excessively" beyond the pale of Argentina legislation, with consequent uneasiness at times when, during the upward phase of the cycles, "demagogues" and "nationalists" with access to state institutions were not lacking.

35. In terms of their high coefficient and demand for foreign exchange, and in spite of their better access to international finance, which allows them to make excellent deals in pre- and post-devaluation periods of acute scarcity of foreign exchange.

36. Even within private capital's oligopolistic faction, the more fully and directly internationalized firms—the subsidiaries of the transnational corporations—are usually the largest (in capital and sales), the fastest-growing, and the most capital-intensive; see especially Sourrouille, "El impacto." Of course this is not peculiar to Argentina; on Mexico see Fernando Fajnzylber and Trinidad Farrago, *Las empresas transnacionales: expansión a nivel mundial y proyección en la industria mexicana* (Mexico City: Fondo de Cultura Económica, 1976); and Carlos Von Doellinger and Leonardo Cavalcanti, *Empresas multinacionais na industria brasileira* (Rio de Janeiro: IPEA/INPES, 1975).

37. These in turn carried with them a large part of the nonpampean regions, which also had to "contribute" to these income transfers.

Faced with this, the large bourgeoisie repeatedly did what all bourgeoisies do in the absence of a tutelary state to induce them to adopt longer-term strategies: they looked to their short-term economic interests, supported the economic reactivation policies, and thus—we may safely assume—profited in a privileged manner from the economic recovery.[38] In this way they went through a full swing of the pendulum, joining the rest of the urban sector and abandoning the pampa bourgeoisie to a solitary lament for the deterioration of its relative prices;[39] their behavior generated great fluctuations of relative prices.

Although this describes the alternation in alliances of the large bourgeoisie, it is still to be explained. However, it must be added that, apart from their economic consequences, these swings had political implications of the greatest importance: they repeatedly broke up that intrabourgeois cohesion essential for stable political domination. More precisely, they broke the cohesion of its two superior sectors (the urban oligopoly and the pampa bourgeoisie), whose respective capital accumulation bases made them potentially capable of "modernizing" Argentine capitalism. Another no less important aspect, to which I shall shortly turn, is that such swings not only generated the political space for but also were to a large extent the consequence of an alternative alliance which encompassed the weaker factions of the bourgeoisie and the popular sector.

Let me insist on a crucial point. The alliance of the dominant factions of the bourgeoisie could have borne fruit if it had lasted long enough to bring about significant productivity increases in the pampa region. This was prevented by the large fluctuations in relative prices. But in their political demands the pampean bourgeoisie concentrated on the level and not on the stability of their prices, thus contributing to the swings I have described. The productivity increases could have taken place with relatively depressed but stable pampean prices (thus meeting the necessary condition of stability stated above), combined with public policies that would have forced them through by more structural measures. This was the motivation behind the various projects designed to tax the dif-

38. At least, the more concentrated and internationalized industrial branches usually responded more vigorously to the reactivation.

39. Maintaining a fixed exchange rate, or systematically allowing the rate to lag behind domestic prices, was the main mechanism that turned relative prices in favor of the urban sector (including wages and salaries).

ference between the potential and the actual productivity of pampa land.

Such an alternative, obviously conflicting with the short-term interests of the pampa bourgeoisie in its present composition, is not against those of the urban sector as a whole (since it does not presuppose a fall in their relative prices), and in the medium term it could have achieved the sought-after increase in pampa production and productivity. However, the attempts to impose such a tax on the "potential rent of the land" repeatedly failed. This must be contrasted with what has happened in many other Latin American countries, where the state—impelled by and allied with the large bourgeoisie—has usually been able to force through the modernization of agrarian regions and their dominant classes.[40] But those agrarian classes were fundamentally regional ones,[41] and although their production might temporarily fall, their contribution to total exports was not comparable to that of the pampa bourgeoisie. That is why other Latin American states have been able to subordinate those classes, and the regional states they controlled, without simultaneously worsening their balance-of-payments problems.

The case of the pampa bourgeoisie has been very different. I have pointed out its early position as a national class, even with respect to its linkage with a national state. This meant that intrabourgeois struggles usually occurred, in contrast with other Latin American cases, at the very heart of a national state that was continually fractured by them. Besides, the discouragement of the pampa bourgeoisie,[42] caused by the fall in its prices and attempts to restructure it by means of tax mechanisms, had strong immediate repercussions on the balance of payments—at the same time

40. This, of course, did not prevent these processes from being acutely conflicting. The point is that the capacity of these classes to resist was less than that of the pampa bourgeoisie and that, besides, the cost of such policies, in their short-term impact on the level of internal economic activity and exports, was lower.

41. In the case of the enclaves it obviously was not a matter of modernizing the economy's most capital- and technology-intensive sector, but of renegotiating with international capital the percentages that could be retained locally. In the cases in which (1) "excessive" pressures were exerted (reaching or threatening nationalization, above all) and (2) the enclave's product was as important as the pampa production for total exports (in Bolivia and, more recently, Chile), the familiar falls in production and/or prices—equivalent in this sphere to the pampa bourgeoisie's recurrent "discouragements"—unleashed the consequent balance-of-payments crisis.

42. For the pampa bourgeoisie's insistence on its "discouragement" because of its internal prices and the attempts to "smother it" with taxes, it is enough to consult collections of documents of the Sociedad Rural Argentina (SRA) and the Coordinadora de Asociaciones Rurales de Buenos Aires y la Pampa (CARBAP).

that, in the upward phase of the economic cycle, the increase in domestic consumption of exportables further diminished the potentially available exports, before pampean productivity had undergone any substantial improvement. Thus a balance-of-payments crisis ensued, and its alleviation by means of devaluations not only turned relative prices against the urban sector but also entailed the expulsion from the governing alliances of the sectors that had impelled the reactivation of the cycle.

As long as the stabilization programs lasted, the immediate interests of the pampa bourgeoisie weighed heavily in the institutional system of the state. Naturally enough, it opposed any prospect of its own restructuring, centering the issue on a sharp increase in its prices and thus creating the conditions for a renewal of the cycle. In other words, although it has long lost its position as the dynamic vanguard of Argentine capitalism, the pampa bourgeoisie, compared with other Latin American agrarian classes, has retained an unusually central economic and political position. This position was sufficient both to block any attempt to restructure it and to use periodic balance-of-payments crises to bring about massive income transfers for its benefit. Meanwhile, and as a consequence, channels for capital accumulation in Argentina were repeatedly short-circuited and the state danced to the pendular tune of civil society.

This accounts for some of the characteristics of the period beginning in 1966, especially the economic policies followed between March 1967 and May 1969. The minister of economics, Krieger Vasena, transparently carried out the policies of the large bourgeoisie. This entailed, among other things, a large devaluation which for the first time did not benefit the pampa and exporting sector. On the contrary, the March 1967 devaluation of 40 percent was wholly appropriated by the state, which withheld a percentage of the value of pampa exports equivalent to the devaluation. This fiscal revenue was used in a substantial program of investment in physical infrastructure and communications. A fixed peso price of pampean production depressed the internal price of pampean foodstuffs. It also allowed a rapid reduction of inflation and—in contrast with other cases of bureaucratic authoritarianism—only a moderate fall in industrial wages.

Even so, this situation could not be maintained and, after 1970, pampean prices (especially those of beef) rebounded until they reached a very high level in 1971–1972. Krieger Vasena's was the only clear and sustained attempt by the large bourgeoisie unilaterally to subordinate the pampa bourgeoisie to its own accumulation needs.[43] But the result was an internal rupture in the cohesion of the bureaucratic authoritarian state and a political and economic collapse impelled by external social actors. While this attempt marked the limits of a unilateral enforcement of supremacy by the large bourgeoisie, the history of previous devaluations, by pushing the big bourgeoisie into alliances with the urban sector, had shown that it was impossible to return to the good old days of pampean supremacy.[44]

## The Defensive Alliance

If the political and economic centrality of the pampa bourgeoisie marks an important difference from other Latin American countries and their agrarian classes, a no less important difference stems from the greater political vulnerability of the weaker (and genuinely national) factions of the urban bourgeoisie in those countries when faced with the expansion of the large bourgeoisie. The growth of the dominant productive structure, oligopolistic and internationalized, has occurred at the expense of many sectors of national capital, weakening its position vis-à-vis international capital and the state. This has caused complaints and strains but has not, so far, been translated into serious political challenges to such "development" patterns. No such development has taken place in Argentina. The reason for the local bourgeoisie's comparatively greater political capacity is to be found not so much in itself as in the characteristics of the popular sector and in the country's relative national homogeneity. Elsewhere, a less organized and autonomous urban sector deprives the weaker factions of the Latin American bourgeoisie of the extremely important ally they had in Argentina. This point is crucial.

Not only is the Argentine popular sector endowed with greater autonomy and organizational capacity than in most other Latin

43. He even tried to introduce a tax on potential rent but, like so many other things, this disappeared in the social explosions of 1969.

44. Another exception—less clear, but also a telling one—can be found in the economic policy followed during 1964 and 1965. Then high pampean prices coexisted with an improvement of real wages. But this attempt met its own limitations, since it entailed the reduction of profits for the urban bourgeoisie—which actively contributed to the 1966 coup—a large increase in the fiscal deficit, and severe restrictions on imports.

American countries, it also happens that the medium- and long-term alliance of the upper sectors of the bourgeoisie depends on the level and stability of the relative prices of the main internal foodstuffs. This gave the popular sector a precise target for its political action, which has interrupted the accumulation circuits of those upper bourgeois factions. These are necessary but not sufficient conditions for the recurrent breakdown of the latter's alliances. To account for the specificity of the phenomena with which we are concerned we must also see how the popular sector associated itself with the objective interests and political action of the weaker factions of the urban bourgeoisie.

These factions are usually penalized by devaluations and stabilization programs. Given an alleviation of the balance-of-payments squeeze, their immediate interest lies in economic reactivation policies that increase employment, liquidity, and credit availability and give the state an expansionary role once again. This is also a direct effect of wage and salary increases; thus, it is not surprising that the bourgeois faction in control of the most labor-intensive enterprises should support these increases, when the even greater costs to them of recession are taken into account. The concurrence with the unions demanding wage increases is, besides, a token it offers to the popular sector to forge the alliance.[45] Such a bourgeoisie— more or less weak and more or less penalized by the expansion of oligopolistic and internationalized capital—exists in other Latin American countries, but only in Argentina has it found a popular ally whose immediate short-term interests are compatible with its own and which possesses a significant capacity for political action.[46]

The main organizational supports of this alliance have been the

45. Since these wage and salary increases encourage economic activity at the same time that other policies, made possible by the transitory easing of the balance of payments, raise the employment level, the orthodox warnings that all this feeds inflation matter little—particularly since inflation, with a fixed or systematically lagging exchange rate, accelerates the reversal of relative prices in favor of the urban sector.

46. In Uruguay the lower level of industrialization, fundamentally due to the smaller internal market, weakened both agents much more; the local bourgeoisie has in itself been weaker, and in the popular sector the working class has had relatively less weight. In Chile the political expression of the working class in Marxist parties (and the absence of a direct target in the relative price of foodstuffs as in Argentina and Uruguay) made this alliance more ambiguous and discontinuous. In the remaining countries of the region the relative weakness of the popular sector, due to a greater intranational heterogeneity, deprived the local bourgeoisie of that fundamental ally.

CGE, the CGT, and the national leadership of the main unions. Its first, principal, and possibly last expression has been *peronismo*. It was not the only one, since—above all in the periods in which *peronismo* was proscribed—it was channeled through other parties and within state institutions by diverse "nationalist" military and civilian groups. Their banner has been the defense of the internal market, in the sense both of raising the level of its activity and of limiting the expansion of international capital within it.

The characteristics of this popular sector and of this local bourgeoisie cannot be understood in isolation from each other. It has been their conjunction in the multiplying effect of their alliance that has made it possible to impose, again and again, their immediate demands. We can now examine the characteristics and principal consequences of this alliance.

1. The alliance was sporadic but recurrent. It only appeared in the downward phases of the cycle, when demands for wage and salary increases and for diverse measures to relieve "the suffocation of small and medium-sized national enterprise"[47] concurred in the reactivation of the internal market at the expense of the pampean exporting sector. Once the cycle revived the alliance dissolved, partly due to the attempts of the local bourgeoisie and the unions to negotiate special agreements individually with the state and with the large bourgeoisie, partly because of the return of more "normal" class cleavages.

2. The alliance was defensive. It arose against the offensives of the upper bourgeoisie. Its ideology of "nationalist" and "socially just" development overlooked what it was unable to *problematize:* the deeply oligopolistic and internationalized structure of the capitalism of which its members were the weakest components. It was defensive because in its victory it could not create an alternative capital-accumulation system; all it achieved was the transition from the downward phase to the upward phase, under conditions that were doomed to provoke the repetition of the cycle.

3. Despite its defensive nature, and although its victories signified the completion and not a way out of the cycle, this alliance was quite successful. It scored repeated victories, annulling the stabilization programs, limiting the domestic expansion of international capital, and launching economic reactivation policies and new dis-

47. These subjects and terms recur in the CGE's demands and declarations; see, e.g., its *Memorias anuales.*

couragements for the pampa bourgeoisie. Thus, it is not surprising that the wage series should also show erratic behavior; its peaks are the result of victories which soon led to marked reductions in wages. The upward movements of wages were accompanied by growth of the GNP and, in general, by higher profit rates for the industrial bourgeoisie as a whole—although, being subject to the overall cycle, profits also seem to have undergone marked fluctuations.[48] The consequence of these processes may be seen in a phenomenon as intrinsically political as it is economic: the inflation, which is even more remarkable for its fluctuations than for its generally high level.

More basically, the defensive alliance was victorious because it managed to destroy the alliance between the two dominant factions of the bourgeoisie. The large bourgeoisie, when the time came to weigh the immediate benefits from a revival of the economy against the threat of a political abyss entailed in aligning with the pampa bourgeoisie and the exporting sector when the remainder of civil society had joined forces against them, opted to support a new upward phase. Repeatedly the defensive alliance—politically—broke "from below" the cohesion of the dominant factions and—economically—blocked the only alliance that could create a new capital-accumulation system and move the economy off its cyclical path.

4. The alliance was polyclassist, in the sense that it included the popular sector (with a strong working-class component) and various bourgeois factions. Its repeated successes were based on this conjunction. However, this ensured that its orientation was nationalistic and capitalist.[49] Its polyclass character, based on the achievement of shared tactical goals, offered a popular base for the demands of the weak bourgeoisie. This faction thus appeared as a progressive one which, contrasting with the large bourgeoisie's "efficientist" orientation and the landholding oligarchy's archaism, seemed to embody the possibility of development with social justice. On the other hand, the popular sector (especially the unions and the working class) gained, through the polyclassist nature of

48. At least if the relationship between urban wholesale prices and wages can be used as an indicator.
49. Basically, it was prevented from uniting to defend the domestic market against the internationalized character of export-related activities and of the large bourgeoisie.

the alliance, access to resources and mass media which it could not otherwise have had.

In particular, the bourgeois respectability of the alliance made more difficult the harsh repression which has been directed at the popular sector elsewhere in Latin America when it has acted in isolation and/or in pursuit of more radical goals. The impact of this alliance stemmed from the multiplying effect of the concurrence of social actors who had their own resource base and who could cooperate on very concrete and short-term goals. In other Latin American countries, the absence of these joint conditions has meant that the local bourgeoisie has lacked popular support and that the popular sector (weaker, in any case, because of greater intranational heterogeneity) has not enjoyed the political protection of a bourgeois ally. This, in turn, has made it possible for the large bourgeoisie to advance unhindered, encountering protests and conflicts, naturally, but not the limits and oscillations that this peculiar alliance imposed in Argentina.

5. The principal political channel of the defensive alliance, *peronismo*, remained locked within capitalist parameters. This limitation also arose from the experience of repeated victories and subsequent defeats. The political activation of the popular sector in pursuit of the goals of the defensive alliance, the protection granted by its bourgeois component, and the changes in public policies it achieved led, on the one hand, to a positive reinforcement of that activation and, on the other, to the solidifying of the organizational basis—above all, the unions—for the popular sector's action.

6. In historical terms, the alliance stemmed from the fresh memory of previous mobilizations which had managed to reverse the downward trend of real wages and of economic activity. It was also a function of the low deterrent effect of a repression that tended to cease the moment the state, indicating a shift in the governing alliances, launched a new upward phase of the cycle. This increased the popular sector's capacity for and disposition to political activation, but it also led to an equally repetitive experience of defeat: periods of low wages and salaries and of mounting unemployment, during which the spokesmen of the defensive alliance were removed from the governing coalition.

However, in contrast with the transparent stimulus entailed by rising food prices and falling salaries and wages, the reversal of the cycle took place because of problems (such as balance-of-payments crises) and through mechanisms (such as devaluations and restrictions in the money supply) whose functioning and impact were harder to grasp. The benefits derived by the pampa bourgeoisie and the exporting sector, and the initial support lent by the large bourgeoisie to each downward reversal of the cycle, fostered the hostility of the popular sector against both factions and against the internationalization and big business which they embodied. At the same time, the defensive alliance could not abandon its capitalist ideology and goals.

Thus, the interpretation of the sequences of such successes and defeats became a mythology of conspiracies of "powerful interests" which had a magical ability to defeat the "people" and hinder "development." Failure and tension generated in some cases a Fascist ideological syndrome and in others a challenging of the capitalist parameters of the situation. But against these centrifugal tendencies a powerful centripetal force operated: as the CGT, the CGE, and *peronismo* tirelessly repeated, since 1955 they had been prevented from carrying out the kind of "socially just" capitalist development that, "placed on the people's side" and exercising wide control of the state's institutions, the local bourgeoisie and the unions seemed to offer.

The feasibility of uniting the national and the popular against the landholding oligarchy and the international monopolies, which the short-term coincidences of the defensive alliance seemed to confirm, were expressed in *peronismo*'s unusual appeal and were a decisive element in the great wave which in 1973 returned it to power. A further condition for this was that in the previous period the large bourgeoisie, ignoring the limits of its supremacy, had tried to impose it unilaterally, even on the pampa bourgeoisie. The social explosions of 1969 and 1970 sealed the defeat of that attempt and, impelled by a great popular activation, forced the political withdrawal of the large bourgeoisie which, in 1973, for the first time lost its place in the governing alliance. Only then could the alternative that the main spokesmen of the defensive alliance claimed to embody be positively put to the test.

7. Rather than cycles we must now speak of spirals, inasmuch as—politically, above all—each swing of the pendulum, with its succession of temporary victories and defeats, sharpened the conflicts from which they derived. The actors were not classes, factions, and organizations that retained their "structural" characteristics unchanged, beyond these struggles. Rather, they were the

political, organizational, and ideological expression of classes and factions created and transformed during and through this pattern of alliances and oppositions. In particular, the popular sector found in the unions and, politically, in *peronismo* an organizational, ideological, and political expression that corresponded closely to the limits of the situation. The mobilization behind the defensive alliance's demands, with its precise aims and polyclass framework, achieved frequent and spectacular victories. This explains the peculiar combination of impressive popular activation with economistic demands, which emphasized, as a token of its alliance with the local bourgeoisie, its rejection of any leap beyond capitalism. Precisely this militant economism, combined with the weaker factions of the bourgeoisie, permitted repeated defensive victories and perpetuated the illusion of an alternative path of capitalist development.

In contrast, the moments of political victory and reversal, at any point in the economic cycle, were those when the temporary victors took the state apparatus by storm, seeking to strengthen institutional positions from which they would fight battles when the situation was once again reversed—as experience taught them it would be. Of course, the unions were no exception to this: the history of the defensive alliance is also that of the extraction from the state of important institutional concessions. These, in turn, reinforced the possibility of renewing the mobilization of the popular sector. The conquest of institutional positions enabled the unions to cover the popular sector with a fine organizational net by which they could direct it repeatedly toward a militant economism, toward the polyclass alliance, and toward the mirage of that "other" capitalist path which *peronismo* proclaimed.

8. These multiplying fusions of the defensive alliance forced the large bourgeoisie repeatedly to abandon the pampa bourgeoisie to a solitary lament at the falling prices of their products. Such fusions both impelled economic reactivation and opened up the political abyss of a wide and active, national and popular mobilization which had somehow to be reabsorbed. By swinging from support of the pampean bourgeoisie to support of a new upward phase of the cycle, the large bourgeoisie closely followed its short-term economic interests and managed to remain the only stable member of the governing alliance. It did not lose its dominant position, but the peculiar conditions outlined meant that its domina-

tion had to shift continuously backward and forward. At the same time and for the same reasons, the channels of capital accumulation were repeatedly short-circuited. These clues enable us to understand Argentine politics as a less surrealistic phenomenon than its political instability and erratic development might lead one to believe.

As I hope is clear, insofar as this discussion refers to the constitution of the classes, it also refers to the state. It is from this viewpoint—starting from and returning to civil society—that the problem of the state must be approached.

### The State

The state is not merely a set of institutions. It also fundamentally includes the network of relationships of political domination activated and supported by such institutions in a territorially defined society, which supports and contributes to the reproduction of the society's class organization. In the case of Argentina the pendular movements of the large bourgeoisie and the difficulties it has faced in subordinating civil society as a whole are tangible indications of a continued crisis of the state as a system of political domination. So are the defensive alliance's recurrent and partially victorious fusions. Out of this was born a democratization by default, which resulted from the difficulties in imposing the authoritarian "solution" that seemed to offer a chance of extracting Argentine capitalism from its political and economic spirals.

By *governing alliance* I mean an alliance that imposes, through the institutional system of the state, policies conforming to the orientations and demands of its members. The large bourgeoisie was the stable member of the governing alliance, but each phase was marked by a temporary change in its partners and by an alteration of scarcely consistent circuits of capital accumulation. That is why public policies were continually changing and hardly ever implemented, as the state danced to the tune of the dynamics of civil society.

The state was repeatedly razed to the ground by civil society's changing coalitions. At the institutional level, the coalitions were like great tides which momentarily covered everything and which, when they ebbed, washed away entire segments of the state—segments which would later resurface as bastions for piecing together

a new offensive against the coalition that had just forced its opponents into retreat. The result was a state apparatus extensively colonized by civil society. The upper bourgeoisie were not the only
ones to hang onto it; its weakest factions and part of the subordinate classes did the same—another fundamental difference from
other Latin American examples. Civil society's struggles were internalized in the state's institutional system in a way that expressed
not only the weight of upper bourgeoisie but also the peculiar
characteristics of a defensive alliance endowed with a remarkable
capacity for partial victory. As a consequence, this colonized state
was extraordinarily fragmented, reproducing in its institutions the
complex and rapidly changing relationships of dominant and subordinated classes—classes which could use these institutions to fuel
the spiraling movements of civil society.

Such a state could not keep at a distance from the governing
alliance's immediate demands and interests; it could only reinforce
the cycles and swings. It was, quite clearly, a weak state: as a support of social domination, because of the recurrent (and increasing) weakening of such domination implied by the popular sector's
mobilizations and the unions' bargaining power; and as an institutional sphere, because it was deeply colonized and factionalized.
This meant that one possible way out of the cycles, a shift toward
some sort of state capitalism, was blocked; a fairly stable and consolidated bureaucratic apparatus with nonnegligible degrees of
freedom vis-à-vis civil society, which would have been a necessary
condition for such a solution, was not available.

Another obstacle arose from the fact that at times when the
large bourgeoisie was in alliance with the pampa bourgeoisie, the
stabilization programs entailed an anti-statist offensive aimed not
only at slashing the fiscal deficit but also at dismantling the advances that had taken place in a statist direction during the previous phase, when the defensive alliance had been part of the governing alliance. Those attempts blocked any trend toward state
capitalism, by dismantling the institutions that could have encouraged it and by dismissing the technocrats who could have carried
it out, replacing them with others who would issue a string of anti-
statist pronouncements and decisions.

In addition, any movement toward state capitalism by the defensive alliance encountered ambivalence (and, frequently, opposition) from the governing alliance's permanent member, the large
bourgeoisie. Feasible or not, this possibility was blocked *ab initio* by

the dynamic of civil society.[50] It can be said, then, that at all levels the Argentine state of the period from 1956 to 1976 was an example of extremely limited autonomy. Its peculiarities were not only that it basically moved in time with the upper bourgeoisie, but also that it reflected the fluctuating political strength of the subordinate classes in their alliance with the weaker factions of the dominant classes. The limit of the alliance, which shows that it must not be mistaken for an equilibrium of forces, arose from the fact that, on the one hand, it had to cooperate in the governing alliance with the large bourgeoisie and, on the other hand, that it could only be a defensive alliance.

Could this defensive alliance constitute an independent governing alliance, excluding the large bourgeoisie (and, of course, the pampa bourgeoisie)? Only a crude mechanism could lead us to believe this to be impossible on the grounds that the defensive alliance contained Argentine capitalism's weakest and least capitalist factions. In fact, it did happen in 1973, when the defensive alliance achieved an extraordinary but pyrrhic victory.

## Provisional Epilogue

The experiment initiated in 1966 sought, on the one hand, to rebuild capital-accumulation mechanisms which subordinated the whole of society to the large bourgeoisie and, on the other hand, necessarily and correlatively, to introduce a system of political domination which, reversing the preceding situation, would aggressively impose itself on civil society. I have mentioned the collapse of that attempt and how this made possible, for the first time, the conquest of the state's institutional system by the defensive alliance, independent of the large bourgeoisie. Recent history cannot be written here. But it is necessary to point out that this alliance could only briefly ignore the economic supremacy of the large bourgeoisie and the pampa bourgeoisie; a glance at the data al-

50. Even without any change in the capitalist parameters of the situation, tax policies might have cushioned the cycles to an extent that would have modified many of the political aspects we have analyzed. But the ability to extract and reallocate resources by means of fiscal instruments (not only taxes on pampean land) presupposes the medium-term stability of those instruments and their implementation and a fairly consolidated bureaucracy that could ignore immediate pressures from the interests involved. These conditions could hardly be met in the midst of the pendular motions and the consequent colonization and factionalization of the state's institutional system.

ready presented demonstrates how, after a brief pause in 1974, the cyclical fluctuations were repeated much more violently. Even before Perón's death, the intrinsically defensive content and limitations of the alliance had been shown beyond question. The old crisis reproduced itself with unusual acuteness and the local bourgeoisie had to abandon ship without even rescuing its organization. On the other hand, the exacerbation of "union power" could not go beyond a repetition, with increased force after the retreat of the local bourgeoisie, of the practices that had made it what it was: an aggressive economism and a search for new institutional advantages, pursued now from the very heart of the state institutional system. This cumbersome heritage of past victories created ominous gaps between the union leaders and their own class. It also generated conservative reactions that threatened the substantial autonomy the unions and the popular sector had retained throughout this complex process.

Perón's death, a peculiar "palace" irrationality, and a violence that fed on itself helped to shake the foundations of the society and accelerated the spirals of its crisis; this happened with a state that had too obviously failed to guarantee the survival of this capitalism. Beneath those factors was the fact that when the defensive alliance managed, at last, to become the governing alliance, it ran up against its own limitations; the very causes of its extraordinary victory precipitated an unprecedented crisis. The promise of a nationalist and socially just path of capitalist development was subjected to a positive test and the alliance's centrifugal tensions flew off in their opposing directions.

The great victory of the defensive alliance led to the paroxysm of the political and economic crisis, to the ebbing away of the nationalist ideology, to the implantation of a new bureaucratic authoritarian state, and to the dissolution or subjection to government control of the main organizations of the popular sector and the local bourgeoisie. As a result, for the first time the defensive alliance's political, ideological, and organizational supports have been neutralized. This has enabled the dominant factions of the bourgeoisie to explore the possibilities for a long-term reaccommodation on more egalitarian terms—between themselves—than those prevalent in 1967–1969. The implication of and precondition for such a reaccommodation is the dispersal of the defensive alliance. This does not entirely preclude a return of that alliance or of the spirals we have studied. But for such a thing to happen, the local bourgeoisie would have to set itself on a hazardous "road to Damascus," toward a renewed alliance with the popular sectors; and it is not certain that by then the popular sector will still be confined within the ideological and political parameters which cemented the defensive alliance before its greatest and most catastrophic victory.

# 6

# Fissures in the Volcano?
## Central American Economic Prospects

## *Clark W. Reynolds*

Central America presents a fascinating panorama of economies growing side by side. All of them are based on primary product exports and recently established import-substituting industry, yet the political, economic, and social conditions of these countries are widely divergent. One would have to go back to nineteenth-century Mexico to find parallels to the hierarchical class structure, wealth inequality, political rigidity, and positivistic utilitarianism that predominate in the northern countries (Guatemala, El Salvador, and Nicaragua). Yet the southern countries are characterized by a greater degree of political opening and higher income levels for the majority of the population. Costa Rica, the only nonmilitary state, is the most conspicuous example. Historically its export income has been widely shared. Panama and

Reprinted from Clark W. Reynolds, "Fissures in the Volcano? Central American Prospects," pp. 195–221 in Joseph Grunwald, ed., *Latin America and the World Economy: A Changing International Order.* © 1978 by Sage Publications, Inc. Reprinted by permission of Sage Publications, Inc.

Honduras, under military regimes with a populist flavor, have recently increased taxation of their economic enclaves (under foreign ownership rather than a domestic elite) to provide funds for incipient programs of land distribution, rural and urban infrastructure, and other progressive activities. El Salvador is beginning to tilt its policies in a similar direction against the opposition of powerful economic interest groups, but it is restrained by the greater conservatism of its northern neighbors. Recent economic changes in the region have been impressive. One wonders what factors account for the parallel growth of the market economy in rural and urban areas, while at the same time the most basic social and institutional structures remain apparently inert in some countries and show such slow progress in others. Can this divergent process continue?

## Labor Participation in an Export Economy, Central American–Style

In an export economy, the principal income-generating activity is determined by foreign demand as reflected in international prices for the domestic export product (translated into internal prices through the exchange rate). The response of producers to this demand (plus the withdrawing of goods from inventories) causes a derived demand for labor depending on the technology employed and its implicit effect on output per worker. If productivity rises rapidly, the demand for additional workers will be less than proportional to the increase in production, and vice versa. Hence the first and most important employment-initiating activity to examine in such economies is the way exports are produced. The income generated by exports in turn generates payments for domestic factors of production, including labor, capital, land, minerals, entrepreneurship, skills in scarce supply (and other scarcity rents), plus government participation in the form of taxes (net of subsidies). The factor income stream in turn generates final demand within the economy, its form depending on the demand propensities of households, business, and government and their respective shares in the functional distribution of income. This internal demand will lead to a secondary derived demand for labor depending, of course, on the labor intensity of the goods and services desired.

In Central America this export-led pattern of employment demand has characterized the region since independence. The product mix and the institutional conditions under which export goods are produced have had much to do with labor utilization and the share of labor in the economic system. They are also affected by terms of land tenure, technology employed, relative scarcity or abundance of labor (itself determined in part by the availability of land for nonexport or subsistence production), and government policies to tax and subsidize economic activities. Further factors are the responses of domestic and foreign entrepreneurship to economic opportunities, subject to the hegemony of external powers—first Britain, and later the United States.

Exports constituted the foremost factor behind not only employment, but the general prosperity and even the political stability of the republics. The internal economies' response to export performance generated a subsequent set of demands for employment in sectors linked to the export sector or providing goods and services that could be produced domestically (home goods) in competition with relatively abundantly available imports.

During the postwar period, Central American economists and some farsighted politicians wished to reduce the region's vulnerability to fluctuations in export prices and the resultant destabilizing impact on internal economic (and political) conditions. It was not appreciated fully how difficult it is to free small, externally linked economies from physical and financial dependence on the world market (and the major economies, which influence that market by their own internal trade cycles). But in Central America in the 1950s, efforts were made to create a degree of independence in a balanced way, following the lead of the Economic Commission for Latin America (ECLA), which set up "integration industries." These, it was hoped, would have the advantage of being located throughout the region on an equitable basis (in terms of impact on the several economies through production, employment, and foreign-exchange savings), yet would be planned in such a way as to eliminate excess competition. The United States joined with skeptics within the region to cast doubts on the viability of the scheme, and capital was not forthcoming, any more than was the general political will for regionwide planning. Only a handful of such plants were established, and they were not a conspicuous success. This first effort at integration was stillborn. With it died import-substitution industrialization as a means to increase the autonomy of regional economic behavior and to expand the freedom of internal economic policy. Perhaps no small element in the failure of this scheme was a general political fear of planning, which implied surveillance of profit performance and eventual fiscal vulnerability of economic activity in the region. The ECLA mystique associated with Raul Prebisch, its founder, conjured up visions of gradual control of the production process by technocrats imbued with the philosophies of Keynes at best and Marx at worst. It was feared that they would use their planning skills to reduce the high degree of independence of capital from domestic monetary or fiscal controls. While the internal politics of the five countries differed, the laissez-faire capitalism that prevailed in all (including Costa Rica, despite its nationalization of the banking system in 1948) was a common article of faith for those controlling the business and financial communities, especially in the export sectors.

The ultimate test, of course, was the extent to which regional development policies might influence the level and distribution of economic rents (those returns net of normal costs of labor and capital which, in their extreme characterization, may be called surplus, *plusvalía,* or excess profits). Export economies, subject to world price determination, often operate as inframarginal producers and thus are able to earn substantial scarcity rents above the normal costs of factor inputs. Wages are determined by the availability of jobs in the market plus the opportunity of workers to earn a subsistence income on their own land. (Opportunities for migration may, in extreme cases, have a bearing on internal wage levels, but this has not yet seemed to be important for Central American countries, except perhaps for El Salvador and Honduras before 1969.) The opportunity cost of capital is determined by international borrowing rates plus discount for risk, depreciation, and obsolescence. The residual element in unit value above these costs represents a rental income (of the pure Ricardian kind) to be divided among owners of land, capital, entrepreneurship, technology, and financial capital, as well as those with political power to permit or prevent economic activity and those with access to scarce marketing channels.

## Rent Partitioning: A Struggle for Shares

Hence, the strategy of each participating sector in an export economy is to maximize the level of rent subject to its share of the total, goals that are often in conflict. This frequently involves a high level of political activity, with a variety of strategies on the part of participants. The first stage of *rent partitioning* occurs within the traditional export activities, particularly among labor, capital, and government. The political process exists to strengthen or weaken the bargaining position (and even the legality of the institutional representatives) of each party. Often the struggle for rent partitioning will occasion major political clashes and the rise and fall of important parties. The governments of some Central American countries were established or removed as a result of the interests of local and foreign firms in securing rights to produce crops (such as bananas) for export with the greatest possible value of rent. Recent evidence suggests that as late as the 1970s a major banana-exporting company used several million dollars to bribe one Central American president to reduce the export tax on bananas. (This evidence came not from domestic sources but from a congressional investigation in the United States.) Such behavior is to be expected when the level of actual or potential rents is high. With such stakes every possible device is used to maximize the participation of those capable of exercising monopoly or monopsony power.

How much does rent partitioning affect the demand for labor and its share in the distribution of rents? This depends on conditions in the labor market, which is often competitive on the supply side and monopsonistic on the demand side. As a result, wages tend to be pushed down to subsistence levels, leaving the maximum amount of rent to be divided among the government and the owners of capital, natural resources, and marketing firms. Central American countries have historically differed in the extent of monopsony power of export industries in the labor market. They have also differed in the relative abundance of manpower available to be employed in the export sector. In Guatemala, access to land was utilized as a means of forcing workers (especially Indians and *mestizos*) into the wage-labor market in order to permit low-cost production of labor-intensive exports such as coffee. El Salvador, which has little arable land for its large and burgeoning population, has been even more successful at this strategy. The recent mass expulsion of its nationals from Honduras has exacerbated the problem.

The more land-abundant economies of Honduras and Nicaragua have been less able to implement programs encouraging low wage labor based on a limited supply of land. Costa Rica actually adopted policies from the earliest part of the nineteenth century in which a relatively broad distribution of land tenure permitted large segments of the rural population to participate in the rental income from coffee and other exports.

This varying behavior among the five countries and their different levels of wages and social participation in the rental "surplus" of the export sectors indicate that no single model explains the pattern of regional exposed growth. Indeed, the pluralistic policies that have operated in Central America underscore the alternatives open for export development along the lines of social participation in the economic process. The political consequences of these alternatives are also apparent. Costa Rica combined export growth with a long, virtually unbroken tradition of democratic administrations and nominal military intervention, while the other countries were noted for their political-military alliances, which imposed tough regimes to enforce the status quo.

What these alternative approaches suggest is that if the mass of the population is given a larger share of the surplus, this need not have a detrimental effect on the demand for labor (even though its supply cost rises). Along with higher incomes, the process generates higher skill attainments, greater education of the work force (and, therefore, broader political participation), and greater division of labor in home goods production because of a widened market. These benefits compensate for pure cost increases per man-hour of work. Hence the Costa Rican model illustrates the feasibility, *over the long run,* of a growth process with broadened and more equitable social participation in economic rents from the export sector. Despite the evidence from Costa Rica, the conditions in other Central American countries are so different, owing to histories of economic inequality enforced by political dictatorship, that since World War II only Guatemala has attempted a moderate series of reforms. These were imposed from the top down by a new middle-class elite which took power in 1944, and the experiment was abruptly ended by a military coup in 1954. Thus the region was able to reflect on long eras of authoritarian control of export economies, by groups adept at extracting the rents, at the very time that the Central American Common Market (CACM) was introduced in the early 1960s.

## The Central American Common Market

The CACM was designed to permit the region to integrate its market for manufactured (primarily consumer) goods so as to create new trade and to divert existing trade from the rest of the world to producers in the region. Clearly the net gain from such policies would be partly at the expense of international "efficiency" of resource allocation. The counterbalancing objective, however, would be to increase the independence of Central America from swings in world trade cycles and to diversify the production structure so that hitherto redundant domestic resources could be utilized more effectively. In terms of restructuring economic production, the CACM proved to be a considerable success, especially during the 1960s. The manufacturing sector grew relative to agricultural and tertiary activities, although part of this growth was due to a shift in relative prices tending to favor the manufacturing over the primary and tertiary sectors. (Although the internal terms of trade did not shift significantly toward manufacturing, without the CACM the shift in relative prices would probably have been more favorable to agriculture than it was.) Some evidence exists, however, indicating that external tariffs were already inflated beyond the level necessary to protect domestic suppliers. Therefore, by lowering the protection on intermediate imports and raising it on final goods, the CACM permitted trade to grow in manufactured goods and actually lowered unit costs of industrial products below pre-1960 levels. This is the result of trade-creation effects which undoubtedly increased the efficiency of existing manufacturing facilities. The impact of this increase in efficiency outweighed the higher costs caused by trade-diversion effects favoring new industries that would not have been set up without the tariff protection of the CACM.

## Employment Consequences of Central American Integration

During the period of rapid growth from 1960 to 1971, the effects of the CACM policies on employment were most pronounced. The main hypothesis employed in the analysis is that conditions of supply and demand in the labor market, influenced by public policy and degrees of market imperfection that differ among countries, activities, and skill levels, are instrumental in determining the wage structure and level of employment.[1] The earn-

1. Labor supply-and-demand conditions may be influenced by historically determined social and other institutional barriers. For example, the family back-

ings of the working class from employment represent a higher share in the distribution of income and wealth than does their relatively meager income from investments and natural resources. Wage income and other factors associated with employment, including psychological identification with the production process, social and political participation of the worker in his environment, and relative as well as absolute deprivation, are intimately associated with social welfare. It is assumed that the ultimate goal of development is the achievement of maximum gains in social welfare. For this study, welfare is seen to be closely associated with income. Hence, employment and the level and share of wages are important measures of the success of the Central American integration process.

During the past decade and a half of integration, the economic growth of the five Central American countries (Honduras dropped out of the CACM in 1969) has been notable by any standard. Table 1 shows that the rate of growth has, however, been decelerating slightly, particularly in the primary sector, while industrial growth has also lost the momentum of the first eight years. The figures suggest the end of the early burst of growth occasioned by the establishment of the CACM and the recovery of agricultural export markets in the 1960s. This coincides with the apparent general lack of "common market *esprit*" throughout the region in 1976. Even the industrial sector, which used to provide most enthusiastic support for integration, fails to see a bright future for further extension of the CACM, although some observers argue that protection for intermediate-goods production might provide a reasonable next step. The problem is that final-goods producers are benefiting by processing low-duty imports of intermediate goods behind a high tariff wall for finished products. They resist any change that threatens their profitability. (It should be noted

---

ground of workers may rank as highly as training or intellect in qualifications for employment. The formalization of this insight in segmentation theories of the labor market is highly relevant to the analysis of conditions in much of Central America. The assumption here is that such approaches influence the degree but not the direction of market adjustment, such that shortages or surpluses in the supply and demand for labor by skill, activity, and region will be distorted if these conditions exist. Their elimination requires legal and other measures that are difficult to implement until the political process itself becomes more democratic and representative of all levels of the working class. Such conditions are far from those that prevail in most countries of the region, the exception being Costa Rica (but even there, the recent tendency has been to restrain the growing influence of labor in the political process).

**Table 1.**　*Growth of Gross Domestic Product in Central America (constant 1960 C.A. peso values)\**

| | CUMULATIVE % PER ANNUM | | |
| --- | --- | --- | --- |
| | *1960–1968* | *1968–1971* | *1971–1975* |
| Primary production (agriculture, mining) | 4.8 | 4.7 | 3.6 |
| Secondary production (manufacturing, construction, energy, transportation) | 7.8 | 5.7 | 6.3 |
| Tertiary production (commerce, banking, real estate, services, others) | 5.5 | 4.7 | 4.7 |
| Total (= GDP) | 5.9 | 5.0 | 4.9 |
| Exports | 9.5 | 3.4 | 7.7 |
| Imports | 8.1 | 4.0 | 9.0 |

*Source:* For 1960–1971: SIECA, "VI Compendio Estadistico Centroamericano," Guatemala, 1975. For 1971–1975: SIECA, "Centroamerica: estadisticas macroeconómicas 1971–75," SIECA/76/PES/8, Guatemala, June 11, 1976.

\*Costa Rica, El Salvador, Guatemala, Honduras, Nicaragua. The Central American peso is valued at one U.S. dollar.

that effective protection in the region is not as high as that of many other Latin American countries.)

The effect of production growth on employment depends on the associated rate of productivity growth in terms of output per worker. Table 2 indicates that over one-half of the growth in output in the region was due to productivity growth, although labor absorption did increase at the significant rate of 2.7 percent per annum from 1960 to 1971 (the period for which census data permit regional employment growth to be estimated).

The primary activities, agriculture and mining, absorbed little incremental labor compared to the growth in the estimated number of job seekers by 1971. That number grew by an estimated 3.1 percent per year for the region as a whole, ranging from 4.0 percent for Nicaragua and Costa Rica to 2.3 percent for Guatemala (for the basis of these calculations see Table 7). Productivity growth accounted for the highest share of output growth in the primary sector (60 percent), due to the introduction of new techniques of cultivation, including mechanization, irrigation, application of pesticides and fertilizers, and the shift to export crops, which responded well to such measures. As a result, labor was released in large numbers to find work in the secondary and tertiary sectors. This problem was exacerbated by the fact that rural workers are only seasonally employed in the cultivation and harvesting of the export crops. Before the 1960s, many of these workers were given access either to their own land or to land rented at low prices for subsistence cultivation and for production for internal markets. However, the boom of commercial export agriculture, which began in 1960 and has continued to the present, sharply diminished the availability of such land throughout the region. This is reflected in the tripling or quadrupling of real rents charged to the peasants. Consequently, ever-increasing numbers of workers are being forced to rely on the highly uncertain, seasonal, rural wage-labor market. Men, women, and children are faced with the choice between migrating to the cities and taking a chance on rural employment (for somewhat higher real wages than before, but on a sporadic basis). Thus, annual real earnings (reflecting the decline in income from subsistence cultivation on low-rent land which more than offsets a slight rise in real wages) appear to be falling for many landless rural workers in the most labor-abundant regions of El Salvador and Guatemala. Only increased participation of women and children in wage labor permits family incomes to be maintained.

The slack in employment in the rural area has been somewhat

**Table 2.**  *Central American Employment Growth in relation to Production and Productivity, 1960–1971 (Percent per annum)*

|  | Growth of Real Output (value added in constant 1960 prices) | Growth of Employment (man-years) | Growth of Productivity (value added per employed worker) |
|---|---|---|---|
| Primary production | 4.8 | 1.9 | 2.9 |
| Secondary production | 7.2 | 4.2 | 3.0 |
| Tertiary production | 5.3 | 3.5 | 1.8 |
| Total GDP, CACM | 5.6 | 2.7 | 2.9 |

*Source:* See Table 1.

picked up by the secondary sector in Central America. Productivity growth accounts for 42 percent of output growth, due to the very high rate of investment in manufacturing and transportation, as well as the use of relatively capital-intensive technology. Tertiary activities have also absorbed a significant share of the increasing work force, productivity growth accounting for only one-third of the growth in output in this sector. As Table 2 shows, the combined employment growth of the secondary and tertiary sectors averaged almost 4 percent per annum, which was well ahead of the rate of growth of the labor supply. The problem, then, is not one of failure of growing sectors to absorb labor rapidly, but of the failure of the agricultural sector to maintain its share of employment opportunities because of its higher relative rate of growth of output per worker. Hence the primary sector, which employed 62 percent of the work force in 1960, fell to 57 percent in 1971, while the secondary sector rose from 17 to 20 percent and the tertiary sector from 21 to 23 percent. The share of output in the primary sector fell less, from 30 to 27 percent. While the share of the secondary sector grew from 22 to 27 percent, that of the tertiary sector fell from 48 to 46 percent.

The nature of rural production has changed in response to a number of factors: rising world prices for cash crops, integration of previously isolated regions through road and communication grids, and resulting declines in transport costs (at least until the recent rise in petroleum prices), plus improved technology for irrigated farming, pesticides, fertilizers, and expanded marketing outlets. The result amounts to a rural revolution in much of Central America. This revolution has given rise to rapidly increasing economic rents both absolutely and, as we shall see, as a share of factor income. The dislocation of the labor force from land previously farmed for subsistence purposes and for local marketing has swollen the numbers of the rural proletariat. This is keeping wage levels down and permitting a higher rent share for those with access to land. Some of the displaced labor provides a pool for employment in the urban industrial and service sectors. The rest is relegated to land in more distant, less accessible regions, to sporadic employment as field hands, and to very low-productivity tertiary and other occupations.

In short, the Central American countries have always been rural-based export economies, but during the CACM period this dependence has increased substantially, the impressive industrialization notwithstanding. And while low-cost labor is essential to the new cropping patterns that are emerging, the consolidation of land and its mechanization have led to a growing surplus of rural labor that is well in excess of readily available employment opportunities, particularly in the most populous regions. Policies favoring regional migration could alleviate this problem somewhat, and much de facto migration does take place among a number of the countries, from El Salvador to Guatemala and from Guatemala to Mexico seasonally, from El Salvador to Nicaragua and Costa Rica (bypassing Honduras, which expelled scores of thousands of Salvadorians in 1969), and from southern Nicaragua to Costa Rica. However, a formal treaty permitting free labor mobility is unlikely in the near future.

## The Regional Distribution of Productivity Growth

Since productivity growth prevented labor absorption from matching the rate of growth in the work force (despite rapid output growth in all major sectors and countries of the region), it is of interest to trace out the locus of productivity growth among the five countries. It should be stressed that without the opportunity to realize such gains, many investments in land development, plant, equipment, education, and new technology would not have been forthcoming, nor would the output growth they produced. Hence, it is not suggested that productivity growth should be minimized in order to create jobs (in order to perpetuate the curse of Eden), but, rather, that the *potential* surplus created by increasing productivity should be channeled into activities that raise the income and welfare of the working class. To date, however, the working-class participation in factor income has actually declined in relative terms (and apparently in absolute terms for some rural landless workers in the most populated regions) in all countries but Nicaragua. Thus, export-led rural growth and import-substituting industrial growth have not permitted the results of the impressive productivity gains to be shared on an equitable basis. This is not to say that those in charge of the development model intended this result, although private enterprise is, understandably, interested in minimizing wage costs. Rather, the nature of the development process itself (with a minimum of fiscal or financial transfers) has had this effect in four of the five countries. The reasons for this are discussed below.

In Table 3, regional productivity growth (4.2 percent per annum in current prices or 2.9 percent in constant prices) has been broken into its national components in order to determine the relative contribution of each of the five countries. Productivity growth over the eleven-year period averaged 485 C.A. pesos, which represents a nominal gain of 58 percent over the value of output per worker in 1960 and a real gain of 37 percent. Among the five countries, Nicaragua and Costa Rica alone accounted for 42 percent of total regional productivity growth, though their combined work force represented only 21 percent of employed labor in the region (a share which did not change over the period). Lagging far behind were El Salvador and Honduras, with a joint contribution to the regional total of 23 percent, although they had 40 percent of the work force. Guatemala also lagged, but by a smaller amount. What these figures reveal is that above the given output per worker in 1960, and despite the rapid growth of employment during the period 1960 to 1971, there remained an additional 485 C.A. pesos per worker in productivity growth to be apportioned among the government and the owners of capital, natural resources, entrepreneurship, technology, and labor.

## Actual Growth in Demand for Labor in Central America, 1960 to 1971

As we have seen, the demand for labor in the region grew at 2.7 percent per annum between 1960 and 1971, or by a total of 1.1 million workers. In Honduras, the low productivity growth combined with the significant rate of output growth caused the demand for labor to increase by the highest rate in the region, 3.4 percent per year (Table 4). Another reason for this demand could be that the existence of abundant land in Honduras, plus access (until 1969) to the labor pool of El Salvador, where wages were even lower, encouraged the growth of activities in the primary sector that involved little capital formation except in labor-intensive land clearing and planting plus forestry. As other studies have shown, these developments did not depend essentially on the machinery of the Central American Common Market, although a number of processing industries were established around San

**Table 3.** *Country Contributions to Regional Productivity Growth, 1960 to 1971*

| | *(1)*<br>*Growth in*<br>*Output per Worker*<br>*(C.A. pesos in*<br>*current values)* | *(2)*<br>*Share of*<br>*Regional*<br>*Employment* | *(3)*<br>*Contribution to*<br>*Output per Worker*<br>*in C.A. pesos*<br>*([1] × [2])* | *(4)*<br>*Contribution*<br>*Relative to Total*<br>*([3] ÷ sum [3])* | *(5)*<br>*Contribution*<br>*Relative to Share*<br>*of Employment*<br>*([4] ÷ [2])* |
|---|---|---|---|---|---|
| Guatemala | 423 | .38 | 161 | .33 | .87 |
| El Salvador | 280 | .23 | 64 | .13 | .57 |
| Honduras | 289 | .17 | 49 | .10 | .59 |
| Nicaragua | 947 | .11 | 104 | .21 | 1.91 |
| Costa Rica | 1,077 | .10 | 108 | .22 | 2.20 |
| Central America | 485 | 1.00 | 485 | 1.00 | 1.00 |

*Source:* See Table 1. Employment estimates are taken from numerous sources, primarily based on census data for individual countries, as consolidated and adjusted by Gustavo Leiva, SIECA Special Studies Unit, Guatemala, 1975–1976.

**Table 4.** *Actual Growth in Demand for Labor in Central America, 1950–1971*

| | 1960 | 1971 | (1960–1971) | Growth of Employment (%) | Growth of Output (cum. annual rates) (%) | Growth of Productivity (%) |
|---|---|---|---|---|---|---|
| | | | *(thousands of man-years)* | | | |
| Guatemala | 1,254 | 1,593 | 339 | 2.2 | 5.4 | 3.2 |
| El Salvador | 741 | 1,025 | 284 | 2.9 | 5.4 | 2.5 |
| Honduras | 557 | 826 | 259 | 3.4 | 4.5 | 1.1 |
| Nicaragua | 367 | 480 | 113 | 2.4 | 6.8 | 4.4 |
| Costa Rica | 338 | 452 | 114 | 2.6 | 6.3 | 3.7 |
| Central America | 3,257 | 4,376 | 1,109 | 2.7 | 5.6 | 2.9 |

*Source:* See Tables 1 to 3. Figures for employment in 1971 are interpolated from the most recent census, assuming constancy of most recent participation rates and constant demographic growth rates for intercensal years.

Pedro Sula which did benefit from the low-cost imports and other incentives of the CACM.

In general, however, trade diversion raised the cost of imported final goods to Honduras without providing commensurate benefits to local manufacturing. This explains the lack of support for continued participation in the CACM, though it is difficult to explain the embargo on migrant labor from El Salvador on these grounds. The explanation for the expulsion of the Salvadorians lies in the opposition of the local population to competition in the labor market. They also objected to land claims made by their neighbors from the west under the expanding agrarian reform program. The military government appears to have responded reluctantly to these populist pressures to exclude the Salvadorians, justifying its action in terms of preserving national resources for its own citizens. On strictly macroeconomic grounds, both El Salvador and Honduras would have benefited from continued free migration and capital flows (the net flows were probably from El Salvador to Honduras in the 1960s, though they might have reversed later). However, the social pressures resulting from migration were more detrimental to Honduras than to its neighbor before expulsion, while afterward this was reversed.

After Honduras, El Salvador had the greatest increase in labor demand, rising by 2.9 percent per annum, followed by Costa Rica (2.6), Nicaragua (2.4), and Guatemala (2.2). The Guatemalan performance was due to its somewhat slower rate of output growth relative to the leading countries, and its somewhat faster productivity growth in comparison to the lagging countries. Hence, from the point of view of employment, Guatemala had the worst of both worlds. This is partly because Guatemala's growth depended more heavily on industrialization (industry grew at 7.9 percent per annum) than on export agriculture. Its growth of primary production (5.7 percent) exceeded only that of the industrial leader El Salvador (4.3 percent). When this is compared to the large share of its work force in agriculture, the Guatemalan experience contrasts with other rapidly industrializing countries such as Costa Rica, which had growth rates in industry and primary production of 11.0 and 7.4 percent per annum respectively, and Nicaragua, which had rates of 12.5 and 7.0 percent. El Salvador had a higher rate of industrialization than Guatemala (8.3 percent), permitting greater labor absorption into the urban sector.

Due to the unequal land-tenure conditions in Guatemala, its impoverished peasantry, the slow rate of productivity growth, and the low per-capita income for the majority of the population, this country, together with El Salvador, is haunted by the specter of a severe excess in the supply of labor. It also has the lowest wage share of value added in Central America, and that share is falling at the most rapid rate. This contrasts with the evidence that average Guatemalan real wages are rising faster than those of El Salvador and Honduras (though average and marginal earnings per worker need not be correlated, especially when the estimates include all skill levels). What appears to be happening is the growth of a dualistic wage structure as workers in higher-productivity urban and commercial agricultural occupations increase their shares of the wage bill at the expense of the marginal workers. Since the February 1976 earthquake, wages seem to have been rising in real terms (increasing sharply in nominal terms) and jobs in construction have drawn heavily on the wage laborers in agriculture. This is the direct result of the combination of dire necessity, occasioning the use of leisure time for massive do-it-yourself reconstruction, and the availability of subsidized construction materials, machinery, and equipment. Disaster-relief operations supported by many countries have provided these materials, which have reached a large share of the affected population.

There is evidence that the earthquake and the subsequent nationwide relief activities have had a profound impact on social consciousness at the grassroots level. What this will mean in practical terms remains to be seen. Even the poorest Indians from the smallest villages in the earthquake zone are now aware that despite many failures and shortcomings of the relief programs, their welfare was for a brief period a matter not only of national but of international concern. This is likely to create a new force in politics whose voice will become more strident as time goes by. Recent events have also galvanized strong pressures for social reform within the hitherto conservative Church hierarchy. The rural earthquake-relief program of Guatemala and the urban reconstruction of Nicaragua when Managua was devastated by the 1972 earthquake both illustrate that massive public-expenditure programs can provide many additional jobs, although at the expense of severe (if temporary) inflation in the prices of basic consumables. While rising prices hurt those on fixed money incomes, the working class in both countries seems to have benefited from these disaster-relief measures, the first real efforts in either country to mount major deficit-spending programs. From a fiscal point of view, the expenditures were financed by external funds rather than by the unsupported creation of liquidity. Nevertheless, the impact was functionally the same as deficit-spending programs, since capacity was severely constrained by the disaster (especially in the case of Nicaragua). In Guatemala, there was little excess capacity in wage-goods production, so the increase in effective demand pushed up price levels by 30 to 40 percent in 1976 alone, since imports did not increase enough to satisfy the demand.

The forced experiment in earthquake relief was a shock treatment for the fiscally unbelievably conservative governments of each country. The consequences seem to have been favorable to the employment of unskilled labor, although much underemployment still exists, largely because of the seasonal nature of the demand for agricultural workers. The lesson is that deficit spending (and attendant inflation), with foreign assistance for balance-of-payments support, and appropriately flexible exchange rates (a divergence from existing policies), might well allay the underemployment problem. Such expenditure should be directed toward labor-absorbing activities such as construction, small-scale agriculture (including land-distribution programs and labor-intensive infrastructure support), and processing industries in labor-surplus regions. Without the intervention of natural disasters, however, the conservatism of most existing governments in the northern part of Central America and of their supporters from the business, commercial, and landed elites stands in the way of such policies. Some possible exceptions that exist in the case of Honduras and El Salvador will be mentioned later.

### Alternative Labor-Demand Patterns with and without Productivity Growth

In order to assess the potential that the growth of the region provides for the absorption of labor, ignoring the effect of the rapid productivity growth that did occur, I have made the extreme alternative assumption that labor requirements per unit of value added remained constant between 1960 and 1971. (Since there was very little inflation during the period, the calculations are made in current prices, which produces a slight upward bias in the estimated demand for labor for 1971.) With this assumption, Table 5 shows that the growth of the region during the eleven-year period

**Table 5.**   *Hypothetical Growth in Demand for Labor in Central America 1960–1971 (thousands of man-years)*

| | Actual Growth in Employment | Hypothetical Growth in Demand for Labor | Gap |
|---|---|---|---|
| Guatemala | 339 | 1,180 | 841 |
| El Salvador | 284 | 676 | 392 |
| Honduras | 259 | 670 | 411 |
| Nicaragua | 113 | 596 | 483 |
| Costa Rica | 114 | 523 | 409 |
| Central America | 1,109 | 3,645 | 2,536 |

*Source:* Data on employment in 1960 and 1971, productivity in 1960, and output in 1971 are from the sources given for Table 1 to 4. For this table, it is assumed that value added per worker remained constant between 1960 and 1971 in order to calculate hypothetical demand for 1971. This figure was then subtracted from employment in 1960 to obtain hypothetical growth in demand.

would have required 3.6 million additional workers, compared to the actual increase in employment of 1.1 million. In short, the "gap" under these extreme assumptions would have amounted to 58 percent of the economically active population in the region. Of course, without the productivity growth and the rewards it provided to investors, growth in output would certainly have caused the demand for labor in 1971 substantially to exceed the available supply for all countries in the region, including the most labor-abundant. In short, productivity growth permitted the region to avoid a severe constraint in labor supply. However, it did the job too well.

If the hypothetical gap between demand and supply of labor is measured as a percentage of 1971 employment, the countries most affected would have been, in descending order, Nicaragua (101 percent), Costa Rica (90 percent), Guatemala (53 percent), Honduras (50 percent), and El Salvador (38 percent). Thus, without the use of natural-resource and capital-intensive technologies, the growth in output during this period would have produced rapidly rising wage levels. Furthermore, assuming that the elasticity of substitution between labor and capital is less than unity, wages would have taken a larger share of the value added. Without taking into consideration the demand effects of changes in income distribution for the realization of scale economies and thus additional incentives to invest in the internal market, the labor constraint would probably have slowed the rate of growth and introduced a self-correcting element into the demand for labor. The opening up of the regional market and the attractiveness of tariff protection for final manufactures and tariff exemption for intermediate inputs permitted the high rate of productivity growth to occur. Additional factors include tax holidays for new investment and the proliferation of rural and urban infrastructure, together with the availability of new labor-saving technology and methods of increasing the productivity of land in the region.

In Table 6, estimates are presented for the sectoral impact of productivity growth on employment demand. Similar assumptions are made about the amount of labor that would have been required with and without productivity growth. This table reveals the sensitivity to productivity demand of the three major production sectors. The ratio of labor demand without productivity growth to actual demand in the primary sector is 4.4; that is, up to four times as many workers would have been required in agriculture (and mining) to produce the production levels of 1971 if increases in productivity had not been provided by investment, opening of new land to cultivation, shifts in cropping patterns, and technological progress (the seed and fertilizer revolution). Food prices would almost certainly have risen relative to those of industrial goods, with the result that exports would have been reduced while food imports would have increased. Paradoxically, it seems that the growth of secondary activities depended heavily on a revolution in productivity in the primary sector, despite policies to encourage manufacturing which in turn tended to discourage agricultural growth elsewhere in Latin America during the period of import-substitution industrialization. What seems to have happened is that tariff protection for the secondary sector was not accompanied by direct income transfers through fiscal or financial subsidies, as it was in Chile, Uruguay, Argentina, and other countries during the 1950s and 1960s. Instead, the fiscal and financial conservatism of Central America during these years minimized the degree of effective protection and artificial subsidization of the industrial sector, thus permitting agriculture to grow simultaneously.

The labor-saving technologies in the rural sector released additional labor for employment in secondary and tertiary activities.

**Table 6.** *Growth in Demand for Labor by Major Production Sector in Central America, with and without Productivity Growth, 1960–1971 (thousands of man-years)*

| | Primary Sector (agriculture, mining) | Secondary Sector (industry, construction energy, transportation) | Tertiary Sector (commerce, banking, services, others) | Total |
|---|---|---|---|---|
| Change in labor demand without productivity growth but with growth in output, 1960–1971 | 1,998 | 880 | 767 | 3,645 |
| Change in labor demand without growth in output but with productivity growth, 1960–1971 | −780 | −212 | −206 | −1,198 |
| Change in labor demand with combined productivity growth and growth in output | −763 | −340 | −234 | −1,337 |
| Actual change in labor demand, 1960–1971 | 455 | 328 | 327 | 1,110 |

*Note:* This table is calculated from the formula:

$$\Delta D_L = \Delta Q\left(\frac{Q}{L_0}\right) + \Delta\left(\frac{Q}{L}\right)\Delta Q_0 + \Delta\left(\frac{Q}{L}\right)\Delta\left(\frac{Q}{L_0}\right)$$

where $D_L$ is demand for labor
$Q$  is value added
$0$  is base year
$\Delta$  is first difference between year 0 and year $n$
$L$  is quantity of labor

This parallel growth of agriculture and industry in Central America was the major reason for the fifteen years of relatively rapid growth in both output and productivity. The secondary sector would have required 2.7 times as many additional workers without the observed productivity growth, while for tertiary activities the figure would have been 2.1. Overall, 3.3 times as many new workers would have been required without productivity gains. Thus, the economic growth of the Central American Common Market was achieved with productivity gains in all major sectors.

## Growth in the Supply of Labor in Central America

In order to relate the observed changes in employment to likely changes in the availability of labor, Table 7 presents a rough estimate of the increase in the supply of labor from 1960 to 1971. This increase is defined as the number of additional man-years available (with equal weighting for age and sex) based on the crude assumption that the participation rates for the economically active age groups (ages 10 to 64 in all countries except Costa Rica, where it is ages 15 to 64) remained constant from 1960 to 1971. This assumption ignores the fact that the desired participation rates change according to changing income levels, urbanization, shifting age composition of the base population, increased educational demand, and other factors. However the purpose of the table is simply to provide rough orders of magnitude for the increase in supply.

In view of the approximate nature of the estimates in Table 7, a comparison with actual changes in labor demand from Tables 4

**Table 7.** *Estimated Labor Supply Increases, 1960–1971 (thousands of man-years)*

| | |
|---|---|
| Guatemala | 369 |
| El Salvador | 284 |
| Honduras | 292 |
| Nicaragua | 202 |
| Costa Rica | 184 |
| Central America | 1,331 |

and 5 is impressionistic at best. However, subject to this qualification, the figures suggest that the growth in labor supply in the region outstripped demand by more than two hundred thousand workers, a significant margin. In terms of total employment in 1971 (4.4 million), this increase in "excess supply" was only 5 percent. Of course, the effect of the growth in excess supply of labor was almost certainly more serious for the lower skill levels, since the demand for more educated and experienced workers grew rapidly as a proportion of total employment. Hence, the impact on the wage structure was to skew wages, widening the income gap between the lowest and the highest skill level. Regional imbalances were also exacerbated, since although the overall growth rates in the supply and in the demand for labor were similar at the country level, the gaps were more uneven. The next section deals with the average earnings of workers during the same period.

## Labor Income in Central America

The evolution of real wages over the period 1960–1971 reflects the interaction of supply-and-demand conditions, as sketched in the preceding sections, and institutional developments that influenced the relative bargaining positions of capital and labor. Although unionization is one important element in this pattern, there is not space here to go into the complex history of attempts by workers to organize and bargain collectively in the five countries. The pattern is also very uneven among the different countries and even among different activity sectors. Costa Rica is the only country in which labor organization is permitted as an active process influencing wages, hours, and working conditions. Even here the results are mixed when compared with other countries in Latin America where democratic politics permit a greater participation of the workers in the determination of wages at the levels of the single firm and of the whole industry. In general, the imposition of military regimes militates against labor's voice in the decisionmaking process. The other four countries of Central America are no exception. The opposition to independent unionization as opposed to company unionization (the former being associated with communism in many areas) is so strong that even professionals in some of the most progressive institutions are finding it impossible to organize without fear of reprisal. Conditions in the labor markets facilitate strike-breaking, in that excess supply of labor enables greater barriers to labor organization to be imposed. (Monopoly and monopsony power have their roots in underlying market conditions and are strengthened by the political system, its legal structure, and enforcement mechanisms.)

Table 8 shows the levels of wages and salaries per worker for the five countries. The growth of real wages has averaged 2.6 percent per annum for the region as a whole, led by Nicaragua and Costa Rica. They are followed by Guatemala, El Salvador, and Honduras, in that order. It should be noted that wage fluctuation since 1971 has been influenced by two factors: the slowdown in the economic process, and the rapid increase in prices. The latter is due to world inflation and increased costs of imports, domestic deficit spending (in Costa Rica), and natural disasters (Hurricane Fifi in Honduras and the earthquakes of Nicaragua and Guatemala) and subsequent relief expenditures which added to final demand even as capacity was reduced. Hence even without a clear indication of post-1971 trends, there is a consensus that during this period real wages

***Table 8.*** *Annual Average Wage and Salary per Employed Worker*

|  | CURRENT C.A. PESOS | | CUM. ANNUAL RATE OF GROWTH, 1960–1971 (%) | |
| --- | --- | --- | --- | --- |
|  | *1960* | *1971* | *Current Prices* | *Constant Prices* |
| Guatemala | 339 | 470 | 3.0 | 2.5 |
| El Salvador | 328 | 431 | 2.5 | 2.2 |
| Honduras | 266 | 370 | 3.0 | 0.9 |
| Nicaragua | 481 | 991 | 6.6 | 4.5 |
| Costa Rica | 622 | 1,138 | 5.5 | 3.5 |
| Central America | 369 | 568 | 3.9 | 2.6 |

*Source:* Based on wage and salary (and fringe benefit) estimates by Gustavo Leiva, SIECA Special Studies Unit, Guatemala, 1971, 1976, based on SIECA and government sources. The figures are average earnings and do not reflect trends in distribution of the wage bill, which for all countries appears to have become significantly more skewed during the period. Current price estimates are converted to constant prices using the implicit GOP deflators for the respective countries from SIECA, "VI Compendio Estadistico Centroamericano," Guatemala, 1975.

probably declined throughout Central America for the lowest skill levels, with lesser declines and even some increases for higher skills (though at a slower rate than in the 1960s).

## Wages, *Plusvalia*, and the Normal Return on Capital in Central America

It is only possible to provide the most general outlines of the distribution of income in the region among labor, capital, and the owners of natural resources. The share of wages and salaries in value added, when deducted from total value added (less depreciation), leaves a residual which may be apportioned among the owners of physical assets, natural resources, and a scarcity rent for other scarce factors. *Scarcity rent* includes profits in excess of the normal return on capital, wages in excess of the opportunity cost of labor, entrepreneurial income, returns to licensing and patents, and other such factors. The scarcity-rent component in neoclassical economic analysis is analogous to the concept of *plusvalia* commonly found in the more progressive Latin American economic literature. This concept provides a rough measure of the surplus income generated, namely, that component of market price which can be extracted without significantly altering resource allocation. Clearly there are strong differences of opinion, both political and technical, about the extent to which the unimpaired market allocation of scarcity rents is essential to the level and efficiency of production. Setting these debates aside, although statistical evidence is somewhat sketchy, it is of interest to determine the extent to which the pattern of growth in Central America since 1960 has influenced the functional distribution of income (see Table 9). (It should be noted that relatively reliable data are perhaps more abundantly available on a comparable basis for the five Central American countries than for most other nations of Latin America.)

The relationship between the absolute level of wages in 1960 and the wage share of output may be seen by comparing the data in Tables 8 and 9 (see Table 10). These figures reflect the labor-surplus situation in Guatemala and El Salvador. Even though both countries had higher average wages than Honduras, they had a lower wage-share of value added. Guatemala had the lowest share, due primarily to its preponderance of low-productivity agricultural employment. Dualism in the labor markets of both countries also lies behind the figures. This becomes more apparent when

**Table 9.** *Functional Distribution of Income in Central America, 1960 and 1971*

|  | Share of Wages and Salaries | Share of Profits Interest, and Rent (plusvalia) | Total |
|---|---|---|---|
| Guatemala |  |  |  |
| 1960 | .407 | .593 | 1.00 |
| 1971 | .374 | .626 | 1.00 |
| El Salvador |  |  |  |
| 1960 | .426 | .574 | 1.00 |
| 1971 | .412 | .588 | 1.00 |
| Honduras |  |  |  |
| 1960 | .438 | .562 | 1.00 |
| 1971 | .413 | .587 | 1.00 |
| Nicaragua |  |  |  |
| 1960 | .493 | .507 | 1.00 |
| 1971 | .515 | .485 | 1.00 |
| Costa Rica |  |  |  |
| 1960 | .502 | .498 | 1.00 |
| 1971 | .492 | .508 | 1.00 |
| Central America |  |  |  |
| 1960 | .441 | .559 | 1.00 |
| 1971 | .430 | .570 | 1.00 |

*Source:* Calculations prepared by Gustavo Leiva, SIECA Special Studies Unit, Guatemala, 1975–1976, based on source materials cited in previous tables. More detailed estimates of cost on capital and residual (*plusvalia*) are available from the author on request and will appear in a forthcoming study by Clark W. Reynolds and Gustavo Leiva on employment, wages, and income distribution in Central America.

one looks at the wage profiles within both industry and agriculture (lack of space precludes presentation of the findings in this paper). The data indicate that this dualism increases during the period 1960–1971, further exacerbating income inequality. As for Costa Rica, one must qualify the implications of functional distribution of income for the size distribution of income among individuals and households. Land and capital are more evenly distributed in that country, so the share of profits, interest, and rent is more equitably divided among the population. Moreover, the relatively high education of the labor force causes the wage bill to be more

**Table 10.**   *Comparison of Wages and Wage Share of Output, 1960*

|  | *C.A. Pesos per Worker, 1960* | *Wages/Value Added, 1960* |
|---|---|---|
| Guatemala | 339 | .402 |
| El Salvador | 328 | .426 |
| Honduras | 266 | .438 |
| Nicaragua | 481 | .493 |
| Costa Rica | 622 | .503 |
| Central America | 369 | .441 |

evenly distributed than it is in the other four countries of Central America. Nevertheless, the evidence in Table 9 indicates that only Nicaragua experienced a significant rise in the wage share of value added between 1960 and 1971, while that of Costa Rica showed a slight (probably statistically insignificant) decline over the period. All the other countries showed significant declines in the wage share, indicating that the surplus generated by the rapid growth of the 1960s was being distributed to owners of capital and natural resources. Since there is no evidence that this ownership became more equitable during the period, it is quite likely that the size distribution of income also became more skewed, particularly in those countries with a surplus of unskilled labor, for whom real incomes stagnated or declined.

## Possible Future Economic Trends

Since this paper is directed to a survey of future economic trends in Latin America and their implications for the international community, it remains to draw some implications for the future from the foregoing analysis and the experience on which it is based. During the past fifteen years, the CACM region has shown impressive growth in all major sectors and countries. Changes in incentives and the creation of infrastructure have had a significant effect toward balanced growth of primary, secondary, and tertiary production. Without major productivity gains (most notable in agriculture and industry), the rapid growth of the region would have exhausted the supply of labor. The process of labor absorption has not quite kept pace with the rapid growth of the labor supply; labor redundancy rates probably rose by at least five percentage points between 1960 and 1971. Although data are scanty on employment and productivity for post-census years, the trends since 1971 appear to indicate an even greater lag in labor absorption.

The gains of the past decade and a half notwithstanding, the common market is no longer a key issue among most opinion groups in the region, despite laudable efforts of the SIECA administration to keep the idea afloat and to promote the new Tratado Marco, which would further expand the provisions of the CACM to include labor migration, some degree of political coordination, and other advances in integration policy. The reasons for this seem to be a general recognition that the easy gains of the past fifteen years have now been achieved. There is also an awareness, which is not shared equally by all governments or all social and economic classes, that conditions within most of the countries are highly inequitable and that integration has *not* measurably improved the relative economic condition of the workers or the absolute income levels of the poorest households. It is this stark reality that must be faced in the decades to come. And there is little evidence that the integration model pursued until now—based on market incentives to private investment in agriculture, manufacturing, and commerce—will demonstrably alter conditions. This is especially true since growth is unlikely to be maintained at previous rates, while the supply of labor to be absorbed is growing at an ever more rapid pace and will continue to do so for at least another generation.

With this situation in mind, and with public awareness of the economic prospects slowly permeating all social groups from the elite to the peasantry, the military is tightening its grip on the political process in all countries but Costa Rica, and even there rumors exist about the clandestine training of paramilitary units for use in the event of serious internal unrest. Meanwhile policymakers are increasingly looking inward for solutions to the joint economic and social question. Honduras has sealed its border to Salvadorians, and there is no sign that this policy will change in the near future. The opportunities for import substitution are running out (except perhaps for intermediate-goods production), given the present size of the market (which itself is a result of growing inequality in income distribution). The business and commercial elite considers that the most obvious outlet would be to increase external protection or to shift to a program of export promotion. This could be accomplished by direct subsidies or by undervaluation of exchange rates, since the scope for additional tax incentives is relatively limited after over a decade of implementing such policies. In short, the implications for additional expansion of foreign trade in Central America will depend on policies of export promotion, including drawback agreements (following the Brazilian model), integration of local producers with transnational production and marketing operations, and associated fiscal and financial incentives. Such a strategy is unlikely significantly to alter the disintegration of the economy and society that predominates in most regions of Central America, and particularly in Guatemala, Nicaragua, and El Salvador.

An alternative approach, not necessarily inconsistent with the above, would be to follow the Costa Rican model and to attempt to improve the distribution of income through employment-generating programs in construction, labor-intensive manufacturing of wage goods for sale to the working class, state distribution systems for wage goods, the stimulation of agricultural production for domestic consumption, and land-distribution schemes. The last would provide the rural work-force with a higher floor on incomes, based in part on subsistence production and in part on broader access to rental income from the sale of cash crops. This approach would require sharp increases in public expenditure, following the fiscal-policy objectives of Costa Rica, which, despite its difficulties, has made the most effort to achieve progress along distributive lines through active intervention by the public sector. Economic rents would have to be taxed at a higher rate than is now the case, to avoid substantial inflation (some of the countries have tax shares of GDP which are among the world's lowest), and exchange-rate policies would have to become more flexible to avoid increasing balance-of-payments deficits.

In addition, whatever the strategies adopted, Central America cannot continue to borrow at a rate of 5 to 10 percent of GDP (represented by the balance-of-trade deficits on current account in the mid-1970s) to supplement surprisingly low domestic savings rates in both the private and the public sector. The large and growing rental-income stream accruing primarily to the elite is not being tapped through taxation or voluntary financial savings so as to permit noninflationary financing of domestic investment. To do so would require reforms in financial policies equal to or surpassing the fiscal reforms which are also long overdue in the region. At present, regional financial institutions are highly underdeveloped, partly because of ceilings on deposit rates of interest. This discourages voluntary financial savings and diverts domestic funds into foreign financial assets, unproductive investments, or consumption.

Moreover, the financial system is scarcely integrated among the five countries, so funds flow more readily between the region and the rest of the world than between surplus and deficit sectors within Central America. Here improved fiscal and financial policy could go hand-in-hand with employment-generating programs of the private and public sectors, although without the requisite political will, neither would improve social participation in the development process. The military governments of the four countries range from highly reactionary to mildly progressive, but there are some pressures within the regimes for more popular programs, such as the incipient land reforms being introduced in Honduras and El Salvador (against the strenuous opposition of many in the business and agricultural elites).[2] The effectiveness of such programs remains to be seen. Until now they have not encroached upon the prime commercial crop land for export and are unlikely to cut severely into the all-important foreign-exchange earnings on which all of these export economies still depend.

All political groups look to the United States, regardless of the degree of favor or disfavor, as the major constraint or prime mover behind their respective programs. While this consciousness of dependence may have the appearance of rank paranoia to the foreign observer, it comes from a profound sense of history which is difficult for those born outside the region to appreciate. Presidents, political parties, military leaders, industries, and even nation-states have owed their existence to the Colossus, despite its generally benign neglect of their condition or of its influence on it. Hence, prospective foreign-policy developments in the United States are seen as being crucial to the region's economic future. Unarmed and democratic Costa Rica has tried to establish stronger links with Panama and Venezuela in order to counterbalance the growing military conservatism of its neighbors to the north, but these attempts will modify the present balance of power only slightly.

If the United States were to tilt its support from the northern

2. Since this paper was written the El Salvador reform was blocked by the new government.

axis of Nicaragua, El Salvador, and Guatemala toward the southern axis of Costa Rica, Panama, and Honduras, this could have a major influence on the success of efforts within the northern countries to improve the social distribution of economic and political power. Such efforts have faltered under the aegis of the past two U.S. administrations, which have maintained a low profile in the economic and social areas and have actively supported military governments and counterinsurgency efforts, most notably in Guatemala and Nicaragua. In both of these countries, and in El Salvador and Honduras, there are groups (which include university professors, professionals, and members of business, commercial, and rural elites) who would provide support for an opening toward more democratic processes of government with greater inclusion of the workers in political and economic decisions. These policies could vent latent pressures from within the social volcano of Central America and perhaps avoid the cataclysm which otherwise seems inevitable. The neighbors to the north (Mexico) and south (Panama and Venezuela) as well as the east (the Caribbean states) would provide support in varying degrees for such an opening, however much they might deplore the obvious continuing dependence of the region on the United States. In the meantime any forecast of economic trends in Central America must await political decisions to deal with the grave inequalities in income and with the political repression and social malaise that make the region integrated in name only.

# Part III

# Toward a Political Economy of Development

## *Robert H. Bates*

For market-oriented economists, development is a product of efficiency and growth. *Efficient employment of scarce resources* means that no reallocation could increase the total value of goods and services. And *growth* is an increase in the magnitude of the total per capita product. When a society is developed, then, people can enjoy more of the good things of life.

One reason that market-oriented economists tend to deny the centrality of politics to the development process is that they tend to discount problems of distribution. Those who adhere to the efficiency-and-growth position counter that if development produces a maldistribution of income, those who are losers in the short run could become winners in the longer run. Given successful development, the winners could become sufficiently better off that they could compensate the losers. Peasants driven off the land by the commercialization of agriculture, for example, could find their children's education being financed by taxes levied from the new economic order.

Another reason that the efficiency-and-growth school discounts the centrality of politics to the development process is that it views governments as imposing social costs. Thus Deepak Lal writes, in an influential recent book: "What the experience of developing countries does show is that, other things equal, the most important advice that economists can currently offer is . . . : 'Get the prices right.'"[1] The free and unbridled use of the market, unimpeded by political intervention and bureaucratic bumbling, does more to produce development, Lal argues, than do any number of government-backed development programs, advanced in the name of *dirigiste* dogmas.

From this viewpoint, governments are not just irrelevant to the development process, they actually impede it. By altering market prices, governments distort markets; they create incentives for resources to flow into uses other than those in which they would be economically most productive. By regulating entry into markets, governments generate rents, economic premiums which lie above what the market would confer. They thereby create incentives for people to invest, not in activities that are economically productive, but in the search for political favor. Those advocating the unrestricted use of the market, then, tend to treat governments as sources of social costs. Their prescription is less government.[2]

Needless to say, the position of Lal and others revives ethical controversies whose origins lie in the deepest roots of moral philosophy. And since development is a field in which radical and Marxist thought has achieved prominence, their free-market advocacy represents a challenge not only to intellectual but also to political traditions. In the controversies that have resulted, important questions have been ignored. These questions probe very deep, and they require positive rather than normative analysis. Why do people abandon markets and turn to political institutions? Why do governments behave as they do? How are public policies chosen?

The authors of the essays in this section tend to accept the premise shared by Lal and others as to what economic development means. But they steadfastly reject their analysis of the role of politics. Rather than arguing that the efficient allocation of resources requires more market and less government, they examine how public institutions actually behave and how they have come to in-

1. Deepak Lal, *The Poverty of "Development Economics"* (London: Institute of Economic Affairs, 1983), p. 107.

2. For a sophisticated presentation of such thinking, see T. N. Srinivasan, "Neoclassical Political Economy: The State and Economic Development," *Asian Development Review* 3, no. 2 (1985): 38–58.

teract with markets in ways that enhance or impede the productive use of society's resources.

The first essay, by Popkin, explores the role of politics in the largest single sector of the developing world: the rural sector. Where, he asks, do peasant institutions come from? What is the role of politics in small-scale societies? In addressing these questions, Popkin strategically positions his analysis so as to deal in a powerful way with the relationship between economics and politics. The reason for many of the political practices and public institutions we observe in peasant societies, he argues, is the inability of markets to enable people to enhance their welfare. Certainly, all members of these societies would be better off were there irrigation facilities, dams, bridges, roads. But in critical cases rational actors, such as the market requires, find it in their interests *not* to contribute to the formation of such facilities. *There is thus a central disjunction between the social good and individual rationality,* Popkin argues. The political process centers on the creation and enforcement of institutions to bridge that gap. Development may make all people better off, but it still requires coercion, enforcement, and politics.

Popkin focuses on the politics of public goods, that is, goods which, once created, can be enjoyed by everyone, whether or not they have contributed to the costs of their formation. Clean air, for example, is a public good. So is security. Because the benefits of public goods can be consumed by persons who have not contributed to their costs, individuals, behaving rationally, will seek to free-ride on the efforts of others. Were all people to act that way, no one would contribute to the formation of public goods. Though desired and valued, they would therefore not be provided. To secure contributions to the formation of public goods, then, people have to be organized. Political organizations replace markets. It is in the failure of voluntaristic institutions such as markets that Popkin sees the origin of public institutions and the introduction of coercion into economic life.

Popkin's analysis sets the stage for Rogowski's discussion of Mancur Olson's exploration of the developmental impact of cartels and of my own study of the influence of pressure groups. Both extend the logic of public goods, for both are based on the critical insight that market prices and public policies themselves represent public goods. A price in a market is, after all, available to everyone who cares to transact in that market. And a public policy affects everyone in a government's domain. Incentives to collude in setting prices or to cooperate in lobbying a government therefore operate in the same way as those that undermine efforts to form public goods in market settings. Cartels and interest groups therefore also require the kinds of leadership and organization discussed by Popkin.[3]

Development, it is held, is a good thing. Why, then, might it not be supplied by the market? The general answer offered in these essays is that there exists a critical disjuncture between what is socially good and what is individually advantageous. People, behaving as rational individuals, might well fail to contribute to the costs of building roads, dams, and bridges. They might instead attempt to free-ride on the contributions of others. Political leadership, organization and the structuring of coercion through the creation of public institutions: these political elements represent necessary parts of the development process.

Feeny's study and the work of North as discussed by Rogowski extend even further the analysis of the role of government in securing development. Feeny examines the spread of the state bureaucracy into the rural hinterlands of South and Southeast Asia in the late nineteenth century. Following in the footsteps of Hayami and Ruttan, Posner and North, Feeny elaborates a model of how property rights are demanded and secured.[4] Market prices, he argues, establish the value of productive assets, and shifts in market prices alter the relative valuation of assets. In response to shifts in market prices, a demand arises for those assets that have become more valuable. People then invest in securing legal title to the assets which have appreciated in value. As South and Southeast Asia were drawn into the world economy in the late nineteenth

3. As Popkin fully discloses, his reasoning draws upon, even while extending, that of Mancur Olson. See Mancur Olson, Jr., *The Logic of Collective Action* (Cambridge, Mass.: Harvard University Press, 1965).

4. See Yujiro Hayami and Vernon W. Ruttan, *Agricultural Development: An International Perspective* (Baltimore: Johns Hopkins University Press, 1971); Hans Binswanger and Vernon Ruttan, eds., *Induced Innovations: Technology, Institutions, and Development* (Baltimore: Johns Hopkins University Press, 1978); Lance Davis and Douglass C. North, *Institutional Change and American Economic Growth* (Cambridge, England: Cambridge University Press, 1971); Richard Posner, *The Economics of Justice* (Cambridge, Mass.: Harvard University Press, 1981); and Douglass C. North and Robert Paul Thomas, *The Rise of the Western World: A New Economic History* (Cambridge, England: Cambridge University Press, 1973). For an intriguing parallel, see as well Frederick Engels, "Origin of Family, Private Property, and State," in Karl Marx and Frederick Engels, *Selected Works*, vol. 2 (Moscow: Foreign Language Publishing House, 1955).

century, relative prices which prevailed in the world market came to prevail in their domestic economies. The structure of prices favored agriculture, and the result was a shifting of resources into the vesting of rights in land.

The story of the creation and modification of this political institution—land rights—becomes a part of the story of the development process because secure property rights make it in the interests of private agents to act in ways that are socially beneficial. Land without property rights will not be used efficiently. It may be overgrazed, as in the case of commons. Or people may underinvest in it, fearing that the returns to their investments may be expropriated by others. Farmers without secure land rights may fail, for example, to switch to permanent crops or to adopt new technologies, such as irrigation or paddy cultivation, when these would enhance the productivity of the land. When people are certain that they will reap the rewards from the costs they incur, then they are willing to manage society's resources in the economically most productive way.[5]

Feeny's analysis helps to link the economic reward of development to political action. From Feeny's analysis we can understand why there is a demand for state intervention. And yet the analysis remains incomplete, for we also need a theory of supply. Feeny shows how shifts in relative prices led to a demand for new institutions. But what accounts for the willingness of those in control of the public bureaucracy to provide them?

This last point is critical, for it leads closer to the heart of the problem of the *political* origins of *economic* development. If property rights and economic growth are themselves public goods— social conditions that an individual can enjoy for free—what, then, makes it in the private interests of those in power to implement public policies to secure them? What makes it in the political interests of the holders of power to adopt policies that promote development? Feeny, and North, point to several major factors. One is political ideology. Another is the economic interests of political elites. As Feeny points out, Thai officials who invested in the creation of property rights did so at least in part because they them-

5. See A. A. Alchian and H. Demsetz, "The Property Right Paradigm," *Journal of Economic History* 33 (March 1973): 16–27; Harold Demsetz, "Toward a Theory of Property Rights," *American Economic Review* 57 (March–June 1967): 347–73; and John Umbek, "Might Makes Right: A Theory of the Foundation and Initial Distribution of Property Rights," *Economic Inquiry* 19 (January 1981): 38–59.

selves owned land. Third is the need of political elites for public revenues. Political elites may or may not be motivated by "social objectives." But insofar as their fortunes depend on the prosperity of their tax base, they may well find it to their advantage to act in ways that enhance its value. The need for revenues may thus link the social good of prosperity with the private interests of rulers.

It is at this point that my own work becomes relevant. I take a more pessimistic position. From my study of agricultural policies in Africa, I too reject the notion that the social good motivates policy decisions. Like Feeny and North, I find that ideologies significantly shape the patterns of political intervention in markets. But I fail to find in the need for revenues a source of political intervention supportive of development and growth. Rather, I argue, governments in Africa are driven to spend in ways that maintain them in power. And the competition for power appears to have driven political elites to extract resources from agriculture at a rate that has caused private individuals to withdraw resources from that sector or at least to fail to make futher investments in it.

Even more pessimistic is the general framework of my argument. I argue that while political elites are behaving in ways that are economically irrational, they are behaving in ways that are politically rational.[6] The policies they choose may therefore represent optimal solutions to political problems. Nonetheless, quite clearly they impose economic costs of sufficient magnitude to retard development.

A major reason why politically rational choices are not economically optimal is that expenditures that represent economic costs might well be regarded by politicians as political benefits. Thus price distortions may create opportunities for rationing; although it is economically inefficient, rationing allows commodities to be targeted to the politically faithful. And government regulation may transform markets into political organizations, ones in which too few transactions take place at too high a cost but ones that can be used to build organizations supportive of those in power.

Even more than the other articles in this volume, the articles in this section illustrate ways of "doing" political economy.

6. See, as well, Kenneth A. Shepsle and Barry R. Weingast, "Political Solutions to Market Problems," *American Political Science Review* 78 (June 1984): 417–34, and Barry R. Weingast, Kenneth A. Shepsle, and Christopher Johnson, "The Political Economy of Benefits and Costs," *Journal of Political Economy* 89 (1981): 642–64.

# 7

# Public Choice and Peasant Organization

## Samuel L. Popkin

A natural affinity exists between public choice and the study of peasant society. *Public choice* can be defined as the study of nonmarket economics and the extension of the methodology of microeconomics to nonmarket settings. Since so much of peasant studies is concerned with the analysis and design of institutions other than markets, public choice can bridge the chasm between market economists applying rational models of individual decisionmaking to markets and the social scientists who have assumed that the assumptions of economics about individual decisionmaking and the allocation of scarce resources were not applicable to their study of rural institutions.

This paper discusses two aspects of public-choice theories that illuminate patterns of rural relations: first, the free-rider problem in collective action; and, second, the problem of obtaining information about quality or effort in exchanges. The anonymity of the ideal market would make it impossible for an individual to evaluate the quality of some products or some work efforts. Such problems of evaluating quality help to explain why some exchanges have personalized relations and why some crops have more personal-

From Clifford R. Russell and Norman K. Nicholson, *Public Choice and Rural Development* pp. 43–80. © Resources for the Future, Inc.

ized production relations than others. After discussing how free-rider problems and information costs affect the organization of peasant agriculture and markets, these two issues are then related to two subjects normally discussed separately, the breakdown of *haciendas* and estates historically and the breakdown of collective agriculture in China.

The division in the past between economists and the other social scientists was caused in great measure by the disdain economists displayed toward nonmarket institutions and nonmarket arrangements. Market economics gave economists a set of elegant tools with which to discuss economic policy, but economists had no corresponding awareness of the economic role of nonmarket institutions. Although one field worker after another wrote treatises on one or another "traditional institution" and its role in the rural economy, economists were defiantly uninterested in rural institutions other than markets.

Ignoring institutions, however, led a generation of economists astray. A milestone in laissez-faire economic theory, Schultz's *Transforming Traditional Agriculture* is an excellent reference point for a brief discussion of the strengths and weaknesses of the assumptions and focuses the free-market economists used in examining peasant agriculture.[1] In his discussion of the evidence for peasants' response to new opportunities and their allocation of resources at the farm level, Schultz emphasized the responsiveness of peasants to market forces. From the evidence for economic responsiveness at the household level, Schultz argued that there are two major ways to improve the position of the peasantry: through education, and by improved and cheaper technology. As Schultz commented, "Once there are investment opportunities and efficient incentives, farmers will turn sand into gold."[2]

Today it is all too easy to disparage Schultz and belittle his contributions. He wrote at a time when most noneconomists had little or no understanding of the role market forces could play in stimulating agricultural production, when there was little or no appreciation of the responsiveness of the so-called traditional farmer to price incentives, when a large number of development scholars even believed in backward-bending labor supply curves—that as wages or profits increased, peasants would work less.

---

1. Theodore W. Schultz, *Transforming Traditional Agriculture* (New Haven: Yale University Press, 1964).
2. Ibid., p. 5.

Important as Schultz's work is, it is severely limited because of its focus on market forces and a fixed institutional framework. By ignoring the interplay between market forces and national and local institutions, Schultz makes prescriptions that are far too narrow and predictions that are far too optimistic about the beneficial aspects of increased market activity. Peasant households are indeed efficient allocators of their resources, and peasants are indeed responsive to market forces. To stress education and technology, however, as the ways to increase productivity is to ignore other crucial factors.

From the evidence that peasants are efficient resource allocators, Schultz argues that traditional agricultural communities are generally also "efficient but poor."[3] If that were so, then it would be appropriate to stress education and technology as means for raising peasant output and living standards; and institutional analysis would be irrelevant. For if peasants are "efficient but poor," then "no appreciable increase in agricultural production is to be had by reallocating the factors at the disposal of farmers who are bound by traditional agriculture. Another implication is that an outside expert, however skilled he may be in farm management, will not discover any major inefficiency in the allocation of factors."[4] If, that is, villages are production-maximizing for the known state of the art, then the most important measures are to give peasants schooling—so that they can understand new methods—and to develop new and cheaper technology.[5]

As Lipton has shown, however, the conclusion that peasants are production-maximizing does not pay sufficient attention to problems of risk and uncertainty facing the household.[6] The leap from peasant efficiency to village efficiency (or production maximization for a given level of technology), moreover, assumes perfect markets in land, labor, and capital. It also fails to take sufficiently into account the problem of nonmarket goods and insurance.

Individual peasant families, although they are highly efficient at the margin in allocating their labor, land, and capital, pay far more attention to risk and uncertainty than Schultz's work implies. The concern with risk means that improved insurance or welfare schemes may do as much to increase production as education or

3. Ibid., p. 38.
4. Ibid., p. 39.
5. Ibid., pp. 21, 33, 155.
6. Michael Lipton, "The Theory of the Optimizing Peasant," *Journal of Development Studies* 4 (April 1968).

technology will. Farmers concerned about survival will diverge from production maximization; the extent of the divergence will be affected by the quality of their insurance. Both risk and insurance, therefore, require more attention than Schultz gave them.

Peasants' worries about risk and insurance and the economic benefits of institutional remedies to these problems were ignored by most economists, not just by Schultz. For example, the widespread practice of scattering plots was viewed by many economists as irrational. In fact, the scattering of plots substantially reduces the maximum damage that small local disasters or climatic variations can cause in a given season: mildew or rot in one area of the village, an errant herd, exceptionally light or heavy rains, and similar mini-disasters will be less likely to wipe out a peasant's entire crop when fields are scattered. Scattered plots reduce the variance of yield from year to year and thus reduce the probability of losing the entire crop, but scattering also cuts the maximum yield per farmer and for the village as a whole.[7]

When there is no reliable, widespread insurance system, scattered plots are often more desirable than a single plot per family. However, centuries of division sometimes lead to extreme scattering. In Greece, for example, Thompson found that the number and dispersion of plots belonging to the typical family were far greater than was indeed for insurance value and that a majority of villagers in the eighteen villages favored a program of plot consolidation to increase production, decrease family friction over inheritances, reduce violence over access to inside plots, and put land consumed by paths and boundaries back into production. But this majority of villagers believed that a voluntary program of consolidation would not work, because the differences in fertility and soil type, as well as the problems of accurately evaluating the yield (and variance) of plots, made weighting systems for establishing equivalences difficult to establish, and there was little willingness to trust any committee of villagers to arrive at an equitable consolidation. For that reason, the general feeling was that compulsory consolidation was the only way to proceed.[8]

The complex problem of trading and consolidating parcels

---

7. Donald N. McCloskey, "English Open Fields as Behavior toward Risk," in Paul Uselding, ed., *Research in Economic History*, vol. 1 (Greenwich, Conn.: JAI Press, 1976).

8. Kenneth Thompson, *Farm Fragmentation in Greece* (Athens: Athens Center of Economic Research, 1963).

arises whenever an inheritance is shared among two or more off-spring. Lipton describes an Indian village where the farmland runs down the side of a long slope. Soil quality varies from top to bottom of the slope but varies little along a contour of the slope. If plots were divided horizontally along the contours of the hill, plowing would be easier and cheaper, and average output would be higher.[9] Lipton reports that each father, however, avoids the problem of equating contours with different averages and variances by dividing the patrimony into vertical strips: "This saddles each generation of sons with longer, thinner sloping strips, increasingly costly and inconvenient to plough properly, i.e., repeatedly and across the slope."[10]

But designing workable systems of crop insurance has been an almost insurmountable problem. The first approach, derived from welfare economics, followed Kenneth Arrow's dictum that "the welfare case for insurance of all sorts is overwhelming. It follows that the government should undertake insurance where the market, for whatever reason, has failed to emerge."[11] Crop insurance has been proposed in several countries to increase production by protecting peasants against risk. But such direct applications of the principles of welfare economics still did not show an appreciation of peasant society.[12] The very existence of insurance can affect the way farmers work and thus can decrease productivity because it is not always possible to separate the effects of sloth and nature. Farmers, then, can take advantage of crop insurance to decrease their own efforts and total productivity can suffer, as when the accounting units in the People's Republic of China were enlarged to commune or county level.

Here is an example of the potential contribution of collective choice to the analysis of nonmarket supralocal organizations for insuring peasants against crop failure. This theory focuses our attention on the disjunction between collective and individual rationality; it reminds us that although village productivity can theoretically be raised by plot consolidation or insurance schemes, it is in any individual peasant's interest to maximize his benefits while

9. Lipton, "Theory of the Optimizing Peasant," p. 339.
10. Ibid.
11. Cited in Mark Pauly, "The Economics of Moral Hazard: Comment," *American Economic Review* 58 (June 1968): 531.
12. James A. Roumasset, *Rice and Risk: Decision Making among Low Income Farmers* (Amsterdam: North Holland, 1976).

minimizing his contributions to these public goods—in other words, to be a free rider.

Although the peasant may be highly efficient—even individually maximizing—when allocating his resources among various production activities, it does not generally follow that villages are production-maximizing for the known technology. Given the price of water, for example, a peasant may make maximizing decisions about the allocation of resources among water, fertilizer, ploughing, and seed. But irrigation facilities, dams, or canals may be in short supply because of problems of leadership or cooperation. Peasants may use the existing water in the most efficient possible way, but new or different leadership, with no change in technology, might improve cooperation and hence increase the supply of water. The Schultzian technology-*cum*-education approach is inadequate for explaining when and why villages will or will not cooperate to provide such public goods as more water.

The narrow market-economics approach assumes that all goods possess excludability—if you do not pay, you do not get to consume the good. However, it is not always possible to restrict benefits directly to purchasers. In such cases as flood control, forest fire prevention, or the construction of irrigation channels, it is difficult to deny benefits to persons who do not contribute to the project. Whenever there is the possibility of enjoying benefits with or without contributions, there may be free riders.

Many divisible goods also have collective aspects. The existence of a school or hospital or theater, even though payment may be required to use it, has aspects of a collective good. This is particularly true in peasant society, where the limitations on savings and capital accumulation, and the costly and unreliable mechanisms for enforcing contracts, mean that many goods are provided on a quasi-collective rather than a market basis.

But the varieties of institutional arrangements for providing these quasi-collective goods—despite their effects on productivity—were rarely studied by economists. Economists usually limited the domain of economics to explicit markets. This equation of economics and market was accepted by most other social scientists studying rural development. Rural anthropologists, sociologists, and political scientists identified the many nonmarket organizations and personalities within rural society as instances of nonmarket economic behavior, outside the domain of the rational individualistic actor posited by the economists. They talked of the persistence of traditional institutional and community orientations as evidence that much of peasant society was outside the realm of economics.

Much of the realm of peasant society is nonmarket but not noneconomic. It may be outside the domain of conventional market economics, but collective choice, as nonmarket economics, can be the bridge between economics and the study of peasant institutions. Through collective choice we can begin to analyze the effects of incentives on villagers as they make their decisions about economic activity in nonmarket and market settings.

## Free Riders and Collective Goods

The basic question for successful organization is: how, and under what conditions, can the resources for a collective project be gathered together and applied? Any attempt to organize for group action must recognize the distinction between individual interests and group interests and must provide effective leadership, as well as sufficient incentives, to overcome individual resistance to collective action.[13]

Many collective projects benefit an individual whether or not he contributes. When weighing his contribution, a peasant can be expected to take account of several factors relating to costs and benefits. First is expenditure of resources; that is, if a peasant contributes to a collective action, he must expend valuable resources. If a project fails, the peasant loses his investment; additionally, he may be punished for participating if the action (such as rebellion) fails. The second factor is positive rewards, that is, the value of the direct and indirect benefits. Third is the probability of his action leading to reward (efficacy); that is, the effectiveness of a contribution depends on its marginal contribution to the success of the endeavor. This, in turn, depends on how other actions aggregate, on whether they bring the effort sufficiently close to success to make a contribution worthwhile. And the fourth factor is leadership viability and trust; that is, when estimating the probability of success, a potential contributor takes into account not only the volume of resources mobilized but the leadership skill with which they are mobilized.

13. Samuel L. Popkin, *The Rational Peasant: The Political Economy of Rural Society in Vietnam* (Berkeley and Los Angeles: University of California Press, 1979), chapter 5.

Given these considerations, whenever there is coordinated action to produce collective goods, individuals may calculate that they are better off not contributing. As long as they cannot be excluded from the good, there is the potential for free riders, individuals who do not contribute to the provision of goods because they believe they will receive the gain or security even if they do not participate. This divergence between the interest of the group to complete a project and the interest of an individual to benefit without contributing suggests than an individual who attaches no special personal (psychic) benefits to the act of participation and who does not view his contribution as necessary will not contribute without an incentive to do so.

As long as the only results of contributing to the common goals are common advantages, a peasant may leave the contributions to others and expend his scarce resources in other ways. Collective action requires more than consensus or even intensity of need. It requires conditions under which peasants will find it in their individual interests to allocate resources to their common interests—and not be free riders.

The structure of peasant society and the failure of so many development schemes—in both market and nonmarket settings—reflects the problems of coordinating mechanisms for the provision of collective goods. In many situations there are arrangements for providing goods that could, if enacted, leave all better off but that will not be successful because of the problem of free riders. There are times when many collective goods are provided by small groups, although large groups could do better—because neither the necessary skills nor incentives systems exist to maintain larger groups, or because peasants, seeking to avert the risk posed by concentrating resources in the hands of another peasant, are unwilling to invest their resources in large-scale projects.

Under what conditions can resources for collective endeavor be aggregated? Olson has stated the argument in its classic form: "Unless there is coercion or some other special device to make individuals act in their common interest, rational, self-interested individuals will not act to achieve their common or group interest."[14]

This formulates the collective-action problem in its most elegant and straightforward fashion. If an individual assumes that his con-

14. Mancur Olson, Jr., *The Logic of Collective Action* (Cambridge, Mass.: Harvard University Press, 1965), p. 2.

tribution to a collective good has no perceptible impact on the contributions of others, and if the collective good is so expensive that
an individual's contribution will not perceptibly change the level of
the collective good supplied, then special incentives are needed to
produce any action toward group goals (the by-product theory of
collective goods). The by-product theory is best illustrated by the
(simplified) example of the American Medical Association (AMA).
The AMA produces major collective goods, particularly political
power, for the medical profession. Since the results of the AMA's
influence on tax and health legislation, for example, are available
to all doctors, membership in the AMA is not required to receive
its collective benefits. But a doctor receives selective, noncollective
benefits from his membership that justify payment of dues. If the
AMA can provide members with valuable information about new
medicines or tax loopholes, or if it can monopolize the services of
malpractice specialists, then it is in the individual doctor's interest
to join the organization. Thus, no one pays anything for collective
goods; they are provided by the organization as a by-product of
the sale of memberships for individual benefits.[15]

As framed by Olson, the by-product theory implies that efforts
to organize for action can succeed only when the leadership provides selective incentives from whose proceeds the collective goods
are financed. However, even for nonexcludable goods, this formulation is too restrictive. Contributions can occur (1) because persons contribute for reasons of ethics, conscience, or altruism; (2)
because it pays to contribute on a pure cost-benefit basis; (3) because of selective incentives (excludable benefits), which can either
be positive or negative; or (4) because it pays to contribute, given
that the contributions of others are contingent on one's own contribution.[16]

When persons have decided to contribute on the grounds of
ethics, altruism, or conscience, a would-be leader need offer no
selective incentives. Instead, what must be offered to persons
searching for the best way to expend their contributions is efficacy.
That is, a leader must be able to convince persons that making the

---

15. Ibid., pp. 137–41.
16. Norman Frohlich and Joe Oppenheimer, "I Get By with a Little Help from
My Friends," *World Politics* 23 (October 1971); Norman Frohlich, Tom Hunt, Joe
Oppenheimer, and R. Harrison Wagner, "Individual Contributions to Collective
Goods: Alternative Models," *Journal of Conflict Resolution* 19 (June 1975).

contribution through a particular organization or a particular form of participation is the most beneficial.

Selective incentives to include participation also are not needed whenever it pays to contribute on a straight cost-benefit calculation. Olson deals with the pure case of collective goods that benefit all equally and from whose benefits no one can be excluded. Thus, while implicit in Olson's analysis, excludability is separate from the pure problem of collective goods. There are also many collective projects in which some benefits can be restricted to participants. In these cases, no special selective incentives beyond those tied to the collective project are needed to induce participation. An insurance scheme, a planting or harvesting cooperative, or a blood bank—all have collective-goods aspects and the benefits can be restricted to members—can be contrasted with an expedition to kill a marauding tiger, a plot to kill a landlord, or construction of a dike—the benefits from which accrue to participants and nonparticipants alike. *Ceteris paribus*, maintaining membership is easier if to be excluded from an organization is to lose valuable benefits.

Excludability is related to the problem of self-enforcement and to situations in which selective incentives, either positive or negative, are needed for leadership to overcome free-rider problems. A group is not self-enforcing when a member gains more benefits by dropping out than by voluntarily remaining in the group. If an immediate benefit can be derived from defection, an organization formed to pursue a goal can survive only if there is sufficient coercion available to the leadership to enforce discipline, or enough resources to make defection less valuable than remaining in the group. An insurance scheme, for example, is self-enforcing: when a member fails to pay or do his share, he loses his benefits. In direct contrast is the problem of organizing a work stoppage among laborers in order to raise their wages. If all the laborers in an area were simultaneously to withhold their labor from their fellow villagers who are tenants or smallholders, the laborers' share of the crop could be increased. But such coordinated action is not self-enforcing, for there is an incentive for any individual laborer to defect and offer his labor. He will reason that if everyone else withholds his labor, wages will inevitably rise; he will therefore receive the future benefits of the collective action as well as the wages he receives as a strikebreaker.

Where defection brings benefits, a second consideration is the ease with which defections can be monitored. It is easy to detect defectors during a labor boycott, and when resources are available the defectors can be dealt with. Similarly, if each villager is responsible for cleaning (or digging) a specified section of a canal and if all villagers are to do their work on the same day, defections will be more easily monitored than if villagers were not assigned specific sections or if the villagers did not all do their work on the same day. There are many times, however, when it is difficult to detect defections and to apply sanctions to maintain group solidarity. This applies to the problem of interest rates. It is common for writers on peasant society to refer to exorbitant, "usurious" interest rates. If all peasants could agree to borrow only at a given rate and at no higher rate, the interest rate would come down and nonmarket methods would govern the allocation of credit.

Directly affecting the stringency of the means needed to prevent defection is the extent to which opposing interests and resources can be mobilized against nascent organizations. Whereas an insurance scheme or a well-digging group is unlikely to generate immediate, local opposition, attempts to raise laborers' wages have a guaranteed opposition from all tenants and smallholders. Tenants and smallholders are financially able to hold out more easily than laborers, and they are in a better power position because they control more resources. Similarly, tenant movements to destroy or weaken landlords are likely to be more successful in areas where there is no class of permanent laborers for the landlords to use against the tenants.

People will also contribute whenever they believe their contribution will make a big enough difference. There are two main variants to consider: (1) a contribution that might influence other persons to contribute and that therefore has an important, perceptible effect on the overall level of contributions, and (2) situations where each bit is seen as a crucial step in a long process. If a large overall goal can be broken into many small independent pieces, all of which are necessary, the free-rider problem can be overcome, for if each person has a monopoly on a necessary factor for the final goal, all contributions are essential.

Effective leaders may provide only selective incentives, but by coordination of contributions, by manipulation of information, or by breaking up a large overall goal into numerous steps with critical thresholds, they may also elicit contributions not tied directly to selective incentives. Olson's tidy formulation, therefore, can be expanded from a situation in which collective goods are financed solely from funds raised by leaders through selective incentives to situations in which collective goods are financed by convincing persons that their contributions will have a perceptible effect.

For pure incentive situations or for contributions justified on the grounds of perceptible effects, participation (be it a purchase or a contribution) is a gamble. The value of a contribution to a peasant depends not just on the value of the collective good, but also on how likely it is that others will contribute. Yet other situations also often involve gambles. For example, with selective incentives there are cases in which peasants must estimate the probability of actually receiving the selective incentive.

Risk is involved both in purchasing incentives and in contributions; peasants can be expected to evaluate their actions as they would evaluate lotteries. This means consideration of success or failure of the collective good being supplied with and without the individual's contribution, weighing the risk of trading the status quo for a lottery between successful action and failure. (Of course, not contributing is also a risky situation with lottery elements.)

In all situations, then, collective action involves risk and uncertainty. It is logically incorrect to equate intensity of need with the likelihood of collective response without also considering the ability of individuals to gamble on an improvement in the status quo. A peasant with a small surplus can more readily afford to take risks than can a peasant truly against the margin.

## Political Entrepreneurs

When a peasant makes his personal cost-benefit calculations about the expected returns on his own inputs, he is making subjective estimates of the credibility and capability of the organizer, "the political entrepreneur," to deliver.[17] The problem of the supply of collective goods and the choice among alternative patterns of supply make "mechanisms for coordination of expectations and the pooling of resources" a central issue.[18] Hence, the importance of the leader as a political entrepreneur—someone willing to invest his own time and resources to coordinate the in-

17. Norman Frohlich and Joe A. Oppenheimer, *Modern Political Economy* (Englewood Cliffs, N.J.: Prentice-Hall, 1978); Norman Frohlich, Joe A. Oppenheimer, and Oran Young, *Political Leadership and Collective Goods* (Princeton: Princeton University Press, 1971).

18. Frohlich, Oppenheimer, and Young, *Political Leadership*, p. 25.

puts of others in order to produce collective action or collective goods—should not be underestimated.

Leadership itself has aspects of collective goods (and evils) for a group. Even when an organization produces divisible goods for individual consumption, there are collective-goods aspects to the organization itself. Systems of incentives and mechanisms for sharing costs are collective goods that leadership can supply to the benefit of the leader and the peasantry. When improved leadership makes possible incentive systems or cost-sharing mechanisms for self-helf projects such as insurance programs or breeding cooperatives, it is possible to produce benefits for the peasants as well as a surplus which can be applied to broader organization objectives.

Consideration of leadership leads to an enlargement of Olson's central formulation. Discussions of collective goods usually address the problem of whether a particular good will or will not be provided to a group. In practice, many collective goods can be provided in many different ways. Improving the quality of available leadership, for example, can change the way the good is provided, increase benefits for all participants, and supply large amounts of "profit" for the organizers.

Whether the entrepreneur is directly exchanging immediate individual benefits for peasant inputs, providing cost-sharing arrangements, or trying to convince the peasant that his actions can have a perceptible and profitable impact on the collective good, he must be concerned with raising the peasant's estimate of the efficacy of his contribution to secure the promised returns. This means that the peasant's subjective estimates of the would-be entrepreneur's capability and credibility will directly influence the entrepreneur's ability to organize peasants, and that, *ceteris paribus,* a situation with more credible organizers is likely to be a situation with more effective organizations. A would-be organizer must also convince a peasant that his goals are credible, that not only can he and will he do what he promises with the peasant's contributions, but that if he does what he promises, the peasant's lot will be bettered. One way of increasing the credibility of the goals may be to use leaders already well known to the group in contrast to urban officials-*cum*-carpetbaggers.

When an entrepreneur approaches a group of peasants, what features of possible issues are crucial? And how does the "organizability" of an issue vary across areas or social structures? By examining relevant properties of different local issues we can begin to answer this question.

First, an examination of examples of successful organization indicates that one crucial consideration is a focus on local goals and goods with immediate payoffs. This suggests than an important way to increase the peasant's estimate of success and, therefore, the probability of contribution is to decrease the scope of the project for which he is being recruited—and thus shorten the interval before benefits are received. The profits can then be directed by the leadership to goals and projects that take longer to pay off.

Second, there is the timing of contributions. The start-up costs of a project and whether peasants are required to pay before or after collective ends are achieved (that is, whether or not there is outside financing) may determine the potential value of a local issue to organizers. Poor peasants might find their individual benefits from an undertaking very high and might be willing to pay enormous amounts to achieve the benefits, but only if they are able to pay after the fact ("on time") out of the profits.

Third, there is the size of the group that the leadership can manage. Many of the collective goals within peasant society can be achieved within groups of widely varying sizes and structures. Thus, insurance and agricultural efforts can be organized so as to supply benefits with or without exclusion, either inside or outside a market mechanism. With little savings and money, with a lack of trained leadership, and with costly and unreliable mechanisms for enforcing contracts, it is not surprising to find insurance and agricultural cooperatives supplied on a quasi-collective rather than a market basis. Large groups are workable, given problems of excludability and defection, only where there is skilled leadership or enforceable contracts. Almost all the small, insurance-type organizations found among peasants can be organized by very small groups of peasants. But the security and viability of the insurance can sometimes be improved immeasurably if a larger group is also involved. That is, a large insurance company is more likely in the long run to provide the promised benefits than is a small company with few members. Although they may be erratic and offer low-quality insurance compared to villagewide or even intervillage associations, however, the small-group arrangements have the virtue of lower leadership requirements and are often the only organization possible. As Olson has noted, small groups need few, if any, special incentives or leadership because each member's contribution has such a notable effect on the overall output of the group.[19]

19. Olson, *Logic of Collective Action,* pp. 33–34.

In a small mutual-aid group, if one member gains a free ride, the loss of his contribution will be perceptible to all and the group will dissolve.

Without skilled leadership or enforceable contracts, exclusion is possible only in small groups. In an eight-man planting cooperative, if a peasant drops out of the group after the other seven have spent the day helping him plant his crops, he will be blackballed from all similar groups as unreliable. So, while small groups may be far less rewarding over a number of years than larger groups, they are viable when there is little or no trusted leadership, because there are minimal problems of coordination and incentives. If a skilled leader can convince peasants to join a larger mutual-aid group, there is potentially a substantial profit for both the peasants and the leader.

A further issue is the type of reciprocity on which the organization is based. Cooperation can be based on strict or on general reciprocity. Peasants make exchanges when it is certain that all (both) parties will be able to maintain a long-run balance. Colson reports, for example, that "exchanges and contracts are likely to be either highly specific, with an understanding of just what it is each party is expected to do, or they involve people who are in constant contact so that giving and return can be balanced at short intervals and the advantages to each partner easily assessed."[20] In other words, as Potter found in Thailand, if reciprocal obligations are not to be evaded, "records must be kept and sanctions exerted; there is nothing loose or informal about this at all."[21] Strict reciprocity is required for large groups; complex interchanges (general reciprocity) take place among small groups of four or five households. If there is to be general reciprocity in a large group, the demands on leadership will be severe.

Next, schemes can have either fixed or variable returns. The exchange systems common in peasant society, such as labor exchanges or burial societies, have fixed returns. In these groups each peasant receives exactly what he has put into the scheme. Such organizations derive their value from utilities of scale in peasant life: eight days of labor at once by many men in a field make a better rice crop than one man working for eight days, and a few coins from many persons when a parent dies are more valuable for

---

20. Elizabeth Colson, *Tradition and Contract* (Chicago: Aldine, 1974), p. 30.
21. Jack Potter, *Thai Peasant Social Structure* (Chicago: University of Chicago Press, 1976), pp. 163, 171.

meeting religious obligations and avoiding debts than are a few coins on the many occasions when someone else's parent dies. Schemes also can have exact exchange or equivalent exchange—labor for labor, part of someone's pig this month for part of someone else's pig next month, or money for money—rather than exchanges where contributions and payout involve aggreeing on a rate of exchange on more than one item. It is easier to begin cooperation with fixed, exact exchanges, and the less exact and specific the exchanges become, the greater the need for high-quality leadership and record-keeping. (Little management is required for large groups with tasks with large economies of scale, like a bucket brigade, or where only low-quality labor is required, that is, so-called festival labor. Agricultural development and refinement of techniques often lead to smaller exchange groups because higher-quality labor input, and thus more vigilance against slackers, is required.)

Cooperative efforts also vary in the extent to which there is a risk of someone absconding with the assets. A plan can require centralized or decentralized holding of assets, and the assets can be liquid or illiquid. Most peasant cooperation, organization, and insurance generally do not concentrate abscondable assets—peasants seldom give another peasant money to hold for the future, because the peasant can always run away with the money or spend it on himself or his family. Instead, contributions are held by the members and given to the bereaved on the death, or the labor is given to the farmer on the agreed-upon day. To concentrate liquid assets, a would-be leader must convince a peasant that he is not going to take his money and run, supplying neither the collective goods nor the promised incentives. One solution (although it raises distributive questions) is to use villagers with fixed assets for leadership positions. As Potter found in Thailand, "Villagers prefer to have wealthy men as village leaders on the theory that, since they already have money, they are less likely to run off with funds entrusted to them."[22] And in Vietnam during the 1960s, the National Liberation Front for the same reason generally gave positions requiring the handling of large sums of cash to landowning peasants.

Finally, we can also distinguish among schemes where everyone has a chance of benefiting and those in which many persons have little or no probability of any return. Old age, widow, and orphan

22. Ibid., p. 52.

support are likely to have some potential value for all villagers, whereas subsidies for poor households are less likely to be of benefit to all villagers and thus may require coercion to establish and maintain.

There are, however, some dramatic occasions when collective action can occur without leadership or organization. There can be collective action such as slowdowns, wildcat strikes, protest marches, or field clearings with little or no formal leadership to supply incentives or even to provide information. This is most likely when there are few internal conflicts of interest over a goal within the group, when the potential participants' jobs require some particular skill or the area is isolated so that strikebreaking is difficult, when persons live together in one community so that they can communicate easily and decide on "the last straw" and defections can be monitored easily; and when work can be put off without destroying the product, so that crucial wages will not be lost. The demands expressed by such collective action, however, will be limited to highly visible, universal demands and thus are likely to reflect the lowest common denominator of a group, not the full range of interests of its members or even the most important preferences of the members. These conditions are most obviously met among rubber plantation workers.[23] It should also be noted that César Chavez started with vineyard workers in California. Thus, when a group engages in collective action and protest, one should not infer from such demonstrations that they will be able to cooperate easily in the more mundane areas of village life. As a colonial newspaper noted in Vietnam in 1896:

> A whole village comes to an admirable understanding in order to pillage a convoy of Chinese junks or to plunder the house of a rich neighbor. Discretion will be well guarded even in the case of success. But ask this same village to group together to store their rice in one central warehouse and assure themselves of quick and certain benefits. Disorder and bickering will quickly break out in the midst of the group. In a week they will be calling each other thieves.[24]

23. Jeffrey M. Paige, *Agrarian Revolution* (Glencoe, Ill.: Free Press, 1978), pp. 50–58; Chandra Jayawardena, "Ideology and Conflit in Lower Class Communities," *Comparative Studies in Society and History* 10 (1967): 418–23.

24. Quoted in Guy Gran, "Vietnam and the Capitalist Route to Modernity: Village Cochinchina 1880–1940," Ph.D. dissertation, University of Wisconsin, 1973, p. 523.

## Lemons

One factor that influences the forms of rural collective action and economic organization, that of information, has not received the attention it deserves. Often individuals have to assess the quality of other people's work or collective contribution. Information about quality is in many circumstances costly, or uncertain, or even impossible to obtain without long time lags. This information problem has a profound influence on forms of collective action and on production relations and the organization of markets as well.

Whereas the work of Olson has provided the starting point for the analysis of collective action with respect to public goods and free riders, the starting point for our preliminary attempts to analyze the impact of information problems on structure of production, marketing, and profit in agriculture is Akerlof's lemon market.[25]

Akerlof's lemons are found not on trees but in the hands of used car dealers. He coined the phrase the "market for lemons" to deal with problems of information cost and information availability between the two sides in economic exchanges. Akerlof's ideas are a natural complement to the considerations of institutional design that arise when there are problems of divisiblity or excludability, for they go to the very heart of agricultural economics—the linkage of work quality and reward. They can help us to explain why different commodities have different markets and different labor and production structures, and why the distribution of profits between producers and middlemen can vary so much among commercial crops.

Akerlof is specifically concerned with situations where there were difficult-to-overcome asymmetries of information between the two sides of an economic exchange. The most obvious example of this occurs whenever a car is sold to a used-car dealer. Whatever make and model of car you bring the dealer, the dealer has available a certain amount of general information, subjective or objective, about the general value of all such cars. Your particular car, however, can be either a peach, that is, a car in very good condition

25. George Akerlof, "The Market for 'Lemons': Quality, Uncertainty and the Market Mechanism," *Quarterly Journal of Economics* 84 (August 1970); George Akerlof, "The Economics of Caste and of the Rat Race and Other Woeful Tales," *Quarterly Journal of Economics* 90 (November 1976).

with few problems, or a lemon, that is, a car in poor condition with many inherent defects. It is extremely difficult without extensive driving or costly testing for the dealer to ascertain with precision—except in the most obvious cases—whether the car is a peach or a lemon. Because the dealer cannot easily evaluate your car, your information advantage both works to your immediate disadvantage and has a detrimental effect on the entire used car market as well.

If a dealer is unable to rate the product accurately, he is unable to pay differentially for peaches and lemons. Your car may be a peach, but since it is possible that you have a lemon, the dealer is unable to reward you for the care with which you have treated your car. Therefore, for a particular car the dealer pays the average value of all such cars in the used-car market. This means that if your car is a peach you have an incentive to drive it into the ground, since you will never get its full value from a dealer, and if you have a lemon there is an incentive to trade it in early. Therefore, the information asymmetry between seller and buyer not only deprives the seller of "peach bonuses" but it also leads to a marketplace dominated by goods of lower quality than if the seller's information advantage could be eliminated and the information shared with the buyers. Thus what the buyer cannot know hurts the seller and the market, not just the buyer.

It is sometimes difficult to collect timely information about quality, and peasant organizations reflect this difficulty. For example, it is very rare in peasant society to find plough teams shared among families or to find instances where plough animals can be rented without a driver. This is an instance of information problems preventing a form of market from emerging. When the plough animal is returned to the owner (or to the collective), it is easy to tell if the animal has been whipped and lacerated, but beyond looking for these external damages (like kicking fenders and checking the finish) it is difficult to tell whether the animal was treated adequately. If the animal was overworked or underfed, or if it has stepped in a hole and cracked a bone, the damage may not show up for several days. There have been, however, times when villagers have owned stud animals cooperatively because there the problem of damage caused by overwork or abuse is apparently less serious. (The amount of work a stud animal will do is roughly proportional to the number of females in the pen.)

The same principle helps to predict which crops will be grown with wage labor on plantations or *haciendas* and which will be dominated by tenancy systems or smallholdings. When labor quality matters a great deal but is very easy to monitor, then it is possible to use wage labor and reward it with piece rates. If it is hard to measure or assess labor quality directly but the quality can easily be inferred from output, it is also easy to reward wage laborers with piece rates. In one case the workers are watched, and in the other their output is sampled. And, of course, if labor quality matters little, then it is again easy to use wage labor and time rates. There are, however, situations in which labor quality matters, but it is both difficult to assess the labor quality directly and to infer the quality from output, because other, uncontrolled factors also affect total output. Then wage labor systems will not successfully link effort and reward, and there will be a tendency for quality to drop and for "easy riders" to dominate the work force.

Rice, for example, is a crop for which labor quality matters greatly and for which it is difficult to use wage labor in the entire production process because of the difficulty of inferring labor quality from output or of inferring labor quality directly. Large-scale rice plantations have never been as profitable as tenancies on the same land because so much supervision of effort and quality is required. It is more profitable for large landowners to divide a large holding into tenancies than to farm the entire holding with wage labor. What the salesman's commission is to markets that are sporadic or uncertain, tenancy is to agriculture: a way of providing an incentive to perform quality work when direct supervision is unfeasible. Sharing the output with a tenant, rather than paying the same person as a laborer, gives the worker an incentive for self-monitoring when supervised monitoring is too costly and expensive.

The new procedures that are developing for self-monitoring of labor in rice fields planted in the high-yielding varieties illustrate a similar development of incentives for self-monitoring. In the past, for example, in parts of the Philippines, harvesters were paid one-sixth of the harvest as their wage. Now, for two reasons, farmers are trying to pay harvesters less than one-sixth of the harvest. One is that because of the population growth, there is more cheap labor than there used to be as well as laborers who will work for less than one-sixth of the harvest (which, of course, means intraclass conflict among the laborers). Second, high-yielding varieties are easier to harvest. A laborer can do more work in a day because all the grain ripens at the same time and the grain is of uniform height. The same percentage, therefore, would mean a higher daily wage.

There are two ways of changing the wage structure which look equivalent to the outsider. One way is simply to cut the harvest wage from one-sixth of the crop to one-eighth of the crop (and then prepare to fight off the laborers if they try to burn you out the first year). The other way is for the tenant to pay one-sixth of the crop to harvesters, but only allow those to harvest who have weeded the same area for free during the year. The cost of weeding plus harvesting is the same price as cutting the harvest wages from one-sixth to one-eighth, and paying for weeding, so that the two systems are equivalent. But, especially where there are high-yielding varieties, the tendency has been towards free weeding and one-sixth of the output. Because the pay for weeding is not a day's pay but a share of the harvest, the weeder has an incentive to self-monitor the weeding because total pay now depends on how much rice comes up two months later. The laborer is absorbing risk because hail could come in the meantime, but the laborer also has a strong incentive now not to kick the rice during weeding because the laborer will harvest that same plot.[26] These changes are also very similar to the first reforms that were tried in China. Those first reforms were designed so that the same person planted, weeded, and harvested a given area, so that the incentives for self-monitoring would be as high as possible for work that could not easily be monitored directly or indirectly for quality.

The ease or difficulty of determining quality also affects the market structure for different crops, in the form of relations between producer and middleman. There is a tendency to take for granted the problem of measuring agricultural output—to assume it is easy to determine the value of the commodity a producer has for sale. It is straightforward, after all, to weigh rice or count lemons. In some commodities, however, it is not only the quantity that matters, it is the quality of the product. Furthermore, among goods in which the quality matters, it is very easy quickly to determine the quality of some products being offered for sale, such as by a taste test, and difficult to do so for others.

That the relative ease or difficulty of determining quality affects

26. M. Kikuchi and Yujiro Hayami, "Inducements to Institutional Innovations in an Agrarian Society," International Development Center of Japan Working Paper, Series no. A–07 (Tokyo, 1977).

the structure of marketing can be illustrated by contrasting rice and rubber.[27] Quality matters enormously in rice, but it is extremely easy for a potential purchaser to assess it. By rubbing a few grains of rice between two blocks of wood, a prospective buyer can determine moisture content and the size of the grain and get a rough estimate of broken grains. With rubber, however, quality cannot be determined immediately. A prospective buyer can weigh the unsmoked sheets of rubber and get the quantity accurately (except, of course, if the scale is rigged), but the quality of the rubber does not become apparent until several months later, after further processing of the raw, unsmoked rubber. A smallholder who produces high-quality rubber by using quality acid and carefully removing impurities can only get the "peach bonus" for rubber quality by developing a reputation as a man who produces "peachy" rubber as opposed to "lemony" rubber. That requires a good reputation with a buyer, something that is possible only in an ongoing relationship. Since quality is easy to assess instantaneously, rice markets are generally auction markets—immediate, relatively impersonal transactions. Or what Adam Smith thought all capitalism was like—information easily and readily ascertainable, easy switching of buyers, little reason for loyalty to any marketer or to any buyer. The growers' reputations matter relatively little since direct quality assessments are so easy to perform. Rubber (which is supposedly more modern, more commercial, more capitalist) is the commodity dominated by customer markets, where reputations— hence ongoing relations—matter. The difference between rice and rubber is not the difference between traditional and modern, or between capital-intensive and labor-intensive; it is a characteristic of the crop—the cost and availability of timely information quality—that determines whether there are customer markets or auction markets.

Does the difference between customer markets and auction markets matter to the producers? Siamwalla's research suggests that the differences in market structures affect the profit structure, and his reasoning and preliminary results are worthy of further attention. Middleman margins in Thailand, he has found, are

27. Ammar Siamwalla, "Farmers and Middlemen: Aspects of Agricultural Marketing in Thailand," *Economic Bulletin for Asia and the Pacific* (June 1978); Ammar Siamwalla, "An Economic Theory of Patron-Client Relationships, with Some Examples from Thailand," paper presented at the Thai-European Seminar on Social Change in Contemporary Thailand, May 1980.

much lower in auction markets than in the more personal markets with agent-client relationships. At any time a rice buyer can compete for a grower's rice against the grower's previous buyer; timely low-cost quality assessments mean that there are no entry barriers for middlemen at the lowest levels of the rice trade. But a new rubber buyer has a barrier to entry; last year's buyer will not identify the "peaches," and the growers are not going to admit the "lemons." So a grower who switches buyers can get only the lemon price for his raw rubber. Thus, there is a "shifting cost" for growers and a concomitant advantage for the buyer of previous years. Consequently, a grower who switches to a new buyer can receive an increased base price for his rubber, but the shift will cost him his "peach" bonus. Rubber marketing is less competitive at the lowest levels and the middleman's profits are higher than in rice.[28]

It is at points in the agricultural cycle where shifting costs are highest, Siamwalla implies, that cooperative arrangements have the most potential. It is so easy for competing rice buyers to react to the slightest fluctuations in rice prices that their nearly simultaneous adjustments to price information look like collusion to growers (and to noneconomist observers). But the very small margins made by buyers in customer markets like the rice market leave little leeway for cooperative marketing to increase the grower's share of the final price.[29] In the personal, friendly rubber market where, because buyers cannot respond as quickly to new price information, there is no appearance to the growers of collusion, there is more room for cooperative marketing. By collectively keeping records of each grower's quality or by selling processed rubber, all the growers profit by recapturing the advantages which now accrue to buyers from a high shifting cost.

Where work quality matters, there is a similar shifting cost for laborers. An employer bidding for new laborers does not know whether a laborer is a peach or a lemon. Laborers may not earn their full value then because the shifting cost gives their old employee a hold over them. In this context there is potential profit to be made from the formation of teams of laborers. Team members

28. Once the raw latex has been processed by initial buyers, profits along the rest of the marketing chain are no higher than for rice, despite the small number of exporters: Siamwalla, "Farmers and Middlemen," p. 17.

29. The price farmers receive for their rice immediately after the harvest may be 18 to 20 percent lower than the midseason price, but storage costs are likely to run 13 to 14 percent: ibid., p. 14.

can monitor each other as the same tasks are done time and again on numerous farms. Even though the identity of the team members may change from year to year, the team leader's reputation can provide continuity. Roumasset and Uy provide evidence from the Philippines.[30] In Vietnam, teams were more likely to emerge when farmers were dealing with migratory laborers—who would be less well known personally—than with local laborers. Farmers were also more likely to use teams for planting than for harvesting, for planting is harder to monitor than harvesting.

## The Rise and Fall of Collective Agriculture

It was in response to the problems of insurance and collective goods that the commitment to collective agriculture developed in post-liberation China. As a response to problems of insurance and collective goods, however, the agricultural communes dramatically exacerbated the problem of linking effort and reward—that is, the lemons problem.

The system of collective agriculture and work points consolidated scattered plots in many areas of China and provided a system to mobilize manpower for collective projects, particularly in irrigation. Since 1978, Chinese agriculture has been decollectivized because the expected increases in productivity did not materialize and peasants near cities devoted themselves to marketing private-plot produce rather than collective work. Collective agriculture has been replaced by the rural responsibility system, a system similar to tenancy, with the landlord in this case being the collective. The failure of collective agriculture is a failure of quality monitoring— the lemons problem—and parallels the breakdown of communal land systems historically, as well as the decline of latifundias and estates.

Before the most recent Chinese agricultural reforms, throughout China there were "easy riders," peasants who did poor-quality work in the collective fields. Many peasants, especially those in suburban communes, also ignored collective work in order to cultivate their private plots. Wherever peasants could manage individual access to markets, the relative value of working their private plots compared to working the collective fields—generally grain—rose.

30. James A. Roumasset and Marilou Uy, "Piece Rates, Time Rates, and Teams: Explaining Patterns in the Employment Relation," unpublished paper, 1979.

Not surprisingly, some of the most vocal demands for agricultural reforms and the most ignoring of collective fields for private plots came in the areas where individual access to markets was possible. Thus the breakdown of what the Chinese themselves have called feudalism followed the pattern of breakdown of feudalism in Europe and the pattern of *hacienda* breakdown in Latin America.

In the past, to maintain the control of serfs or *haciendados* or of tenants on giant latifundias in colonial Southeast Asia, estate owners attempted forcibly to block peasants from access to markets. The development of market skills, after all, could allow the peasants to learn to do without the lords. In amassing their estates and maintaining forced dependencies, owners of large estates in Southeast Asia forcibly prevented peasants from selling paddy, buffalo or even garden produce on their own.[31] Ironically, a twelfth-century Chinese author advised that to control serfs "one should not allow them to have fields and gardens of their own, for if one does, they immediately become filled with greedy schemes."[32]

The contemporary Chinese agricultural reforms have resulted in a commercial boom. Recently the Chinese press has been filled with articles telling peasants that they should not condemn their neighbors who are becoming rich. The national leadership has also had to condone peasant households that invest their agricultural earnings in new businesses, particularly transport and commerce. Peasants are buying trucks and marketing their neighbors' produce in the cities, sometimes even going to other provinces.

As noted above, tenancy as opposed to wage labor can be viewed as a way of giving peasants an incentive to monitor their labor quality under conditions where external monitoring was costly. When such crops were grown communally, each peasant doing a task received the same number of work points for each day of labor, regardless of the quality of his or her labor. Although the value of each work point depended on total output, thus linking total work and total pay, each individual's "extra effort" was spread over the whole group. The problem of watering down each person's incentive to do quality work was recognized early and the accounting unit, that unit over which work points were related to output, was

31. Popkin, *Rational Peasant,* p. 75.
32. Mark Elvin, *Pattern of the Chinese Past* (Stanford: Stanford University Press, 1973), p. 77.

reduced in size from communes or brigades of thousands of persons to work teams of a few hundred persons. Still the collective wage-labor system failed to inspire high-quality work; even within the team, the smallest collective unit, Chinese peasants still considered themselves to be "eating from too large a pot."[33]

Now families are contracting with the team for plots of land that they are to work themselves. The land is still owned by the collective, but its cultivation is the sole responsibility of one household. The household is paid for the amount of crop it contracts with the collective to produce; anything above that quota is the household's to consume or sell. Because collective draft animals and farm machinery had in the past been poorly maintained and monopolized by those with personal connections to the leadership, they have now been redistributed to private households.

Working land on a tenancy system can raise production compared to the work-point system. Like all forms of tenancy, however, the rural responsibility system will create its own problems. Eventually, as historically has been common in communal land systems, the rotation of land will become a problem. As agricultural techniques develop, greater investment in land is required. Maximum benefit from irrigation, for example, requires countless hours of fine grading of land. Unless the land is to be farmed by the same family for a number of years, the work to maximize the value of the land does not pay off. In Vietnam, for example, land owned by the village that was periodically allotted to families was less productive than private land, because peasants did not want "to set a table for someone else to eat." More generally, the development of agricultural techniques and investments such as grading the land or planting long-range crops like coffee can be predicted, in China as elsewhere, to lead to a system of de facto private, unrotated land or to a failure to adopt new techniques and crops.[34] Futhermore, as land reallocation breaks down in China it is easy to predict that there will emerge a system of local markets in land and rights to land. As credit becomes more important, peasants can also be expected to demand land titles in-formal long-term contracts that can be used as pledges to obtain credit.

Although the tenancy system has raised productivity by more

33. Richard Madsen, *Chen Village* (Berkeley and Los Angeles: University of California Press, 1983); John Burns, work in progress on Chinese agricultural reforms, 1983.

34. Popkin, *Rational Peasant*, p. 68.

successfully linking effort and reward, a new problem has emerged. Commune, brigade, and team officials are having trouble getting peasants to contribute time and money to collective goods. Many peasants are reluctant to pay into the local accumulation fund and are too busy to contribute time to maintain or construct waterworks. This means a whole new system for metering water or forcing peasants to contribute will be needed. And as many families experience periodic labor shortages, "new" forms of cooperation are emerging which are similar to the small groups so common earlier among peasants. Despite the official view that hired labor is synonymous with exploitation, many families are also hiring labor to meet peak demand.

## Conclusion

In this paper I have laid out implications for the study of rural institutions that follow from two issues that have been raised in nonmarket economics. Both the free rider and the lemon are problems that can require nonmarket solutions. But *nonmarket* does not mean *noneconomic*. Effective institutions are institutions that are free rider–proof, not free rider–prone; and appropriate divisions of labor can minimize problems with lemons. As the recent experience of China indicates, old dichotomies between public and private, between market and nonmarket, between economic and noneconomic are as outmoded as the distinction between traditional and modern. The linkage between effort and reward is central to changes in the organization of peasant society. It is necessary to recognize the limits of markets to provide collective goods and deal with problems of quality, and it is necessary to recognize the role of economic rationality in nonmarket settings as well.

# 8

# The Development of Property Rights in Land:

## A Comparative Study

### *David Feeny*

This chapter studies changes in property rights. It elaborates a simple model of induced institutional change and tests it against experiences in South and Southeast Asia. The chapter takes advantage of the comparative studies to show how contrasting systems of property rights have led to different responses to a common set of relative prices. In so doing, it explores the impact upon the domestic economies of this region of its entry into the world economy.

Previous versions of this paper have been presented at the thirty-fifth annual meeting of the Association for Asian Studies, 25 March 1983, and to the Council on Southeast Asian Studies, Yale University; the Economic Growth Center, Yale University; the Center for the Comparative Study of Development, Brown University; and the economics department, Northeastern University. The author has benefited from the comments of the participants at these presentations. In addition, helpful suggestions were made by Richard Barichello, Fred Carstensen, Victor Doherty, Robert Evenson, Yujiro Hayami, Samuel Popkin, Carl Pray, Louis Putterman, and James C. Scott.

## A Supply-and-Demand Model of Induced Institutional Change

A demand for institutional change arises when some gain cannot be captured under current institutional arrangements.[1] In the specific case of the system of property rights, an appreciation in the relative price of a factor will induce an increase in the demand for an institution to define property rights in that factor. It will also increase the benefits to be derived from the utilization of that system of property rights. A rise in the relative price of a factor thus will increase the demand for the establishment of a system of property rights to govern the use of that factor.

The analysis of the demand for institutional change concerns situations in which there are potential benefits to some party that are only attainable through the creation of a new set of institutional arrangements. The factors that affect the demand for change are then the factors that serve to create the potential benefits for the users of institutional arrangements. Whether change will indeed occur depends, however, on the supply of institutional change, that is, the willingness and capability of the fundamental institutions of government to provide new arrangements.[2] The ca-

1. Seminal demand-induced models of institutional change include Yujiro Hayami and Vernon W. Ruttan, *Agricultural Development: An International Perspective* (Baltimore: Johns Hopkins University Press, 1971); Lance Davis and Douglass C. North, *Institutional Change and American Economic Growth* (Cambridge, England: Cambridge University Press, 1971); and Douglass C. North and Robert Paul Thomas, *The Rise of the Western World: A New Economic History* (Cambridge, England: Cambridge University Press, 1973).

2. Works that explicitly or implicitly include the supply of institutional change include Vernon W. Ruttan, "Induced Innovation and Agricultural Development," *Food Policy* 2 (1979): 196–216; Vernon W. Ruttan, "Induced Institutional Change," in Hans Binswanger and Vernon W. Ruttan, eds., *Induced Innovations: Technology, Institutions, and Development* (Baltimore: Johns Hopkins University Press, 1978); Vernon W. Ruttan, "Institutional Innovations," in Theodore W. Schultz, ed., *Distortions of Agricultural Incentives* (Bloomington: Indiana University Press, 1978); Vernon W. Ruttan, "Some Empirical Evidence on Induced Technical Change in Agriculture," in Herbert Giersch, ed., *International Economic Development and Resource Transfer: Workshop 1978* (Kiel: Institut für Weltwirtschaft von der Universität Kiel, 1978); Vernon W. Ruttan, "Induced Institutional Innovation," *Agricultural Economic Research* 31 (1979): 32–35; Vernon W. Ruttan, "Bureaucratic Productivity: The Case of Agricultural Research," *Public Choice* 35 (1980): 529–47; and Vernon W. Ruttan, "Three Cases of Induced Institutional Innovation," in Clifford S. Russell and Norman K. Nicholson, eds., *Public Choice and Rural Development* (Washington, D.C.: Resources for the Future, 1981); David Feeny, "Technical and Institutional Change in Thai Agriculture, 1880–1940," Ph.D. dissertation, University of Wisconsin, 1976; David Feeny, "Induced Technical and Institutional Change: A Thai Case Study," in

pability depends in part on the cost of institutional innovation. As in the technical-change case, the cost depends in part on the stock of existing knowledge about the design and operation of institutions. The stock of knowledge in turn depends on past experience in production, trade, and distribution as well as the previously existing set of institutions and the nature and degree of research on institutions. Just as investments in basic science research can affect the supply of technical change, investments in educational institutions and research (especially in legal studies and the social sciences) can affect the supply of institutional change through both the creation and the borrowing of new ideas in institutional design. In addition to the effects of the stock of knowledge, the cost of supplying new institutions depends on the prices of the factors used in institutional design. Implementation costs will also affect the supply.

The willingness to provide new arrangements does not depend solely on the cost; it also depends greatly on the private benefits and costs of providing the change that accrue to the agents who are in a position to provide change, that is, the elite decisionmakers of government. The fundamental institutions of a society and the initial distribution of power will thus have a significant impact on the kinds of new institutional arrangements that are supplied. In some cases the elite's interests will be compatible with actions that serve to maximize social welfare; in other cases they may not be.

The provision of new institutional arrangements has a public-good characteristic. In addition to being affected by the demand for change (arising out of subjects' self-interests) and the supply of change (in part reflecting the self-interests of the elite), it is also affected by ideology and conventional wisdom.[3] Notions of how the

Gordon P. Means, ed., *The Past in Southeast Asia's Present* (Ottawa: Canadian Society for Asian Studies, 1978); David Feeny, *The Political Economy of Productivity: Thai Agricultural Development 1880–1975* (Vancouver: University of British Columbia Press, 1982); Joel M. Guttman, "Interest Groups and the Demand for Agricultural Research," *Journal of Political Economy* 86 (1978): 467–84; Joel M. Guttman, "Villages as Interest Groups: The Demand for Agricultural Extension Services in India," *Kyklos* 33 (1980): 122–41; Yujiro Hayami and Masao Kikuchi, "Investment Inducements to Public Infrastructure: Irrigation in the Philippines," *Review of Economics and Statistics* 60 (1978): 70–77; Yujiro Hayami and Masao Kikuchi, *Asian Village Economy at the Crossroads: An Economic Approach to Institutional Change* (Tokyo: University of Tokyo Press, 1981); Douglass C. North, *Structure and Change in Economic History* (New York: W. W. Norton, 1981); and James A. Roumasset, "The New Institutional Economics and Agricultural Organization," *Philippine Economic Journal* 17 (1978): 331–48.

3. See North, *Structure and Change in Economic History.*

world should and how it does operate affect institutional design. North argues that ideology is used by the state to ameliorate the free-rider problem, to reduce the incentives to act only on the basis of narrow self-interest. Ideology thus facilitates the organization of collective action. In the colonial property-rights-development setting, different colonial powers had different ideologies concerning the organization of property rights, and those ideologies, as well as the conventional wisdoms that accompanied them, changed over time.

Institutional change, then, arises through the interaction of the demand for and the supply of change in dynamic sequences. The institutional response in one period becomes part of the initial conditions in the next period, thus affecting the subsequent path of change. In the case of property rights there was often a gradual evolution from simple changes to increasingly elaborate and complicated systems. The approach is summarized below.

*Endogenous Variables*

Institutional arrangements: legal provisions defining property rights in land and in particular the degree of security of land rights

Utilization of the existing institutional arrangements: the degree to which cultivators or owners made use of the system

*Exogenous Variables*

Demand for institutional change
    Relative product and factor prices
    Basic rules of government
    Technology
    Size of market
Sources of gains from innovation
    Capital gains
    Amelioration of incomplete markets, externalities, market failure, and common-property-resource problems
    Risk-sharing
    Achievement of economies of scale
    Reductions of transaction cost
Supply of institutional change
    Cost of innovation
    Stock of knowledge
    Implementation costs
    Basic institutions
    Ideology
    Conventional wisdom
    Private returns to elite decisionmakers

*Interaction of Demand and Supply: Dynamic Sequences*

## Nineteenth- and Twentieth-Century Asian
## Trends in Relative Product and Factor Prices

In the supply-and-demand model of institutional change briefly sketched above, attention is focused on the important role of trends in relative factor prices in determining the demand for the establishment of more elaborate systems of property rights. Thus in order to apply the model, an examination of those trends is needed.

In an effort to provide some preliminary documentation on these trends, both direct and indirect evidence will be utilized. The indirect evidence comes from the trends in the terms of trade, that is, the ratio of the export price of land-intensive agricultural products to the import price of manufactured goods. The terms of trade measure the incentives afforded to an economy by the opportunity of engaging in international trade. The trends in the terms of trade reflect the division of the gains from trade between the two trading partners. The gains from trade are increases in real income made possible by trading.

In a closed economy (no international trade), real land rents (the charge for the use of the services of land in production) are sensitive to population density. As population density rises there is a tendency for real land rents to appreciate with respect to real wages. At low population densities real wages tend to be high relative to real land rents. This close association between real land rents and population density is, however, broken when the economy engages in large-scale international trade. Now relative produce prices are determined on world markets rather than within the economy. Real land rents are now linked to the endowments of land, labor, and capital, to production technology, and to the external terms of trade. Thus it is possible to use a simple general-equilibrium model with two goods (agricultural and manufactured) and three factors of production (land specific to agriculture, mobile capital, and labor) to predict the trends in relative factor prices.[4] While the results for the trends in real wages are somewhat ambiguous, the results for the trend in real land rents are relatively

---

4. The general-equilibrium model is developed in Glenn R. Hueckel, "The Napoleonic Wars and Their Impact on Factor Returns and Output Growth in England,

clear-cut. Real land rents are very sensitive to the trend in the terms of trade (a result of assuming that land is specific to agriculture). This follows because as the relative price of the agricultural product rises, resources move from the other sector (manufacturing) into agriculture. Labor and capital are, however, imperfect substitutes for land. Thus as people seek to expand agricultural output in response to favorable prices, land rents are bid up. Thus we can use the trend in the terms of trade as a proxy for the trend in real land rents.

Data on the terms of trade are presented in Table 2. The data on the Thai terms of trade have the advantage of directly reflecting the ratio of the price of the agricultural to the manufactured product and cover a long period of time. The data indicate a relative appreciation of agricultural prices from the 1860s to 1912, a decline over the period from 1912 to 1925, and finally appreciation from the mid-1920s to the end of the 1930s. Overall, the relative price of the agricultural product appreciated.

On the basis of the trends reflected in these terms-of-trade indices, one would expect that in periods during which the terms of trade were improving, real land rents would have been appreciating, and that the overall trend in real land rents would have been one of appreciation. Evidence confirming the predictions will be discussed below.

Much the same trends in the terms of trade evident for Thailand are also apparent for Burma (see Table 1). From the 1870s to 1912 the ratio of the price of rice or paddy to the prices of imported goods rose. From 1912 to 1925 the terms of trade declined and then rose for one series and fell for the other over the 1925 to 1940 period. Again, overall the terms of trade appreciated.

Data on the Indian terms of trade presented by Bhatia and by Appleyard and Birnberg and Resnick for the later period give much the same impression as the Thai and Burmese indices: an appreciation from the 1860s to the 1910s and a decline in the interwar period (see Table 1). These terms-of-trade indices for India are not ideal, in that manufactured goods were both exported and imported, as were agricultural products; more disaggregated

---

1793–1815," Ph.D. dissertation, University of Wisconsin, 1972, and is applied to the Thai case in Feeny, "Technical and Institutional Change," and Feeny, *Political Economy of Productivity*.

**Table 1.** *Nineteenth- and Twentieth-Century Trends in the Terms of Trade*

| | Rate of Change (% per year) | | Rate of Change (% per year) |
|---|---|---|---|
| *Thailand* | | *India* | |
| 1865–1867 to 1912 | 1.41 or 1.55 | 1861–1869 to 1906–1914 | 0.90 |
| 1912 to 1925 | −3.39 or −1.92 | 1906–1914 to 1931–1939 | −0.79 |
| 1925 to 1939 | 1.03 or 1.18 | 1861–1869 to 1931–1939 | 0.29 |
| 1865–1867 to 1939 | 0.47 or 0.85 | 1903–1908 to 1934–1939 | −0.14 or −0.51 |
| 1865–1867 to 1940 | 1.52 or 1.95 | 1888 to 1914 | 1.12 |
| | | 1914 to 1936 | 0.08 |
| *Burma* | | 1888 to 1936 | 0.65 |
| 1870–1871 to 1912–1913 | 1.90 | *Philippines* | |
| 1890–1892 to 1912–1913 | 1.62 | 1902 to 1925 | 0.51 |
| 1912–1913 to 1925–1926 | −1.33 or −1.44 | 1925 to 1938 | −2.86 |
| 1925–1926 to 1939–1940 | −0.41 or 0.82 | | |
| 1870–1871 to 1939–1940 | 0.81 | 1902 to 1938 | −0.77 |
| 1890–1892 to 1939–1940 | 0.55 | | |

*Sources:*

*Thailand:* The figures represent the export price of rice divided by the import price of white or grey shirting, respectively. The data are taken from David Feeny, *The Political Economy of Productivity: Thai Agricultural Development 1880–1975* (Vancouver: University of British Columbia Press, 1982), pp. 17, 131.

*Burma:* The data represent either the external terms of trade (an index of export prices divided by an index of import prices) or the internal terms of trade (an index of domestic paddy prices divided by an index of the unit value of consumer goods imports). The data are taken from Aye Hlaing, "Trends of Economic Growth and Income Redistribution in Burma, 1870–1940," *Journal of the Burma Research Society* 47 (1964): 145–48.

*India:* The first set of data represents the net barter terms of trade (an index of export prices divided by an index of import prices) and are taken from B. M. Bhatia, "Terms of Trade and Economic Development: A Case Study of India—1861–1939," *Indian Economic Journal* 16 (1969): 417–19.

The figures for 1903–1908 to 1934–1939 represent, respectively, Laspeyres and Paasche indices of terms of trade and are drawn from Dennis R. Appleyard, "Terms of Trade and Economic Development: A Case Study of India," *American Economic Review* 58 (1968): 190.

The remaining figures represent Paasche indices of the terms of trade and are drawn from Thomas B. Birnberg and Stephen A. Resnick, *Colonial Development: An Econometric Study* (New Haven: Yale University Press, 1975).

*Philippines:* The data represent Paasche indices of the terms of trade and are drawn from Birnberg and Resnick, *Colonial Development.*

indices would be desirable. Still, the bulk of the exports are land-intensive goods relative to the import bundle.

Finally, Birnberg and Resnick present evidence on the terms of trade for the Philippines (see Table 1). There appears to have been an appreciation over 1902–1925, a sharp decline from 1925 through 1938, and a decline overall.

The sample of trends in the terms of trade presented in Table 1 points to an appreciation over the period from the mid-nineteenth century until World War I. Therefore one would expect that over the period production and specialization in export activities would have increased and real land rents would have appreciated. Each of these predictions will be examined.

Data on the trends in rice exports and cotton goods imports for Thailand and Burma are presented in Table 2. Rice exports do appear to have increased, especially in periods during which the terms of trade were increasingly favorable. Similarly there was a rapid expansion of cotton-goods imports (the leading import in both countries). While rice-export data are only an indirect indicator of paddy production trends, there is evidence that production responded to the price incentives reflected in the terms of trade. The conclusion is corroborated by the accounts and measures (largely for the twentieth century) of the rapid increases in the area under paddy cultivation in both Burma and Thailand.[5]

Thus it appears that production trends followed the terms of trade. But what happened to real land rents, measured in rice or manufactured goods? In Table 3 two crude measures of real-land-rent trends are presented. The use of the price of land rather than actual rent assumes that the trend in land rents is reflected in the trend in land prices.[6] While data on actual land rents would be preferable, long time series on rents are generally not available. For purposes of fleshing out the broad trends, however, the real-land-price series should be more than adequate.

5. For the Burmese case see Michael Adas, The Burma Delta: Economic Development and Social Change on an Asian Rice Frontier, 1852–1941 (Madison: University of Wisconsin Press, 1974), and Cheng Siok-Hua, The Rice Industry of Burma 1852–1940 (Singapore: University of Malaya Press, 1968). For the Thai case see James C. Ingram, Economic Change in Thailand; 1850–1970, second edition (Stanford: Stanford University Press, 1971), and Feeny, Political Economy of Productivity.

6. The assumption that the trend in real land rents is accurately approximated by the trend in real land prices further assumes that there was no sharp decline in the real rate of interest. For the Thai case this appears to be a very reasonable assumption; see Feeny, Political Economy of Productivity.

**Table 2.**   *Growth of Agricultural Exports and Manufactured Goods Imports (Average percent per annum)*

|  | Quantity of Rice Exports | Value of Rice Exports |  |
| --- | --- | --- | --- |
| *Thailand* |  |  | Value of Cotton-Goods Imports |
| 1864 to 1910 | 4.43 | 5.64 | 4.36 |
| 1910 to 1925 | 1.78 | 4.14 | 6.10 |
| 1925 to 1940 | −0.85 | −3.80 | −3.19 |
| 1864 to 1940 | 2.84 | 3.41 | 3.16 |
| *Burma* |  |  | Quantity of Cotton-Goods Imports |
| 1870–1875 to 1905–1910 | 3.21 | 5.95 |  |
| 1876–1880 to 1911–1915 |  |  | 3.51 |
| 1905–1910 to 1920–1925 | 1.06 | 3.88 |  |
| 1911–1915 to 1921–1925 |  |  | −2.95 |
| 1920–1925 to 1935–1940 | 1.21 | −3.29 |  |
| 1921–1925 to 1936–1940 |  |  | 2.72 |
| 1870–1875 to 1935–1940 | 2.25 | 3.27 |  |
| 1876–1880 to 1936–1940 |  |  | 2.21 |

*Sources:*

*Thailand:* The data are from David Feeny, *The Political Economy of Productivity: Thai Agricultural Development 1880–1975* (Vancouver: University of British Columbia Press, 1982), pp. 127–30.

*Burma:* The data are from Aye Hlaing, "Trends of Economic Growth and Income Distribution in Burma, 1870–1940," *Journal of the Burma Research Society* 47 (1964): 89–148.

The results presented in Table 3 conform to our predictions. When the terms of trade appreciated, real land prices appreciated; when the terms of trade declined, so did real land rents. Thus it appears to be reasonable to use the terms of trade as a proxy for the trend in real land rents when direct evidence is unavailable. This conclusion is further corroborated by the widespread reports

**Table 3.**   *Rate of Change in Real Land Prices (% per year)*

|  | Land Price Deflated by Price of Rice | Land Price Deflated by Price of Manufactured Goods |
|---|---|---|
| *Thailand* | | |
| 1915 to 1925 | −0.31 | −1.09 or −0.14 |
| 1925 to 1940 | 2.58 | 4.17 or   4.55 |
| 1915 to 1940 | 1.41 | 2.03 or   2.65 |
| *Burma* | | |
| 1889–1890 to 1920–1921 | 3.25 | 2.52 |

*Notes and sources:*

*Thailand:* The figures in the second column represent the land prices as deflated by the price of white or grey shirting, respectively. The data are drawn from David Feeny, *The Political Economy of Productivity: Thai Agricultural Development 1880–1975* (Vancouver: University of British Columbia Press, 1982), pp. 20, 33.

*Burma:* The figures in the second column represent the land price deflated by the unit value of consumer goods imports. The data are drawn from Aye Hlaing, "Trends of Economic Growth and Income Distribution in Burma, 1870–1940," *Journal of the Burma Research Society* 47 (1964): 128, 147–48.

of an appreciation of land prices from the mid-nineteenth to the early twentieth century.

## Case Studies

Given the generally favorable terms-of-trade movements over the last half of the nineteenth century and the concomitant appreciation in real land rents and expansion of the production of land-intensive agricultural products, the simple supply-and-demand model of institutional change predicts an increase in the demand for more elaborate and secure systems of property rights in land and a greater utilization of the institutional arrangements of that system. The evidence on the trends in the demand for property rights in land and the responses of the central authorities to those demands will now be examined.

The strategy here is to describe the "traditional" indigenous system of property rights in land that existed in the early nineteenth century and then to trace the major changes that occurred over time. The trends in Thailand, Burma, India, and the Philippines will be sketched briefly.

## Thailand

The early-nineteenth-century system of property rights in land in Thailand was essentially one of usufruct rights. As long as the cultivator continued to use the land he (or she) had the right to exclude others from using it, sell it, pass it on to the person's heirs, or offer it as collateral to obtain a loan. The maintenance of the rights depended on the payment of land taxes. If the land was abandoned for more than three consecutive years, rights were forfeited.

Over the first half of the nineteenth century the degree of commercialization of the Thai economy gradually increased, as did ties to regional and world markets.[7] During the fourth reign (1851–1868) land rights were made more formal through the issuance of title deeds based on paddy-land-tax receipts. In 1867–1868, titles for paddy land for which the tax was based on the area harvested were introduced. In 1882–1883, for some major Central Plain rice-producing provinces, titles based on the area owned rather than harvested were issued for the first time. Such a title could be obtained by presenting to officials the tax receipts for the previous ten years. Documents were also available to give cultivators of newly cleared areas the right to exclude others while developing the land for three years; if the area had not been developed by that time, the rights were forfeited.

The appreciation of land prices continued and deficiencies in the property-rights system became apparent. Frequent land disputes occurred (the expected gain from obtaining ownership rose and justified the transaction cost of disputation). During the 1880s the government responded by issuing standard forms and prescribing standardized procedures. The lack of a central place for land records meant, however, that more than one set of titles could be issued for the same piece of land, and disputes became increasingly frequent.

7. Trends in Thailand's international trade and in particular the Sino-Thai trade in the first half of the nineteenth century are described in Viraphol Sarasin, *Tribute and Profit: Sino-Siamese Trade, 1652–1853* (Cambridge, Mass.: Council on East Asian Studies, Harvard University, 1977); see also Ingram, *Economic Change in Thailand*. Developments in Thai property rights are described in Feeny, *Political Economy of Productivity*.

The response was the passage of a more comprehensive land law in 1892. It created nine types of land, including land held by religious institutions, royal land, residential land, agricultural land, land used for mining, forest and jungle land, and waterway land. The agricultural-land category included three types of orchards and gardens, upland land, two types of paddy land, and garden lands. Provisions were made for transferable title deeds which could be used as collateral, and documents and procedures were created for the registration of such transactions. Homesteading provisions were included, as well as procedures for converting old documents to the newly created ones. The 1892 land law replaced the earlier rather ad hoc system with a more comprehensive one.

However, major deficiencies in the legislation and its administration remained. The lack of central land-title offices and precise descriptions of the boundaries of the lands in question meant that disputes over ownership could not easily be resolved and land could not be identified unambiguously. These problems became conspicuous in the Rangsit area (a major commercial rice-exporting region in the Central Plain to the northeast of Bangkok) during the boom of the 1890s, when a number of bitter land disputes arose. As a result the Royal Survey Department was diverted from its work on mapping and in 1896 began cadastral surveys, initially concentrating on the Rangsit area but later expanding into most of the major rice-exporting areas in the Central Plain.

In 1901 the Torrens system of land titling, with central provincial land-record offices and cadastral surveys, was formally adopted. Between 1901 and 1909 eleven land-record offices were established. By 1909–1910, 593,069 title deeds had been issued in the Central Plain (637,001 in the kingdom as a whole) and the area surveyed was 1,605,000 hectares (1,671,000 hectares for the whole kingdom). The work was carried out by European experts (mainly on loan from the Indian Civil Service) who in addition to conducting the survey work also provided training to the Thai staff. After 1909 the Royal Survey Department was transferred back to its original mapping duties and the rate of increase in the surveyed area plunged. The number of title deeds on file (primarily in the Central Plain) did, however, continue to increase; the rate of increase of title deeds on file for the kingdom was 4.69 percent per year over the period from 1905–1906 to 1941.

The system was incompletely realized. A lack of diligent record-keeping and administration reduced the benefits. Not all farmers obtained or were able to obtain the proper documents for land that they held. Areas outside the Central Plain were especially incompletely served by cadastral surveys.

After 1909 a number of minor changes were made in the system implemented during the pre–World War II period. Administrative procedures were changed and fees were instituted on land transfers. Restrictions were placed on the sale of public lands in 1916 and 1919, with the intent of curbing land speculation. Finally, in 1938–1939, a new schedule of agricultural land taxes was established.

A more major change was made in 1936 when the 1901 law was amended to allow the registration of claims on unsurveyed lands. Traditionally, claims on apparently unclaimed lands were registered with the village headman, but the 1936 law required registration at the Land Department. The 1936 law represented a compromise between the elaborate European cadastral survey system of the 1901 law and the incomplete implementation of that system. The compromise was extended in 1954 when a new comprehensive land law was enacted. It provides for a variety of land documents that give different levels of security of land rights. Occupation certificates are issued by village headman and commune leaders and allow the holder temporarily to exclude others from using land as long as it is being developed. Reserve licenses issued by district officers also give rights for temporary occupation subject to utilization. Exploitation testimonials (again issued by district officers) confirm that utilization of previously reserved land has taken place and confer rights that are transferable and inheritable. Finally, full title deeds issued by cadastral survey and providing for the recording of land transactions are issued by officials in the provincial capital. The 1954 code is the basis of the current system of land rights in Thailand. The major changes in the Thai property-rights system are summarized below.[8]

| Period | Institutional Change |
|---|---|
| Early nineteenth century | Usufruct rights, existing system |
| 1851–1868 | Issue title deeds based on the area harvested |
| 1882–1883 | Issue title deeds based on the area owned |

8. See Feeny, *Political Economy of Productivity.*

| | |
|---|---|
| 1880s | Prescribe standardized forms and procedures in an effort to reduce land disputes |
| 1892 | Enact a comprehensive land law with provision for title deeds and use of land as collateral |
| 1901 | Institute a Torrens system of land registration and conduct cadastral surveys |
| 1936 | Amendment to 1901 law, allowing for ownership, based on registration with the Land Department, of claims on unsurveyed lands |
| 1954 | Enact a new land law providing for a variety of documents and levels of security of land rights |

Even within the parameters of the compromise embodied in the 1954 code, the system is still incomplete. Ingram reports estimates for the late 1960s of the area covered by three types of land documents. Only 12 percent of the total area had full title deeds, 4 percent had reserve licenses, 18 percent had exploitation testimonials, and 65 percent had no formal legal documentation at all.[9]

Disputes over conflicting claims to the same piece of land played an important role in causing the government to develop more systematic and elaborate systems of land rights in Thailand. In the early twentieth century, differential access to the formal system and

9. Ingram, *Economic Change in Thailand*, p. 266. See also Feeny, *Political Economy of Productivity;* Webster V. Johnson, *Agricultural Development of Thailand with Reference to Rural Institutions* (Bangkok: Division of Land Policies, Department of Land Development, 1969); M. B. Hooker, *Legal Pluralism: An Introduction to Colonial and Neo-Colonial Laws* (Oxford: Oxford University Press, 1975); David Phillip Gisselquist, "A History of Contractual Relations in a Thai Rice Growing Village," Ph.D. dissertation, Yale University, 1976; David M. Engel, *Code and Custom in a Thai Provincial Court* (Tucson: University of Arizona Press, 1978); Jeremy H. Kemp, "Legal and Informal Land Tenures in Thailand," *Modern Asian Studies* 15 (1981): 1–23; Toru Yano, "Land Tenure in Thailand," *Asian Survey* 8 (1968): 853–63; and Khambanonda Chalermrath, *Thailand's Public Law and Policy for Conservation and Protection of Land with Special Attention to Forests and Natural Areas* (Bangkok: National Institute of Development Administration, 1972).

the ability of powerful government officials to manipulate the land-records system allowed elites to obtain ownership of land that under the traditional system would have been controlled by home-steading cultivators. Today intrafamilial manipulation of the system has allowed some heirs to gain at the expense of others.[10] The traditional system of equal inheritance by all surviving children is frequently subverted by more literate and knowledgeable siblings—a clash between the use of the "modern" system and traditional inheritance practices. The central government has been increasingly involved in the adjudication of local disputes which in former times would have been settled by local officials.

In the Thai case the appreciation of land prices led to an increase in the demand for a more systematic set of procedures for defining property rights in land. The government in fact responded to the demands and gradually a new system of property rights evolved.

In part the new system evolved as a practical solution to the land disputes that became so common as land became more valuable. The cost of supplying a new set of institutions was lowered by the availability of European systems and officials—by the existence of a stock of knowledge and practice on the organization of property rights in land. Over time that system was increasingly indigenized. While it has never been vigorously exploited in Thailand, a better cadastral system also gave the government an enhanced land-tax-revenue base. Finally, private and social interests coincided. Government officials participated in the land boom and benefited from the more secure system of property rights in land. They had an incentive to supply the new system because they too would share in the gains. By separating land ownership from land use, members of the elite could become noncultivating landowners with secure title and thus capture the capital gains. Under the traditional usufruct system this was not possible.

During the period between 1850 and 1912, the Thai government made another fundamental change in its property-rights systems. It gradually dismantled a system of property rights in man (corvée and debt slavery). The change was facilitated by a significant decline in real wages over the period.[11] The development of

10. Engel, *Code and Custom in a Thai Provincial Court.*
11. Real wages in rice declined by 1.04 percent per year between 1864 and 1912. For more on the trends in Thai human property rights, see Feeny, *Political Economy of Productivity.*

more efficient wage-labor markets and the immigration of Chinese workers made corvée a less attractive form of taxation. With the general rise in commercialization, money taxes could be substituted for taxes in kind and in labor services. The rise of property rights in land created a new asset for use as collateral. The motivations of the monarch in abolishing slavery included humanitarian goals and the desire to be seen as progressive in an international setting in which slavery was increasingly condemned. Domestic political factors were important as well. By gradually abolishing slavery and corvée, the king could remove the control of labor services from powerful opposition nobility and thus consolidate his position with respect to the nobles. Thus both economic (decline in real wages, rise in factor and product markets) and political (both domestic and international) factors underwrote a sweeping transformation of the Thai property-rights system from one of property rights in man to one of property rights in land.

## Burma

The property-rights systems in land and man in precolonial Burma were not unlike the systems in Thailand.[12] There were systems of property rights in man in the forms of corvée and debt slavery. Traditional property rights in land were largely usufruct rights, that is, rights were retained only through use, although technically land had to have been abandoned for twelve years before it was available for use by others. Land could often be sold, mortgaged, or inherited, although in some districts land could only be sold to someone from the same district. There was a significant amount of regional variation in the property-rights system. As in the Thai case, all land belonged to the king but the populace was allowed to clear land and retain it and obtain title documents. An additional category was land that was the absolute

12. The discussion for Burma is based on J. S. Furnivall, "Land as a Free Gift of Nature," *Economic Journal* 19 (1909): 552–62; B. H. Baden-Powell, *The Land-Systems of British India: Being a Manual of the Land-Tenures and of the Systems of Land-Revenue Administration Prevalent in the Several Provinces*, 3 vol. (Oxford: Oxford University Press, 1892); Frank N. Trager and William J. Koenig, *Burmese Sit-tans 1764–1826: Records of Rural Life and Administration* (Tucson: University of Arizona Press, 1979); Adas, *Burma Delta;* and J. Russell Andrus, "Three Economic Systems Clash in Burma," *Review of Economic Studies* 3 (1936): 140–46. The focus here is on lower Burma.

property of the king; it was often allocated for crown service or to local officials. Vacant lands were available for clearing and usufruct rights. Finally, glebe land rights did not depend on continued occupation.

The British were perplexed by the system of shifting cultivation practiced by Burman farmers and were opposed to the frequent abandonment of fields. Furnivall reports that the traditional usufruct system, under which a cultivator could exclude others from using land only while it was in fact in use, in interaction with the fallow system of shifting cultivation, did sometimes result in insufficient fallow periods. As a result of British opposition to the abandonment of fields and in a desire to create a peasant proprietary system, special homesteading and fallow tax rates were built into the land rights and revenue system. British motivation included the desire to build a land-tax-revenue base to support government operations. Policy can also be seen as a reaction to previous experience in India, in that officials wanted to create a class of peasant cultivators. The basic assumptions underlying land policy were a belief in the efficiency of private property rights and a laissez-faire ideology.

Newly cleared land was initially exempt from land taxes. Low tax rates applied to land that was registered as being fallow. On unregistered fallow land, higher tax rates were charged. When the land had been occupied and the land taxes paid for twelve years, title deeds were issued and the land could then be used as collateral.

The use of the British system of property rights in land increased significantly during the rice-export boom of the late nineteenth century. From the 1870s on, farmers decided with increasing frequency to pay taxes on fallow land, in order to retain their rights. As land was used for collateral, land alienation became increasingly frequent over the 1908–1930 period and increased rapidly during the depression of the 1930s. In the late 1930s and early 1940s, the colonial government responded with tenancy legislation, thus restricting the property rights in land which they had earlier created.

In Burma the ideology of the colonial power interacted with the indigenous systems of property rights and farming to create a new system with alienable rights in land but also with provisions for homesteading and fallow periods. The motivations included the creation of a society of peasant cultivator-owners who would have the incentive to cultivate efficiently. The desire to avoid concentration of ownership was somewhat thwarted by the 1930s trend in land alienation.

As in the Thai case, the increase in land prices did create a demand for more secure property rights in land and greater utilization of that system. Because the provision and operation of that system were in the ideological and economic interests of the colonial government, changes in the property rights system and the administrative system with which to operate it were forthcoming. The institutional arrangements designed for Burma also reflected compromises that explicitly took into account the traditional fallow practices and traditional rights to clearing "waste" land.

### India

Generalizations about the system of property rights in land in India and the trends in that system are quite hazardous and will probably fail to do justice to the regional, ethnic, and temporal diversities found there. With that major caveat in mind, the broad trends will nonetheless be examined.[13]

The traditional system that the British encountered was one of inalienable hereditary resident cultivator rights. In Bengal a class of revenue collectors known as *zamindars* acted as intermediaries between the cultivators and the rulers. In Oudh the *talqudars* acted as intermediaries above the village level with land-revenue collection rights.

British law and practice varied considerably within India and over time. In general, however, the British sought to make land private, alienable property with individual property rights being assigned to the person responsible for paying the land tax. Like Indian governments before them, the British East India Company and the colonial government relied heavily on land tax revenues. The development of property rights in land was thus inextricably

13. The discussion for India is based on Thomas R. Metcalf, *The Aftermath of Revolt: India, 1857–1870* (Princeton: Princeton University Press, 1964); Thomas R. Metcalf, *Land, Landlords, and the British Raj: Northern India in the Nineteenth Century* (Berkeley and Los Angeles: University of California Press, 1979); Eric Stokes, *The English Utilitarians and India* (Oxford: Oxford University Press, 1959); Tom G. Kessinger, *Vilyatpur 1848–1968: Social and Economic Change in a Northern Indian Village* (Berkeley and Los Angeles: University of California Press, 1974); Baden-Powell, *Land-Systems of British India*, and Dietmar Rothermund, *Government, Landlord, and Peasant in India: Agrarian Relations under British Rule 1865–1935* (Wiesbaden: Franz Steiner, 1978).

linked to revenue policy. As the British administrative "frontier" moved within India for over one hundred years, experience in "older" areas affected practice in the newly governed regions. Thus Madras experience affected Bombay, Uttar Pradesh experience was carried over to the Punjab, and Bengal practice was transferred to Banaras. Local conditions also affected the system adopted and in particular its actual practice. In addition, the degree to which the colonial government thought it was expedient to co-opt the loyalty of the indigenous elite in governing the country often affected land settlements profoundly. Thus the post-Mutiny period witnessed a number of policy reversals.

Finally, an important variable in the determination of the land system was the prevailing ideology of the responsible British officials in London and in India. The rise and decline of utilitarian thought were reflected in British policy in India.

As a sweeping generalization, two basic paradigms of British practice may be distinguished. In the *zamindar* system, land rights were given to the tax collectors as a landed gentry who then became the landlords to the cultivators. In the *ryotwari* system, land rights were instead invested in the peasant cultivators themselves.

The *zamindar* system was first created by Lord Cornwallis in Bengal in 1793 and was congruent with his Whig belief in the superiority of government by a landed gentry who would in turn supervise the cultivators to ensure efficient practice. The relatively low transaction cost of this strategy made it quite attractive. Rather than having to determine the ownership of each piece of land and keep track of each individual land transaction, large areas could be administered by dealing with a single landowner. The political advantages included the enhanced loyalty of the traditional elite. Cornwallis encountered a very entrenched class of *zamindars* in Bengal who had thwarted earlier attempts at direct settlement with the cultivators. It is easy to understand his choice of settlements.

The *zamindar* system was first used in Bengal. An important component of the Bengal *zamindar* settlement, the distribution of land rights to *zamindar* revenue collectors as landlords, was copied in parts of Madras and in Uttar Pradesh. It was later extended to a number of areas after the 1857 Mutiny, in an effort to restore order and loyalty.

The *ryotwari* system was gradually developed in Madras in the 1790s by Munro and copied in the Bombay Presidency in the 1830s. It arose in part because there was no existing class of local *zamindars.* Its demands for thorough knowledge of the area and the ability to conduct detailed settlement surveys were met by military officers like Munro who had extensive experience in Madras and a knowledge of the indigenous language. In addition the land revenue system in Madras was designed to allow the cultivator to designate (at the beginning of the year) the fields for which he would be responsible for the payment of land taxes.

The northwest was originally settled through the *zamindar* system; the *ryotwari* system was introduced in the 1843–1853 period of utilitarian reforms. After the Mutiny, the *zamindar* system was reinstituted in Oudh and the Punjab. In addition to being politically expedient, the policy reversal resulted from a growing dissatisfaction on the part of British officials with the imposition of alien (British) concepts of property and their growing appreciation and knowledge of indigenous institutions and concepts of property.

The *ryotwari* system required detailed cadastral surveys and a much more complex administrative machinery. Ricardian rent theory affected the thinking of Mill and many other British officials in the early nineteenth century. In the Bombay Presidency the implementation of that thinking was especially vigorous. A complex cadastral survey was begun in 1835. It classified land into nine soil-quality categories and also based its relative land-quality rankings on climate, market access, distance from village, village population, and likely availability of manure. While the detailed land and title surveys gave relative rent rankings, the government still needed a way of determining the absolute rent. Officials decided to use trial and error. If taxes were set above the level of rent, land abandonment and declines in cultivation would follow. If taxes were set below the rents, cultivation would expand. By examining the revenue history of an area, the absolute level of taxes needed to capture the Ricardian rents for the government could be determined. Technically the land belonged to the government and the cultivators paid taxes as rent on the land. Officials believed that efficiency would be enhanced by assessing rents that were approximately equal to the Ricardian rent.

The agricultural sector in the Bombay Presidency (or at least those areas that have been carefully studied) performed well. Capital accumulated, cultivation increased, and land prices rose. Clear titles were issued and tenure was made more secure. Taxes were rationalized and lowered in the process. How much of the success was due to the adherence to Ricardian rent theory and how much was due to the favorable agricultural prices experienced is, however, difficult to determine.

The introduction of secure property rights in land in India created new credit markets. Over the nineteenth century the economy experienced the spread of "law and order," a marked reduction in transport costs, a rise in commercial agriculture, and a rise in land prices. In some areas land taxes were set at high levels and *zamindars* fell into arrears, often losing land to moneylender and commercial castes. Land alienation often significantly altered the distribution of land holdings from that originally envisaged by the British.

Colonial officials also increasingly became concerned over tenant rights. Beginning in 1886, a series of laws to grant greater security to tenants were passed. Many of these provided for hereditary tenant rights after twelve continuous years of occupation. Of course, landlords could easily circumvent the restrictions by "rotating" their tenants.

In India we can see that political expediency, utilitarian and Whig ideologies, indigenous systems, and the practical considerations of transaction cost in creating and administering a land-rights-revenue system all interacted to produce a number of distinct systems which then had their own individual evolutions. Creating alienable land also had a quite significant impact on the Indian society as well as on the operation of its agricultural markets.

### Philippines

In pre-Spanish times the Philippines had traditional communal ownership of land and a fairly elaborate system of property rights in man.[14] Individuals held usufruct rights in land. There were several categories of debt slavery under which slaves owed their owners fixed shares of their crop output.

The Spanish viewed debt slavery as the product of antisocial usury and moved to abolish it. They also introduced private individual property rights in land and alienability. Title to the formerly

14. The discussion for the Philippines is based on John Leddy Phelan, *The Hispanization of the Philippines: Spanish Aims and Filipino Responses 1565–1700* (Madison: University of Wisconsin Press, 1959), and John A. Larkin, *The Pampenejans: Colonial Society in a Philippine Province* (Berkeley and Los Angeles: University of California Press, 1972).

communal lands was generally issued to the indigenous chief. In addition, some royal land was donated to religious estates and some was made available for homesteading under the provision that failure to keep it in use caused the title to revert to the crown. Over time the alienability of land often resulted in *mestizo* money-lenders accumulating control of land through loan defaults.

While in the technical sense land was the property of the state until the late nineteenth century, in practice private ownership, sale, lease, and inheritance prevailed. With the sugar-export boom of the nineteenth century and the rise in land values that accompanied agricultural commercialization, land disputes became more common. In response the colonial government began issuing clear land titles in 1885. Confusion, however, remained.

The next major step came with the new colonial government of the United States. In response to the confusion in the documentation of land rights, a cadastral act was passed in 1913, followed by a survey which took six years to complete. Provision was made for the homesteading of vacant lands, and the mechanism was used frequently during the sugar-export boom. The desire to avoid land taxes did, however, lead to a failure to acquire formal title to occupied lands. As in Thailand and Burma, in the Philippines literate elites were often able to manipulate the formal system to acquire legal title to lands that had been cleared by others, thus contributing to a more unequal distribution of land.

## Conclusions

Several inductive conclusions follow from this brief discussion of the trends in property-rights systems. First, the rising value of land increased interest in acquiring land and utilizing the system of property rights. This in turn led to disputes over ownership that often exposed weaknesses in the prevailing system of identifying and administering land rights. A number of attempts at administrative solutions typically followed, often finally resulting in the institution of a full cadastral survey.

In this context it is useful to distinguish between the effects of rising land values on land already under cultivation and their effects on hitherto uncultivated land. In the former case traditional or existing institutions to define property rights in land came under less pressure for change. In settled communities, ownership boundaries tended to be well known and thus there was less uncertainty about how land disputes would be adjudicated. De facto rights were often enforceable even in the absence of de jure documents. Under these circumstances the major advantage of obtaining formal documentation of land rights was its usefulness as collateral.

On the frontier where settlements were new, boundaries were not well known to all and there was great uncertainty about the outcome of land disputes. In a sense the formal procedures and documents of the government partly substituted for the local knowledge and enforcement mechanisms that existed in the settled communities. Thus on the frontier the demand for more precise and secure property rights in land tended to be greater. New institutional arrangements were in fact frequently provided in response to the demand articulated through land disputes.

Second, differential access to the increasingly formal and legalistic system provided an important avenue through which unequal patterns of land ownership could emerge. Elites were often very successful in manipulating land records in their favor. This appears to have happened in Burma, the Philippines, Cochin China, and the Rangsit area in central Thailand.[15] Inequality was also created (although frequently eroded through alienation) by the initial distribution of land to elite groups in the Philippines, Bengal, and Northwest India. On the other hand, alienation appears to have promoted land concentration in Burma.

Third, in many cases a major motivating factor of the government in the creation and administration of the land-rights system was the desire to collect land tax revenues. The taxpayer was defined as the owner, thus often converting an indigenous political intermediary of the traditional system into a full owner under the new system.

Fourth, in virtually all cases the legal provisions "exceeded" administrative practice in the degree of sophistication and precision of the land rights. This occurred for two reasons. First, the transactions cost of establishing and operating the systems were considerable and much higher than the costs of enacting the enabling legislation. Cadastral surveys took years and even decades to com-

15. For the Cochin China case see Samuel L. Popkin, *The Rational Peasant: The Political Economy of Rural Society in Vietnam* (Berkeley and Los Angeles: University of California Press, 1979); for the Thai case see Feeny, *Political Economy of Productivity*, and Thai National Archives, Sixth Reign, Ministry of Agriculture Documents 5/1–5/12.

plete and, as we can see from the Thai evidence, many are still incomplete. Second, colonial powers (and thus the stock of knowledge of institutions from which the Thais directly borrowed) came from different economic and institutional (as well as ecological) environments. Relative land scarcity and relatively high land values often had prevailed for centuries. In addition, higher stocks of human capital made more administratively demanding systems of land rights feasible. Naturally there was a tendency to introduce something like the "home" system, which was often overly sophisticated. Often explicit compromises were made (for homesteading, for instance) in the legislation and additional compromises emerged in the implementation of the systems and subsequent revisions in the legislation. The 1954 Land Code in Thailand can be seen as an example of such a compromise.

Finally, in all the cases it appears that the rise in the terms of trade and the growth of the population were indeed associated with a rise in real land prices. That increase was in turn associated with an increase in the demand for more precise land rights and a greater utilization of the existing system to increase the security of land rights. A more secure system of land rights gradually evolved. Greater security typically came in two forms. First, uncertainty about the outcome of the adjudication of land ownership disputes was reduced. Second, owners had greater assurance that they would be able to retain long-term rights in the land.

The evolution of the system of land rights was affected by political expediency, ideology and conventional wisdom, transaction costs, and the system that immediately preceded it. In short, both the supply of and the demand for institutional change played important roles in the nineteenth- and twentieth-century development of property rights in land in Asia.

## Implications for Future Research

This chapter provides an interpretation of the comparative development of property rights in land in South and Southeast Asia during the nineteenth and twentieth centuries. The implications of the approach have, however, not been fully exploited. Further research is needed in order to construct a more complete interpretation.

First, the stock of qualitative and, in particular, of quantitative evidence on the trends in property-rights systems, relative product prices, and relative factor prices needs to be augmented. Quantitative measures of institutional change need to be created to test crude hypotheses—for example, measures of the degree of utilization of the land-rights system, such as the percentage of the area under cultivation that is titled, would be invaluable.

Second, a number of implications of the model need to be explored. For instance, the demand-induced model of institutional change is based on the premise that innovations in institutional arrangements are made in order to capture gains previously unobtainable. In the case of property rights in land, those gains include the capital gains resulting from the appreciation in land rents, enhanced incentives to invest in land productivity–increasing improvements, and improved access to credit markets. From the point of view of the state, property rights in land provided a lucrative source of tax revenues as well as potential political benefits in the form of loyalty to the regime.

Evidence on the magnitude and trends in each of the gains should be sought. Greater precision and security of land rights should enhance incentives for land development. Thus evidence on rates of investment in land development and productivity differentials between areas with more and less secure land rights should be sought. Of course, to the extent that land rights are first provided in more fertile and commercialized areas, a simultaneity problem complicates the drawing of inferences.

Another benefit of more secure land rights is the ability to use land as collateral, thus improving access to credit markets. This would be shown by longer debt maturities and/or lower real interest rates resulting from land titling. (Once again, there is a simultaneity problem.)

Finally, if the appreciation in real land rents followed the appreciation of the terms of trade and induced the development of more secure property rights in land, what happened when the terms of trade declined and why was a reversal in the property-rights developments not observed? Several tentative answers suggest themselves. First, real land rents in fact depend on more than the terms of trade; in particular, the downward pressure on land rents was in part blunted in many cases by technical changes that served to increase the productivity of land. Similarly, irrigation development and falling transportation costs helped to offset the downward pressure on land rents that occured when the terms of trade declined. Furthermore, institutional change is not instantaneous. It is subject to lags. Thus the periods of declining real land rents may not have been of sufficient duration to have induced major changes in the institutional arrangements. Declines should, however, be observable in the marginal rate of utilization of the "sticky" institutional arrangements. In addition, each new institutional arrangement becomes part of the status quo, now often with vested interests committed to its maintenance. Thus the incentives for parties who seek to reverse earlier institutional innovations need to be powerful. As a result, during the periods of declining terms of trade and real land rents, not a dismantling of the system of property rights in land, but instead a period of quiescence, might be expected.

In sum, more work is needed in order fully to elaborate and test the induced model of institutional change against the nineteenth- and twentieth-century Asian experience. While economic history can be a powerful research tool for the testing of theory, especially in the mainly nonexperimental disciplines of the social sciences, the analysis must also be applied to the contemporary world.

Many of the historical transformations described are still occurring today. Technical change in the forms of mechanization and of development of modern fertilizer-responsive varieties of rice are powerful forces contributing to the evolution of labor-market institutions for the recruitment and supervision of harvesting labor in Indonesia and the Philippines. Hayami and Kikuchi describe the disequilibrium in traditional harvest-labor institutions created by the higher-yielding varieties.[16] With the introduction of those varieties, traditional shares for harvest workers substantially exceeded real wages in the local economy. Mechanization of harvest operations, the hiring of extravillage harvest wage-labor teams, and new share-harvest arrangements are the three primary responses to the disequilibrium, with the choice depending in large part on the degree of social cohesion in the village. In the process, the division of the gains from the introduction of the new varieties is being assigned.

Increasing population density and the spread of transportation and communication infrastructure are creating disputes over land ownership in many areas in the less developed world today. For instance, in northern Thailand the spread of cultivation, by ethnic Thai lowlanders, up the slopes of the mountains is coming into

16.  Hayami and Kikuchi, *Asian Village Economy.*

conflict with the swidden cultivation practices of ethnic-minority hill tribesmen. The situation is further complicated by the open-access nature of the forests in Thailand.[17] While in theory forest lands belong to the state, with some provision for traditional use of forest products for home consumption, the state's property rights in increasingly scarce forest land cannot be adequately enforced. Because forest land that is brought under cultivation is not supposed to be converted into private property, farmers have little security and few incentives to invest in land development. When titles or other land-registration documents are issued, the unequal access to the Thai bureaucracy generally means that ethnic Thai are favored in the distribution of property rights in land. The general insecurity in land rights has meant, according to recent World Bank observers, that farmers have continued to use environmentally damaging extensive means of cultivation when all parties recognize that it would be in the long-run interests of the farmers themselves, as well as of the people downstream who suffer from increased flooding and siltation, if more intensive modes of cultivation were used. Property-rights issues lie at the heart of many open-access and/or common-property resource disputes in the Third World today. Innovations in institutional arrangements to ameliorate these market-failure problems in the use of land, water, forests, and fisheries should therefore be a high priority on the political economy research agenda. The supply-and-demand model of induced institutional change outlined above is one possible approach to this issue.

17. For more on land disputes and forest resource problems in northern Thailand see Peter Kinstadter, E. C. Chapman, and Sanga Sabhasri, eds., *Farmers in the Forest: Economic Development and Marginal Agriculture in Northern Thailand* (Honolulu: University Press of Hawaii, 1978), and David Feeny, "Agricultural Expansion and Forest Depletion in Thailand, 1900–1975," paper presented at the conference on the World Economy and the World Forests in the Twentieth Century, National Humanities Center, Research Triangle Park, North Carolina, April 1983.

# 9

## Structure, Growth, and Power:
### Three Rationalist Accounts

### *Ronald Rogowski*

Robert Gilpin, *War and Change in International Politics.* Cambridge, England: Cambridge University Press, 1981.
Douglass C. North, *Structure and Change in Economic History.* New York: W. W. Norton, 1981.
Mancur Olson, *The Rise and Decline of Nations: Economic Growth, Inflation, and Social Rigidities.* New Haven: Yale University Press, 1982.

These three ambitious works all address the same broad and timely questions: Why do national economies grow and contract? How is economic growth affected by, and how does it affect, the domestic structures and policies and the international power of states? What is the relation between economic health and political tranquillity, within and between states? All three volumes, moreover, claim to proceed from the same perspective, namely, that of rational choice—applied by Olson to individual subjects, by Gilpin to state leaderships, and by North to both. Finally, all apply to their

Reprinted with permission from *International Organization*, volume 37, Ronald Rogowski, "Structure, Growth and Power: Three Rationalist Accounts." © 1983, The MIT Press.

chosen subjects an impressive historical erudition, which draws as effortlessly on evidence from ancient empires and primitive tribes as on that from the present day.

To the adherent of rational-choice theory, Olson's volume will be what the Jacobin Terror was to Dickens. It is an "awful" work in both the archaic and the modern senses of the word, stunning in its deductive rigor and power, calamitously wrong in many of its implications. North, while less ineluctible in his logic. less often errs: the slightly less parsimonious and precise model is justified by the greater accuracy of its implications. Gilpin's contribution, as he himself emphasizes at the outset, is not intended as an effort in deductive theory but at most as an "analytical framework" (p. 2). Tentative in its rationalism and discursive in its argument, it is likely to be dismissed by more formal theorists as "wisdom litera- ture." That would be wrong, even if not wholly unjust, for it *is* wise, powerful in its insights, and accurate in its chief conclusions. Its overgrown logic, in which the path of the argument often disap- pears, can be pruned into order and clarity.

None of the three authors, of course, fully answers all, or indeed any, of the large questions he addresses. (Only Olson aims so high.) Yet I think, and shall try to show, that something very close to a full explanation can be discerned in the agreements and complemen- tarities of these three works. What one or two of them ignore, the third usually addresses; where one errs, another corrects.

I shall therefore proceed in an unconventional and somewhat dialectical way, bringing each work into constructive discourse with the others. In this endeavor I shall take up the volumes not in any order of perceived merit but according to the levels on which their respective analyses are focused: Olson first, as dealing principally with the importance of groups within states; North, who elaborates a powerful theory of the state, second; and last Gilpin, who alone concentrates on the explanation of transactions among states.


## Olson and the Theory of Groups

Because, in contrast to almost all my friends and col- leagues, I found much to admire in Olson's *Rise and Decline of Na- tions*, I shall concede at once that there is also in it much that alien- ates: the tone is pompous (what other living author, one wonders, would have had the brass to appropriate for one of his own previous works the short title *The Logic*,[1] or to concede amiably that his own momentous contribution has been possible only because he "stands on the shoulders of giants"?);[2] the name-dropping quickly becomes tiresome (are "helpful conversations and correspondence" with the likes of Senator Daniel Patrick Moynihan really acknowledged because they were helpful, or because they were with Moynihan?); and the evidence deployed is frequently either not to the point or of doubtful accuracy (of which more below). Still, as I have by now frequently rejoined, the *model* is a thing of beauty and power, capable of generating many quite precise, and some wonderfully accurate and counterintuitive, predictions. It is good enough and right just often enough to make us wonder why it is sometimes so wrong; and to make us try to correct rather than to abandon it.

The model, to outline it very summarily, elaborates deductively the economic and social effects of what Olson calls "distributional coalitions," that is, cartels, guilds, and unions that seek to raise not their members' productivity or expertise but their share of what society already produces. (Following Olson, I shall frequently use *cartel* as a convenient generic equivalent of *distributional coalition*.) Almost without exception, the proliferation of such groups will reduce efficiency, increase social inequality, make politics less stable, curtail economic growth, increase "normal" unemployment, and make depressions more severe and inflation more likely.[3] Why?

First, to the extent that a group succeeds in gaining greater compensation than the market would provide, it obviously diverts to itself resources and talents that could find more efficient uses. (This effect could be avoided only if, magically, *all* groups were "symmetrically" organized, so as to be able to block each other's above-market demands. See immediately below.) Second, as Olson's *Logic of Collective Action* demonstrated, distributional coalitions are far likelier to succeed among small and wealthy groups

1. Mancur Olson, Jr., *The Logic of Collective Action* (New York: Schocken Books, 1968).
2. Olson attributes the apothegm in this form to Newton. It seems to have originated with Didacus Stella (as quoted in Lucan *Civil War* 2.10) in the rather less self-flattering form "*pigmei* gigantum humeris impositi plusquam ipsi gigantes vident" (my emphasis). See John Bartlett, *Familiar Quotations,* 14th ed. (Boston: Little, Brown, 1968), p. 134.
3. A cartel can increase social efficiency only if it acts to curtail the power of some existing cartel—for example, if a coalition of shippers achieves deregulation of trucking.

than among large and poor ones: lawyers form tougher guilds earlier than do bank clerks; steel owners cartelize more easily and more powerfully than steelworkers. Hence the net effect of cartelization in any society is ordinarily to make the rich richer and the mighty mightier. (More generally, lawyers and intellectuals, as possessors of superior organizational skills, are rewarded even more disproportionately in cartelized societies.) Third, distributional coalitions, as special-interest groups par excellence, are likely to be "passionate" minorities in Anthony Downs's sense;[4] and, hence, by Olson's logic, a society that contains more such groupings is likelier to have unstable majorities and intransitive collective preferences ("Arrow" or Condorcet cycles). Fourth, if an existing cartel is threatened by some new technology, it will invest in slowing the innovation or raising its price, as in the familiar cases of featherbedding and anti–department store legislation; but even when a new technology would increase demand for a group's services, the group will often retard its adoption by restricting entry and extracting even higher monopoly wages or rents. Hence a more cartelized society will innovate more slowly and grow less rapidly.

In general, distributional coalitions prefer to fix prices and restrict entry rather than to regulate amounts marketed by their members, simply because the former aspects are easier to police—as OPEC has by now discovered. The net effect of these tendencies is threefold. They divert some available demand from the less to the more cartelized sectors of the economy; the classic parallel might be tariffs or price supports that, by raising the cost of food, depress consumer demand in other sectors. They force some available labor into those sectors of weaker demand. And they motivate employers of over-market-price labor to hire only the most productive and skilled workers available. In Olson's analysis, which is better supported technically than I am indicating here, these effects lead to a higher "normal" unemployment, whose burden falls, against conventional economic assumptions, disproportionately on the young, the less skilled, the less productive, and the already less advantaged.

At the same time, distributional coalitions usually can decide their affairs only consensually and slowly; hence the prices they set tend to be "sticky" and, of course, especially resistant to decreases.

4. In *An Economic Theory of Democracy* (New York: Harper and Row, 1957), pp. 55–69.

This being so, any unexpected disinflation or slump in aggregate demand especially dislocates a cartelized society. Because prices in the organized sectors resist change, they exceed market levels by even more than before; hence those sectors quickly display unused capacity and high unemployment. At the same time, the whole burden of price-cutting and of attempting to soak up unemployed labor falls on the unorganized "flexprice" sectors (the term was coined by Sir John Hicks), so that in the Great Depression agricultural prices dropped far more than industrial ones and unemployed workers indeed turned to the (unorganized) retailing of fruit.

Unanticipated inflation or stimulation of demand has of course the opposite effect. While cartel prices are stickier downward, they are still sticky upward (major U.S. unions, for example, typically sign three-year contracts); hence an unanticipated general price rise often *reduces* their premium over market. This change frees demand in the uncartelized sectors (consider again the parallel effects of a sharp reduction in a food tariff), reduces unemployment, and benefits particularly the young, less skilled, and less advantaged workers. For all these reasons demand-stimulation is an attractive remedy—not, as Keynes had argued, in *all* depressed economies but in the special case of *highly cartelized* ones. (*Mutatis mutandis*, monetarism, according to Olson, is a theory that can work only in the special case of relatively uncartelized societies.) Where cartelization is far advanced, however, Olson contends, quite drastic inflation will be required to combat a sharp contraction in demand. Thus, after the slump created by the oil price increases of 1973, the moderate inflation resorted to in much of the West had only slight effects on unemployment, leading to a predictable "stagflation" and to "negative Phillips curves." (Obviously, in Olson's analysis, the general shape of any country's Phillips curve must be a function of its level of cartelization.)

Finally, however, an important Olsonian stipulation: the evil effects of cartels will be obviated to the extent that they are "encompassing," that is, that they organize a very large share of any sector's or any society's (or, he somewhat curiously suggests in a reference to Japan [p. 49], any *firm's*) work force or productive capacity. Cartels of this kind can, for reasons that again flow directly from Olson's *Logic of Collective Action*, find it worth their while not only to claim a larger share for their members but to direct them toward greater productivity and innovation. Hence the Swedish LO is less malign than the British TUC or the American AFL-CIO.

Now, I submit that to have advanced a parsimonious, precise, and logically consistent explanation of societies' different rates of efficiency, growth, political stability, inequality, unemployment, and inflation, while along the way subsuming and seeming to resolve the Keynesian-monetarist controversy, entitles a man to sound a little pompous. (There remain substantial problems of evidence, but let us defer those for now.) Yet Olson does not stop here but offers a separate account of *why* societies are more or less cartelized. Five factors seem important, principal among them simply time: in any society that remains stable in its politics and its boundaries, the number and power of distributional coalitions tend to increase. Second, consanguinity or shared ethnicity makes cartelization more likely: thus the more rapid and more effective organization of European nobilities, Indian castes, and white South African workers. What decisively breaks down cartels is, in Olson's view, a third set of factors, namely, foreign occupation, social revolution, and totalitarian rule. Also tending to weaken cartels is integration into a larger political unit (a mere common market will not be nearly so effective). Here the argument could be drawn directly out of (but is not attributed to) *The Federalist*, No. 10: factions are weaker in a larger unit and are especially slow to coordinate their efforts in a large unit newly joined. Fifth, Olson allows that various kinds of state action can accelerate or retard cartelization. High tariffs, as economists know, favor cartelization by excluding possible competitors; so do restrictive immigration policies. The state may directly organize cartels, as did the National Recovery Agency in the early New Deal, or may stimulate the formation of coalitions by grants of privileged access (the "consultation of affected interests"). Conversely, a state committed to the market may discourage coalitions. In these respects indirect effects of regime form and ideology may be noted: colonial or authoritarian regimes (India and Hong Kong under British rule; France under Napoleon III?) have often resisted or impeded cartels more effectively than indigenous and democratic ones; and Liberal ideology in Britain delayed cartelization in the late nineteenth and early twentieth centuries.

By connecting these two elements of this theory, Olson is able to make some quite specific predictions about which of the world's economies ought to have grown most rapidly at which times and which ought be most resistant to inflation and recession, which societies ought to be the most nearly equal, and which polities the most stable. Specifically, those societies without substantial racial or ethnic divisions that most recently underwent foreign occupation, social revolution, or totalitarian rule and that were incorporated into a larger juridical unit should perform best on all indices. Conversely, the most dismal performances may be expected of societies with long records of political stability, fixed boundaries, and immunity from invasion; deep and multiple divisions of ethnicity or race;[5] and high tariffs, strict limits on immigration, or other state policies that encourage cartelization.

If these conclusions were correct, they would fully justify the pessimism that pervades Olson's volume: precisely those societies that most consistently escaped totalitarianism, conquest, and revolution would, *ceteris paribus,* perform worst economically, politically, and socially and would eventually be pushed aside by more vigorous competitors. Every Britain must suffer Britain's fate.

Fortunately, Olson's evidence, and that of his supporters in a balanced and useful volume of discussion and criticism edited by Dennis Mueller, is far from convincing.[6] In the contemporary world, Olson argues, West Germany, France, and Italy, all with histories of foreign occupation, totalitarian rule (if in the case of France we count Vichy), and recent incorporation into the European Community, ought to be at or near the top in economic performance; so should Japan, with recent totalitarian rule and foreign occupation, and Belgium and the Netherlands, which have undergone foreign occupation and been integrated into a larger unit. At the low end of the scale of anticipated performance, all with stable boundaries and politics over long intervals, stand Australia and New Zealand (also with high tariffs and restrictive immigration), Canada (with high tariffs and ethnic and regional divisions), Britain (with policies that strongly favor interest-group formation, plus substantial restrictions on immigration), and the United States. Indeed, the first group has had the highest rates of growth and the greatest resistance to cyclical recession; the second group has done worst on both scores. Moving to historical evidence, Olson attributes the very rapid growth of Germany and Japan at the end of the nineteenth century largely to their then-recent consolidation into authentically national states, both having

5. The proviso "multiple" is important. In South Africa, for example, one could argue that whites form an "encompassing" coalition; in India, pretty clearly no caste does.
6. Dennis C. Mueller, ed., *The Political Economy of Growth* (New Haven: Yale University Press, 1983).

previously been highly decentralized. The seemingly countervailing case of Sweden (stable boundaries and politics, long national integration) is accounted for by its "encompassing" coalitions.

Olson, however, sees as the strongest evidence in support of his claims a regression analysis (pp. 92–117) that relates the economic performance of the fifty United States to their political "age," that is, to the time elapsed since their admission to the Union or (in the case of the former Confederate states) since the end of Reconstruction, which Olson sees as analogous to foreign occupation. The same tack is taken with respect to today's nation-states by Olson's former student Kwang Choi, writing in the Mueller volume (chapter 3), with similarly heartening results.

About all that this highly selective use of evidence shows is a surprising ignorance of recent comparative history. If revolution and foreign conquest really conduce to rapid economic growth in ethnically homogeneous societies, why did France's economy grow so slowly both after 1815 and after 1870?[7] If stable states with high tariffs must grow slowly, why did Sweden's great expansion come *after* its adoption of protection in 1887–1892 and *before* any significant growth of "encompassing" coalitions?[8] If incorporation into a larger juridical unit is so economically helpful, why has Australia done better outside the European Community than West Germany has done within it?[9] If the Civil War and Reconstruction were the boons to the South that Olson claims, why did it take eighty years for their benefits to be felt? (As Frederick Pryor has asked, can Olson seriously contend that his regression of the fifty states' economic growth rates, if run on the data of 1900 or even 1920, would show similar results?)[10] Finally, there are the other variables of the theory, which, not surprisingly, are neglected in Olson's empirical testing: that recent totalitarian or foreign rule makes societies more equal or more resistant to inflation will come as a surprise to

7. See, for example, Eric J. Hobsbawm, *The Age of Revolution: 1789–1848* (New York: New American Library, 1962), pp. 212–13; and Henry W. Ehrmann, *Politics in France*, 4th ed. (Boston: Little, Brown, 1983), p. 18.

8. M. Donald Hancock, *Sweden: The Politics of Postindustrial Change* (Hinsdale, Ill.: Dryden Press, 1972), p. 23.

9. Between 1960 and 1980, real GDP grew on average 4.2 percent annually in Austria, 3.7 percent annually in West Germany. The difference in growth in per capita GDP was even sharper, 3.9 as against 3.2 percent per year: Organization for Economic Cooperation and Development, *Historical Statistics, 1960–1980* (Paris: OECD, 1982), p. 40.

10. In Mueller, *Political Economy of Growth*, chapter 5, at p. 91.

the French, the Italians, and the Japanese, who have since World War II suffered some considerable bouts of inflation and whose distributions of wealth and income are often counted among the developed world's more unequal ones.[11]

Part of the problem is, of course, that element of Olson's theory which tries to predict societies' degrees of cartelization. There is simply no evidence that totalitarian rule or foreign occupation always breaks the grip of social coalitions, and indeed some prominent cases—including ones erroneously cited by Olson as supporting his position—speak for exactly the contrary thesis. The regimes of Fascist Italy and Vichy France, for example, are widely believed to have strengthened interest-group representation and power.[12] And few scholars of either postwar Japan or West Germany, so far as I am aware, have been able to share Olson's judgment that the Allied occupation "emasculated or abolished" their preexisting coalitions (p. 75). On the contrary, it is usually held that the "enterprise groups" and cartels, if affected at all, rapidly came back as strong as before.[13] In any event, to claim that those societies today have weaker coalitions than does the United States—and this is exactly the implication of Olson's claim about the effects of totalitarianism and conquest—is ludicrous. (However, Olson may well be right about the effects of ethnicity and state action.)

If in fact postwar France, Italy, Japan, and West Germany have some unusually *strong* social coalitions while the United States has unusually weak ones—and that, surely, is much closer to the

11. On inflation in the Fourth Republic see Alfred Cobban, *A History of Modern France*, vol. 3, *France of the Republics, 1871–1962* (Harmondsworth: Penguin, 1965), pp. 210, 213. In 1974, the year after the first great increase in oil prices, inflation in Japan was 21 percent, in Italy 19 percent, in France 11 percent; on average in the European OECD countries, it was 12 percent: OECD, *Historical Statistics, 1960–1980*, p. 72. According to one widely disseminated estimate, the Gini indices of inequality of personal income in 1962 were France, .52; West Germany, .48; Netherlands, .44; Britain and Sweden, both .40; and the United States, .35. See Karl W. Deutsch, *Politics and Government: How People Decide Their Fate*, 2d ed. (Boston: Houghton Mifflin, 1974), p. 138.

12. For example, Joseph La Palombara, *Interest Groups in Italian Politics* (Princeton: Princeton University Press, 1964), pp. 132–33; Charles S. Maier, *Recasting Bourgeois Europe: Stabilization in France, Germany, and Italy in the Decade after World War I* (Princeton: Princeton University Press, 1975), p. 85; and Philip M. Williams, *Crisis and Compromise: Politics in the Fourth Republic* (Garden City, N.Y.: Anchor, 1966), p. 393.

13. Chitoshi Yanaga, *Big Business in Japanese Politics* (New Haven: Yale University Press, 1968), pp. 35–41; Arnold J. Heidenheimer and Donald P. Kommers, *The Governments of Germany*, 4th ed. (New York: Thomas Y. Crowell, 1975), p. 47.

truth—what becomes of the main part of Olson's theory, which attempts to link superior economic, social, and political performance to *weak* cartelization? Only the possibility, to which Olson occasionally resorts in speaking of Japan and Germany, that the coalitions in the more successful economies have been unusually "encompassing." That answer, however, brings Olson close to the position of such students of modern corporatism as Philippe Schmitter, who has tried to show that in the postwar period, powerful interest groups have made societies more governable.[14]

Astonishingly, however, Olson never really tries to test directly his best-argued propositions. His evidence about the extent of cartelization in particular societies is entirely anecdotal, and he confesses to some uncertainty about how even to operationalize his crucial independent variable (count the number of groups? the size of their memberships? somehow gauge their power?). Failing that, he turns to the indirect tests already mentioned, taking time, stability, and absence of totalitarian episodes as surrogates of his real describing variable; and in this way he comes to grief.[15]

Something is cooking here, but its tastes are subtler than Olson appreciates. Few would deny that Britain has been crippled, economically and politically, by powerful and selfish pressure groups. At the other extreme, West Germany, Belgium, the Netherlands, Norway, Austria, and (as Olson admits and explains) Sweden have flourished, so most students agree, largely *because* of their powerful interest associations, which can enforce bargains that guarantee wage and price stability,[16] promote productivity and quality, and accelerate technical adaptation. Japan, Italy, and France appear to have found half the recipe of corporatist success, with strong organizations of capital and management but weak ones of labor; thus their growth has been attended by greater inequality, greater social unrest, and (a little surprisingly, in light of Olson's arguments on this head) a greater propensity to inflation.

---

14. Philippe C. Schmitter, "Interest Intermediation and Regime Governability in Contemporary Western Europe and North America," in Susan Berger, ed., *Organizing Interests in Western Europe: Pluralism, Corporatism, and the Transformation of Politics* (Cambridge, England: Cambridge University Press, 1981).

15. This pitfall is, fortunately, avoided by most of the contributors to the volume edited by Mueller, *Political Economy of Growth*. Especially valuable are the comparative essays by Moses Abramowitz (chapter 4) and Pryor (chapter 5).

16. For example, Bruce W. Headey, "Trade Unions and National Wages Policies," *Journal of Politics* 32 (1970): 407–39; cf. Franz Lehner, chapter 10 in Mueller, *Political Economy of Growth*.

We can, however, be a little more precise. In 1970 Bruce Headey proposed and applied to thirteen of the European and North American advanced industrial societies a measure of "organizational centralization" of trade unions, that is, of the power of their central offices. Schmitter later applied Headey's index to two more societies; and, for the total of fifteen, combined it into a broader measure of "corporatism." In an exercise, I ranked the fifteen societies according to Headey's measure of centralization and Schmitter's index of corporatism. I then compared those rankings with those of average annual growth in per capita gross domestic product (GDP)—the measure of growth that Olson prefers—over the period 1960–1980, as reported by the OECD. In both cases the rank-order correlations proved *positive*, rather than, as Olson would presumably predict, negative; indeed, the estimated correlation between economic growth and Headey's measure of centralization was—for whatever interest it may hold—about 1.38 times its standard error, for a significance level of about .08. Ordinarily negative findings of this strength are not counted as confirmatory, even in the social sciences.

## North on States, Firms, and Ideologies

For North, here as in his important work with Thomas, the principal determinant of economic growth is the extent to which prevailing property rights relate individual to social benefits and costs.[17] The specification of maximally efficient property rights varies, as before, with population density and capital stocks so that demographic growth remains the great engine of social and political change. Yet North has here substantially refined the previously almost implicit theory of the state, has introduced new theories of ideology and of the firm, and has extended and revised the earlier historical discussion so that he now ranges from the origins of human society to the early part of the present century. He has produced what, despite flaws, must be acknowledged as a work of brilliance and of overwhelming erudition, one that over the next decade or less will become part of the essential armory of every student of politics or history.

Begin, as North does, with the state: an "organization with a

17. Douglass C. North and Robert Paul Thomas, *The Rise of the Western World: A New Economic History* (Cambridge, England: Cambridge University Press, 1973).

comparative advantage in violence" over some geographic area (p. 21), it trades protection and the enforcement of property rights for taxes. Because, except in the most primitive hunter-gatherer societies, there are economies of scale in the provision of these two services, the existence of a state can increase a society's total income. At the same time, rulers are of course motivated to maximize their profits, that is, the surplus of their revenues over the costs to them of providing protection and justice. Yet rulers are constrained against simple depredation by the requirements of social efficiency and the availability of substitutes. If, that is, rulers impose grossly inefficient or arbitrary property rights, they may so impoverish the society as to diminish their own long-term rents or to weaken the state against rivals; and external or internal rivals will compete against the incumbent rulers in part by trying to offer equal or better services at lower cost.

On the other hand, even rulers inclined to enforce maximally efficient property rights ordinarily cannot do so, partly for reasons that relate closely to Olson's argument. First of all, rulers act as "discriminating monopolists." Admitting that some groups in the society are strategically more important—that is, that their cooperation is vital to the functioning of the state or the society—rulers buy their aid with grants of lower taxes or a greater share of power in what North now calls the "constitution" of the state. These privileges will often themselves be economically inefficient, as was the exemption of the French aristocracy from the *taille;* and, as more and more groups "capture an interest in the state" in this way (p. 43), conflict over property rights will become more open and the rights themselves less certain. By both routes, efficiency and growth decline.

Now, it is reasonable to think that as societies grow more complex, the number and power of such "strategic groups" must rise. More important as sources of injurious pluralism, however, are mobilization and the decline of shared ideology. In a society, or indeed in any sizable organization, North contends, enforcement costs soon become impossibly high. If constituents operated only on a calculus of evasion, detection, and punishment, free-rider problems would soon sabotage all cooperation. In practice, every large organization has found more cost-effective the inculcation of some coherent set of beliefs, according to which the existing order is fair, just, and natural and every betrayal of it is base or perverse. (Rivals to the existing leaders must undermine this ideology, ordinarily by supplying one of their own.) North goes so far as to assert that "the stability of any society requires a [shared] ideological superstructure" (p. 182).

Shared ideology, however, can arise and persist only "when the individuals of a universe have similar experiences" (p. 205). The more specialized and differentiated a society's work force becomes, the less likely it is to retain a common ideology (p. 51). A second factor is sheer economic dislocation, which can generate "massive ideological alienation" and "[activate] groups to participate in control of the state." Exactly this combination of specialization and dislocation has characterized the workings of modern markets, North believes, thus accounting for the "diverse ideologies" and the pluralist struggles for control of the state that we now observe (pp. 181–83).

More generally, then, and in contrast to Olson, North seemingly would predict powerful and greedy coalitions—and hence lower rates of growth, greater instability, and the rest—not particularly in old and secure states, but in highly specialized economies subject to extreme market fluctuations.[18] Growth should, in any event, be slower in societies with deep ideological divisions.

At the same time, North emphasizes that powerful groups are not the only source of inefficiency and economic decline. At least as important are, first, the prevailing and largely technologically determined costs of protection, agency, enforcement, and collection—the economically optimal tax may be too expensive to collect, economically efficient property rights impossibly costly to enforce—and, second, the "stickiness" of constitutions and property rights, which, no less than Olson's cartel prices, are hard to alter once established. Again much of the cause, according to North, is ideology, which, once inculcated, is like one of Thomas Kuhn's scientific paradigms: while it economizes information and permits concentration on day-to-day problems, it prevents consideration of fundamental alternatives and, indeed, often makes them literally "unthinkable."

Together these factors of cost and stickiness imply short-term instability and long-term decline for virtually all states. Over the short term, unpredictable innovations, particularly in military technology, may drastically alter the costs of protection, agency, or enforcement, or the strategic importance of particular social

18. North, however, does not really attempt a comparative application of his theory, instead examining secular decline in efficient property rights.

groups—as did, for example, the introduction of the phalanx, the stirrup, and the cannon. When that occurs, states that can adapt, even if only by revolutionary change, survive and grow; but, owing to the tenacity of acquired rights, most fail.

Even states that escape these perils are doomed over the longer run. If from the beginning they maintain inefficient property rights, they will fail to grow economically and will be eclipsed. If they do grow, they may face political upheaval or economic stagnation even sooner, for their very growth will so increase population and capital stocks as to make their previously efficient property rights a fetter on further growth. Because the now inefficient rights cannot be changed within the existing ideology and constitution, revolution or decline must ensue (pp. 28–29 and 208).

From this part of North's analysis, it seems to me, we can safely draw three general hypotheses. First, economic growth will generally be more rapid in states strong and autonomous enough to adapt their property rights to changing conditions, yet challenged (or wise) enough not to become predatory. Second, *some* social revolutions—in particular, those that install strong states and property rights better suited to the society—will spur economic growth; others will not. Third, extremely rapid growth is its own nemesis; moderate rates are more likely to be sustained.

However, the cases of Japan, Italy, and France raise doubts about all five of the hypotheses (these three and the two stated earlier) that North's analysis seems to imply. Japan has had to develop a highly specialized economy, and many of the shocks of the international market—most memorably, of course, the oil crisis of 1973—have hit it very hard; yet growth has barely slowed, nor has "massive ideological alienation" become manifest.[19] Neither has Japan's extremely rapid growth seemed to bring it up against limits sooner than, say, West Germany's more moderate rate. Italy, on the other hand, is frequently portrayed as almost the quintessentially weak and penetrated state, in which property rights are always conditioned by political machinations;[20] and its ideological divisions, if now mellowed, are still among the deepest in Western Eu-

19. Japan's rates of annual growth in real GDP since 1973 (in percentage) have exceeded the average of the seven major industrial states (including Japan) as follows: in 1974, Japan -1.0 against the average 0.3; 1975, 2.3 and -0.5; 1976, 5.3 and 5.2; 1977, 5.3 and 4.2; 1978, 5.0 and 4.1; 1979, 5.1 and 3.5; and 1980, 4.4 and 1.1 (OECD, *Historical Statistics, 1960–1980*, p. 40).

20. For example, by P. A. Allum, *Italy—Republic without Government?* (New York: W. W. Norton, 1973).

rope. Yet the Italian economy has consistently grown more rapidly than, for example, that of the far more stable and more ideologically homogeneous Federal Republic of Germany. Finally, the French Revolution created more rational and efficient property rights, and certainly a more powerful and autonomous state; yet, as I have already noted, the French economy grew very slowly for most of the nineteenth century.

These cases raise fundamental issues. First, do differences in property rights really account for recent variations in growth and prosperity? Writing with Thomas, North was plausible in claiming that superior English and Dutch property rights explained those states' sixteenth- and seventeenth-century ascents. But does Germany overtake Britain after 1880 because of a comparative advantage in property rights? Can more efficient property rights explain American or Japanese episodes of rapid growth? By the logic of North's whole argument this must be so—he asserts pretty plainly that U.S. decline since about 1900 is due to abridgments of property rights (pp. 193–98)—but we get no direct argument of the proposition. At one point North actually suggests that efficient property rights had only a brief heyday and that they have by now been substantially diluted everywhere (p. 184), from which it ought of course to follow that economic performance must be dismal everywhere.

Even more doubtful, I think, is the importance North now wants to assign to ideology. Too often it becomes here, as it has for others before North, a euphemism for ignorance: whatever seems at first glance to defy rational explanation—such as the support of middle-class reformers in the United States for measures to alleviate the sufferings of the poor (pp. 197–98)—is at once attributed to "ideology." Nor is there good reason to believe that ideology is so "sticky" or so potent as North now believes. If ardently free-trading Junker could be converted to protection in a matter of months, if devoutly monarchist English gentlemen could become republicans, or if conservative farmers in North Dakota and Saskatchewan could be converted to socialism—and all these changes do indeed seem to have occurred[21]—then one is entitled to a cer-

21. Hans-Ulrich Wehler, *Das Deutsche Kaiserreich 1871–1918* (Göttingen: Vendenhoeck and Ruprecht, 1973), p. 48; Christopher Hill, *The Century of Revolution: 1603–1714* (New York: W. W. Norton, 1966), pp. 173–76; Robert I. Morlan, *Political Prairie Fire: The Nonpartisan League, 1915–1922* (Minneapolis: University of Minnesota Press, 1955); and Seymour Martin Lipset, *Agrarian Socialism: The Co-operative*

tain skepticism about the persistence and perhaps about the effectiveness of such beliefs. Even Kuhnian paradigms, we should recall, do get overthrown. Finally, the claim that political and social
stability is impossible without a common "ideological superstructure" is refuted by powerful evidence, as political scientists have
been demonstrating now for two decades with evidence from such
cases as the Netherlands, Norway, and Eastern Europe.[22] North
offers nothing that would counter those demonstrations.

Despite these seeming failures, the core of North's work—his
analysis of the state and, as I shall indicate below, of the firm—
remains a vast and essential contribution, which cannot possibly be
discarded. Because, as North has elsewhere observed, the state is
so singularly lacking in Olson's book, we have reason to try North
as its corrective; and Olson's analysis of group influence may similarly help to complete North.[23]

## The Counterpoint: North and Olson

The central mystery remains that of the relations among
the state, organized groups, and economic performance. On this
North's analysis of the firm sheds much light. The firm after all is
a group, if a highly specialized one, and it resembles the state in its
reliance on supervision, command, and ideology. To economic historians the central question is why hierarchy of this kind should so
generally have supplanted the market. Why, for example, does the
simple textile broker, purchasing from many competing producers
and paying by quality and quantity of output, give way to the textile firm, which controls every phase of production, pays by input
(hours worked), and must bear heavy costs of supervison and
agency? North suggests three main motivations: new economies of
scale, for example in the vertical integration of production; a
greater need for uniform quality, coupled with high costs of post-

---

Commonwealth Federation in Saskatchewan (Berkeley and Los Angeles: University of
California Press, 1971).

22. Arend Lijphart, The Politics of Accommodation: Pluralism and Democracy in the
Netherlands, 2d ed. (Berkeley and Los Angeles: University of California Press, 1975),
chapter 2; Harry Eckstein, Division and Cohesion in Democracy: A Study of Norway
(Princeton: Princeton University Press, 1966), especially chapter 3; cf. Brian Barry,
Sociologists, Economists and Democracy, 2d ed. (Chicago: University of Chicago Press,
1978), pp. 86–87.

23. Douglass C. North, "A Theory of Economic Change," review of Olson, Rise
and Decline of Nations, Science 219 (14 January 1983): 163–64.

production inspection; and the need to avoid bottlenecks and post-contract cheating by highly specialized and essential classes of producers.

All of this is highly plausible, indeed too plausible to confine to the firm. If workers and managers can be motivated in these ways to accept hierarchy, why not other classes of producers or, for that matter, other groups? If the state happens to be the form of hierarchy that can best meet these three problems, why should not the state, rather than firms, assume the functions? If firms can develop ways of avoiding the bottlenecks that greedy groups of producers might create, why cannot states or coalitions do the same?

I am suggesting that we regard states, firms, and social coalitions merely as aspects of a single phenomenon, namely, that of rationally accepted subordination. (North himself implies in his concluding chapter that all three are really parts of the "structure," or institutional framework, of his title.) In practice, certainly, no rigid separation is possible: the Renaissance guilds acted as pressure groups within their cities and appropriated parts of state power; they also closely resembled firms in their reliance on wage labor and in their concern with product quality. More recently the Irish state has guaranteed the quality of exported butter and the Mexican state the quality of handicrafts; pressure groups, notably the bar and local medical associations, have governed important questions of property rights; and in not a few cases, particularly in southern Italy, Detroit, and Las Vegas, organizations not exactly coterminous with the state have enjoyed a "comparative advantage in violence."

On this point Olson and North correct each other: groups can readily gain control of property rights without, or even against, state action (Olson's example of the Indian castes will persuade at least those who have read Bailey or Dumont), but—and here North's analysis of the firm must be generalized to correct Olson—even small groups need not pursue merely distributional goals. As was just noted, the guilds, despite their narrowness, had as a major function the certification of quality, and so do present-day professional associations.[24] Farmers' cooperatives in late-nineteenth-century Denmark sought, not protection from the market, but greater quality and productivity.[25] Not only in Sweden but in West

24. On the guilds see North and Thomas, *Rise of the Western World*, p. 57.

25. Alexander Gerschenkron, *Bread and Democracy in Germany* (Berkeley and Los Angeles: University of California Press, 1943), pp. 37–40.

Germany and Japan, trade unions have frequently held back wage demands and helped to boost quality in the interests of export promotion, not only for the economy as a whole but for their particular firm or sector.[26]

Since even narrow coalitions can act to achieve greater efficiency—*productively* rather than *distributionally*—Olson's theory must be modified. The evil consequences he predicts indeed ensue when distributional coalitions proliferate; but since Olson is wrong in relating distributional orientation only to size and proliferation only to age, we must try anew to analyze why coalitions will grow and why some will pursue productivity, others only a bigger share.

North offers no definite answer, but the beginnings of one are not far to seek in his framework. As North and Thomas had observed, and as Olson admits (pl. 132ff.), cartels cannot long flourish without insulation from a larger market; and protection, whether by tariffs or by more covert methods, cannot succeed where autarky is impossible.[27] Hence, to the extent that a country's factor endowments require it to trade, we might expect, its coalitions will seek efficiency and quality rather than a bigger share.[28] The sole exception would logically be those economies whose exports, usually in the simplest primary products, are subject to little variation in quality and hence to little improvement.

If this argument is correct, Olson's conclusions are all but reversed. Postwar Germany, Italy, and Japan succeed economically, not because of totalitarian episodes or foreign occupation or integration into larger units, but because *losses* of territory, of empire, or of the hope of empire left them with factor endowments that indisputably forced them to trade. Britain and the United States fall behind precisely because they remain so long in the contrary position: possessed of dominions that made autarky seem achievable—in 1953 over half, and in 1965 still one-third, of Britain's trade was with the Empire and Commonwealth, and until 1973 trade was less than 10 percent of U.S. gross national product

26. Guido S. Goldman, "The German Economic Challenge," in Andrei S. Markovits, ed., *The Political Economy of West Germany: Modell Deutschland* (New York: Praeger, 1982), p. 18, and John Holusha, "Japan's Productive Car Unions," *New York Times*, 30 March 1983, p. 27.

27. That is, tariffs in trade-dependent countries cannot serve distributional goals. They can of course be used initially by such economies as part of a larger strategy to achieve competitiveness, as the experiences of Sweden (see above) and Japan have conclusively demonstrated.

28. Cf. Peter J. Katzenstein, "The Virtues of Necessity: Small States in the International Economy" (tentative title of a forthcoming book).

(GNP)—their coalitions, even if weaker, could concern themselves more with distribution and less with production and quality.[29] Perhaps at the greatest advantage were such small states as Belgium and the Netherlands, whose situations had long condemned them to trade and whose coalitions were therefore old hands at the enhancement of productivity.[30]

In this light, the European Community also assumes a different aspect. While the separate-state coalitions were indeed initially weakened, exactly as Madison would have foretold, any advantage thus conferred (and in already free-trading nations like Belgium it was probably nil) will quickly have been outweighed by an opposite effect, namely, the real possibility of European self-sufficiency.[31] That half of the Community's trade in 1980 was internal suggests a potential for cartelization and protection that has perhaps already begun to be exploited, at least in agriculture and steel.[32]

Olson thus revised can also lend substance and precision to North's account of the rise of state intervention and the supposed decline of efficient property rights in most advanced economies since about 1890. Olson contends that wherever strong coalitions have managed *within* a country to insulate one sector's prices from market fluctuations, those caught in the now more violently fluctuating "flexprice" sectors have quickly turned to the state for relief; for example, U.S. farmers' support for populism. The same logic ought, however, to apply *internationally:* those societies most dependent on the international market, and particularly those

29. A useful contrast is this: in 1954, trade outside the Commonwealth and Empire was equivalent to 18 percent of British GDP; by contrast, in 1957, the last year before the creation of the EEC, trade amounted to 30 percent of West Germany's GDP. See, for these and figures in the text: OEEC, *Economic Conditions in the United Kingdom* (Paris: OEEC, 1955), pp. 9, 15; OECD, *Historical Statistics of Foreign Trade* (Paris: OECD, 1982), pp. 84–85; and OEEC, *Economic Conditions in the Federal Republic of Germany* (Paris: OEEC, 1960), pp. 30–35.

30. Ever since 1973, these two countries' increases in productivity, measured as growth in real value added per person employed, have been among the five highest in the OECD in both the manufacturing and the industrial sector: OECD, *Historical Statistics of Foreign Trade,* p. 44.

31. In Madison's day the construction of effective distributional coalitions over large areas doubtless took much longer. Modern means of communication have made organization far easier and more rapid. (I owe this point to my colleague Marvin Hoffenberg.)

32. On internal trade see OECD, *Historical Statistics of Foreign Trade,* pp. 38–39. A modified version of Olson's second chief proposition may eventually prove to be true, namely, that distributional coalitions tend to gain strength at a constant (if secularly increasing) rate in *self-sufficient* societies.

whose products are subject to the most violent price fluctuations, ought also to incline most, not necessarily, as North contended, to "massive ideological alienation," but to state intervention. David Cameron has presented evidence to show that the state has indeed grown most rapidly in recent decades in those countries most exposed to world trade; and in the American (and, until World War I, British) "exceptional" resistance to socialism, there is supporting historical evidence.[33]

Taken together, these results imply that highly trade-dependent economies, at least to the extent that they export more than undifferentiated primary products, will have both interventionist states and dense networks of powerful productive coalitions,[34] often closely entwined and interpenetrated—a picture very different from Olson's, but one to be encountered in the Low and Scandinavian countries, in postwar West Germany, and, with reservations already suggested, in Japan and Italy.

Less trade-dependent countries may be expected to have powerful distributional coalitions, but it does not follow that in such cases the state will be weak in all senses or the mere plaything of competing interests. States may gain and hold wide powers, both North's analysis and the history of European absolutism teach us, as much (or more) because of foreign threats as because of the vicissitudes of markets. When states are thus strengthened in societies with powerful distributional coalitions, the conflict between state and society is likely to be sharp and continual. Theda Skocpol's work, which deals precisely with relatively self-sufficient empires under conditions of military threat, can be read as a chronicle of the most intense moments of such conflicts; and the whole history of modern France can be understood—at least Charles de Gaulle so understood it—as an unceasing struggle between the needs of national survival and the greed of domestic interests.[35] In societies of this kind, as both North and Olson would expect, the

33. David R. Cameron, "The Expansion of the Public Economy: A Comparative Analysis," *American Political Science Review* 72 (December 1978): 1243–61.

34. In fact, unions in open economies tend to be more powerful and centralized—a curious finding, if they are as distributional as Olson would imply. See Geoffrey K. Ingham, *Strikes and Industrial Conflict* (London: Macmillan, 1974), p. 42.

35. Theda Skocpol, *State and Social Revolutions: A Comparative Analysis of France, Russia, and China* (Cambridge, England: Cambridge University Press, 1979), especially pp. 40–41, 47–48, and Charles de Gaulle, *Memoirs of Hope: Renewal and Endeavor*, trans. Terence Kilmartin (New York: Simon and Schuster, 1971), pp. 147–48, 308.

economy performs best when the state is powerful, autonomous, and threatened by readily available substitutes: France under Napoleon III and de Gaulle, Germany under the Empire.[36] Paradoxically, however, the extreme powers that states of this kind achieve in wartime often prove disastrous for them over the longer run: for reasons that Olson's earlier work can also make clear, distributional coalitions will often behave as productive ones under conditions of total war. When they do so, embattled governments are tempted to relate to them accordingly: Germany in World War I, Britain in World War II.[37] When, once the emergency is past, the coalitions revert to type, the state has often lost all power to resist and can regain it, if at all, only by a breach of the existing constitution.

More ominously, the view taken here implies also that in countries of "borderline autarky"—ones that approach but do not achieve self-sufficiency—distributional coalitions may arise but will necessarily advocate conquest of the lacking resources as part of their program: Japan and perhaps Germany (as I discuss below) in the 1920s and 1930s may serve to illustrate the point.

Olson and North thus combined and amended can, I think, also account for the frequently tyrannical governments and insecure property rights of today's Third World countries. Their exposure to trade keeps government strong and distributional coalitions weak (the sole exceptions, predictably, have been countries with some potential for self-sufficiency, such as Brazil and Argentina); and the almost invariant quality of their exports provides little incentive for the development of productive coalitions. As Tocqueville might have put it, here the state is strong and society is weak.

Finally, we should observe that the theory so amended no longer entails either Olson's or North's pessimistic predictions. To the extent that states become and remain dependent on trade, exporting goods differentiable in quality, nothing in the theory so far excludes continued growth. Yet there may be other reasons for pessimism, as we shall see.

36. On Napoleon III's France see, for example, J. C. Asselain and Christian Morrisson in Mueller, *Political Economy of Growth*, chapter 8, at p. 167.

37. Gerald D. Feldman, *Army, Industry, and Labor in Germany, 1914–1918* (Princeton: Princeton University Press, 1966); Samuel H. Beer, *British Politics in the Collectivist Age* (New York: Vintage, 1969), pp. 212–16.

## Gilpin on Hegemony and Systemic Change

Olson and North both seem implicitly to assume that a state's international power depends almost wholly on its economic health and growth. This Gilpin denies. Moreover, he focuses on two problems largely neglected by the other two theorists: first, the governance, and the impact on individual states' economic choices, of the international system; and second, the likely incidence and effects of war.

Following McNeill,[38] Gilpin first observes that military and economic power can actually be inversely related, since for long centuries less advanced economies routinely plundered wealthier ones. The extent to which wealth translates into power in fact varies, Gilpin contends, with three main factors: economic development and growth; structures of social organization and governance; and the available technologies of warfare, transportation, and communication. The rise of the nation-state, a new and more effective form of governance, mobilized greater power from the same resources. The introduction of new weaponry and new infantry techniques in the seventeenth century gave the advantage to more expensive standing armies and hence made wealth matter more, a tendency that was accelerated by the even more expensive technologies of the nineteenth and, until recently, the twentieth century—improved artillery and armor, steam and steel battleships, aircraft. (Nuclear weapons, on the other hand, Gilpin speculates, may have substantially divorced military from economic power by giving even quite modestly endowed states enormous destructive potential.) In transportation, the advent of the railroad, by permitting more rapid deployment of soldiers and weapons, strengthened such continental powers as Germany, Russia, and the United States independently of any increase in their wealth and thus positioned them better to challenge Britain's sea-based hegemony.

Such changes matter, according to Gilpin, because they profoundly affect the stability of the international system and the likelihood of armed conflict. Gilpin takes it as axiomatic—and this is of course his fundamental break with most previous analyses of

38. William H. McNeill, *Past and Future* (Chicago: University of Chicago Press, 1954).

these issues—that states strive to change the international system only to the extent that the benefits of doing so outweigh the costs. State leaderships, in other words, behave *rationally*. Only when every power estimates the costs of change as equal to or greater than the benefits will the system be stable or, what Gilpin defines as the same thing, "legitimate" (pp. 10–12, 50–51). When any power anticipates that benefits will exceed costs, the system will be unstable. And what principally lowers the cost of a challenge is some shift in power that favors the challenger.

*What* is sought is change that raises the prestige or the position in the international division of labor of the dissatisfied power, or that modifies the rules of the system in its favor. *How* change is sought varies with the type of international system. While other systems have been known historically and are still theoretically possible (empires, true balances of power), the international arena since at least 1815 has been hegemonic; that is, its boundaries, basic rules, hierarchy, and international division of labor have been primarily determined by a single leading power. Barring what Gilpin calls systems change—transformation into a nonhegemonic system—alterations either will be at the relatively trivial level of interactions change, a category to which Gilpin relegates not only shifts of alliance by most so-called changes of regime, including those analyzed by Robert Keohane and Joseph Nye, or will be systemic change, displacement of the previous hegemonic power and fundamental revision of boundaries, rules, and all the rest (pp. 39–44). While such a displacement might in theory be attempted or achieved peacefully, it has historically occurred only as a consequence of what Gilpin, following Raymond Aron, calls hegemonic war—a general and unlimited conflict for domination of the system (chapter 5, especially pp. 207–8).

What, then, can make it rational for a state's leadership to risk hegemonic conflict? By the logic of Gilpin's assumptions, it can obviously only be some antecedent change that lowers the costs or raises the benefits of doing so. We have already seen what usually lowers the costs: as the hegemon weakens or a rival gains strength, the rival's estimated costs of a challenge decrease. In contrast, four chief factors raise the benefit of a challenge to the existing system (or, what is the same thing, raise the opportunity costs of continued acceptance) and thus also decrease stability in the system: first, innovations that radically increase economies of scale, especially in the provision of defense and other public goods (for example, the military revolution of the seventeenth century, which made not only wealth but size more important); second, the rise of costly externalities that are beyond the reach of the existing state (the Athenians' desire to make their allies pay a larger share of the common defense); third, domestic political upheavals, often a consequence of economic growth, which bring to power persons or groups who see larger opportunities or who simply have different memories (as perhaps in the French and Soviet revolutions); and fourth, the grounded perception that some "window of opportunity" is about to close forever (observable, Gilpin thinks, in the "race for empire" of the late nineteenth century and, frequently, in the hegemonic power's contemplation of preemptive war against a rising potential contender).

Independently of these factors, Gilpin contends—and here he shares the neo-Malthusian pessimism of North—all powers tend over time to weaken, and hegemonic powers tend to do so particularly. Thus, cyclical hegemonic conflict is all but inevitable. In part this weakening flows from a universal tendency to economic decline, which in turn Gilpin sees as due to the exhaustion of cheaply exploited factors of production and of existing property structures *à la* North (a fate that in Gilpin's view, however, can be postponed by societies with open frontiers, such as the United States, Russia, and China, for much of their history); and from the randomness and clustering of crucial innovations, which rarely tend to occur successively in the same society. Specific to hegemonic powers are two further factors: the tendency of military and administrative expenditures to increase more rapidly than income; and the displacement of investment by both private and public consumption. Increasing military expenditure is caused by the diffusion of military technology, by increasing costs of agency, by tendencies toward suboptimization (secession or autonomy), and, not least, by decreasing martial virtue among the citizens of the (secure) hegemon. Decreasing investment stems both from military consumption and from Veblenesque effects of affluence in the society at large.

From all of this it must follow—although here I am inferring from Gilpin rather than summarizing him—that the most dangerous situation of all will be one in which a hegemonic power is declining economically while its costs of defense are rising and while a rapidly rising rival is benefiting not only from economic growth but from changes in transportation and in economies of scale in defense; and in which negative externalities, for example in trade, are growing—in short, exactly the situation that characterized the rivalry of Britain and Germany at the turn of the present century.

Gilpin's is obviously a rich and insightful work, but it is also a sprawling and eclectic one, whose logic has more leaks than the *Mary Rose*. Exactly because—as with Olson, albeit for quite different reasons—I want to defend the book and emphasize its worth, I shall at once concede its faults. First, Gilpin's grasp, not only of economics but of comparative history, seems less sure than North's. One never feels quite certain that Gilpin understands indifference curves or the law of diminishing returns, and uncertainty turns to impatience when to his hesitant recapitulations of the familiar is added the zeal of the convert. In his historiography Gilpin falls into such solecisms as claiming that trade was insignificant in the "command economies" of all previous empires, presumably including the fiercely trading one of Rome (pp. 127 and 133);[39] describing secure property rights across national boundaries— which, if one accepts Keynes's description, almost certainly reached their zenith in the nineteenth century[40]—as a "revolutionary feature of the modern world," exercised in the 1980s on an unparalleled scale (p. 25); or taking for granted that the present-day United States suffers from comparatively "high taxation" (p. 232), when in fact its rate is one of the lowest (roughly tied with Japan's) among the major industrial powers.[41]

Far more serious than such slips as these is the work's lack of deductive rigor and parsimony. To accept Gilpin's central conclusions, we are required to grant at least half a dozen weakly supported premises: for example, that crucial innovations arise randomly and tend to cluster, that the effects of innovations on military power can rarely be foreseen, that the hegemon's citizens always lose their martial virtue, that Veblen was right about conspicuous consumption, that costs of agency must always rise in large states. One objects to these claims not so much because they are doubtful (although I think most are) but because they are necessary to the argument. Unless Einstein was wrong, and God is

39. See, for example, Frank Burr Marsh, *A History of the Roman World from 146 to 30 B.C.*, 3d ed. (London: Methuen, 1963), pp. 3–5.
40. John Maynard Keynes, *The Economic Consequences of the Peace* (New York: Harcourt, Brace, and Howe, 1920), pp. 11–16.
41. OECD, *Historical Statistics, 1960–1980*, p. 59.

malicious as well as cunning, reality cannot be *this* complex—so, at least, the scientist in us protests. Gilpin's conclusions may well be right and, indeed, I shall argue presently that most of them probably are, but his argument for them is too cluttered, too remote from deductive clarity, to be convincing.

### The Fugue of the Art: Gilpin, North, and Olson

Gilpin's central contention requires only two assumptions: if most states value hegemony more than peace and if every hegemon eventually weakens, then recurrent hegemonic wars are indeed likely. Gilpin, however, wants to go beyond this, as should we, to identify factors that accelerate or retard the inevitable cycle.

North and Olson offer ways of tidying up Gilpin's argument. Most of its sprawl arises from his efforts to account for innovation and military power as independent variables. With respect to innovation, North observes that many technological advances, from agriculture to the three-field system to steam power, appear to have lain unused for decades or centuries, until shifts in relative prices made their employment profitable. From this he suggests the radical simplification that technology is ordinarily a *dependent* variable in human affairs rather than the basic cause that its historians at their most zealous have made it out to be.[42] Innovation, as use and not merely as invention, is almost entirely determined by the incentives to individual innovators—the extent to which they are enabled to appropriate a share of the social benefits of their work—and by relative prices, which determine whether there is a social benefit.

Military technology, it must be stressed, is for North the significant exception. Given states' obvious interest in coercive power, innovations in this field tend to go unused only when a regime supposes itself to be invulnerably protected by the older technology or when, as Gilpin observes (p. 63), introduction of the new weaponry seems as likely to ruin existing elites as would military defeat.

If North's view is the correct one, Britain's hegemonic decline

42. For example, Lynn White, Jr., *Medieval Technology and Social Change* (New York: Oxford University Press, 1966), especially pp. 69–76.

has little to do with German railroads—and the railroad itself, as Hobsbawm has shown, resulted less from any technological break-through than from a growth of markets and a surfeit of capital— and almost everything to do with the British failure to innovate, either militarily or economically, in, for example, large-scale steel production and the new chemical and electrical industries.[43] (In fact in this case power waned quite directly with wealth: British politicians debated repeatedly, beginning with Gladstone's final fall from office in 1894, whether they could afford to keep pace with the German navy, while Germany comfortably supported that navy along with an army that dwarfed Britain's.)[44]

British military failure, to the extent that it was independent of economics, is explained readily enough from North's perspective: military innovation is less likely to be valued by states that are, or think themselves, secure. British economic failure was due not to any random "clustering" of innovations in other lands but to Brit-ain's long-term neglect of technical education and of investment in basic research[45]—in short, from a social failure to lower the costs or to increase the incentives for innovators. The more basic ques-tion is, then, why did Britain fail to offer the requisite facilities and incentives? Gilpin, who does not deny the significance of failures to innovate, attributes them in general to ill-defined "institutional rigidities" (p. 189). Olson's logic, we can now recall, is clearer and more informative: innovation and growth (and, one suspects, in-vestment) are less likely in societies dominated by distributional coalitions, that is (as has been argued above), in societies that are or can easily be economically self-sufficient and whose military se-curity denies the state any claim to countervailing strength.[46]

Taken together these propositions imply, as I think Charles Maier first phrased it, that "hegemony corrupts." The secure state,

43. Hobsbawm, *Age of Revolution*, pp. 63–67; on military innovation see Philip Magnus, *King Edward the Seventh* (Harmondsworth: Penguin, 1964), chapter 17; on economic innovation see David S. Landes, *The Unbound Prometheus: Technological Change and Industrial Development in Western European Economies from 1750 to the Pres-ent* (Cambridge, England: Cambridge University Press, 1972), pp. 262–76, 281–90.

44. Philip Magnus, *Gladstone: A Biography* (New York: E. P. Dutton, 1954), pp. 414–20.

45. Landes, *Unbound Prometheus*, pp. 339–58.

46. For an enlightening contrast between the British Empire's relative self-sufficiency and Germany's growing dependence on insecure trade before World War I see David Calleo, *The German Problem Reconsidered: Germany and the World Order, 1870 to the Present* (Cambridge, England: Cambridge University Press, 1978), pp. 35, 83.

with guaranteed access to raw materials and markets, grows less rapidly, rewards innovation less, and neglects the arts of war. This is Gilpin's result without Gilpin's tenuous logic, and it implies a stricter corollary: that decline will set in almost immediately after hegemony, or at least secure self-sufficiency, is achieved. This seems to hold for both Britain and the United States, which Gilpin takes as the only two historical cases of hegemony. Probably it also applies to the recent experience of the Soviet bloc.[47] This much of the shared pessimism thus seems warranted, but we have still no reason to think, as Olson and North do, that *all* highly developed economies must eventually decline.

It can be fairly asked, no less of Gilpin's account than of the one I am offering, why such a seemingly poisoned apple as hegemony should be so avidly sought. Gilpin's answer, while predictable, is only partly persuasive: leading powers seek hegemony to keep international markets open, which it is in their interests to do (pp. 138–39). This can account for Britain's rise, but only imperfectly for Germany's subsequent challenge or for the long hesitancy of some plausible challengers, notably including the United States.[48] I suspect, rather, that states do not really seek hegemony except, as Gilpin describes empire-seeking in another context, "preclusively": to prevent an economically existing hegemon from excluding its more efficient competitors from crucial markets or resources. This, at any rate, is David Calleo's account of the nineteenth-century German challenge, which was advocated (as Kehr showed with respect to naval expansion) more by the free-trading than by the protectionist forces within the Reich.[49] If challenges are generally so motivated, the struggle for hegemony becomes a classic example of the prisoner's dilemma. All advanced states would be better off and would continue to grow more rapidly if free trade were preserved without hegemony; yet each, fearing that some other will restrict it adversely, seeks hegemony.

On one other significant point, however, Gilpin's analysis sets limits to those of Olson and North. Because changes in international hegemony can alter the conditions and the stability of trade and the range of "permitted" activities in the international division

47. Cf. Pryor, in Mueller, *Political Economy of Growth*, chapter 5, especially pp. 96–97.

48. David Lake, "The International Economic Structure and American Foreign Economic Policy, 1887–1934," *World Politics* 35 (July 1983).

49. Calleo, *German Problem Reconsidered*, chapter 4.

of labor, hegemonic instability or displacement can also profoundly affect the prosperity of economies, the policy choices open to governments, the strength of contending domestic groups and coalitions, and, indeed, states' particular forms of property rights. Osvaldo Sunkel and Pedro Paz have argued that Latin America's industrialization was first accelerated by world depression and war and then retarded and reversed by the slump in export earnings that resulted from the final shift from British to U.S. hegemony after World War II.[50] Russia's economic policy and progress before World War I depended no less on other powers' trade policies and on whether British hegemony would survive the growing German challenge. And David Abraham has recently claimed that even so profound an alteration of domestic power, property rights, and the international system as the rise to power of national socialism in Germany may find its explanation in shifting international governance: the dynamic and export-oriented industrial sectors in Weimar Germany, which for reasons of self-interest had allied with workers to support the democratic regime, were fatally weakened by the rise of international protectionism after 1929, and their collapse may have so vitiated the Weimar Coalition of interests as to make possible Hitler's seizure of power.[51]

While general observations on these points are still difficult, we can perhaps advance three claims. First, stable hegemony helps, and instability harms, nearly all economies that export quality-differentiable products.[52] Second, within borderline autarkical economies (defined earlier), stable hegemony strengthens trade- and productivity-oriented sectors, while instability increases the weight of protectionist forces and distributional coalitions. Third, where an exporter of primary products enjoys complementarity with the hegemonic power—as did the United States before the Civil War and Argentina before 1914—it will be less subject to market fluctuation and hence, by our earlier reasoning, likely to have a weaker state than its situation would otherwise imply.

If we grant that different hegemonies can affect the interna-

50. Osvaldo Sunkel and Pedro Paz, *El subdesarrollo latinoamericano y la teoría del desarrollo,* 4th ed. (Madrid: Siglo Veintiuno Editores, 1973), pp. 71, 436ff.
51. David Abraham, *Collapse of the Weimar Republic: Political Economy and Crisis* (Princeton: Princeton University Press, 1981).
52. The principal exception is of course the hegemon itself, which for reasons already advanced may be expected to decline under stable hegemony and may actually be stimulated by instability—as was Britain after 1931. (I am grateful to Peter Gourevitch and Calum MacDonald for having called this instance to my attention.)

tional division of labor differently, we must also substantially qualify Gilpin's general assertion of the likelihood of war in situations of "eroding hegemony."[53] The threat that a rising power presents to a hegemon, and hence the likelihood that the hegemon will strike preemptively or the challenger preclusively, must vary with the presumptive role of the old hegemon in its successor's "new order." That such British statesmen as Cecil Rhodes and Stanley Baldwin looked far more equably on an American than on a German succession is to be explained not only by cultural ties (which had notably failed to prevent conflict when Prussia supplanted Austrian regional domination) but, surely, by relative American disinterest in many of those regions and sectors that most concerned the British.[54]

What, finally, do these works tell us about the value of the rational-choice approach? The answer of course depends on the goal, on what one regards as good theory. The traditional standard demands simultaneous high marks on at least five criteria: parsimony, power, rigor, precision, and empirical accuracy. A useful second-best criterion has recently been proposed by Brian Barry, namely, that theory "should help us to interpret and understand some complex social phenomenon by seizing on some crucial aspect of it and enabling us to think more clearly and systematically about it than we would have been able to do without the theory."[55] By this less demanding measure, North's volume succeeds: its model of the rent-seeking state, of the firm, and even of ideology does enable us to think more clearly and systematically about wide ranges of social phenomena and thus lends credence to the rational-choice perspective that underlies it.

By the more rigorous traditional demands, paradoxically, Olson's theory may deserve higher praise, for it meets four of the five standards, failing only on the (alas, essential) one of accuracy. Yet even it, and a fortiori the efforts of North and Gilpin, fails to make

53. Gilpin himself, interestingly, draws back from the implications of his arguments for the present day, claiming that hegemonic war between a declining United States and a rising Soviet Union is unlikely because of a series of fortunate coincidences (pp. 234–40).

54. On British attitudes see Edward Hallett Carr, *The Twenty Years' Crisis, 1919–1939: An Introduction to the Study of International Relations* (New York: Harper Torchbooks, 1964), pp. 232–33.

55. Brian Barry, "Review Article: Crisis, Choice, and Change," *British Journal of Political Science* 7 (1977): 99–113, 217–53.

a convincing case for the rational-choice approach as applied to questions of international politics and economic growth. Only when some rational-choice theory as parsimonious, powerful, rigorous, and precise as Olson's also demonstrates great and surprising accuracy will—or should—a skeptical world be convinced. These efforts bring us palpably near, but not to, the goal.

# 10

# Governments and Agricultural Markets in Africa

## *Robert H. Bates*

Governments in Africa intervene in agricultural markets in characteristic ways: they tend to lower the prices offered for agricultural commodities, and they tend to increase the prices that farmers must pay for the goods they buy for consumption. And although African governments do subsidize the prices farmers pay for the goods they use in farming, the benefits of these subsidies are appropriated by the rich few: the small minority of large-scale farmers.

Other patterns, too, are characteristic of government market intervention. Insofar as African governments seek increased farm production, their policies are project-based rather than price-based. Insofar as they employ prices to strengthen production incentives, they tend to encourage production by lowering the prices

Research for this essay was supported by the Division of Humanities and Social Sciences of the California Institute of Technology and by the National Science Foundation, Grant no. SOC 77–08573A1. The paper draws extensively on materials presented in Robert H. Bates, *Markets and States in Tropical Africa: The Political Basis of Agricultural Policies* (Berkeley and Los Angeles: University of California Press, 1981), and Robert H. Bates, *Essays on the Political Economy of Rural Africa* (Cambridge, England: Cambridge University Press, 1983).

of inputs (that is, by lowering costs) rather than by increasing the prices of products (that is, by increasing revenues). A last characteristic is that governments intervene in ways that promote economic inefficiency: they alter market prices, reduce market competition, and invest in poorly conceived agricultural projects. In all of these actions, it should be stressed, the conduct of African governments resembles the conduct of governments in other parts of the developing world.

One purpose of this paper is to describe more fully these patterns of government intervention. A second is to examine a variety of explanations for this behavior.

## The Regulation of Commodity Markets

It is useful to distinguish between two kinds of agricultural commodities: food crops, many of which can be directly consumed on the farm, and cash crops, few of which are directly consumable and which are instead marketed as a source of cash income. Many cash crops are in fact exported; they provide not only cash incomes for farm families but also foreign exchange for the national economies of Africa.

### Export Crops

An important feature of the African economies is the nature of the marketing systems employed for the purchase and export of cash crops. The crops are grown by private farm families, but they are then sold through official, state-controlled marketing channels. At the local level, these channels may take the form of licensed agents or registered private buyers; they may also take the form of cooperative societies or farmers' associations. But the regulated nature of the marketing system is clearly revealed in the fact that these primary purchasing agencies can in most cases only sell to one purchaser: a state-owned body, commonly known as the marketing board.

*Background*    The origins of these boards are diverse. In some cases, particularly in the former settler territories, they were formed by farmers themselves. At the time of the Great Depression, commercial farmers banded together in efforts to stabilize the markets for cash crops; in effect, with the support of the colonial states they dominated, they sought to create producer-run cartels. More commonly, the origins of the marketing boards lay in an alternative source of cartel formation: in the efforts of the purchasers and exporters of cash crops to dominate the market and to force lower prices on farmers.[1]

In either case, World War II led to the institutionalization of the regulation of export markets. During the war, Britain sought to procure agricultural commodities and raw materials from her colonial dependencies. Some materials, such as food for troops in North Africa, were needed for the war effort; others were needed to generate foreign exchange for the purchase of armaments from North America; and the purchase of still other goods was required to provide prosperity for the colonial areas and thereby to lessen the likelihood of political instability at a time when British armed forces were already spread perilously thin. To secure the regularized purchase of raw materials, the British government created a ministry of supply. The ministry signed bulk-purchasing agreements with the colonial governments in each of the African territories. To administer the terms of these agreements, the colonial authorities created official marketing agencies. In those territories in which large-scale producers had already begun to operate market-stabilizing schemes, the producer associations running these schemes were recruited to staff and administer the state marketing boards. In the territories where purchasers' cartels held a predominance of market power, the state procurement schemes in effect conferred legal standing on the merchant-based cartels; the cartels became the instruments for securing raw materials.[2]

In either case, upon independence many African governments found themselves the inheritors of bureaucracies that held an official monopoly over the purchase and export of commodities in the most valuable sector of their domestic economies. These new states possessed extremely powerful instruments of market intervention. They could purchase export crops at an administratively

1. P. T. Bauer, *West Africa Trade* (London: Routledge and Kegan Paul, 1964); William O. Jones, "Agricultural Trade within Tropical Africa: Historical Background," in Robert H. Bates and Michael F. Lofchie, eds., *Agricultural Development in Africa: Issues of Public Policy* (New York: Praeger, 1980).

2. Charlotte Leubuscher, *Bulk Buying from the Colonies: A Study of the Bulk Purchase of Colonial Commodities by the United Kingdom Government* (London: Oxford University Press, 1956); Elspeth Huxley, *No Easy Way: A History of the Kenya Farmers' Association and Unga Limited* (Nairobi: private printing, 1957), pp. 137ff.; and Bauer, *West Africa Trade.*

set, low domestic price; they could then market these crops at the prevailing world price; and they could accumulate the revenues generated by the difference between the domestic price at which the goods were purchased and the world price at which they were sold.

*Government Taxation*    Initially, the revenues accumulated by the marketing boards were to be used for the benefit of the farmers, in the form of price assistance funds. At times of low international prices, these funds were to be employed to support domestic prices and so to shelter the farmers from the vagaries of the world market. For example, 70 percent of the western Nigerian marketing board's revenues were to be retained for such purposes. But commitments to employ the funds for the benefit of the farmers proved short-lived. They were overborne by ambitions to implement development programs and by political pressures on governments from nonagricultural sectors of the economy.

The Cotton Price Assistance Fund, for example, was accumulated by the Lint Marketing Board in Uganda. In the 1950s it was employed to stabilize prices, but thereafter it was increasingly used for other purposes. In the pre-independence period, for example, it was used to secure revenues for the building of the Owen's Falls Dam; although the fund purchased shares in the Uganda Electricity Board, the agency responsible for the dam, it has received no dividends from these shares (and they have declined in value). In the 1960s, the fund "lent" 100 million Uganda shillings to the government for investment in the capital budget, interest free. Still later, it was employed to capitalize the Cooperative Development Bank by contributing twelve million shillings interest free, repayable over thirty-five years.[3]

In West Africa, too, the revenues of the marketing boards were increasingly diverted to uses other than the stabilization of farmers' incomes. In Nigeria, for example, funds were first loaned to the regional governments; later, they were given to these governments in the form of grants; later still, the legislation governing the use of these revenues was altered such that the boards became

3. Uganda, Treasury Department, "Statement of Cotton Price Assistance Fund at 31st October 1977," 11 November 1977 (typescript); David Walker and Cyril Ehrlich, "Stabilization and Development Policy in Uganda: An Appraisal," *Kyklos* 12 (1959): 341–53.

instruments of direct taxation.[4] We have already noted that the statutes governing the marketing boards in western Nigeria reserved 70 percent of the trading surpluses for price stabilization; an additional 7.5 percent was to be employed for agricultural research, and the remaining 22.5 percent for general development purposes. But Helleiner notes that, following self-government,

> the Western Region's 1955–1960 development plan announced . . . the abandonment of the "70–22.5–7.5" formula for distribution of the Western Board's right to contribute to development, and provided for 20 million in loans and grants to come from the Board for the use of the Regional Government during the plan. . . . [The Board] was now obviously intended to run a trading surplus to finance the regional Government's program. The Western Region Marketing Board had by now become . . . a fiscal arm of the Western Nigerian Government.[5]

This transition was followed as well in Ghana, where "the government decided to remove . . . legal restrictions on its access to the funds of the Board."[6]

The movement from an instrument of price stabilization largely for the benefit of farmers to an instrument of taxation with the diversion of revenues to nonfarm sectors can be seen as well in changes in the price-stabilizing policies employed by the marketing boards. Investigations clearly suggest that what was stabilized was not the domestic price paid to farmers but, rather, the difference between the domestic and the world price, that is, the off-take from the farmer which was appropriated by the government.[7]

### Food Crops

African governments also intervene in the market for food crops. And, once again, they tend to do so in ways that lower the prices of agricultural commodities.

One way African governments attempt to secure food cheaply is by constructing bureaucracies to purchase food crops at govern-

---

4. H. M. A. Onitiri and Dupe Olatunbosun, *The Marketing Board System* (Ibadan: Nigerian Institute of Social and Economic Research, 1974).

5. Gerald K. Helleiner, *Peasant Agriculture, Government, and Economic Growth in Nigeria* (Homewood, Ill.: Richard D. Irwin, 1960), pp. 170–71.

6. Bjorn Beckman, *Organizing the Farmers: Cocoa Politics and National Development in Ghana* (New York: Holmes and Meier, 1976), p. 199.

7. See Bates, *Markets and States*.

ment-mandated prices. A recent study by the United States Department of Agriculture examined the marketing systems for food crops in Africa and discovered a high incidence of government market intervention. In the case of three of the food crops studied, in over 50 percent of the countries in which the crop was grown the government had imposed a system of producer price controls, and in over 20 percent the government maintained an official monopsony for the purchase of that food crop (Table 1); in these instances, the government was by law the sole buyer of the crop.

Regulation of food markets entails policing the purchase and movement of food stocks and controlling the storage, processing, and retail marketing of food. An illustration is offered by the maize industry of Kenya; according to subsection 1 of section 15 of the Maize Marketing Act, "All maize grown in Kenya shall, subject to the provision of this Act, be purchased by and sold to the Board, and shall, without prejudice to the Board's liability for the price payable in accordance with section 18 of this Act, rest in the Board as soon as it has been harvested."

According to the Maize Marketing (Movement of Maize and Maize Products) Order, all movements of maize require a movement permit, which is only valid for twenty-four hours and which must be obtained from the Maize and Produce Board. The sole

**Table 1.**  *Patterns of Market Intervention for Food Crops in Africa*

|  | COUNTRIES IN WHICH CROP IS GROWN | COUNTRIES WITH PRODUCER PRICE CONTROLS | | COUNTRIES WITH LEGAL MONOPOLY | |
| --- | --- | --- | --- | --- | --- |
|  | Number | Number | % | Number | % |
| Rice | 26 | 25 | 96 | 11 | 42 |
| Wheat | 12 | 8 | 67 | 4 | 33 |
| Millet and sorghum | 38 | 9 | 24 | 7 | 18 |
| Maize | 35 | 24 | 69 | 9 | 26 |
| Roots and tubers | 33 | 6 | 18 | 1 | 3 |

*Source:* United States Department of Agriculture, *Food Problems and Prospects in Sub-Saharan Africa* (Washington, D.C.: USDA, 1980), p. 173.

exceptions are the movement of maize or maize products within the boundaries of the farm; the movement of not more than two bags (180 kg) accompanied by the owner; and the movement of not more than ten bags within the boundaries of a district, accompanied by the owner and intended for consumption by the owner or his family.[8]

The controls over the market for food crops increase the costs of marketing. In part, this is because the government-imposed barriers to entry confer excess profits on the public agents who operate in the market. Their nature and magnitude are perhaps most vividly illustrated by the bribes they extract from farmers and traders.[9] A second major consequence of the regulated maize market is that many consumers pay higher prices and many producers receive lower prices than would be the case were maize to be moved more easily between places and over time.

More directly relevant to the concerns of this paper, however, is the impact of food marketing controls on food prices. For insight into this subject we can turn to Doris Jansen Dodge's study of NAMBoard, the food marketing bureaucracy in Zambia. Over the years studied by Dodge (1966–1967 to 1974–1975) NAMBoard depressed the price of maize by as much as 85 percent; that is, in the absence of government controls over maize movements, the farmers could have gotten up to 85 percent higher prices for their maize than they were able to secure under the market controls imposed by NAMBoard. Gerrard extends Dodge's finding for Zambia to Kenya, Tanzania, and Malawi; Dodge herself extends them to eight other African countries.[10] The result is a weakening of incentives to produce food.

*Projects*   In order to keep food prices low, governments take additional measures. In particular, they attempt to increase food supplies. This can be done either by importing food or by

8. Guenter Schmidt, "Maize and Beans in Kenya: The Interaction and Effectiveness of the Informal and Formal Marketing Systems," Institute for Development Studies, University of Nairobi, Occasional Paper No. 31, 1979.

9. Ibid., p. 68.

10. See Doris J. Jansen, "Agricultural Pricing Policy in Sub-Saharan Africa of the 1970s," unpublished paper, 1980 (mimeo.); Christopher David Gerrard, "Economic Development, Government Controlled Markets, and External Trade in Food Grains: The Case of Four Countries in East Africa," Ph.D. dissertation, University of Minnesota, 1981; and Doris Jansen Dodge, *Agricultural Policy and Performance in Zambia* (Berkeley: Institute of International Studies, 1977).

investing in food production projects. Foreign exchange, however, is scarce; especially since the rise of petroleum prices, the cost of imports is high. So as to conserve foreign exchange, then, African governments attempt to become self-sufficient in food. To keep prices low, they invest in projects that will yield increased food production.

In some cases, governments turn public institutions into food production units: youth-league farms and prison farms provide illustrative cases. In other instances, they attempt to provide factors of production. In Africa, water is commonly scarce and governments invest heavily in river-basin development schemes and irrigation projects. Capital equipment is also scarce; by purchasing and operating farm machinery, governments attempt to promote farm production. Some governments invest in projects to provide particular crops: rice in Kenya, for example, or wheat in Tanzania. In other instances, governments divert large portions of their capital budgets to the financing of food production schemes. Western Nigeria, for example, spent over 50 percent of the Ministry of Agriculture's capital budget on state farms over the period of the 1962–1968 development program.[11]

### Nonbureaucratic Forms of Intervention

Thus far I have emphasized direct forms of government intervention. But there is an equally important, less direct form of intervention: the overvaluation of the domestic currency.

Most governments in Africa maintain an overvalued currency.[12] Foreign money therefore exchanges for fewer units of local currency. A result is to lower the prices received by the exporters of cash crops. For a given sum earned abroad, the exporters of cash crops receive fewer units of the domestic currency. In part, overvaluation inflicts losses on governments; deriving a portion of their revenues from taxes levied by the marketing boards, the governments command less domestic purchasing power as a result of overvaluation. But because their instruments of taxation are mo-

---

11. Frances Hill, "Experiments with a Public Sector Peasantry," *African Studies Review* 20 (1977): 25–41; and Werner Roider, *Farm Settlements for Socio-Economic Development: The Western Nigerian Case* (Munich: Weltforum, 1971).

12. International Bank for Reconstruction and Development, *Accelerated Development in Sub-Saharan Africa: An Agenda for Action* (Washington, D.C.: IBRD, 1981); and Franz Pick, *Pick's Currency Yearbook, 1976–1977* (New York: Pick Publishing, 1978).

nopolistic agencies, African governments are able to transfer much of the burden of overvaluation: they pass it on to farmers, in the form of lower prices.

In addition to lowering the earnings of export agriculture, overvaluation lowers the prices paid for foreign imports. This is, of course, part of the rationale for a policy of overvaluation: it cheapens the costs of importing plant, machinery, and other capital equipment needed to build an industrial sector. But items other than plant and equipment can be imported, and among these other commodities is food. As a consequence of overvaluation, African food producers face higher levels of competition from foreign foodstuffs. And in search of low-price food, African governments do little to protect their domestic food markets from foreign products—products whose prices have artificially been lowered as a consequence of public policies.

### Industrial Goods

In the markets for the crops they produce, African farmers face a variety of government policies that serve to lower farm prices. In the markets for the goods that they consume, however, they face a highly contrasting situation: they confront prices for consumers that are supported by government policy.

In promoting industrial development, African governments adopt commercial policies that shelter local industries from foreign competition. To some degree they impose tariff barriers between the local and the international markets. To an even greater extent, they employ quantitative restrictions. Quotas, import licenses, and permits to acquire and use foreign exchange are all employed to conserve foreign exchange, on the one hand, while, on the other, protecting the domestic market for local industries. In connection with the maintenance of overvalued currencies, these trade barriers create incentives for investors to import capital equipment and to manufacture domestically goods that formerly had been imported from abroad.[13]

---

13. J. Dirck Stryker, "Ghana Agriculture," paper for the West African Regional Project, 1975 (mimeo.); Scott R. Pearson, Gerald C. Nelson, and J. Dirck Stryker, "Incentives and Comparative Advantage in Ghanaian Industry and Agriculture," paper for the West African Regional Project, 1976 (mimeo.); International Bank for Reconstruction and Development, *Kenya: Into the Second Decade* (Washington, D.C.: IBRD, 1975); and International Bank for Reconstruction and Development, *Ivory Coast: The Challenge of Success* (Washington, D.C.: IBRD, 1978).

Not only do government policies shelter industries from low-cost foreign competition, they shelter them from domestic competition as well. In part, protection from domestic competition is a by-product of protection from foreign competition. The policy of allocating licenses to import in conformity with historic market shares provides an example of such a measure. The limitation of competition results from other policies as well. In exchange for commitments to invest, governments guarantee periods of freedom from competition. Moreover, governments tend to favor larger projects; seeking infusions of scarce capital, they tend to back the proposals that promise the largest capital investments. With the small markets typical of most African nations, the result is that investors create plants whose output represents a very large fraction of the domestic market; a small number of firms thus come to dominate the market. Finally, particularly where state enterprises are concerned, governments sometimes confer virtual monopoly rights upon particular enterprises. The consequence of all these measures is to shelter industries from domestic competition.

One result is that inefficient firms survive. Estimates of the use of industrial capacity range as low as one-fifth of the single-shift capacity of installed plant.[14] Another consequence is that prices rise. Protected from foreign competition and operating in non-competitive market settings, firms are able to charge prices that enable them to survive despite operating at very high levels of cost.

### Farm Inputs

By depressing the prices offered farmers for the goods they sell, government policies lower the revenues of farmers. By raising the prices that consumers—including farmers—must pay, governments reduce the real value of farm revenues still further. As a consequence of these interventions by governments, then, African farmers are taxed. Oddly enough, while taxing farmers in the market for products, governments subsidize them in the market for farm outputs.

Attempts to lower input prices take various forms. Governments provide subsidies for seeds and fertilizers, the level of the latter

14. Ghana, *Report of the Commission of Enquiry into the Local Purchasing of Cocoa* (Accra: Government Printer, 1967); and Tony Killick, *Development Economics in Action: A Study of Economic Policies in Ghana* (New York: St. Martin's Press, 1978), p. 171.

running from 30 percent, in Kenya, to 80 percent, in Nigeria. They provide tractor-hire services at subsidized rates—up to 50 percent of the real costs in Ghana in the mid-1970s.[15] They provide loans at subsidized rates of interest for the purchase and rental of inputs. And they provide highly favorable tax treatment for major investors in commercial farming ventures.[16] Moreover, through their power over property rights African governments have released land and water to commercial farmers at costs that lie below the value they would generate in alternative uses. The diversion of land to large-scale farmers and of water to private tenants on government irrigation schemes, without paying compensation to those who had employed these resources in subsistence farming, pastoral production, fishing or other ventures, represents the conferring of a subsidy on the commercial farmer— and one that is paid at the expense of the small-scale, traditional producer. This process has been documented in northern Ghana,[17] Nigeria,[18] Kenya,[19] Ethiopia,[20] and Senegal.[21] It was, of course, common in settler Africa as well.

In the case of land and water use, then, a major effect of government intervention in the market for inputs is to augment the fortunes of large-scale farmers at the expense of small-scale farmers. To some degree, this is true of programs in support of chemical and mechanized inputs as well. And even where there is no direct redistribution, it is clear that government programs that seek to increase food production by reducing the costs of farming reach only a small segment of the farming population: the large

15. Stryker, "Ghana Agriculture"; C. K. Kline, D. A. G. Green, Roy L. Donahue, and B. A. Stout, *Industrialization in an Open Economy: Nigeria 1945–1966* (Cambridge, England: Cambridge University Press).

16. See, for example, David Onaburekhale Ekhomu, "National Food Policies and Bureaucracies in Nigeria: Legitimization, Implementation, and Evaluation," paper presented at the African Studies Association Convention, Baltimore, Maryland, 1978 (mimeo.).

17. *West Africa*, 3 April 1978.

18. Ekhomu, "National Food Policies"; Janet Girdner and Victor Oloransula, "National Food Policies and Organizations in Ghana," paper presented to the annual meeting of the American Political Science Association, New York, 1978.

19. Apollo I. Njonjo, "The Africanization of the 'White Highlands': A Study in Agrarian Class Struggles in Kenya, 1950–1974," Ph.D. dissertation, Princeton University, 1977.

20. John Cohen and Dov Weintraub, *Land and Peasants in Imperial Ethiopia: The Social Background to Revolution* (Assen: Van Gorcum, 1975).

21. Donal B. Cruise O'Brien, *The Mourides of Senegal: The Political and Economic Organization of an Islamic Brotherhood* (Oxford: Clarendon Press, 1971).

farmers. In part, this is by plan. The programs are aimed at the "progressive farmers" who will "make best use of them." Because the large farmers have the same social background as those who staff the public services, the public servants feel they can work most congenially and productively with these people.[22] Moreover, to favor the large farmer is politically productive. I will elaborate this argument below.

## Discussion

Governments intervene in the market for products in an effort to lower prices. They adopt policies which tend to raise the price of the goods farmers buy. And while they attempt to lower the costs of farm inputs, the benefits of this policy are reaped only by a small minority of the richer farmers. Agricultural policies in Africa thus tend to be adverse to the interests of most producers.

Studies in other areas suggest that this configuration of pricing decisions is common in the developing nations.[23] Indeed, it is argued by some that the principal problems bedeviling agriculture in the developing areas originate from bad public policies. In the words of Theodore Schultz, given the right incentives, farmers in the developing world would "turn sand into gold."[24] "Distortions" introduced into agricultural markets by governments, he contends, furnish the most important reasons for their failure to do so.[25] While Schultz's position is perhaps an extreme one, it nonetheless underscores the importance of understanding why Third World

22. See David M. Leonard, *Reaching the Peasant Farmer: Organization Theory and Practice in Kenya* (Chicago: University of Chicago Press, 1977); and H. U. E. Van Velzen, "Staff, Kulaks and Peasants," in Lionel Cliffe and John Saul, eds., *Socialism in Africa*, vol. 2 (Dar es Salaam: East African Publishing House, 1973).

23. Raj Krishna, "Agricultural Price Policy and Economic Development," in M. Southworth and Bruce F. Johnston, eds., *Agricultural Development and Economic Growth* (Ithaca: Cornell University Press); United States General Accounting Office, *Disincentives to Agricultural Production in Developing Countries* (Washington, D.C.: Government Printer, 1975); Carl Gotsch and Gilbert Brow, "Prices, Taxes and Subsidies in Pakistan Agriculture, 1960–1976," World Bank Staff Working Paper no. 387 (Washington, D.C.: World Bank, 1980); Keith Griffin, *The Green Revolution: An Economic Analysis* (Geneva: United Nations Research Institute, 1972); Michael Lipton, *Why Poor People Stay Poor: Urban Bias in World Development* (Cambridge, Mass.: Harvard University Press, 1977).

24. Theodore W. Schultz, *Transforming Traditional Agriculture* (New York: Arno Press, 1976), p. 5.

25. Theodore W. Schultz, ed., *Distortions of Agricultural Incentives* (Bloomington: Indiana University Press, 1978).

governments select this characteristic pattern of agricultural policies. In the remaining sections, I will advance several explanations for their choices.

## Governments as Agents of the Public Interest

The first approach derives from development economics. Public policy represents a choice by government made out of a regard for what is socially best. The overriding public interest of poor societies is in rapid economic growth. And the policy choices of Third World governments represent their commitment to rapid development, a commitment that implies supplanting agriculture with industry.

In common with most political scientists, I remain skeptical of such a benevolent theory of government. It is therefore unsettling to have to admit that, *confining attention to export crops,* the implications of this approach are consistent with many of the facts.

All the governments of Africa seek industrial development. Most seek to create the social and economic infrastructure necessary for industrial growth and many are committed to the completion of major industrial and manufacturing projects. To fulfill their plans, governments need revenues; they also need foreign exchange. In most of the African nations, agriculture represents the single largest sector in the domestic economy; and in many it represents the principal source of foreign exchange. It is therefore natural that in seeking to fulfill these objectives for their societies, the governments of Africa should intervene in markets in an effort to set prices in a way that transfers resources from agriculture to the "industrializing" sectors of the economy: the state itself and the urban industrial and manufacturing firms.

An explanation based on the development objectives of African regimes is thus consistent with the choices made in the markets for export goods. It is also consistent with other well-known facts. The policy choices that have been made are, for example, in keeping with the prescriptions propounded in leading development theories. According to these theories, to secure higher levels of per capita income, nations should move from the production of primary products to the production of manufactured goods. Savings take place out of the profits of industry and not out of the earning of farmers. Resources should therefore be levied from agriculture and channeled into industrial development. And agriculture in the

developing areas, it is held, can surrender revenues without a significant decline in production. These were, and remain today, critical assertions in development economics. Many policymakers in
Africa were trained by development specialists; and important advocates of these arguments have served as consultants to the development ministries of the new African states. It is therefore credible
to account for the policy choices made by African governments—
ones that systematically bias the structure of prices against agriculture and in favor of industry—as choices made in accordance with
prescriptions of how best to secure the welfare of people in poor
societies.

Such an approach ultimately proves unsatisfactory, however, for
it fails to generate explanatory power, and where it does offer explanations, they are often wrong. Although the social welfare–
maximizing interpretation of government could not be rejected on
the basis of the actions exhibited by governments concerning export crops, the deficiencies of this approach become apparent
when it is applied to government policies concerning food crops.

To secure social objectives, governments can choose among a
wide variety of policy instruments; and knowledge of the public
objectives of a program fails to give insight into why a particular
policy instrument is chosen. For example, an important objective
of African governments is to increase food supplies. To secure
more supplies, governments could offer higher prices for food or
they could invest the same amount of resources in food production
projects. There is every reason to believe that the former is the
more efficient way of securing the objective. But governments in
Africa systematically prefer project-based policies to price-based
policies.

To strengthen the incentives for food production, African governments can increase the price of farm products or subsidize the
costs of farm implements. Either would result in higher profits for
producers. But governments systematically choose the latter policy.

To increase output, African governments finance food production programs. But given the level of resources devoted to these
programs, they often create too many projects; the programs then
fail because resources have been spread too thin. Such behavior is
nonsensical in terms of the social objectives of the program.

To take a last example: in the face of shortages, governments
can either allow prices to rise or maintain lower prices while imposing quotas. In a variety of markets of significance to agricul-

tural producers, African governments exhibit a systematic preference for the use of quotas—a preference that cannot readily be accounted for in terms of their development objectives.

A major problem with an approach that tries to explain agricultural policies in terms of the social objectives of governments, then, is that the social objectives that underlie a policy program fail to account for the particular form the policies assume. The approach thus yields little in the way of explanatory power. A second major difficulty is that when explanations of governmental behavior are made in terms of the objectives of public policy, they often prove false.

This problem is disclosed by the self-defeating nature of many government policies. To secure cheaper food, for example, governments lower prices to producers; but this only creates shortages which lead to *higher* food prices. To increase resources with which to finance programs of development, governments increase agricultural taxes; but this leads to declines in production and to shortfalls in public finances and foreign exchange. And to secure rapid development, governments seek to transfer resources from agriculture to industry; but this set of policies has instead led to reduced rates of growth and to economic stagnation.

The policy instruments chosen to secure social objectives are thus often inconsistent with the attainment of these objectives. And yet the choices of governments are clearly stable; despite undermining their own goals, governments continue to employ these policy instruments. Some kind of explanation is required, but one based on factors other than the social objectives of governments.

## Governments as Agents of Private Interests

An alternative approach would not view governments as agencies that maximize the social welfare. Rather, it would view them as agencies that serve private interests. And, rather than interpreting government policies as choices made out of a regard for the public interest, it would instead view them as decisions made in order to accommodate the demands of organized private interests. This approach would view public policy as the outcome of political pressures exerted by groups that seek satisfaction of their private interests from political action.

Particularly in the area of food price policy, this approach has much to recommend it. Put bluntly, food policy in Africa appears to represent a form of political settlement, one designed to bring about peaceful relations between African governments and their urban constituents. And it is a settlement in which the costs tend to be borne by the mass of the unorganized: the small-scale farmers.

The urban origins of African food policies are perhaps most clearly seen in Nigeria. If one searches out the historical origins of government food policy in Nigeria, one is drawn to the recommendations of a series of government commissions—the Udoji Commission, the Adebo Commission, and the Anti-Inflation Task Forces, for example—which were impaneled to investigate sources of labor unrest and to resolve major labor stoppages.[26] The fundamental issue driving urban unrest, they noted, was concern with the real value of urban incomes and the erosion of purchasing power because of inflation. While recommending higher wages, these commissions also noted that pay increases represented only a short-run solution; in the words of the Adebo Commission, "It was clear to us that, unless certain recommended steps were taken and actively pursued, a pay award would have little or no meaning." "Hence," in the words of the commission, "our extraordinary preoccupation with the causes of the cost of living situation."[27] As part of its efforts to confront the causes of the rising cost of living, the commission went on to recommend a number of basic measures, among them proposals "to improve the food supply situation."[28] The origins of many elements of Nigeria's agricultural program lie in the recommendations of these reports.

Urban consumers in Africa constitute a vigilant and potent pressure group demanding low-priced food. Because they are poor, much of their income goes for food; some studies suggest that urban consumers in Africa spend between 50 and 60 percent of their incomes on food.[29] Since changes in the price of food have a major impact on the economic well-being of urban dwellers in Africa, they pay close attention to the issue of food prices.

Urban consumers are potent because they are geographically

26. See Nigeria, Federal Ministry of Information, *Second and Final Report of the Wages and Salaries Review Commission, 1970–71* (Lagos: Ministry of Information, 1971); Nigeria, *Public Service Review Commission* (Lagos: Government Printer, 1974); Nigeria, Federal Ministry of Information, *First Report of the Anti-Inflation Task Force* (Lagos: Government Printer, 1978).

27. Nigeria, *Public Service Review Commission*, p. 10.

28. Ibid., p. 93.

29. Hiromitsu Kaneda and Bruce F. Johnston, "Urban Food Expenditure Patterns in Tropical Africa," *Food Research Institute Studies* 2 (1961): 229–75.

concentrated and strategically located. Because of their geographic concentration, they can be organized quickly; and because they control transport, communications, and other public services, they can impose deprivations on others. They are therefore influential. Urban unrest frequently heralds a change of government in Africa, and the cost and availability of food supplies are major factors promoting urban unrest.

It should be noted that it is not only the workers who care about food prices. It is also the employers. Employers care about food prices because food is a wage good; with higher food prices, wages rise and, all else being equal, profits fall. Governments care about food prices not only because they are employers in their own right but also because as owners of industries and promoters of industrial development programs they seek to protect industrial profits. Indicative of the significance of these interests is that the unit that sets agricultural prices often resides not in the Ministry of Agriculture but in the Ministry of Commerce or of Finance.

When urban unrest begins among food consumers, the political discontent often spreads rapidly to upper echelons of the polity: to those whose incomes come from profits, not wages, and to those in charge of major bureaucracies. Political regimes that are unable to supply low-cost food are seen as dangerously incompetent and as failing to protect the interests of key elements of the social order. At times of high prices, influential elites are likely to ally with the urban masses, to shift their political loyalties and replace those in power. Thus it was that protests over food shortages and rising prices formed a critical prelude to the coups and coup attempts in Ghana, Liberia, Kenya, and Guinea.

It is ironic but true that among those governments most committed to low-cost food are the "radical" governments in Africa. Despite their stress on economic equality, they impose lower prices on the commodity from which the poorest of the poor, the peasant farmers, derive their income. A major reason for their behavior is that they are deeply committed to rapid industrialization; moreover, they are deeply committed to higher real wages for urban workers and have deep institutional ties to organized labor.

We can thus understand the demand for low-cost food. Its origins lie in the urban areas. It is supported by governments, both out of political necessity and, on the part of more radical ones, out of ideological preference. Food is a major staple and higher prices for such staples threaten the real value of wages *and* profits.

Partially confirming these contentions is statistical evidence concerning government controls over the retail price of rice. Taking the presence or absence of retail price controls for rice as a dependent variable, I have taken as independent variables the ideological preferences of the various governments, data as to whether or not rice was an urban staple, and measures of the domestic rate of inflation.[30] Employing these variables in a probit analysis, I secured results suggesting that insofar as rice is a staple of urban consumption, governments are more likely to subject it to retail price control; and the greater the rate of domestic inflation, the more likely are governments to attempt to control the price of rice. Moreover, Socialist and Marxist governments are more likely to impose price controls than are governments of no discernible ideological stance; capitalist governments are less likely to do so. I obtained similar results for my analysis of government control over the retail price of maize, with one exception: inflation was not significant. But, interestingly, a measure of the concentration of urban dwelling was: the greater the proportion of urban dwellers concentrated in the nation's largest city, the more likely the government was to have retail price controls for maize.

There are thus fundamental political reasons for governments to seek to lower the price of food. There are also real limitations on their ability to do so. One limitation is political: insofar as farmers themselves are powerful, they are likely to resist the efforts of governments to lower agricultural prices. Only occasionally, however, are farmers powerful. In West Africa, urban/bureaucratic elites have entered rice farming; and where they have done so, they have won protected commodity prices and subsidized prices for farm inputs.[31] In East Africa, similar elites maintain large-scale wheat farms; they too have employed their political influence to avoid adverse pricing policies. But most farms are owned by members of the peasantry, not the elite; they are small-scale, not large-scale; and the farmers are politically weak, not strong. Rarely, then, are farmers powerful; and most often they are taxed.

Political power on the part of farmers thus occasionally influences the pricing decisions of governments. A more common influ-

---

30. The ideological preferences of governments were assessed by Crawford Young, *Ideology and Development in Africa* (New Haven: Yale University Press, 1982). Measures of inflation and urbanization were taken from IBRD, *Accelerated Development*. Measures of government market intervention were taken from United States Department of Agriculture, *Food Problems and Prospects in Sub-Saharan Africa* (Washington, D.C.: Government Printer, 1980).

31. Scott R. Pearson, J. Dirck Stryker, and Charles P. Humphreys, *Rice in West Africa* (Stanford: Stanford University Press, 1981).

ence is the limitation of governmental resources. When lower price levels are imposed on farmers, consumers may face shortages; indeed, food production tends to be highly price-elastic. A necessary corollary to low-food-price policies in Africa is thus the use of public resources to produce or to import food. But most African governments are poor and have little foreign exchange. Governments therefore lack the resources with which to make up the shortfalls resulting from their pricing policies, and this places a major limitation on the degree to which they can lower agricultural prices.

Evidence for these arguments is contained in the recent work of Gerrard.[32] Gerrard finds that when the self-sufficiency price for a given crop lies below the world price, as is the case with maize, then governments tend to set the domestic price at the self-sufficiency price. They also do so when the self-sufficiency price lies above the world price, as is the case with wheat. Gerrard interprets these results as suggesting that African governments regulate prices in order to secure self-sufficiency. But, rather than interpreting these results as suggesting a systematic search by governments for social objectives, I would instead interpret them as the consequence of the interplay between political pressures on governments and financial constraints. Wheat producers are large-scale farmers; often they are members of the political elite and they employ their power to secure government pledges for self-sufficiency. This political commitment secures them sheltered markets and production subsidies. Maize is produced by small-scale farmers who lack political power; they therefore face lowered prices. The primary limit to the subsidies for the relatively powerful is the cost to government of production subsidies; the primary limit to the low-food-price policy for the weak is the cost to government of food imports. Caught between the political pressures for price changes and the financial costs of securing alterations in prices, governments tend to act as if their goal were self-sufficiency.

Self-sufficiency for wheat producers therefore represents a political triumph for farmers; for maize producers, it represents a political defeat. For both, the limits to the political outcome are the financial costs to the government. This interpretation covers the facts, as recorded by Gerrard, while resting on a pressure-group rather than a welfare-maximizing theory of public policy.

Pressure groups form only one component of a pluralist model

---

32. Gerrard, "Economic Development."

of politics.[33] A second is competitive elections. Clearly, were competitive elections contested by rival parties in Africa, agricultural policy could not be so strongly biased against rural dwellers. With less than 10 percent of their population in cities, most nations would contain electoral majorities composed of farm families; and electoral incentives would almost inevitably lead politicians to advocate pro-agrarian platforms in their efforts to secure votes and to win power.

Evidence of the significance of electoral incentives is to be found in Zambia. From 1964 to 1972, the government of Zambia devoted on average over 70 percent of its capital budget to expenditures in the urban areas. In the years prior to national elections, however, the government reallocated its capital program: over 40 percent of the capital budget was then spent in the rural districts. Moreover, it was in the years prior to elections that major rural-development programs were announced: the creation of zones of intensive rural development, new credit programs, mechanization schemes, the decentralization of rural administration. The commitment to rural development was thus tied to the electoral cycle. Having periodically to face a rural constituency, the government periodically recommitted itself to the enhancement of their fortunes.[34]

There is thus a tension between the two components of the pluralist model. In the African context, the impact of organized interest groups works to the detriment of agrarian interests, whereas competitive elections work to their advantage. In recent years the frequency of the return to democratic forms of government among the African states has been more than matched by the frequency of the demise of competitive party systems. Electoral incen-

33. A more systematic analysis of pressure-group politics, based on more rigorous microeconomic foundations, is contained in Robert H. Bates and William P. Rogerson, "Agriculture in Development: A Coalitional Analysis," *Public Choice* 35 (1980): 513–27; and Bates, *Markets and States*. The first deals primarily with the demand for price intervention; the second, with the supply. Both attempt to explain the relative inefficacy of farmers in pressure-group politics in the developing areas. A major source of relevant theorizing for this portion of the analysis is the capture-theory approach to industrial regulation. See George Stigler, "The Theory of Economic Regulation," *Bell Journal of Economics and Management Science* 3 (1971): 3–21; Sam Peltzman, "Toward a More General Theory of Regulation," *Journal of Law and Economics* 19 (1976): 211–40.

34. See Robert H. Bates, *Rural Responses to Industrialization: A Study of Village Zambia* (New Haven: Yale University Press, 1978).

tives have little opportunity to counter the biases produced by interest-group politics.

## Governments as Agencies That Seek to Retain Power

The interest-group model thus accounts for major elements of the food policies maintained by African governments. It explains the political pressures for low food prices and thus helps to explain why, when governments want more food, they prefer to secure it by building more projects rather than offering higher prices. By the same token, it helps to account for the governments' preference for production subsidies rather than higher food prices as incentives for food production.

Nonetheless, an interest-group explanation too is incomplete. Its primary virtue is that it helps to account for the essentially draconian pricing policies adopted by African governments. Its primary limitation is that it fails to explain how governments get away with such policies. How, in nations where the majority of the population are farmers and the majority of the resources are held in agriculture, are governments able to succeed in implementing policies that violate the interests of most farmers? In search of answers to this question, a third approach is needed, one that looks at agricultural programs as part of a repertoire of devices employed by African governments in their efforts to secure political control over their rural populations and thus to remain in power.

### Organizing a Rural Constituency

We have already seen that adopting policies in support of higher prices for agricultural commodities would be politically costly to African governments. It is also important to note that such a stance would generate few political benefits. From a political point of view, conferring higher prices offers few attractions for politicians, for the benefits of the measure could be enjoyed by rural opponents and supporters alike. The benefits could not be restricted to the faithful or withheld from the politically disloyal. Pricing policies therefore cannot be employed by politicians to organize political followings.

Project-based policies suffer less from this liability. Officials can exercise discretion in locating projects; they can also exercise discretion in staffing them. Such discretion allows them to bestow benefits selectively on those whose political support they desire. Politicians are therefore more likely to be attracted to project-based policies as a measure of rural development.

The relative political utility of projects explains several otherwise puzzling features of government agricultural investments. One is the tendency to construct too many projects, given the budgetary resources available. A reason for this proliferation is that governments often wish to ensure that officials in each administrative district or electoral constituency have access to resources with which to secure a political backing.[35] Another tendency is to hire too large a staff or a staff that is technically untrained, thus undercutting the viability of the projects. A reason for this is that jobs on projects—and jobs in many of the bureaucracies involved with agricultural programs, for that matter—represent political plums, given by those in charge of the programs to their political followers. State farms in Ghana were staffed by the youth brigade of the ruling Convention People's Party, and the cooperative societies in Zambia were formed and operated by the local and constituency-level units of the governing party, to offer just two examples of the link between staffing and political organization.

Again and again, from an economic point of view, agricultural projects fail; they often fail to generate earnings that cover their costs or, when they do so, they often fail to generate a rate of return comparable to that obtainable through alternative uses of government funds. Nonetheless, public agencies revive and reimplement such projects. A major reason is that public officials are frequently less concerned with using public resources in a way that is economically efficient than they are with using them in a way that is politically expedient. If a project fails to generate an adequate return on the public investment but nonetheless is privately rewarding for those who build it, provision it, staff it, or hold tenancies in it, then political officials may support it, for the project will serve as a source of rewards for their followers and as an instrument for building a rural political organization.

35. See Bates, *Rural Responses;* Jerome C. Wells, *Agricultural Policy and Economic Growth in Nigeria, 1962–1968* (Ibadan: Oxford University Press for the Nigerian Institute of Social Science and Economic Research, 1974); Alfred John Dadson, "Socialized Agriculture in Ghana, 1962–1965," Ph.D. dissertation, Harvard University, 1970.

### Disorganizing the Rural Opposition

We have seen that government policies are often aimed at establishing low prices for agricultural products. Particularly in the market for cash crops, governments maintain monopsonistic agencies and use their market power to lower product prices. They therefore impose deprivations on all producers. What is interesting, however, is that they return to selected members of the farm community a portion of the resources which they thus exact. Some of the earnings taxed from farmers are returned to a privileged few, in the form of subsidies for farm inputs. While imposing collective deprivations, governments thus confer selective benefits.

These benefits serve as side-payments: they compensate selected members of the rural sector for the losses they sustain as a consequence of the government's programs. They thereby make it in the private interests of particular members of the rural sector to abide by policies that are harmful to rural dwellers as a whole. By so doing, they secure the defection of favored farmers from a potential rural opposition and their adherence to the governing coalition, which implements agricultural programs that are harmful to farming as a whole.

Agricultural producers are both subsidized and taxed. What is of concern at this point is the use of subsidy programs for political purposes. In northern Ghana in the late 1970s, for example, subsidized credit was given to large-scale, mechanized producers who were close allies of the military government. In Senegal, the rural base of the governing party is dominated by the Mourides, a religious sect that earns much of its income from the production of groundnuts; its adherence to the government in power, and to the government's pricing policies, is in large part secured by the conferral upon its leaders of massive amounts of subsidized credit, land, machinery, and other farm inputs.[36] In Zambia, access to subsidized inputs could best be obtained by most rural dwellers by membership in agricultural cooperative societies. The societies were formed by local units of the governing party and are now dominated by them; access to inputs is therefore contingent on political loyalty. The rural loans program, moreover, was run and staffed at the local level by former party militants who helped to

36. Cruise O'Brien, *Mourides*.

ensure that the fruits of independence were given to those who contributed to the cause of the party in power. In Ghana, to cite one last example, the collective resistance of cocoa producers to low cocoa prices in the 1950s was broken in part by the "secret weapon" of the Convention People's Party, the notorious United Ghana Farmers' Council. By distributing gammalin, cutlasses, and other farm inputs to those who would support the government and its policies, and by restricting credit to the politically faithful, the Farmers' Council helped to break the resistance of the farming population to the government and its agricultural programs.[37]

It should be noted, incidentally, that the bestowal of privileged access to farm inputs was a technique employed by the colonial governments as well. And the exchange of political loyalty for access to these inputs was widely recognized to be part of the bargain. In Northern and Southern Rhodesia, for example, the colonial governments used revenues secured by their monopsonistic maize marketing agency to subsidize the costs of inputs, which they then lavished upon a relatively small number of so-called improved or progressive farmers. The nationalist movements presciently labeled these farmers stooges of the colonial regimes. They saw that the apportionment of the inputs had been employed to separate the interests of these privileged farmers from the interests of the mass of rural producers and to detach their political loyalties from those of their fellow Africans.

By conferring selective benefits in the markets for farm inputs while imposing collective deprivations in the markets for products, governments secure the deference of a privileged few to programs that are harmful to the interests of most farmers. By politicizing farm-input programs and making access to their benefits contingent upon political loyalty, the governments secure acquiescence to those in power and compliance with their policies. The political efficacy of these measures is underscored by the fact that they are targeted to the large producers, who have the most to gain from a change in pricing policy and who might otherwise provide the leadership for efforts on the part of farmers to alter the agricultural policies of their governments.

37. Ghana, Jibowu Commission, *Report of the Commission of Enquiry into the Affairs of the Cocoa Purchasing Company* (Accra: Government Printer, 1956); Ghana, *Local Purchasing of Cocoa.*

## Markets as Instruments of Political Organization

As we have seen, in the markets for agricultural products, public monopsonies depress the prices of commodities below the market prices. At these prices, demand exceeds supply. Those in charge of the market can then bestow the right of entry. Those who are permitted to secure the good at the government price can reap the benefit of selling it at the market price. Persons given access to the regulated market thus come to owe their fortunes to the favor of those in charge. Members of the Cocoa Marketing Board in Ghana, for example, frequently allowed private trading by persons whose political backing they wished to secure. Such persons came from the highest levels of the Ghanaian government. In the Kenya maize market, issuance of movement permits by the director of the Maize and Produce Marketing Board was used to create an indebted and loyal political following.[38] Granting access to a market where the price of commodities has been artificially lowered as a matter of government policy thus becomes a valuable instrument in the accumulation of political influence.

Regulation of product prices also facilitates political control, by yielding the capacity to disorganize those most hurt by the measure: the farmers themselves. For a portion of the gains, the bureaucrat in charge of the market can turn a blind eye while farmers make sales at market-clearing prices. The structure of regulation vests legal powers in the bureaucrats; the farmers have no right to make such sales. Only by securing an individual exception to the general rule can the farmer gain access to the market-clearing price. Within the framework established by marketing policy, farmers thus do best by securing individual exceptions. The capacity for discretion thus allows the bureaucrat to separate the individual interests of particular producers from the interests of their class, and collective organization on the part of rural producers becomes more difficult. In addition, the structure of regulations creates for the government essential elements of political power: by allowing exceptions to the rules, the bureaucracy grants favors; by preparing to enforce the rules, it threatens sanctions. Market regulations thus become a source of political control, and this, in a sense, is most true when they are in the process of being breached.

38. Kenya, *Report of the Maize Commission of Inquiry, June 1966* (Nairobi: Government Printer, 1966).

Governments seek to depress prices for inputs as well; the result, once again, is the enhancement of their capacity for political control. When they lower the prices of inputs, private sources furnish lesser quantities, users demand greater quantities, and the result is excess demand. One consequence is that the inputs acquire new value; administratively created shortages give an economic premium to those who acquire the scarce inputs. Another consequence is that, at the mandated price, the market cannot allocate the inputs; they are in short supply. Rather than being allocated through a pricing system, they must be rationed. Those in charge of the regulated market thereby acquire the capacity to exercise discretion and to confer special benefits on those whose favor they desire.

On occasion, governments place political heavyweights in charge of these programs. The result often is that the elite-level figures then appropriate the premium: they sell the inputs at the prices they can command in the market. By allowing the corruption of farm programs the governments secure the fealty of potent political figures. In other cases, governments forbid such corruption and instead allocate the inputs at their officially mandated prices. The result then is the securing of political loyalty from lower-level political figures, the intended clients and beneficiaries of the subsidy programs, for it is they who then secure the economic premium.[39] Moreover, because of excess demand, those who distribute the inputs can make demonstrations of political loyalty a prerequisite for their allocation. Thus it is that public programs that distribute farm credit, tractor-hire services, seeds, and fertilizers and that bestow access to government-managed irrigation schemes and public lands become instruments of rural political organization.

## Conclusion

Governments in Africa, like governments elsewhere in the developing world, intervene in agricultural markets in ways that violate the interests of most farmers. They tend to adopt low-price policies for farm products; they tend to increase the prices farmers

---

39. In Zambia, one of the cooperative societies I studied in Luapula purchased subsidized fertilizers. It then reaped the rental premium associated with the subsidy by selling the fertilizer at market clearing prices to the local commercial farmers.

must pay for the goods they consume. And while they subsidize the prices of goods that farmers use in production, the benefits of these subsidies are appropriated by the richer few. In addition, the farm policies of African governments are characterized by a stress on projects rather than prices; when price policies are used, by a preference for lowering farm costs rather than increasing farm revenues; and by widespread economic inefficiency.

I have examined several political explanations for this configuration of agricultural policies. I conclude by commenting on their durability.

The pattern of price interventions, I have argued, represents the terms of a political pact among organized political interests, the costs of which are transferred to unorganized interests who are excluded from the price-setting coalition. Members of the pact are labor, industry, and government; small-scale farmers constitute its victims; and large-scale farmers stand as passive allies, politically neutralized through subsidy programs.

No member of the winning coalition possesses an incentive to alter its political demands unilaterally. Organized labor, for example, will not unilaterally alter its demand for cheap food. Nor will industry call for reforms that raise food prices, and thus wages, unless other members of the coalition make credible commitments to offsetting concessions. In the short term, then, the coalition and the price structure that supports it appear stable.

Over the longer run, however, the structure of the payoffs achieved by the coalition changes. Farmers adjust; in response to pricing policies, they produce less. The result in food markets is lower supplies at higher prices. The result in export markets is fewer exports and less foreign exchange. The costs which once were externalized upon the unorganized agrarian sector are now internalized, through the operation of markets, onto the dominant coalition. The farmers have transferred the costs of the political settlement to the intended beneficiaries. And as these costs mount, the pact among them becomes less stable.

As the payoffs from this basis for governance in Africa erode, opportunities arise for the introduction of new pricing policies. And as the costs of the present policies are disproportionately borne by one of the more influential of the coalition partners, the governments themselves, the likelihood of policy changes is enhanced. To support low food prices, governments must provide additional supplies, either by subsidizing local production or by financing imports from abroad. But, throughout Africa, states are undergoing a fiscal crisis; they lack both revenues and foreign exchange. One consequence is that governments are less willing or able to bear the costs of current agricultural policies. Another is the reallocation of political power. At moments of fiscal crisis, finance ministers and directors of the central banks gain greater influence over public policy. Moreover, they find allies among foreign donors and international creditors, who pressure governments to make adjustments that will lessen their burden of debt. In league with international agencies, these figures have assumed greater influence over public policy.

The set of public policies described in this paper have thus formed the basis for a political pact among organized interests. But they have set in motion economic forces which erode their economic and political value. Moreover, the fiscal crisis in contemporary Africa has restructured power relations within African governments and has brought new players into the policymaking process. The result is that the commitment to these policies may not be stable and they may in fact be subject to change.

# Selected Readings

*The items listed here were suggested by scholars who were asked to nominate the most influential writings on development published over the past several years.*

ADELMAN, IRMA, M. J. D. HOPKINS, S. ROBINSON, G. B. RODGERS, AND R. WERY. "A Comparison of Two Models for Income Distribution Planning." *Journal of Policy Modeling* 1 (1979): 37–82.

ADELMAN, IRMA, AND CYNTHIA T. MORRIS. *Economic Growth and Social Equity in Developing Countries.* Stanford: Stanford University Press, 1973.

ADELMAN, IRMA, AND SHERMAN ROBINSON. *Income Distribution Policy in Developing Countries.* New York: Published for the World Bank by Stanford University Press, 1978.

AHUWALIA, MONTEK S. "Income Inequality: Some Dimensions of the Problem." In *Redistribution with Growth,* edited by Hollis Chenery et al. New York: Oxford University Press, 1974.

———. "Inequality, Poverty and Development." *Journal of Development Economics* 3 (1976): 307–42.

AHUWALIA, MONTEK S., AND HOLLIS CHENERY. "The Economic Framework." In *Redistribution with Growth,* edited by Hollis Chenery et al. New York: Oxford University Press, 1974.

ALAVI, HAMZA. "The State in Post Colonial Societies: Pakistan and Bangladesh." *New Left Review* 74 (1972): 59–81.

ALBRIGHT, DAVID E. "A Comparative Reconceptualization of Civil-Military Relations." *World Politics* 32 (1980): 553–76.

ALSCHULER, LAWRENCE R. "Satellization and Stagnation in Latin America." *International Studies Quarterly* 20 (1976): 39–82.

AMIN, SAMIR. "Underdevelopment and Dependence in Black Africa—Origins and Contemporary Forms." *Journal of Modern African Studies* 10 (1972): 503–24.

AMSDEN, ALICE. "Taiwan's Economic History." *Modern China* 5 (1979): 341–80.

ANDREWS, BRUCE. "The Political Economy of World Capitalism: Theory and Practice." *International Organization* 36 (1982): 135–63.

BAER, WERNER, RICHARD NEWFARMER, AND THOMAS TREBAT. "On State Capitalism in Brazil: Some New Issues and Questions." *Inter-American Economic Affairs* 30 (1976): 69–91.

BALASSA, BELA. "The Changing International Division of Labor in Manufactured Goods." World Bank Staff Working Paper no. 329. Washington, D.C.: World Bank, 1979.

———. "Disequilibrium Analysis for Developing Economies: An Overview." *World Development* 10 (1982): 1027–38.

———. "The Newly-Industrializing Developing Countries after the Oil Crisis." *Weltwirtschaftliches Archiv* 117 (1981): 142–94.

———. "The Process of Industrial Development and Alternative Development Strategies." World Bank Staff Working Paper no. 438. Washington, D.C.: World Bank, 1980.

———. "Prospects for Trade in Manufactured Goods between Industrial and Developing Countries, 1978–1990." *Journal of Policy Modeling* 2 (1980): 437–55.

———. "Structural Adjustment Policies in Developing Economies." *World Development* 10 (1982): 23–38.

———. "The Tokyo Round and the Developing Countries." *Journal of World Trade Law* 14 (1980): 437–55.

———. "Trade in Manufactured Goods: Patterns of Change." World Bank Reprint Series no. 180. From *World Development* 9 (1981): 263–75.

BALL, NICOLE. "Understanding the Causes of African Famine." *Journal of Modern African Studies* 14 (1976): 517–22.

BANGUERO, HAROLD. *Columbia 2000: A Framework for Population, Employment, Growth, Income Distribution and Essential Human Needs Planning*. Bogota, Columbia: University of Los Andes, 1981 (mimeo.).

BARRETT, RICHARD E., AND MARTIN KING WHYTE. "Dependency Theory and Taiwan: Analysis of a Deviant Case." *American Journal of Sociology* 87 (1982): 1064–89.

BATES, ROBERT H. *Markets and States in Tropical Africa*. Berkeley and Los Angeles: University of California Press, 1981.

———. "Some Core Assumptions in Development Economics." Paper presented to the inaugural conference of the Society of Economic Anthropology, Bloomington, Indiana, 1981.

BAUMGARTNER, T., AND T. R. BURNS. "The Structuring of International Economic Relations." *International Studies Quarterly* 19 (1975): 125–59.

BECKER, DAVID G. "Development, Democracy, and Dependency in Latin America: A Post-Imperialist View." *Third World Quarterly* 6 (1984): 411–31.

———. "State, Power, and Class Forces in Peru, 1968–1972." Paper presented at the annual meeting of the American Political Science Association, Denver, 2–5 September 1982.

BENJAMIN, ROGER. *Limits of Politics: Collective Goods and Political Change in Postindustrial Societies.* Chicago: University of Chicago Press, 1980.

BENNETT, DOUGLAS, AND KENNETH SHARPE. "The State as Banker and Entrepreneur: The Last-Resort Character of the Mexican States' Economic Intervention, 1917–1976." *Comparative Politics* 12 (1980): 165–89.

BERG, ELLIOT J. "Socialism and Economic Development in Tropical Africa." *Quarterly Journal of Economics* 78 (1964): 549–73.

BIENEN, HENRY. "Military Rule and Political Process: Nigerian Examples." *Comparative Politics* 10 (1978): 205–25.

BIERSTEKER, THOMAS J. *Distortion or Development? Contending Perspectives on the Multinational Corporation.* Cambridge, Mass.: M.I.T. Press, 1978.

———. "The Illusion of State Power: Transnational Corporations and the Neutralization of Host Country Legislation." *Journal of Peace Research* 17 (1980): 207–21.

———. "Self-Reliance in Theory and Practice in Tanzanian Trade Relations." *International Organization* 34 (1980): 229–64.

BLITZER, CHARLES R., PETER B. CLARK, AND LANCE TAYLOR, EDS. *Economy-Wide Models and Development Planning.* New York: Oxford University Press, 1975.

BORNSCHIER, VOLKER. "Dependent Industrialization in the World Economy." *Journal of Conflict Resolution* 25 (1981): 371–400.

BORNSCHIER, VOLKER, AND THANH-HUYEN BALLMER-CAO. "Income Inequality: A Cross-National Study of the Relationships between MNC-Penetration, Dimensions of the Power Structure and Income Distribution." *American Sociological Review* 44 (1979): 487–506.

BORNSCHIER, VOLKER, CHRISTOPHER CHASE-DUNN AND RICHARD RUBINSON. "Cross-National Evidence of the Effects of Foreign Investment and Aid on Economic Growth and Inequality: A Survey of Findings and a Reanalysis." *American Journal of Sociology* 84 (1978): 651–83.

BOUSQUET, NICOLE. "From Hegemony to Competition: Cycles of the Core?" In *Processes of the World System,* edited by Terrence K. Hopkins and Immanuel Wallerstein, vol. 3, *Political Economy of the World System Annuals.* Beverly Hills: Sage Publications, 1980.

BOZZOLI, BELINDA. *The Political Nature of a Ruling Class: Capital and Ideology in South Africa, 1890–1933.* London: Routledge and Kegan Paul, 1981.

BRADBY, BARBARA. "The Destruction of Natural Economy." *Economy and Society* 4 (1975): 127–61.

BRENNER, ROBERT. "Agrarian Class Structure and Economic Development in Pre-Industrial Europe." *Past and Present* 70 (1976) 30–75.

BRETON, ALBERT. "The Economics of Nationalism." *Journal of Political Economy* 72 (1964): 376–86.

BREWSTER, HAVELOCK. "Economic Dependence: A Quantitative Interpretation." *Social and Economic Studies* 22 (1973): 90–95.

BRITTAN, SAMUEL. "The Economic Contradictions of Democracy." *British Journal of Political Science* 5 (1975): 129–59.

CAPORASO, JAMES A. "Dependence, Dependency, and Power in the Global System: A Structural and Behavioral Analysis." *International Organization* 32 (1978): 13–43.

———. "Dependency Theory: Continuities and Discontinuities in Development Studies." *International Organization* 34 (1980): 605–28.

———. "Industrialization in the Periphery: The Evolving Global Division of Labor." *International Studies Quarterly* 25 (1981): 347–84.

———. "Introduction to the Special Issue of *International Organization* on Dependence and Dependency in the Global System." *International Organization* 32 (1978): 1–12.

———. "The State's Role in Third World Economic Growth." *Annals of the American Academy of Political and Social Science* 459 (1982): 103–11.

———. "The World Bank Country Studies: Reactions of a Political Scientist." Paper prepared for delivery at National Science Foundation conference, Minneapolis, October 1981.

CARDOSO, FERNANDO H. "Associated-Dependent Development: Theoretical and Practical Implications." In *Authoritarian Brazil,* edited by Alfred Stepan. New Haven: Yale University Press, 1973.

———. "Dependent Capitalist Development in Latin America." *New Left Review* 74 (1972): 83–95.

———. "Industrialization, Dependency and Power in Latin America." *Berkeley Journal of Sociology* 17 (1972–1973): 79–95.

———. "On the Characterization of Authoritarian Regimes in Latin America." In *The New Authoritarianism in Latin America,* edited by David Collier. Princeton: Princeton University Press, 1979.

———. "The Originality of a Copy: CEPAL and the Idea of Development." *CEPAL Review,* no. 4 (1977): 7–40.

CARDOSO, FERNANDO H., AND ENZO FALETTO. "The Consumption of Dependency Theory in the United States." *Latin American Research Review* 12 (1977): 7–24.

———. *Dependency and Development in Latin America.* Translated by Marjory M. Urquidi. Berkeley and Los Angeles: University of California Press, 1979.

CHAMBERS, R. "Rural Poverty Unperceived: Problems and Remedies." *World Development* 9 (1981): 1–19.

CHASE-DUNN, CHRISTOPHER. "Core-Periphery Relations: The Effects of

Core Competition." In *Social Change in the Capitalist World Economy,* edited by Barbara H. Kaplan. Beverly Hills: Sage Publications 1978.

———. "The Effects of International Economic Dependence on Development and Inequality: A Cross-National Study." *American Sociological Review* 40 (1975): 720–38.

CHASE-DUNN, CHRISTOPHER, AND RICHARD RUBINSON. "Cycles, Trends, and New Departures in World-System Development." In *National Development and the World System: Educational, Economic, and Political Change, 1950–1970,* edited by John W. Meyer and Michael T. Hannan. Chicago: University of Chicago Press, 1979.

———. "Toward a Structural Perspective on the World-System." *Politics and Society* 7 (1977): 453–76.

CHENERY, HOLLIS B. "Patterns of Industrial Growth." *American Economic Review* 50 (1960): 624–54.

———. "Transitional Growth and World Industrialization." In *The International Allocation of Economic Activity,* edited by B. Ohlin. New York: Holmes and Meier, 1977.

CHENERY, HOLLIS, AND MOISES SYRQUIN. *Patterns of Development, 1950–1970.* New York: Oxford University Press, 1975.

CHENERY, HOLLIS, ET AL. *Redistribution with Growth.* New York: Oxford University Press, 1974.

CHILCOTE, RONALD H., AND JOEL EDELSTEIN, EDS. *Latin America: The Struggle with Dependency and Beyond.* Cambridge, Mass.: Schenkman, 1974.

CHOUCRI, NAZLI, AND ROBERT C. NORTH. *Nations in Conflict.* San Francisco: W. H. Freeman, 1975.

CHRISTENSEN, CHERYL. "World Hunger: A Structural Approach." *International Organization* 32 (1978): 745–74.

CLAIRMONTE, FREDERICK F. "Bananas." In *Commodity Trade of the Third World,* edited by Cheryl Payer. New York: John Wiley and Son, 1975.

CLARK, CAL. "Dependent Development: A Socialist Variant." *International Studies Quarterly* 27 (1983): 271–93.

———. "Economic Development in Taiwan: Implications for Political Economy Theories." Paper presented at the twenty-fifth annual conference of the International Studies Association, Atlanta, March 1984.

CLARKE, SIMON. "Capital, Fractions of Capital and the State: 'Neo-Marxist' Analysis of the South African State." *Capital and Class* 5 (1978): 32–77.

CLEAVER, HARRY M., JR. "The Contradictions of the Green Revolution." *American Economic Review* 62 (1972): 177–86.

CNUDDE, CHARLES F., AND DEANE E. NEUBAUER. "New Trends in Democratic Theory." In *Empirical Democratic Theory,* edited by Charles F. Cnudde and Deane E. Neubauer. Chicago: Markham Publishing, 1969.

COHEN, JOHN M. "Effects of Green Revolution Strategies on Tenants and Small Scale Landowners in the Chilalo Region of Ethiopia." *Journal of Developing Areas* 9 (1975): 335–58.

COLBURN, FORREST D. "Current Studies of Peasants and Rural Development: Applications of the Political Economy Approach." *World Politics* 34 (1982): 437–49.

COLLIER, DAVID. "Overview of the Bureaucratic-Authoritarian Model." In *The New Authoritarianism in Latin America,* edited by David Collier. Princeton: Princeton University Press, 1979.

COLLIER, DAVID, ED. *The New Authoritarianism in Latin America.* Princeton: Princeton University Press, 1979.

COLLIER, RUTH BERINS. "Parties, Coups, and Authoritarian Rule: Patterns of Political Change in Tropical Africa." *Comparative Political Studies* 11 (1978): 62–93.

COOPER, FREDERICK. "Africa and the World Economy." *African Studies Review* 24 (1981): 1–86.

COX, ROBERT W. "Ideologies and the New International Economic Order: Reflections on Some Recent Literature." *International Organization* 33 (1979): 257–302.

CRANE, GEORGE T. "The Taiwanese Ascent." In *Ascent and Decline in the World System,* edited by Edward Friedman. Beverly Hills: Sage Publications, 1982.

CUMINGS, BRUCE. "Interest and Ideology in the Study of Agrarian Politics." *Politics and Society* 10 (1981): 467–95.

———. "The Origins and Development of the Northeast Asian Political Economy: Industrial Sectors, Product Cycles and Political Consequences." *International Organization* 38 (1984): 1–40.

CURRIE, LAUCHLIN. "Is There an Urban Bias? Critique of Michael Lipton's *Why Poor People Stay Poor: Urban Bias in World Development.*" *Journal of Economic Studies* 6 (1979): 86–105.

DAHRENDORF, RALF. *The New Liberty: Survival and Justice in a Changing World.* Stanford: Stanford University Press, 1975.

DE JANVRY, ALAIN. "Inducement of Technological and Institutional Innovations: An Interpretative Framework." In *Resource Allocation and Productivity in National and International Agricultural Research,* edited by Thomas M. Arndt, Dana G. Dalrymple, and Vernon W. Ruttan. Minneapolis: University of Minnesota Press, 1977.

DERVIS, KEMAL, AND SHERMAN ROBINSON. "The Foreign Exchange Gap, Growth and Industrial Strategy in Turkey: 1973–83." World Bank Staff Working Paper no. 306. Washington, D.C.: World Bank, 1978.

DERVIS, KEMAL, JAIME DE MELO, AND SHERMAN ROBINSON. *General Equilib-*

*rium Models for Development Policy.* Cambridge, England: Cambridge University Press, 1982.

DIAMANT, ALFRED. "Bureaucracy and Public Policy in Neocorporatist Settings: Some European Lessons." *Comparative Politics* 14 (1981): 101–24.

DÍAZ ALEJANDRO, CARLOS F. "Delinking North and South: Unshackled or Unhinged?" In *Rich and Poor Nations in the World Economy,* edited by Albert Fishlow et al. New York: McGraw-Hill, 1978.

———. *Essays on the Economic History of the Argentine Republic.* New Haven: Yale University Press, 1970.

DOLAN, MICHAEL B., AND BRIAN W. TOMLIN. "First World–Third World Linkages: External Relations and Economic Development." *International Organization* 34 (1980): 41–63.

DORE, R. P. "Late Development or Something Else? Industrial Relations in Britain, Japan, Mexico, Sri Lanka, and Senegal." Unpublished paper, 1974.

DUVALL, RAYMOND D. "Dependence and *Dependencia* Theory: Notes toward Precision of Concept and Argument." *International Organization* 32 (1978): 51–78.

DUVALL, RAYMOND D., AND JOHN R. FREEMAN. "The State and Dependent Capitalism." *International Studies Quarterly* 25 (1981): 99–118.

———. "The Techno-Bureaucratic Elite and the Entrepreneurial State in Dependent Industrialization." *American Political Science Review* 77 (1983): 569–87.

DUVALL, RAYMOND, STEVEN JACKSON, BRUCE M. RUSSETT, DUNCAN SNIDAL, AND DAVID SYLVAN. "A Formal Model of '*Dependencia*' Theory': Structure and Measurement." In *From National Development to Global Community: Essays in Honor of Karl W. Deutsch,* edited by Richard L. Merritt and Bruce M. Russett. London: Allen and Unwin, 1981.

ECKSTEIN, SUSAN. "Capitalist Constraints on Cuban Socialist Development." *Comparative Politics* 12 (1980): 253–74.

EVANS, PETER B. *Dependent Development: The Alliance of Multinational, State and Local Capital in Brazil,* Princeton: Princeton University Press, 1979.

———. "Foreign Investment and Industrial Transformation: A Brazilian Case Study." *Journal of Development Economics* 3 (1976): 119–39.

———. "Recent Research on Multinational Corporations." *Annual Review of Sociology* 7 (1981): 199–223.

———. "Reinventing the Bourgeoisie: State Entrepreneurship and Class Formation in Dependent Capitalist Development." Unpublished paper, 1981.

FAGEN, RICHARD R. "Equity in the South in the Context of North-South Relations." In *Rich and Poor Nations in the World Economy,* edited by Albert Fishlow et al. New York: McGraw-Hill, 1978.

————. "Studying Latin American Politics: Some Implications of a *Dependencia* Approach." *Latin American Research Review* 12 (1977): 3–26.

FALK, RICHARD. "A World Order Perspective on Authoritarian Tendencies." *Alternatives: A Journal of World Policy* 5 (1969): 127–93.

FEENY, DAVID H. "Competing Hypotheses of Underdevelopment: A Thai Case Study." Working Paper no. 78–22, 1978, Department of Economics, McMaster University, Hamilton, Ontario, Canada.

————. "Infrastructure Linkages and Trade Performance: Thailand, 1900–1940." *Explorations in Economic History* 19 (1982): 1–27.

————. *The Political Economy of Productivity: Thai Agricultural Development, 1881–1975.* Vancouver: University of British Columbia Press, 1982.

FIELDS, GARY S. *Poverty, Inequality and Development.* Cambridge, England: Cambridge University Press, 1980.

FISHLOW, ALBERT, CARLOS F. DÍAZ ALEJANDRO, RICHARD R. FAGEN, AND ROGER D. HANSEN, EDS. *Rich and Poor Nations.* New York: McGraw-Hill, 1978.

FOSTER-CARTER, AIDAN. "The Modes of Production Controversy." *New Left Review* 107 (1978): 47–77.

FOX, M. LOUISE. "Income Distribution in Post-1964 Brazil." *Journal of Economic History* 43 (1983): 261–71.

FRANK, ANDRE GUNDER. *Capitalism and Underdevelopment in Latin America: Historical Studies of Chile and Brazil.* New York: Monthly Review Press, 1967.

FREEMAN, JOHN R. "State Entrepreneurship and Dependent Development." *American Journal of Political Science* 26 (1982): 90–112.

FRIEDEN, JEFF. "Third World Indebted Industrialization: International Finance and State Capitalism in Mexico, Brazil, Algeria, and South Korea." *International Organization* 35 (1981): 407–31.

FRIEDMAN, DAVID. "A Theory of the Size and Shape of Nations." *Journal of Political Economy* 85 (1977): 59–77.

FROBEL, FOLKER, JURGEN HEINRICHS, AND OTTO KREYE. *The New International Division of Labor.* Cambridge, England: Cambridge University Press, 1980. Originally published in German as *Die neue internationale Arbeitsteilung: Strukturelle Arbeitslosigkeit in den Industrielandern und die Industrielisiering der Entwicklungslander.* Hamburg: Rowohlt Taxchenbach, 1977.

FURTADO, CELSO. *The Economic Growth of Brazil: A Survey from Colonial to Modern Times.* Berkeley and Los Angeles: University of California Press, 1963.

GALLAGHER, CHARLES. "The Shape of Things to Come." *American Universities Field Staff Report,* no. 33 (1979).

GEORGE, ALEXANDER L. "Case Studies and Theory Development: The Method of Structured Focused Comparison." In *Diplomacy: New*

*Approaches in History, Theory, and Policy,* edited by Paul Gordon Lauren. New York: Free Press, 1979.

GEREFFI, GARY. "Drug Firms and Dependency in Mexico: The Case of the Steroid Hormone Industry." *International Organization* 32 (1978): 237–86.

GERSCHENKRON, ALEXANDER. *Economic Backwardness in Historical Perspective.* Cambridge, Mass.: Harvard University Press, 1962.

GILPIN, ROBERT. *U.S. Power and the Multi-national Corporation.* New York: Basic Books, 1975.

GO, EVELYN. "International Reserves: Factors Determining Needs and Adequacy." Asian Development Bank Economic Staff Paper no. 1. May 1981.

GOTSCH, CARL H. "Technical Change and the Distribution of Income in Rural Areas." *American Journal of Agricultural Economics* 54 (1972): 326–41.

GOUREVITCH, PETER. "The Second Image Reversed: The International Sources of Domestic Politics." *International Organization* 32 (1978): 881–912.

GRINOLS, EARL, AND JAGDISH BHAGWATI. "Foreign Capital, Savings and Dependence: A Reply to Mr. Wasow." *Review of Economis and Statistics* 61 (1979): 154–56.

HAGELBERG, G. B. "Sugar." In *Commodity Trade of the Third World,* edited by Cheryl Payer. New York: John Wiley and Son, 1975.

HART, KEITH. *The Political Economy of West African Agriculture.* Cambridge, England: Cambridge University Press, 1982.

HECHTER, MICHAEL. "Karl Polyani's Social Theory: A Critique." *Politics and Society* 10 (1981): 339–429.

HIBBS, DOUGLAS A., JR. *Mass Political Violence.* New York: Wiley-Interscience, 1973.

HIGGOTT, RICHARD A. "From Modernization Theory to Public Policy: Continuity and Change in the Political Science of Political Development." *Studies in Comparative International Development* 15 (1980): 26–58.

———. "Structural Dependence and Decolonization in a West African Land-Locked State: Niger." *Review of African Political Economy* 17 (1980): 43–58.

HIRSCHMAN, ALBERT O. "Beyond Asymmetry: Critical Notes on Myself as a Young Man and on Some Other Old Friends." *International Organization* 32 (1978): 45–50.

———. *Essays in Trespassing: Economics to Politics and Beyond.* Cambridge, England: Cambridge University Press, 1981.

———. "The Political Economy of Import-Substitution Industrialization in Latin America." In *A Bias for Hope,* edited by Albert Hirschman. New Haven: Yale University Press, 1971.

———. "The Rise and Decline of Development Economics." In *Essays in*

*Trespassing.* Cambridge, England: Cambridge University Press, 1981.

———. "The Turn to Authoritarianism in Latin America and the Search for Its Economic Determinants." In *The New Authoritarianism in Latin America,* edited by David Collier. Princeton: Princeton University Press, 1979.

HIRSCHMAN, ALBERT O., AND MICHAEL ROTHSCHILD. "The Changing Tolerance for Economic Inequality in the Course of Economic Development." *Quarterly Journal of Economics* 87 (1973): 544–66.

HO, SAMUEL P. S. "South Korea and Taiwan: Development Prospects and Problems in the 1980s." *Asian Survey* 21 (1981): 1175–96.

HOPKINS, MICHAEL F., AND ROLPH VAN DER HOEVEN. "Policy Analysis in a Socioeconomic Model of Basic Needs Applied to Four Countries." *Journal of Policy Modeling* 4 (1982): 425–55.

HOPKINS, RAYMOND F. "Securing Authority: The View from the Top." *World Politics* 24 (1972): 271–92.

HSIUNG, JAMES C., ET AL., EDS. *Contemporary Republic of China: The Taiwan Experience, 1950–1980.* New York: American Association for Chinese Studies, 1981.

HUGHES, BARRY B. "GLOBUS 6 Economic Model." GSIS, University of Denver. Unpublished paper, 1984.

———. *International Futures Simulation.* Iowa City: CONDUIT, 1982.

———. *World Modeling.* Lexington, Mass.: Lexington Books, 1980.

———. "World Models: The Bases of Difference." GSIS, University of Denver. Unpublished paper, 1984.

HUNTINGTON, SAMUEL P. "The Change to Change: Modernization, Development, and Politics." *Comparative Politics* 3 (1971): 283–322.

HYMER, STEPHEN H. *The Multinational Corporation: A Radical Approach.* Cambridge, England: Cambridge University Press, 1979.

INKELES, ALEX. "Convergence and Divergence in Industrial Societies." In *Directions of Change: Modernization Theory, Research, and Realities,* edited by Mustafa O. Attir, Burkart Holzner, and Zdenek Suda. Boulder: Westview Press, 1981.

———. "Modernization and Family Patterns: A Test of Convergence Theory." In *Family History,* vol. 1, *Conspectus of History,* edited by Dwight W. Hoover and John T. A. Koumoulides. Muncie: Ball State University Department of History, 1980.

INKELES, ALEX, AND LARRY DIAMOND. "Personal Development and National Development: A Cross-National Perspective." In *The Quality of Life: Comparative Studies,* edited by Alexander Szalai and Frank M. Andrews. Beverly Hills: Sage Publications, 1980.

ISENMAN, PAUL J., AND HANS W. SINGER. "Food Aid: Its Potential Disincentives to Agriculture." *Development Digest* 15 (1977): 15–24.

JACKMAN, ROBERT W. "Dependence on Foreign Investment and Economic Growth in the Third World." *World Politics* 34 (1982): 175–96.

————. "Politicians in Uniform: Military Governments and Social Change in the Third World." *American Political Science Review* 70 (1976): 1078–97.

JACKSON, STEVEN, BRUCE RUSSETT, DUNCAN SNIDAL, AND DAVID SYLVAN. "Conflict and Coercion in Dependent States." *Journal of Conflict Resolution* 22 (1978): 627–57.

JACKSON, STEVEN, AND DUNCAN SNIDAL. "The Calculus of Coercion: International Capital, Domestic Coalitions, and Coercion as Public Policy in Dependent Countries." Paper prepared for delivery at the annual meeting of the American Political Science Association. New York, September 1981.

JODICE, DAVID A. "Sources of Change in Third World Regimes for Foreign Direct Investment, 1968–1976." *International Organization* 34 (1980): 177–206.

JOHNSON, CHALMERS A. "Introduction—The Taiwan Model." In *Contemporary Republic of China: The Taiwan Experience, 1950–1980*, edited by James C. Hsiung et al. New York: American Association for Chinese Studies, 1981.

————. *MITI and the Japanese Miracle: The Growth of Industrial Policy, 1925–1975*. Stanford: Stanford University Press, 1982.

JOHNSON, WILLARD R., AND ERNEST J. WILSON. "The 'Oil Crises' and African Economies: Oil Wave on a Tidal Flood of Industrial Price Inflation." *Daedalus* 3 (1982): 211–41.

JOHNSTON, BRUCE F., AND WILLIAM C. CLARK. "Rural Development Programs: A Critical Review of Past Experience." Paper prepared for the Eighteenth International Conference of Agricultural Economists, Jakarta, Indonesia, August–September 1982.

JOLLY, RICHARD. "International Dimensions." In *Redistribution with Growth*, edited by Hollis Chenery et al. New York: Oxford University Press, 1974.

JORGENSEN, DALE W. "Testing Alternative Theories of the Development of a Dual Economy." Reprinted in *Development Economics and Policy*, edited by Ian Livingstone. London: George Allen and Unwin, 1967.

JOWITT, KENNETH. "Scientific Socialist Regimes in Africa." In *Socialism in Sub-Saharan Africa: A New Assessment*, edited by Carl G. Rosberg and Thomas M. Callaghy. Berkeley: Institute of International Studies, 1979.

KASFIR, NELSON. "Explaining Ethnic Political Participation." *World Politics* 31 (1979): 365–88.

KATZENSTEIN, PETER J. "International Relations and Domestic Structures: Foreign Economic Policies of Advanced Industrial States." *International Organization* 30 (1976): 1–45.

KAUFMAN, ROBERT R. "Industrial Change and Authoritarian Rule in Latin America: A Concrete Review of the Bureaucratic-Authoritarian

Model." In *The New Authoritarianism in Latin America,* edited by David Collier. Princeton: Princeton University Press, 1979.

KAUFMAN, ROBERT R., HARRY I. CHERNOTSKY, AND DANIEL S. GELLER. "A Preliminary Test of the Theory of Dependency." *Comparative Politics* 7 (1975): 303–30.

KEOHANE, ROBERT O. "The Demand for International Regimes." *International Organization* 36 (1982): 325–55.

———. "Hegemonic Leadership and U.S. Foreign Economic Policy in the 'Long Decade' of the 1950s." In *America in a Changing World Political Economy,* edited by William P. Avery and David P. Rapkin. New York: Longman, 1982.

KERKVLIET, BENEDICT J. "Martial Law in a Nueva Ecija Village, the Philippines." Unpublished paper, 1980.

KLEIN, PHILIP A. "Confronting Power in Economics: A Pragmatic Evaluation." *Journal of Economic Issues* 14 (1980): 871–96.

KNIGHT, PETER T., ET AL., EDS. "Implementing Programs of Human Development." World Bank Staff Working Paper no. 403. Washington, D.C.: World Bank, 1980.

KORTEN, DAVID C. "Community Organization and Rural Development: A Learning Process Approach." *Public Administration Review* 5 (1980): 480–511.

———. "Social Development: Putting People First." In *Bureaucracy and the Poor: Closing the Gap,* edited by David C. Korten and Felipe B. Alonso. New York: McGraw-Hall, 1981.

———. "Toward a Technology for Managing Social Development." In *Population and Social Development Management: A Challenge for Management Schools,* edited by David C. Korten. Caracas, Venezuela: Instituto de Estudios Superiores de Administración, 1979.

KRASNER, STEPHEN D. "State Power and the Structure of International Trade." *World Politics* 28 (1976): 317–47.

KREININ, MORDECHAI E., AND J. M. FINGER. "A Critical Survey of the New International Economic Order." *Journal of World Trade Law* 10 (1976): 493–512.

KREUGER, ANNE O. "The Political Economy of the Rent-Seeking Society." *American Economic Review* 64 (1974): 291–303.

KUBO, YUJI, JEFFREY D. LEWIS, JAIME DE MELO, AND SHERMAN ROBINSON. "Multisector Models and the Analysis of Alternative Development Strategies: An Application to Korea." World Bank Staff Working Paper no. 563. Washington, D.C.: World Bank, 1983.

KURTH, JAMES R. "Industrial Change and Political Change: A European Perspective." In *The New Authoritarianism in Latin America,* edited by David Collier. Princeton: Princeton University Press, 1978.

———. "The International Politics of Postindustrial Societies: The Role of the Multinational Corporation." In *Stress and Contradiction in Modern Capitalism: Public Policy and the Theory of the State,* edited by

Leon N. Lindberg et al. Lexington, Mass.: Lexington Books, 1975.

———. "Political Consequences of the Product Cycle: Industrial History and Political Outcomes." *International Organization* 33 (1979): 1–34.

KUZNETS, SIMON. "Economic Growth and the Contribution of Agriculture: Notes on Measurement." In *Agriculture in Economic Development*, edited by Carl Eicher and Lawrence Witt. New York: McGraw-Hill, 1964.

———. "Economic Growth and Income Equality." *American Economic Review* 45 (1955): 1–28.

———. "Growth and Structural Shifts." In *Economic Growth and Structural Change in Taiwan: The Postwar Experience of the Republic of China*, edited by Walter Galenson. Ithaca: Cornell University Press, 1979.

———. *Quantitative Aspects of the Economic Growth of Nations: Distribution of Income by Size*, vol. 11, no. 2, pt. 2. Chicago: University of Chicago Press, 1963.

LACLAU, ERNESTO. "Feudalism and Capitalism in Latin America." In *Politics and Ideology in Marxist Theory: Capitalism-Fascism-Populism*, edited by Ernesto Laclau. London: New Left Books 1977.

———. "Teorías marxistas del estado: debates y perspectivas." In *Estado y política en América Latina*, edited by Norbert Lechner. Mexico City: Siglo Veintiuno, 1981.

LALL, SANJANAYA. "Is 'Dependence' a Useful Concept in Analysing Under-development?" *World Development* 3 (1975): 799–810.

LANGDON, STEVEN. "The Multinational Corporation in the Kenya Political Economy." In *Readings on the Multinational Corporation in Kenya*, edited by Raphael Kaplinsky. Nairobi: Oxford University Press, 1978.

LEE, EDDY. "Changing Approaches to Rural Development." *International Labour Review* 119 (1980): 99–114.

LEFF, NATHANIEL H. "Economic Development through Bureaucratic Corruption." *American Behavioral Scientist* 8 (1964): 8–14.

———. "Entrepreneurship and Economic Development: The Problem Revisited." *Journal of Economic Literature* 17 (1979): 46–64.

———. *Underdevelopment and Development in Brazil: Reassessing the Obstacles to Economic Development*. London: Allen and Unwin, 1982.

LEHMANN, DAVID. "The Death of Land Reform: A Polemic." *World Development* 6 (1978): 339–45.

LELE, UMA. "Cooperatives and the Poor: A Comparative Perspective." *World Development* 9 (1981): 55–72.

LENSKI, GERHARD E. *Power and Privilege: A Theory of Social Stratification.* New York: McGraw-Hill, 1966.

LEVI, MARGARET. "The Predatory Theory of Rule." *Politics and Society* 10 (1981): 431–65.

LEWIS, W. ARTHUR. "The Slowing Down of the Engine of Growth." *American Economic Review* 70 (1980): 555–64.

———. "The State of Development Theory." *American Economic Review* 74 (1984): 1–10.

LEYS, COLIN. "Political Perspectives." In *Development in a Divided World,* edited by Dudley Seers and Leonard Joy. Harmondsworth: Penguin, 1970.

———. "Underdevelopment and Dependency: Critical Notes." *Journal of Contemporary Asia* 7 (1977): 92–107.

LIBBY, RONALD T. "Theoretical Perspectives on 'Form of the State' in Africa and Latin America." University of Notre Dame. Unpublished paper, 1982.

———. "Transnational Class Alliance in Zambia." University of Notre Dame. Unpublished paper, 1982.

LIBBY, RONALD T., AND MICHAEL E. WOAKES. "Nationalization and the Displacement of Development Policy in Zambia." *African Studies Review* 23 (1980): 33–50.

LIEBERMAN, SAMUEL S. *Rural Development and Fertility Transition in South Asia: The Case for a Broad-Based Strategy.* New York: Population Council, 1980.

LIPIETZ, ALAIN. "Marx or Rostow?" *New Left Review* 132 (1982): 48–58.

LIPSET, SEYMOUR M. "Racial and Ethnic Tensions in the Third World." In *The Third World: Premises of U.S. Policies,* edited by W. Scott Thompson. San Francisco: Institute for Contemporary Studies, 1978.

———. "Some Social Requisites of Democracy: Economic Development and Political Legitimacy." *American Political Science Review* 53 (1959): 69–105.

———. "Values, Education, and Entrepreneurship." In *Elites in Latin America,* edited by Seymour M. Lipset and Aldo Solari. New York: Oxford University Press, 1967.

LIPSON, CHARLES. "The Transformation of Trade: The Sources and Effects of Regime Change." *International Organization* 36 (1982): 417–55.

LIPTON, MICHAEL. "Urban Bias and Food Policy in Poor Countries." *Food Policy* 1 (1975): 41–50.

LOEHR, WILLIAM. "Economic Growth: Distribution and Incomes of the Poor." University of Denver. Unpublished paper, 1978.

LOFCHIE, MICHAEL F. "Agrarian Crisis and Economic Liberalisation in Tanzania." *Journal of Modern African Studies* 16 (1978): 451–75.

———. "Political and Economic Origins of African Hunger." *Journal of Modern African Studies* 13 (1975): 551–67.

————. "The Uganda Coup—Class Action by the Military." *Journal of Modern African Studies* 10 (1972): 19–35.

LOWENTHAL, ABRAHAM F. "United States Policy toward Latin America: Liberal, Radical and Bureaucratic Perspectives." *Latin American Research Review* 8 (1973): 3–25.

MCCARTHY, F. DESMOND. "General Equilibrium Model for Egypt." In *Modeling Growing Economies in Equilibrium and Disequilibrium*, edited by Allen C. Kelly, Warren C. Sanderson, and Jeffrey G. Williamson. Durham, N.C.: Duke University Press, 1983.

MCCLINTOCK, CYNTHIA. *Peasant Cooperatives and Political Change in Peru.* Princeton: Princeton University Press, 1981.

MCGOWAN, PATRICK J., AND DALE L. SMITH. "Economic Dependency in Black Africa: An Analysis of Competing Theories." *International Organization* 32 (1978): 179–235.

MAHLER, VINCENT A. *Dependency Approaches to International Political Economy: A Cross-National Study.* New York: Columbia University Press, 1980.

MALLOY, JAMES M., ED. *Authoritarianism and Corporatism in Latin America.* Pittsburgh: University of Pittsburgh Press, 1977.

MANN, MICHAEL. "Review Article: The Pre-Industrial State." *Political Studies* 28 (1980): 297–304.

————. "State and Society, 1130–1815: An Analysis of English State Finances." In *Political Power and Social Theory*, vol. 1. Greenwich, Conn.: JAI Press, 1980.

MARINI, RUY MAURO. "Brazilian Sub-Imperialism." *Monthly Review* 9 (1972): 14–24.

MARTIN, ANDREW. "Political Constraints on Economic Strategies in Advanced Industrial Societies." *Comparative Political Studies* 10 (1977): 323–54.

MAXWELL, S. J., AND HANS W. SINGER. "Food Aid to Developing Countries: A Survey." *World Development* 7 (1979): 225–47.

MENDONÇA DE BARROS, JOSE ROBERTO, AND DOUGLAS H. GRAHAM. "The Brazilian Economic Miracle Revisited: Private and Public Sector Initiative in a Market Economy." *Latin American Research Review* 13 (1978): 5–38.

MERKX, GILBERT W. "Recessions and Rebellions in Argentina, 1870–1970." *Hispanic American Historical Review* 53 (1973): 285–95.

MESAROVIČ, MIHAJLO, AND EDWARD PESTEL. *Mankind at the Turning Point.* New York: E. P. Dutton, 1974.

MEYER, JOHN W., AND MICHAEL T. HANNAN. "National Development in a Changing World System: An Overview." In *National Development in the World System*, edited by John W. Meyer and Michael T. Hannan. Chicago: University of Chicago Press, 1979.

MORAN, THEODORE H. "Multinational Corporations and Dependency: A

Dialogue for *Dependentistas* and Non-*Dependentistas*." *International Organization* 32 (1978): 79–100.

———. *Multinational Corporations and the Politics of Dependence: Copper in Chile*. Princeton: Princeton University Press, 1974.

———. "Transnational Strategies of Protection and Defense by Multinational Corporations: Spreading the Risk and Raising the Cost for Nationalization in Natural Resources." *International Organization* 27 (1973): 273–87.

MURRAY, ROBIN. "The Internationalization of Capital and the Nation State." *New Left Review* 67 (1971): 84–109.

MYTELKA, LYNN K. "Technological Dependence in the Andean Group." *International Organization* 32 (1978): 101–39.

NAYER, BALDEV RAJ. "Political Mainsprings of Economic Planning in the New Nations: The Modernization Imperative versus Social Mobilization." *Comparative Politics* 6 (1974): 341–66.

ODELL, JOHN S. "Latin American Trade Negotiations with the United States." *International Organization* 34 (1980): 207–28.

O'DONNELL, GUILLERMO. "Comparative Historical Formations of the State Apparatus and Socio-Economic Change in the Third World." *International Social Science Journal* 32 (*On the State*) (1980): 717–29.

———. *Modernization and Bureaucratic Authoritarianism: Studies in South American Politics*. Berkeley: Institute of International Studies, 1973.

———. "Reflections on the Patterns of Change in the Bureaucratic-Authoritarian State." *Latin American Research Review* 13 (1978): 3–38.

———. "States and Alliances in Argentina, 1956–1976." *Journal of Development Studies* 15 (1978): 3–33.

O'DONNELL, GUILLERMO, AND DELFINA LINCK. *Dependencia y autonomía*. Buenos Aires: Amorrortu, 1973.

OLIVIERA CAMPOS, ROBERTO DE, AND RAPHAEL VALENTINO. "Brazil." In *The Political Economy of New and Old Industrial Countries*, edited by Christopher Saunders. London: Butterworth, 1981.

OLSON, MANCUR, JR. "Rapid Growth as a Destabilizing Force." *Journal of Economic History* 23 (1963): 529–52.

———. *The Rise and Decline of Nations*. New Haven: Yale University Press, 1982.

OXAAL, IVAR, TONY BARNETT, AND TONY BOOTH. *Beyond the Sociology of Development*. London: Routledge and Kegan Paul, 1975.

PAIGE, JEFFERY M. "One, Two, or Many Vietnams? Social Theory and Peasant Revolution in Vietnam and Guatemala." CRSO Working Paper no. 275. Center for Research and Social Organization, Ann Arbor, 1982.

PALMA, GABRIEL. "Dependency: A Formal Theory of Underdevelopment or a Methodology for the Analysis of Concrete Situations of Underdevelopment?" *World Development* 6 (1978): 881–924.

PAPANEK, GUSTAV F. "The Effect of Aid and Other Resource Transfers on Savings and Growth in Less Developed Countries." *Economic Journal* 82 (1972): 934–50.

PARSON, JACK. "Theory and Reality in the Periphery: The State in Contemporary Botswana." Paper presented at the annual meeting of the American Political Science Association, Denver, September 1982.

PAUKERT, F. "Income Distribution at Different Levels of Development: A Survey of Evidence." *International Labor Review* 108 (August–September 1973): 97–126.

PAYER, CHERYL. "Coffee." In *Commodity Trade of the Third World*, edited by Cheryl Payer. New York: John Wiley and Son, 1975.

PETERSON, WILLIS L. "International Farm Prices and the Social Cost of Cheap Food Policies." *American Journal of Agricultural Economics* 61 (1979): 12–21.

PETRAS, J. "State Capitalism and the Third World." *Development and Change* 8 (1977): 1–17.

PFEFFERMANN, GUY, AND RICHARD WEBB. "Poverty and Income Distribution in Brazil, 1960–1980." *Review of Income and Wealth*, Series 29 (1983): 101–24. Also in *Revista Brasileira de Economia* 37 (1983): 145–75.

PREISER, E. "Property, Power and the Distribution of Income." In *Power in Economics: Selected Readings*, edited by Kurt Wilhelm Rothschild. Harmondsworth: Penguin, 1971.

PRZEWORSKI, ADAM. "Material Bases of Consent: Economics and Politics in a Hegemonic System." *Political Power and Social Theory* 1 (1980): 21–66.

———. "Material Interests, Class Compromise, and the Transition to Socialism." *Politics and Society* 10 (1980): 125–53.

———. "Proletariat into a Class: The Process of Class Formation from Karl Kautsky's *The Class Struggle* to Recent Controversies." *Politics and Society* 8 (1977): 343–401.

PRZEWORSKI, ADAM, AND JOHN SPRAGUE. "Class Mobilization in Selected Western European Political Systems." Paper presented at the annual meeting of the American Political Science Association, New York, August–September 1978.

RANIS, GUSTAV. "Equity with Growth in Taiwan: How 'Special' is the 'Special Case'?" *World Development* 6 (1978): 397–409.

RAPKIN, DAVID P., AND WILLIAM P. AVERY. "U.S. International Economic Policy in a Period of Hegemonic Decline." In *America in a Changing World Political Economy*, edited by William P. Avery and David P. Rapkin. New York: Longman, 1982.

REYNOLDS, CLARK W. "Bankers as Revolutionaries in the Process of Development." In *Debt and the Less Developed Countries*, edited by Jonathan D. Aronson. Boulder: Westview Press, 1979.

———. "The New Terms of Trade Problem: Economic Rents in International Exchange." In *Economics in the Long View: Essays in Honour of Walter W. Rostow,* edited by Charles P. Kindleberger and Guido di Tella, vol. 1. New York: New York University Press, 1982.

——. "Social and Political Interaction in the Economic Development of a Disequilibrium System: Some Latin American Examples." *Food Research Institute Studies in Agricultural Economics, Trade, and Development* 10 (1971): 89–108.

RODGERS, GERRY, MIKE HOPKINS, AND RENÉ WERY. *Population, Employment and Inequality.* Farnborough: Saxon House for the International Labour Office, 1978.

ROGOWSKI, RONALD. "Rationalist Theories of Politics: A Midterm Report." *World Politics* 30 (1978): 296–323.

ROKKAN, STEIN. "Territories, Nations, Parties: Toward a Geoeconomic-Geopolitical Model for the Explanation of Variations within Western Europe." In *From National Development to Global Community: Essays in Honor of Karl W. Deutsch,* edited by Richard L. Merritt and Bruce M. Russett. London: Allen and Unwin, 1981.

RUBINSON, RICHARD. "The World-Economy and the Distribution of Income within States: A Cross-National Study." *American Sociological Review* 41 (1976): 638–59.

SAMUELSON, PAUL A. "International Trade and the Equalization of Factor Prices." *Economic Journal* 58 (1948): 163–84.

SCHATZBERG, MICHAEL G. "The Insecure State in Zaire: Resistance Within, Resistance Without." Paper prepared for delivery at the annual meeting of the American Political Science Association, Denver, September 1982.

SERRA, JOSÉ. "Three Mistaken Theses regarding the Connection between Industrialization and Authoritarian Regimes." In *The New Authoritarianism in Latin America,* edited by David Collier. Princeton: Princeton University Press, 1979.

SHEAHAN, JOHN. "Market-Oriented Economic Policies and Political Repression in Latin America." *Economic Development and Cultural Change* 28 (1980): 267–91.

SKIDMORE, THOMAS E. "Politics and Economic Policy Making in Authoritarian Brazil, 1937–71." In *Authoritarian Brazil,* edited by Alfred Stepan. New Haven: Yale University Press, 1973.

SKLAR, RICHARD L. "The Nature of Class Domination in Africa." *Journal of Modern African Studies* 17 (1979): 531–52.

SKOCPOL, THEDA. "A Critical Review of Barrington Moore's *Social Origins of Dictatorship and Democracy.*" *Politics and Society* 4 (1973): 1–34.

——. "What Makes Peasants Revolutionary?" *Comparative Politics* 14 (1982): 351–75.

SLATER, CHARLES C., GEOFFREY WALSHAM, AND MAHENDRA SHAH, EDS. *KENSIM: A Systems Simulation of the Developing Kenyan Economy 1970–78.* Boulder: Westview Press, 1977.

SMITH, TONY. "The Underdevelopment of Development Literature: The Case of Dependency Theory." *World Politics* 31 (1979): 247–88.

SNIDAL, DUNCAN. "Springboard or Plank? The 'Korean' Model for Export Platform Development." Paper presented at the Midwest Political Science Association Meeting, Milwaukee, April 1982.

SNIDAL, DUNCAN, RAYMOND DUVALL, STEVEN JACKSON, BRUCE RUSSETT, AND DAVID SYLVAN. "Testing 'Dependencia': An Overview of the Yale Dependence Project." German translation published in *Weltgesellschaft und Sozialstruktur: Festschrift zum 60. Geburtstag von Peter Heintz*, edited by Guido Hischier, René Levy, and Werner Obrecht. Diessenhofen: Rue gger, 1980.

SOUTHALL, AIDAN. "General Amin and the Coup: Great Man or Historical Inevitability?" *Journal of Modern African Studies* 13 (1975): 85–105.

———. "Social Disorganization in Uganda: Before, during, and after Amin." *Journal of Modern African Studies* 18 (1980): 627–56.

STALLINGS, BARBARA. "Euromarkets, Third World Countries and the International Political Economy." In *The New International Economy*, edited by Harry Makler, Alberto Martinelli, and Neil Smelser. Beverly Hills: Sage Publications, 1982.

STANILAND, MARTIN. "The Underdevelopment of Political Economy." Working Paper no. 32. Los Angeles: Center for International and Strategic Affairs, 1981.

STEPAN, ALFRED. "The New Professionalism of Internal Warfare and Military Role Expansion." In *Authoritarian Brazil: Origins, Policies, and Future*, edited by Alfred Stepan. New Haven: Yale University Press, 1973.

STEWART, FRANCES, AND PAUL STREETEN. "New Strategies for Development: Poverty, Income Distribution and Growth." *Oxford Economic Papers* 28 (1976): 381–405.

STINCHCOMBE, ARTHUR L. "Review Essay: The Growth of the World-System." *American Journal of Sociology* 87 (1982): 1389–95.

STONE, CARL. *The Caribbean and the World Economy: Patterns of Insertion and Contemporary Options*. Working Paper no. 1. San German, Puerto Rico: Universidad Interamericana de Puerto Rico, 1983.

SUNDARAM, JOMO KWAME. "The Ascendance of Bureaucratic Capitalists in Malaysia." *Alternatives: A Journal of World Policy* 7 (1982): 467–90.

SUNKEL, OSVALDO. "The Development of Development Thinking." In *Transnational Capitalism and National Development*, edited by José J. Villamil. Atlantic Highlands, N.J.: Humanities Press, 1979.

———. "Transnational Capitalism and National Disintegration in Latin America." *Social and Economic Studies* 22 (1973): 132–76.

SUNKEL, OSVALDO, AND PEDRO PAZ. *El subdesarrollo latinoamericano y la teoría del desarrollo*, 8th ed. Mexico: Siglo Veintiuno Editores, 1975.

SYLVAN, DAVID, DUNCAN SNIDAL, BRUCE RUSSETT, AND STEVEN JACKSON. "A Formal Model of 'Dependencia' Theory: Some Empirical Results." Paper prepared for the 1979 meeting of the American Political Science Association, Washington, D.C., August 1979.

SYLVAN, DAVID, ET AL. "The Peripheral Economies: Penetration and Economic Distortion, 1970–1975." In *Contending Approaches to World System Analysis*, edited by William R. Thompson. Beverly Hills: Sage Publications, 1983.

TAYLOR, LANCE. *Macro Models for Developing Countries.* New York: McGraw-Hill, 1979.

TIMMER, C. PETER. "The Political Economy of Rice in Asia: Indonesia." *Food Research Institute Studies* 14 (1975): 197–231.

TIMMER, C. PETER, AND WALTER P. FALCON. "The Political Economy of Rice Production and Trade in Asia." In *Agriculture in Development Theory*, edited by Lloyd G. Reynolds. New Haven: Yale University Press, 1975.

TODERO, MICHAEL P. *Economic Development in the Third World*, 2d. ed. New York: Longman, 1981.

TRIMBERGER, ELLEN KAY. "A Theory of Elite Revolutions." *Studies in Comparative International Development* 7 (1972): 191–207.

TYLER, WILLIAM G., AND J. PETER WOGART. "Economic Dependence and Marginalization." *Journal of Inter-American Studies and World Affairs* 15 (1973): 36–45.

VALENZUELA, J. SAMUEL, AND ARTURO VALENZUELA. "Modernization and Dependency: Alternative Perspectives in the Study of Latin American Underdevelopment." *Comparative Politics* 10 (1978): 535–57.

VENIERIS, YIANNIS P., AND DIPAK K. GUPTA. "Sociopolitical and Economic Dimensions of Development: A Cross-Sectional Model." *Economic Development and Cultural Change* 31 (1983): 727–56.

VERNON, RAYMOND. "International Investment and International Trade in the Product Cycle." *Quarterly Journal of Economics* 80 (1966): 190–207.

VINER, JACOB. "Power versus Plenty as Objectives of Foreign Policy in the Seventeenth and Eighteenth Centuries." *World Politics* 1 (1948): 1–29.

WALLERSTEIN, IMMANUEL. "Dependence in an Interdependent World: The Limited Possibilities of Transformation within the Capitalist World-Economy." *African Studies Review* 17 (1974): 1–26.

———. "The Rise and Future Demise of the World Capitalist System: Concepts for Comparative Analysis." *Comparative Studies in Society and History* 16 (1974): 387–415.

———. "Semiperipheral Countries and the Contemporary World Crisis." In *The Capitalist World Economy*, edited by Immanuel Wallerstein. Cambridge, England: Cambridge University Press, 1979.

WALLERSTEIN, MICHAEL. "The Collapse of Democracy in Brazil: Its Economic Determinants." *Latin American Research Review* 15 (1980): 3–40.

WARREN, BILL. "Imperialism and Capitalist Industrialization." *New Left Review* 81 (1973): 3–44.

WARWICK, DONALD. "Integrating Planning and Implementation: a Transactional Approach." Development Discussion Paper no. 63. Cambridge, Mass.: Harvard Institute for International Development, June 1979.

WASOW, BERNARD. "Saving and Dependence with Externally Financed Growth." *Review of Economics and Statistics* 61 (1979): 150–54.

WATERBURY, RONALD. "Non-Revolutionary Peasants: Oaxaca Compared to Morelos in the Mexican Revolution." *Comparative Studies in Society and History* 17 (1975): 410–42.

WEEDE, ERICH, AND HORST TIEFENBACH. "Some Recent Explanations of Income Inequality: An Evaluation and Critique." *International Studies Quarterly* 25 (1981): 255–82.

WEEKS, JOHN. "Employment, Growth, and Foreign Domination in Underdeveloped Countries." *Review of Radical Political Economics* 4 (1972): 59–70.

WEISSKOPF, THOMAS E. "The Impact of Foreign Capital Inflow on Domestic Savings in Underdeveloped Countries." *Journal of International Economics* 2 (1972): 25–38.

WILSON, WALLACE W. "Financing International Mineral Development Projects." *Mining Engineering* 25 (1973): 91–95.

WOLPE, HAROLD. "Towards an Analysis of the South African State." *International Journal of the Sociology of Law* 8 (1980): 399–421.

WOLPIN, MILES D. "Cuban Political Science in the Seventies." *Polity* 6 (1974): 424–41.

———. "Egalitarian Reformism in the Third World vs. the Military: A Profile of Failure." *Journal of Peace Research* 15 (1978): 89–107.

———. "Legitimizing State Capitalism: Malian Militarism in Third-World Perspective." *Journal of Modern African Studies* 18 (1980): 281–95.

———. "Marx and Radical Militarism in the Developing Nations." *Armed Forces and Society* 4 (1978): 245–64.

———. "Militarism, Socialism and Civilian Rule in the Third World: A Comparison of Development Costs and Benefits." *Current Research on Peace and Violence* 7 (1977): 105–33.

———. "Military Dependency versus Development in the Third World." *Bulletin of Peace Proposals* 8 (1977): 137–41.

———. "Military Professionalism and Leftist Political Movements." *Current Research on Peace and Violence* 4 (1981): 33–54.

———. "Military Radicalism in Latin America." *Journal of Inter-American Studies and World Affairs* 23 (November 1981): 395–428.

WORSELY, PETER. "One World or Three? A Critique of the World System Theory of Immanuel Wallerstein." In *Socialist Register,* edited by Ralph Millis and John Saville. London: Merlin Press, 1980.

WRIGHT, CHARLES L. "Income Inequality and Economic Growth: Examining the Evidence." *Journal of Developing Areas* 13 (1978): 49–66.

ZOLBERG, ARISTIDE R. "Dilemmas at the Gate: The Politics of Immigration in Advanced Industrial Societies." Paper prepared for delivery at the fourth annual Earl Warren Memorial Symposium, University of California at San Diego, November 1982.

———. "Strategic Interactions and the Formation of Modern States: France and England." *International Social Science Journal* 32 (1980): 687–716.

# Contributors

*Alice H. Amsden* is on the faculty of the Graduate School of Business Administration of Harvard University. The author of many articles, she has published *International Firms and Labour in Kenya* (London: Frank Cass, 1971) and is preparing, with Linsu Kim, a volume on the industrial revolution in South Korea.

*Robert H. Bates* is Henry R. Luce Professor in the Department of Political Science of Duke University. He is the author of a forthcoming study on agricultural development in Kenya, entitled *Beyond the Miracle of the Market: The Political Economy of Agrarian Development in Kenya* (Cambridge, England: Cambridge University Press).

*David Feeny* is associate professor of economics and clinical epidemiology and biostatistics at McMaster University. He is the author of *The Political Economy of Productivity: Thai Agricultural Development, 1881–1975* (Vancouver: University of British Columbia, 1982).

*Charles Lipson* is a member of the Department of Political Science at the University of Chicago and co-director of the university's Program on International Political Economy. He is the author of *Standing Guard: Protecting Foreign Capital in the Nineteenth and Twentieth Centuries* (Berkeley and Los Angeles: University of California Press, 1985).

*Paul Mosley* is professor of development economics and policy at the University of Manchester. He has been an economic adviser to the Kenyan Treasury and the Overseas Development Administration of the United Kingdom. He is the author of *The Settler Economies: Studies in the Economic History of Kenya and Southern Rhodesia, 1900–1963* (Cambridge, England: Cambridge University Press, 1983) and *Overseas Aid: Its Defence and Reform* (London: Harvester Press, 1986).

*Joan Nelson* received her doctorate from Harvard University in 1960. Since 1982 she has been a Fellow of the Overseas Development Council, where she has focused on the political economy of stabilization. She has published books and articles on development assistance and policy dialogue, migration, political participation, and the politics of economic stabilization.

*Guillermo O'Donnell* is Helen Kellogg Professor of Government and Sociology and academic director of the Helen Kellogg Institute for International Studies of the University of Notre Dame, and senior researcher at Centro Brasileiro de Analise e Planejamento in Brazil. His most recent book is *Transitions from Authoritarian Rule: Latin America and Southern Europe* (Baltimore: Johns Hopkins University Press, 1986), co-authored with Philippe Schmitter and Laurence Whitehead.

*Samuel L. Popkin* is a member of the Department of Political Science of the University of California, San Diego. He is the author of *The Rational Peasant* (Berkeley and Los Angeles: University of California Press, 1979); co-author with Ithiel de Sola Pool and Robert P. Abelson of *Candidates, Issues and Strategies* (Cambridge, Mass.: M.I.T. Press, 1964); and co-editor of *Chief of Staff* (Berkeley and Los Angeles: University of California Press, 1986).

*Clark W. Reynolds* is a professor at the Food Research Institute and director of the United States–Mexico Project and coordinator of the Americas Program at Stanford University. His work has focused on the political economy of Latin America. His books include *The Mexican Economy: Twentieth Century Structure and Growth* (New Haven: Yale University Press, 1970) and *The United States and Mexico: Economic and Social Aspects* (Stanford: Stanford University Press, 1983).

*Ronald Rogowski* is chair of the Department of Political Science at the University of California, Los Angeles. Author of *Rational Legitimacy: A Theory of Political Support* (Princeton: Princeton University Press, 1974) and co-editor, with Edward Tyriakian, of *New Nationalisms of the Developed West: Toward Explanation* (Boston: Allen and Unwin, 1985), he currently writes on theoretical issues in comparative politics.

# Index

Page numbers followed by "t" denote tables.

Adjustment loans. *See* Structural adjustment loans
Advanced capitalist states: cartelization of, 304–10; economic growth of, 314; Euromarket and, 17–18; IMF and, 31; industrial dualism in, 171; recession in, 9; trade incentives for, 317–18, 327. *See also* Capital markets; *specific nations; specific sectors*
Africa: agricultural policies in, 244, 331–58; debts of, 23. See also *specific nations; specific regions*
Agriculture sector: cash vs. food crops, 332–35, 338; collective action and, 261–70; commercialization of, 145, 158, 174, 185, 239, 349; crop insurance, 248–49; fixed-capital in, 154; Green Revolution in, 146, 154–55, 172–73; investment of earnings, 269; in LDCs, 110–11, 342–43; market structures and, 246, 265, 331–38; mechanization of, 174; price-fixing and, 303–4; project-based policies, 333–38, 351–52; real land rents, 277; reforms in, 152–53, 268–69, 292; shifting cultivation, 289; programs; social objectives and, 342–45; surplus transfers in, 157–58; wage structures, 265. *See also* Peasants; Property rights; Stabilization; Subsidy; *specific countries; specific crops; specific regions*
Akerlof, George, 262
American Medical Association (AMA), 253
Amsden, Alice, 11
Apthorpe, R., 156

Argentina, 176; agriculture in, 177–78; balance of payments, 188–90; bourgeois alliances in, 177, 184–201; capitalism in, 176; consumption in, 179, 182–83, 185, 196; currency devaluation in, 188, 193; democratization of, 201; economic peculiarities of, 182–84; foreign investment in, 183–84; governing alliances, 201–3; GNP growth for, 197; nationalization in, 180n; national state structure of, 179–82, 194; pampas power in, 178, 181, 185, 190–93; *peronista* government, 183; stabilization in, 193; subsidies in, 180n; unions in, 196; urban vs. rural economies of, 184–89; wage goods exports, 184
Artificial price structures, 303, 312, 331–58
Asia: industrialization of, 147–48; product-factor price trends, 276–82; terms of trade trends, 278t. See also *specific nations*
Auction markets, 266–67
Austerity programs, 14, 81, 87; budget discipline and, 101; debt service, 18; labor unions and, 115; public opinion and, 10; timeliness of, 99. *See also* Structural adjustment loans; *specific nations*
Autarkical economies, 317, 320, 328

Balance-of-payments, 14, 52, 92; financing of deficits, 19, 37, 52–53; Latin America crises, 183, 185, 188–90, 193, 195, 223; offshore markets and, 14; Taiwan and, 163. *See also*

Capital markets; Debt crises; Structural adjustment loans

Bank(s). *See* Capital markets; Euromarket; *specific banks*

Bank for International Settlements (BIS), 41

Barter arrangements, 157–58

Bilateral aid agreements, 33, 49, 83, 97–98. *See also* Conditionality

Bombay Presidency, 292

Brazil, 179n, 181. *See also* Latin America

Bribery, 210, 337

Budgets. *See* Austerity programs; Debt crises

Burden-sharing, 32–33

Bureaucracy, state, 242; authoritarianism and, 193, 204; management of, 101–2; property rights and, 242, 272–99; private enterprise and, 162–63, 166; regulated markets and, 156, 331–58. *See also* Nation states

Burma: import-export growth, 281t; paddy cultivation in, 280; property rights in, 288–90; real land price changes, 282t; terms of trade, 277, 278t

By-product theory, 253

CACM. *See* Central American Common Market

Cadastral Act (1913), 294

Cadastral survey system, 146, 285, 287, 292, 294–96

Cameron, David, 319

Canadian International Development Agency (CIDA), 49

Capital accounts, IMF and, 30

Capitalism. *See* Advanced capitalist states

Capital markets: bonds in, 15n; capital accumulation, 143, 156, 166, 177, 193, 203; capital-exporting states, 17; debt negotiations, 26–35; domestic, 18; floating-rate loans, 20; foreign currency liabilities, 19; IMF borrowing in, 36; interdependence in, 27; lender autonomy and, 37, 46; money-market banks, 19, 46; normal return in, 230–32; opportunity cost of capital, 209; petrodollar market, 8, 14, 25–26, 36–37; politics of, 7–12, 19, 40–41; reporting in, 41; reserve requirements, 13; supervision of, 41;

syndicates in, 8, 16, 27–30; in United States, 12, 19; urban bourgeoisie and, 190. *See also* Euromarket; Foreign exchange; Offshore credit markets; *specific banks; specific agencies*

Caribbean states, 236. See also *specific nations*

Cartelization: African, 350–51; economic effects of, 301–10; EEC, 318; innovation and, 326; producer-run, 333; rationale for, 305; Taiwanese, 165; threats to, 303; trade and, 320. *See also* Interest groups

Cash crops: marketing systems, 332–35; overvalued currency and, 338–39; self-sufficiency price, 349; *See also* Agriculture

Central America, 208; CACM, 211–17, 235; capital ownership in, 232; democratization in, 179–80, 236; dictatorships in, 211; employment growth in, 215t, 216; export economy of, 206–11, 215, 233–34; GDP, 214–15t; income distribution in, 231t; labor in, 218, 220t, 221–23, 227–28t, 232–33, 262t; laissez-faire capitalism in, 209; monopsony power of exporters in, 210; regional productivity growth, 219t; rent partitioning in, 209–11; wages in, 229t, 232t. *See also* Latin America; *specific countries; specific sectors*

Central American Common Market (CACM), 211–17, 235

China: collectivization in, 268–71; migrations to Taiwan, 149–52

Citibank Corporation, 36

Classes. *See* Social class

Closed economies, 276

Coercion, in loan negotiations, 75

Collective action: agricultural, 147, 156, 251–52, 257–58, 268–71, 293; banking, 16, 26–29, 31, 43–44; by-product theory and, 253; CACM, 211–17, 235; Condorcet cycles, 303; defection from, 254–55; easy-riders and, 268; EEC, 318; family contracts and, 270; ideology and, 275; incentives for, 254–56, 258; information and, 262–68; land disputes and, 299; leaderless, 261; in nonmarket economies, 251–56, 259–60; quality and, 266–67, 316; reciprocity, 259

Collective choice analysis, 3, 249–50

Colonialism: economic growth and, 144–49, 171, 306; marketing agreements and, 333; patronage and, 354; property rights and, 275, 289–94. See also *specific nations*

Command-and-control approach, of analysis, 8

Commercial banks. *See* Capital markets

Commercial farms, 145, 158, 174, 185, 239, 349

Commodities. *See* Prices: *specific sectors*

Communism, 97, 149, 151

Competition, neoclassical theory and, 155–56, 160

Comprehensive land law, Thailand, 284

Conditional development aid, 47–79, 106. See also *specific agencies; specific nations*

Conditionality: defined, 10, 30, 47; development aid and, 47–79; games theory and, 56–69; IMF and, 30–31, 36, 39, 43, 49–51; output changes, 54t; politics and, 38, 63–64; slippage, 10, 63–64; tightness of, 59–64, 69–70, 74–75; types of, 50t. See also Loan negotiations; Structural adjustment loans

Conspicuous consumption, 324

Consumer markets: in Africa, 339–40, 346–47; auction markets vs., 266–67; CACM and, 211–12; hegemonic societies and, 323; in Latin America, 179, 182–83, 192; public goods and, 241; stabilization programs and, 110

Cooperative Development Bank, 334

Cooperatives. *See* Collective action

Corporatism, index of, 310

Corvée, 287–88

Costa Rica: income distribution in, 229t, 231–32t, 284; land tenure in, 211; as nonmilitary state, 206; work force of, 210–11, 218

Cotton Price Assistance Fund, 334

Credit: contraction spirals, 45; debt stock vs., 40; in India, 293; peasants and, 270; private financing and, 23–28; restriction of, 111; syndicate banks and, 8, 16, 20, 27–30. *See also* Capital markets; Debt crises

Crop insurance, 248, 249

Cross-default clauses, 27, 28

Currency: overvaluation of, 338–39. *See also* Devaluation; Foreign exchange

Current-account balances: commercial banks and, 12; IMF role, 30; OPEC surpluses and, 24–25. *See also* Debt crises

Debt crises, 10–17; bilateral agreements, 33–34; burden-sharing, 32; creditor conferences, 27, 29, 34, 43; defaults, 16, 27–30, 44, 71; Euromarket and, 16–22, 26–29, 42; international monitoring of, 8–9, 16, 29–40, 44–46; management of, 26, 29–35, 81; Paris Club and, 34; private creditors and, 26–36; profile of, 22–26; rescheduling and, 13, 34–35; sanctions and, 8, 29, 44. *See also* Conditionality; International Monetary Fund; Loan negotiations; Structural adjustment loans

Debt slavery: in Burma, 28; in Philippines, 293; in Thailand, 287–88

Default, on loans, 16, 27–30, 44, 71

Defense. *See* Military; National security

de Larosière, Jacques, 39

Democracy: in Africa, 350–51; by default, 201; in Latin America, 180, 206, 210, 228, 236

Dependency theory, 2; Argentina and, 177; Taiwan paradox and, 142–43, 171–72

Devaluation: in Argentina, 188, 193; economic theory and, 92; exporters and, 110–12; in Ghana, 91, 94–95, 104, 113, 116; in Jamaica, 94, 114. *See also* Stabilization programs

Developing nations. See *specific nations; specific regions; specific sectors*

Development: African protectionism and, 339–40; allocation of resources, 239–240, 243–44, 250; capital markets and, 7–46; cartelization and, 301–10; conditional aid to, 47–79; IMF role, 9, 11; manufacturing and, 343–44; national wealth-power relations, 321; property rights and, 272–99, 310–20; public corporations and, 167–71; risk analysis and, 11; social participation in, 211; statist intervention costs and, 97; theories of, 1–3, 142–43, 171, 239–44, 301, 310, 326, 343–44; World Bank role, 9, 49. *See also* Patronage; Stabilization programs; *specific nations*

Dictatorships, 211

Direct loans, in LDCs, 111
Disaster relief, 222–23
Disinflation, 304
Distributional coalitions. *See* Cartelization; Interest groups
Dodge, Doris Jansen, 337

Earthquakes, 222, 229
East Africa, 337, 348. *See also* Africa
Easy riders, in collective agriculture, 268–69
Economic Commission for Latin America (ECLA), 208–9
Economic conservatism, in Central America, 225
Economic growth theories. *See* Development, theories of
Economic policy: in Africa, 62n, 331–58; in Central America, 211–13, 225, 234–35; distortions in, 1; revolution and, 313. *See also* Development; *specific programs; specific sectors*
Economic rents: agricultural output and, 277; defined, 209; equity in, 177, 209–11; population density and, 276; scarcity rent, 230; taxation of, 234
Economies of scale, firms and, 315
Elections, African policy and, 350
Elites, political, 100, 105, 244, 287, 295. *See also* Patronage; *specific nations*
El Salvador: income distribution in, 231t; labor demand in, 220t, 224t; political structure of, 206; regional productivity growth and, 218, 219t; wage-labor market, 210, 221, 229t, 230, 232t. *See also* Central America
Embargoes, 12, 221
Employment. *See* Labor force
Enclaves, Latin American, 177–78, 181
*Estancias,* 177, 185–86. See also *specific nations*
*Etatisme. See* Nation states
Euromarket: central role of, 14–17; creditor clubs, 29–35; development of, 18–22; LIBOR and, 21; restrictions of, 41; syndicates in, 8, 16, 27–30. *See also* Offshore credit markets
European Economic Community (EEC), 318
Exchange rate. *See* Foreign exchange
Exchange systems, in peasant society, 259–60
Exports: African, 332–35; Argentinian, 177, 181, 184–85; Central American,

207–9, 215, 233–34; debt-service payments and, 10; economic rents and, 209–11; expansion of, 87; of primary products, 176–77, 182; state power and, 165–66, 319–20. *See also* Devaluation; Trade
Extended Fund Facility Agreement, 89

Fascism, 199
Feeny, David, 242
Fertilizer, barter arrangements for, 157–58
Feudalism, 269
Firms: analysis of, 314–15; multinational, 7, 16, 168, 190n
Flexprice-sectors, 304, 318
Floating-rate loans, 20
Food crops: cash crops vs., 332–35; production projects, 333–38, 345–51. *See also* Agriculture
Food production projects, 333–38, 345–51
Foreign aid: conditional, 47–79; redirection of, 23; retroactive terms, 35. *See also* Development; *specific agencies*
Foreign exchange: imports and, 9, 338–39, 343, 349; interest repayment and, 24; NICs need for, 24; reserve depletion, 81; stabilization programs and, 87, 89–90, 92; urban industrialization and, 183–84. *See also* Balance of payments; Devaluation
Foreign investment. *See* Capital markets
Foreign policy. *See* Colonialism; Imperialism; *specific nations*
Forest lands, resource disputes and, 299
Free markets, 209, 239–40, 246
Free riders, public goods and, 241, 250–56, 275

Game theory, loan negotiations and, 56–69
GDP. *See* Gross Domestic Product
General-equilibrium analysis, 276–77, 328
Ghana: debt in, 94–95, 109; devaluation in, 91, 94–95, 103–4, 116; elite unity in, 100; National Liberation Council, 93–94; patronage in, 102, 105, 352; stabilization programs, 11, 86, 90–93; subsidy programs, 353; taxation in, 104; United Farmers' Council, 354. *See also* Africa

Gilpin, Robert, 40, 300–301, 321–30
Governing alliances, Latin American, 201–4
Government. *See* Nation states; *specific nations; specific sectors*
Grant of near-grant terms, 49
Great Britain: colonialism of, 289, 293, 333; hegemonic decline of, 325–26; Indian land rights and, 290–91; ODA, 49; pressure groups in, 309; trade incentives of, 317, 327
Great Depression, 304, 332
Greece, 248
Green Revolution, 146, 154–55, 172–73
Gross Domestic Product (GDP): Central American, 214t; SALs and, 52. See also *specific nations*
Gross National Product (GNP), 49, 86, 317–18
Group(s), theory of, 301–10
Group of, 77, 34
Guatemala: disaster relief in, 222–23; economic reforms in, 211; labor demand in, 220t, 224t, 226–27t, 230; land access in, 210; regional growth and, 219t; structural problems of, 206; U.S. support of, 236; wages in, 229t, 231–32t. *See also* Central America

*Hacienda* system, 176–78, 264, 269
Heady, Bruce, 310
Hegemony, 317, 321–26. See also *specific nations*
Hla Myint, 161–62
Hobbesian analysis, 15
Homesteading, 284, 289, 294
Honduras: CACM and, 213; development policy and 207, 236; immigration policy of, 233; import prices, 218; labor demand, 220t, 227t; regional growth and, 219t; trade diversion in, 221; wages in, 229t, 231–32t. *See also* Central America

Ideology, development and, 88, 311–14
IMF. *See* International Monetary Fund
Immigration, 149, 233, 305–6
Imperialism, 7, 144–49, 171, 289–93. *See also* Colonialism
Imports: Argentinan demand for, 183; cost of, 218, 338–40; duty free, 148; exchange rates and, 112; oil price shocks and, 9; restrictions on, 92;

substitution, 111, 164, 166, 182, 208–9, 217. See also *specific sectors*
Incentives: collective action and, 254; for debt repayment, 16, 27–28; electoral, 350; for food production, 337, 342, 344–45; trade, 317–18, 327
Income: Africa, 346; Argentina, 183, 188, 193; Central American 229t, 231–25; Chinese, 269; Costa Rican model, 234; maldistribution of, 239; in Taiwan, 160t, 175; urban, real value of, 346. *See also* Wages
India: credit access in, 292; property rights systems of, 277, 280, 290–93
Indifference curves, 324
Industrialization: financing of, 19; import substitution and, 208–9; incentives, 328; locational advantage and, 148; OECD study of, 164, 165n; programs, 19. *See also* Capital markets; Development; Technology; *specific nations*
Inflation: demand and, 304; economic growth and, 309; Nigerian Task Forces on, 346; real wages and, 229
Information: collective action and, 262–68; joint analysis of, 98
Infrastructure: in Central America, 225; transportation and, 321. See also *specific nations*
Inheritance, of land, 249, 287
Innovation: British failure in, 326; costs of, 274. *See also* Technology
Institutional change: hegemonic societies and, 326–27; property rights and, 283–99; quantitative measures of, 297; supply-demand model of, 273–76
Insurance, crop, 247–48, 258–59
Integration, economic: Central American, 211–13; Latin American, 208
Interest groups, 309; African, 350–51; in LDCs, 108, 110–11; as passionate minorities, 303. *See also* Cartelization
Interest rates, 209; collective action and, 255; external debt, 13, 23–24; floating-rate loans, 20; peasants and, 161–62; reform, 92–93; rise in, 80. *See also* Capital markets
International agencies, 8; conditionality and, 30–31, 36, 39, 43, 49–56; policy impact of, 97–98; political involvement of, 83. See also *specific agencies*
International Monetary Fund (IMF): creditor clubs and, 29–35; Extended

Fund Facility Agreements, 89; national voting weights in, 38; new demands on, 35–40; performance criteria, 30, 39; political involvement of, 89, 98–99; quota reviews by, 38; role of, 9, 11; stabilization and, 86, 93; standby arrangements, 31–32, 89, 101. *See also* Stabilization programs; Structural adjustment loans

Intrinsic sanctions, 44

Investment: displacement of, 323; of farm earnings, 269; in research, 274. *See also* Development

Iran, debts of, 17

Jamaica: devaluation in, 94, 114; GNP, 86; patronage in, 105; power struggles in, 100, 104; stabilization programs of, 90, 95–96

Japan: cartelization in, 306–9; domination of Taiwan, 144–49; rapid growth of, 313

Joint ventures, 98

Kaunda, Kenneth, 102–3

Keyna: economic assessments by, 97; elite unity in, 100; Kenya African National Union (KANU), 102; loan negotiations with, 60n; maize market in, 355; patronage in, 105; stabilization programs in, 11, 86. *See also* Africa

Kenyatta, Jomo, 102

Keynes, John Maynard, 209, 304–5, 324

Kikuyu, 102

Labor force: absorption of, 232–33; Adebo Commission, Nigeria, 346; CACM, 212–17, 224–25, 230–32; Central American technology and, 224–25; common ideology of, 312; dislocation of, 216; dualism in, 230–32; export economies and, 207–9; full employment problems, 174; growth of, 227–28; international division of, 329; Latin American demand for, 179, 212n; productivity growth and, 223–27; quality of, 264; rent partitioning and, 210; shortages of, 174; surpluses, 163, 222; wage labor, 160, 210–11, 215, 264, 270

Labor unions, 114; austerity programs and, 115; in Central America, 204,

228; in Latin America, 195, 199, 204; organizational centralization of, 310; price changes and, 304

Laissez-faire economic theory, 209, 239–40, 246

Land: access in Guatemala, 210; in Burma, 290; forest disputes, 299; Indian classification of, 292; inheritance of, 249, 287; landlords, 145–47, 152, 255; in Latin American, 177–78, 185–86; in Philippines, 294; prices of, 280–81, 283, 290; reforms, 268–69, 292; rents, 276–77; smallholdings, 152, 174, 264, 349; surveys of, 146, 285, 287, 292, 294–96; in Thailand, 283–88, 296, 299; tenure systems, 145–46, 208–11, 264, 269–71. *See also* Property rights

Latin America: balance-of-payments, 183; coalitions in, 201; class stratification in, 177, 194, 202; ECLA, 208–9; economic surplus, 182; enclaves, 181; *hacienda* breakdown, 269; homogeneity of economy, 178n; import substitution, 182; integration industries in, 208; plantations, 181; primary export products, 182; state economic policies, 191, 202; taxation in, 203n; unrest, 198; world market and, 179, 181. *See also* Central America: *specific countries*

LDCs. *See* Less developed countries

Lemon market analysis, 262–68

Less developed countries (LDCs), 22, 86–87; agricultural policy in, 342–43; austerity measures, 14, 87; capital markets and, 7–11; conditional development and, 9, 47–56; debts of, 12–46; direct loan reliance, 111; political opposition in, 104; populations of, 110; structural adjustment operations, 55t; syndicated banks and, 8, 16, 20, 27–30; trade dependence of, 87. *See also* Interest groups; Stabilization programs; *specific nations; specific regions; specific sectors*

Leverage. *See* Conditionality, of loans

Lint Marketing Board, 334

Lipson, Charles, 8

Lipton, Michael, 247

Loan negotiations, 10, 30–37; coercion in, 75; commercial vs. official, 33–34; conditional development aid and, 49–56; economic reform and, 71; game theory analysis of, 56–69; limi-

tations of, 98; most-favored nations in, 32–33; mutual agreement on, 71; Nash product, 61; risk and, 31–32, 60–62; tightness of requirements, 10, 56–63; World Bank study of, 35. *See also* Conditionality; Structural adjustment loans
London Inter-Bank Offer Rate (LIBOR), 21

McKinnon, Ronald, 41
Maize, price control of, 336, 348–49, 355
Market forces, 106, 247; anti-market bias, 93; development and, 240; economic analysis and, 239, 250; government intervention and, 11, 240, 246, 331–58; ideologies and, 88, 199, 244, 311–14; macroeconomic variables, 39–40; neoclassical theory and, 155, 165, 171, 230; political organization and, 355–56; social costs and, 239–40. See also *specific nations; specific sectors*
Marketing Board, African, 332–35
Marx, Karl, 209, 240
Mayer, Helmut, 42
Middlemen, margins of, 266–67
Migrant labor: Central American embargo on, 221; teams of, 268
Military: Central American politics and, 233, 235; economic power relation and, 116, 321–25; government by, 144–49, 207, 233–36, 310–21; technology and, 321, 325
Moi, Daniel Arap, 102
Monetarism theory, 303–5
Monopoly, 158, 210, 229, 311, 353–54. *See also* Cartelization
Monopsony, 158, 299
Mosley, Paul, 9–10
Mueller, Dennis, 306
Multilateral institutions, 16, 31, 37. See also *specific agencies*
Multinational banks. *See* Capital markets
Multinational corporations, 7, 190n, 168, 314–15

NAMBoard, Zambia, 337
Nash product, 61
Nash-Zeuthen bargaining process, 66
National Development Levy, 104, 113
Nationalism, 149, 152, 204

Nationalization, 180n
National Recovery Agency, 305
National security: costs of, 323; military innovation and, 326
Nation states: alliances, 180–82, 191; anti-statism, 202; capital accumulation and, 143, 156, 166, 177, 196, 203; firms vs., 315–16; integration efforts, 208; military power in, 116, 144–49, 207, 233–36, 320–21; nonstate actors and, 16; political security risks, 90; property rights and, 310–20; protectionism by, 164, 317, 328, 339–40; public interest and, 343–45; sovereign borrowers, 20, 29; systemic change and, 321–29. *See also* Debt crises; *specific nations; specific organizations; specific regions; specific sectors*
Natural disasters, 222–23, 229
Ndegwa Report, 97
Nelson, Joan, 10
Neoclassical economic analysis, 155, 165, 171, 230
Newly industrializing countries (NICs), 24. See also *specific countries*
Nicaragua: CACM and, 211–17; debt rescheduling by, 32n; disaster relief, 222–23; labor demand in, 220t, 224t, 227t; political structure of, 206; productivity growth, 217–18, 219t; rent partitioning, 210; wage labor in, 210, 229t, 231–32t. *See also* Central America
Nigeria, food policies of, 334–35, 346. *See also* Africa
Nonmarket economies, 246; collective choice theory and, 249–50; cooperatives and, 258–59; insurance organizations and, 258–59
North, Douglas C., 300–301, 310–20
North Africa, 333. See also *specific nations*

O'Donnell, Guillermo, 11
OECD. *See* Organization for Economic Cooperation and Development
Offshore credit markets, 8, 12; defined, 14n; petrosurpluses and, 25; state actions and, 19, 40–41. *See also* Euromarket
Oil: importing states, 40; joint ventures, 168; 1973 embargo, 12; price shocks, 9, 25, 80, 304, 338
Oligarchies, 177, 181, 187

Olson, Mancur, Jr., 258, 300–320
OPEC. *See* Organization of Petroleum Exporting Countries
Open-access property disputes, 299
Opposition parties, 104; collective action and, 255; in LDCs, 108; in Sri Lanka, 97
Organization of Petroleum Exporting Countries (OPEC): cartel theory and, 303; IMF and, 38; 1973 embargo, 12; petrodollar market, 8, 14, 24–26, 36–37. *See also* Oil

Paddy-land tax, 283
Pampas, *estancia* vs. *hacienda*, 177. *See also* Argentina
Panama, economic reform in, 206–7. *See also* Central America
Parastatals, 19, 101, 106
Paris Club, 33–34
Patrimony, 249, 287
Patronage, 9; African, 102, 105, 150, 352–55; foreign exchange demand and, 11. *See also* Elites, political
Peasants: allocation of resources and, 250; credit and, 161–62, 270; economic responsiveness of, 246; exchange systems, 259–60; farming methods of, 155–56, 247–49; free rider problem and, 251–56; in Latin America, 182; market access for, 269; political entrepreneurs, 256–61; public choice theory and, 245. *See also* Collective action; *specific nations; specific regions*
Peng Ming-min, 150–52
Perón, Juan, 183, 204
*Peronismo*, 196–200
Peru: austerity measures in, 115; debt payment crisis, 35–36; oligarchy in, 181; stabilization and, 114. *See also* Latin America
Petrodollar market, recycling in, 8, 14, 21, 24–26, 36–37
Petroleum. *See* Oil
Philippines: property rights in, 293–94; terms of trade, 278t, 280; wage structures, 264–65
Phillips curves, negative, 304
Planning, political fear of, 209
Plantations, 177, 181, 264
Pluralist model, of politics, 349–51
*Plusvalia* economics, 230–32
Political economy of development theory, 1–3, 85, 239–44

Political entrepreneurs, 256–61
Political organization: African markets and, 355–56; capital markets and, 10; Central American parties, 210; lack of support base for, 102–7; risk management and, 34–36, 107–20; stabilization programs and, 82–88, 99; SALs and, 11. *See also* Nation states; *specific nations*
Population: land rents and, 276; in LDCs, 110; migration of, 149, 217, 233, 305–6. See also *specific nations*
Prebisch, Raul, 209
Pressure groups. *See* Cartelization; Interest groups
Prices: Asian trends in, 276–82; cartels and, 303–4; controls, 2, 92, 158, 188, 303, 312, 331–58; influence on consumption, 183; general-equilibrium analysis of, 276–77; of land, 280–81; market entry and, 240; SAL distortions of, 74t; technology and, 325. See also *specific sectors*
Private debt, 23, 33–37
Privatization, of economy, 93, 345–51
Productivity: collective action and, 317; easy riders and, 268–69; factor prices and, 276–82; regional growth in Central America, 214–15t, 217–18, 219–20t. See also *specific sectors*
Profit motive, 93. *See also* Economic rents
Project-based food policies, 351–52
Property rights, 8; in Burma, 288–90; cadastral survey and, 285, 287, 292, 294–96; commercial farmers and, 341; economic growth and, 310–20; evolution in, 275; frontier demands for, 295; in India, 290–93; in Philippines, 293–94; relative factor price and, 273, 276–82; state control and, 311; in Thailand, 283–88
Protectionism: African, 339–40; aid and, 48; autarky and, 317; Taiwanese, 164; Weimar Germany and, 328. *See also* Tariffs
Public choice theory, 244–45, 249, 251–56
Public corporations, 101
Public goods: for creditors, 31; free riders and, 241, 250–56, 275; institutional change and, 274–75; politics of, 241, 245; rational choice and, 300–330
Public interest. *See* Social wefare

Quotas, for IMF-member lending, 38

Radical governments, African, 347
Rational choice theory, 300–301; cartelization and, 301–10; collective choice
and, 249; firms and, 315–16; social
good and, 241; trade incentives and,
317, 327; value of, 329
Rationing, 11, 158
Recessions, 8–9, 80, 189–91
Refinancing, 29–30. See also Loan ne-
gotiations
Reform movements: agricultural, 152–
53, 268–69, 292; IMF, 36; development programs, 51; interest-rate
and, 92–93; in loan negotiations, 58–
63, 71; social costs of, 11
Regions: development policies, 209; ,
Latin American autonomy, 180; markets, 225. See also specific regions
Regulated markets, 8, 93, 332–38, 355
Rents. See Economic rents; Tenancy
land systems
Repression, political, 144–52, 198
Research, investment in, 274
Revenue policy. See Taxation
Revolution: debtors and, 17, 20, 29,
32n; economic growth and, 2, 198,
200, 216, 307, 313; rent partitioning
and, 210; Sri Lanka and, 104n; Taiwan and, 151
Rhodesia, 354
Ricardian rent theory, 292
Rice: barters of, 157; labor quality and,
264–66; market intervention and,
336t; price controls, 348; property
rights and, 284
Risks: analysis of, 10, 247, 270; asset
depletion and, 260; of austerity measures, 87; in capital markets and, 8,
14, 19–20, 39; on conditional aid, 48,
64; devaluation and, 94; peasant production and, 248; political, 34–36,
107–20; SAL limits, 10, 57, 60, 62,
66; of stabilization, 11, 89–91
Rogowski, Ronald, 241
Rubber, 266–67
Rural sector: African food policy and,
351–54; bourgeois urban alliances,
177, 184–201; LDCs population,
110; responsibility system, 268; role
of politics in, 241–42, 245–71. See
also Peasants; specific nations
Russia, 328
Ryotwari system, 291

SALs. See Structural adjustment loans
Sanctions, debt, 8, 16, 29, 44
Saudi Arabia, IMF and, 38
Savings, in Central America, 234
Scarcity rent, 230
Schultz, Theodore W., 246–48, 342
Senegal, subsidy programs in, 353
Shifting cultivation, in Burma, 289
Siamwalla, Ammar, 266–67
Social class: alliances, 177, 184–201;
development and, 172; equity
among, 88, 209–11; rural landlords,
152–53, 156; stratification, 162, 179,
191, 194, 202
Social welfare: in Central America,
213; government intervention and,
342–45; individual rationality and,
241; Taiwan and, 159; welfare economies, 249, 261
Solomon, Anthony, 31
Spain, Philippines colonialism and,
293–94
Special interest groups. See Interest
groups
Sri Lanka: communal riots in, 104n;
elite unity in, 100; failed reform efforts in, 96; government strength in,
109; political opposition in, 89–91,
97, 104; stabilization programs, 11,
86, 88–90
Stabilization programs, 11, 43, 81; anti-
statism and, 202; economic risks and,
91–95, 112, 190–91; equity in, 88;
factors encouraging, 95–100; failure
of, 82, 96; IMF guidelines, 30; leaders' commitment to, 88–89; political
risk of, 87, 89–91, 110–13; public reactions to, 105, 107–10; sanctions
and, 16; structural adjustment and,
88; substainability of, 85–88, 99;
Tanzania, 59n; wages and, 114. See
also Conditionality; International
Monetary Fund; specific nations
Stagflation, 188, 304. See also Inflation
Standby Agreements, IMF, 31–32, 89,
101
Strikes, union, 228
Structural adjustment loans (SALs), 9–
10; balance of payments and, 52;
commitment to, 88, 99; as conditions
of aid, 106; energy prices and, 36;
increases in, 84; market incentives of,
93; objectives of, 51–52; output
changes predicted, 54t; risk, 57; slippage, 63–64, 76–78t; tightness of

conditions, 70, 72–74t. *See also* World Bank
Sub-Saharan Africa, 96–97
Subsidy programs: African, 331, 340–41, 349, 353–54; Argentine, 180n; Central American, 225; consumer goods, 112; flexprice sectors and, 318
Subsistence production, 208, 234
Sugar cane production, 145, 158
Supply-and-demand analysis, 273–76
Surplus value extraction, 143, 159–63
Syndicate banks: cross-default clauses, 27–28; IMF role, 30; overlapping, 28; role of, 8, 29; sanctions by, 16; sovereign borrowers and, 20, 29

Taiwan, 11; agricultural sector, 146, 152–63, 174; Chinese Nationalist corruption in, 150–51; export boom in, 168; foreign investment in, 168–69, 172; Formosan nationalism in, 149–52; income distribution in, 153, 159–60, 163; industrialization of, 163–67; Japanese occupation of, 144–49; Land-to-the Tiller Act, 152, 158, 173; leading economic indicators, 145t; liberalization policy, 165–66; manufacturing productivity, 170t; net domestic product by origin, 161t; police role in, 157; protectionism in, 164–65; state enterprises in, 158, 167–71; taxation burdens, 157–58, 159t; trade deficits, 163, 172; U.S. aid to, 171
Tanzania, 59n, 62n
Tariffs, 212–13, 303, 305, 317
Taxation: African Marketing Boards and, 334–35, 339; cartelization and, 305; economic rents and, 209, 211, 234; in Ghana, 104; hidden, 158; land rights and, 192, 291–93, 295, 311
Technology: in Central America, 208, 224–25; capital accumulation and, 143; costs of, 274; Green Revolution, 154–55; and labor, 224–25; peasant production and, 247–48; price shifts and, 325; research investments, 274; in Taiwan, 146–47; technocrats, 11, 95
Tenancy land systems, 152, 211, 264, 269, 271
Terms of trade, 145–46, 158, 212, 276–77, 280–82

Thailand: agricultural prices, 277; import-export growth, 281t; middlemen margins in, 266–67; peasant reciprocity, 259–60; property rights in, 283–88; real land price changes, 282t; terms of trade trends, 278t, 280; Torrens land titling system, 284–85
Thomas, Robert P., 310, 314
Threat-and-Inducement strategies, 65–69
Tightness, of conditionality, 65, 69–70, 74–75
Torrens land titling system, 284–85
Totalitarian rule, economic growth and, 306, 308
Trade: CACM and, 211–12; concentration, 166; diversion in Honduras, 221; incentives to, 317, 319, 327; LDCs and, 86–87, 111; peripheral underdevelopment and, 143; protectionism, 164, 303, 305, 317, 328, 339–40. *See also* Capital markets; *specific countries*
Transnational corporations, 7, 16, 168, 190n, 314–15
Turkey, debts of, 13

Uncertainty. *See* Risk, analysis of
Underemployment, 223
Unemployment, cartelization and, 302–3. *See also* Labor force
United Ghana Farmers' Council, 354
United States: Central American policy of, 210, 235–36; colonialism in Philippines, 294; economic growth analysis, 307, 314; GNP, 318; USAID, 49–56
Unions. *See* Labor unions
Urban sector: African, 346–47; bourgeois alliances, 177, 184–201; LDCs, 110
Uruguay, 177–78
Usufruct rights, 288–89

Vasena, Krieger, 193
Vietnam, 260–61, 268, 270

Wages: adjustments, 113; in Argentina, 178, 184; Central American, 209–10, 212, 229–30; labor unions and, 115, 195; in Latin American, 178; restraints, 103, 115; stabilization programs and, 114; in Thailand, 288

Wang, Sung Hsing, 156–57
War: hegemonic, 323–25; Taiwan and 147–50, 166; in Zimbabwe, 94
Warrenite economics, 2
Welfare. *See* Social welfare
West Africa, 34, 348
Wheat, 248, 349
Working class: in Central America, 209–17; in Latin America, 179; stabilization, equity and, 88. *See also* Peasants
Work point system, 269
World Bank, 18; changing perspectives and, 97–98; conditionality and, 9–10, 48–49, 71; cooperative financing with, 36–37; debtor bargaining and, 10, 35; and economic growth, 48, 53;

IDA, 49. *See also* Structural adjustment loans

Young, Oran, 45–46

Zaire, 34
Zambia, 11; cooperative societies, 352–53; development policy, 350; elite unity in, 100; GNP, 86; IMF Standby Agreement, 86; NAMBoard, 337; patronage in, 105; stabilization programs, 94, 95, 102, 103; subsidy programs, 353–54; United National Independence Party, 103, 105. *See also* Africa
*Zamindar* system, 291–93
Zeuthen's Principle, 60–61
Zimbabwe, war in, 94